A Foreigner's Cinematic Dream of Japan

A Foreigner's Cinematic Dream of Japan

Representational Politics and Shadows of War in the Japanese–German Co-production *New Earth* (1937)

Iris Haukamp

BLOOMSBURY ACADEMIC
NEW YORK • LONDON • OXFORD • NEW DELHI • SYDNEY

BLOOMSBURY ACADEMIC
Bloomsbury Publishing Inc
1385 Broadway, New York, NY 10018, USA
29 Earlsfort Terrace, Dublin 2, Ireland

BLOOMSBURY, BLOOMSBURY ACADEMIC and the Diana logo
are trademarks of Bloomsbury Publishing Plc

First published in the United States of America 2021
This paperback edition published in 2022

Copyright © Iris Haukamp, 2021

For legal purposes the Acknowledgements on p. xi constitute an extension
of this copyright page.

Cover design: Louise Dugdale
Cover image © Kawakita Memorial Institute

All rights reserved. No part of this publication may be reproduced or
transmitted in any form or by any means, electronic or mechanical, including
photocopying, recording, or any information storage or retrieval system,
without prior permission in writing from the publishers.

Bloomsbury Publishing Inc does not have any control over, or responsibility for, any third-party websites referred to or in this book. All internet addresses given in this book were correct at the time of going to press. The author and publisher regret any inconvenience caused if addresses have changed or sites have ceased to exist, but can accept no responsibility for any such changes.

The Acknowledgements on pp. xi–xii constitute an extension of this copyright page

Library of Congress Cataloging-in-Publication Data
Names: Haukamp, Iris, author.
Title: A foreigner's cinematic dream of Japan: representational politicsand shadows of war in the Japanese-German coproduction New Earth (1937)/ Iris Haukamp.
Description: New York ; London : Bloomsbury Academic, 2020. |
Includes bibliographical references, filmographies, and index.
Identifiers: LCCN 2020013015 | ISBN 9781501343537 (hardback) |
ISBN9781501343551 (pdf) | ISBN 9781501343551 (ebook)
Subjects: LCSH: Atarashiki tsuchi (Motion picture) | Itami, Mansaku, 1900-1946. |
Fanck, Arnold, 1889-1974. | Motion pictures–Japan–History–20th century. |
Motion pictures–Germany–History–20th century. | Japan–Relations–Germany. |
Germany–Relations–Japan.
Classification: LCC PN1997.A83 H38 2020 | DDC 791.43/72–dc23
LC record available at https://lccn.loc.gov/2020013015

ISBN: HB: 978-1-5013-4353-7
PB: 978-1-5013-6930-8
ePDF: 978-1-5013-4355-1
eBook: 978-1-5013-4354-4

Typeset by Deanta Global Publishing Services, Chennai, India

To find out more about our authors and books visit www.bloomsbury.com
and sign up for our newsletters.

一人の外国人が海を越えて日本に来た。	A foreigner crossed the oceans and came to Japan.
彼は自分の眼で日本を見た。	He saw Japan with his own eyes.
そして日本を愛した。	And fell in love with Japan.
彼は愛する日本の夢を土臺として彼らしい一つの現實を描いた。	Based on the dream about the Japan he loved, he painted one subjective reality.
其の現實がこの映画である。	This film is that reality.
而も是は一刷毛に描いた略図である。	And yet, it is a rough sketch, painted in one stroke of the brush.
従って例えば現實的その他の矛盾は篇中随所に之を指摘する事が出来る。	Therefore, one can discern factual and other inconsistencies all throughout the piece.
但し諸君の雅量は苦笑と共に是等を看過して下さる事と信ずる。	However, Ladies and Gentlemen, I trust in your generosity to overlook these with a wry smile.

(Itami Mansaku, epigraph to *New Earth*, 1937)

I'd rather scale calving icebergs in Greenland or float around on ice-floes than shoot a film here in Japan.

(Arnold Fanck, 02.09.1936)

CONTENTS

List of figures viii
Acknowledgements xi
Note on sources and translation xiii
Timeline of related cinematic and political events xv

Introduction 1

1 Film export and international (mis-)understanding 25

2 Producing *New Earth*: People, stories, inconsistencies 53

3 A pact of the silver screen 85

4 The politics of authenticity: Representing others, recognizing selves 107

5 International stars and national landscapes: Authentic star personas? 125

6 Itami's version of Fanck's dream 157

7 Repercussions: Coming to terms with *New Earth* 193

Conclusion 213

Appendix 1: Plot summary and credits 225
Appendix 2: Feature films shown to Fanck in Japan (February–March 1937) 228
Appendix 3: Filmography Arnold Fanck 230
Appendix 4: Filmography Itami Mansaku 234
References 238
Filmography 262
Index 267

FIGURES[1]

0.1 The film's climax, shot on an active volcano in the Northern Japan Alps 2
0.2 'Announcing [our] true values to the world: Japan's greatest and finest masterpiece!' 3
0.3 Teruo driving a Komatsu tractor 4
0.4 Yamato Iwao explaining the principles of the family state to Gerda Storm 6
0.5 The Asia Express 10
0.6 The protagonists arriving on a steamship 10
0.7 The film team's commemorative picture on completion 12
0.8 Impressions of 'Japan' superimposed in Fanck's credit sequence 15
0.9 The miniature model of Japan 16
0.10 Journalist Gerda capturing Japan 18
1.1 German advertisement for *Yakichi the Woodcutter* aka *Eternal Heart* 33
1.2 Credit titles in *Nippon* 35
1.3 Yuasa Hatsue as the 'singer' in *Nippon* 37
1.4 Special effects in *Nippon* 38
1.5 Fast swordplay by Hayashi Chōjirō in *Samimaro* 39
1.6 The hero's manic laughter in *Bonfire* 40
1.7 Mitsuko's dream of Teruo leaving on a ship 46
1.8 Teruo torn between East and West 46
2.1 Cameraman Sepp Allgeier on location (ca. 1930) 54
2.2 Gerda and Teruo watch troops marching through Tokyo 59
2.3 Members of the crew during a location shoot (names and place unclear) 60
2.4 Shooting a 'Hotel Europe' scene (J.O. Studios) 64
2.5 Announcement of the nationwide release in Shōchiku SY chain theatres 70

---

[1] Figures 1.2–1.6 are by courtesy of the Cinémathèque Suisse. Figures 2.1 and 4.2 are in the public domain, as the authors are unknown and the copyright has expired. Figures 6.20 and 6.21 are from the National Film Archive of Japan Collection. All other images are by courtesy of the Kawakita Memorial Film Institute Tokyo.

2.6   Itami's absence from the premiere programme's cover 72
2.7   From the Kawakitas' photo album: Sightseeing in Manchukuo and on the Trans-Siberian Railway 75
2.8   Invitation to the premiere on 23 March, 6.00 pm, issued by the German–Japanese Society, Ufa and Terra 76
2.9   The Kawakitas 'in front of Cologne Cathedral' (1937) 80
2.10 Kawakita Kashiko and Hara Setsuko in Central Park 82
3.1   The map of 'Manchuria' (*Mandschurei*) 92
3.2   Reception at the Mainichi Shinbun Office (8 February 1936): Hack is the first person from the right 97
3.3   Shots of steelworks 99
3.4   Shot of a silk factory 100
3.5   The 'geisha party'? Fanck, Hack, Eweler, Elisabeth Fanck, Kawakita, others unknown 100
4.1   Teruo proving himself on the volcano 109
4.2   Location shooting for *Storms over Mont Blanc*: Left to right: Hans Schneeberger, Leni Riefenstahl, Richard Angst, Sepp Allgeier, Arnold Fanck 117
4.3   Angst operating the telephoto lens 119
5.1   Kosugi as a thoughtful Teruo 126
5.2   Promotional picture of Hayakawa as Yamato Iwao 128
5.3   Promotional picture of Eweler 129
5.4   Production snapshot of Hara 131
5.5   A production still of the modern kitchen in the Yamato house 133
5.6   The set of the 'Yamato house' 133
5.7   The first shot of Mitsuko 135
5.8   Mount Asama erupting 138
5.9   Tokyo by night 139
5.10 Hideko and Kanda in modern Tokyo 140
5.11 The old underscoring the new 141
5.12 Hanshin Railway and Misakaya in Tokyo? 143
5.13 Teruo returns to his roots 144
5.14 Helping Manchukuo to her feet through construction 148
5.15 'Manchukuo' 152
5.16 Manchukuo's large, fertile plains 153
5.17 The film team (including Fanck, Itami and Kawakita) on location. Cameraman Angst (second row, middle) is wearing a Kwantung army costume 154
6.1   Mitsuko running through the garden 162
6.2   The globe scene 163
6.3   Mitsuko serving dinner 165
6.4   Teruo's injured feet 166
6.5   Teruo picks up Mitsuko – Itami uses the same shot, minus the superimposition 168

6.6   Superimpositions signifying Teruo's dream 169
6.7   Mitsuko playing the *koto* 169
6.8   Teruo waking up beneath Mount Fuji 172
6.9   Little Emiko being scared 173
6.10 Spatial logic 176
6.11 A detail from a Tōwa advertisement for 'Japan's premiere [*sic*] export film' 177
6.12 Itami uses the same setting, with the Hakenkreuz and Imperial Army flags replaced by the Stars and Stripes and Hinomaru respectively 178
6.13 Fanck violating the 180-degree rule (Itami here uses the Stars and Strips and the Hinomaru, and in a sense keeps the spatial logic) 179
6.14 Shooting the naginata scene 180
6.15 'A dangerous storm is blowing across the world' 180
6.16 The 'donkey-mill' in Fanck's version, with the small boy out of frame 184
6.17 The soldier guarding the settlers 185
6.18 Mrs Kanda receives the telegram 187
6.19 His birth family is disappointed by Teruo's attitude 187
6.20 The first impression of the soldier in Itami's *New Earth* (Courtesy of the National Film Archive of Japan) 189
6.21 Itami's soldier as a small silhouette in the background (Courtesy of the National Film Archive of Japan) 190
7.1   Angst, Itami and Staudinger shooting on location 199
7.2   The meeting in Karuizawa. Left to right: Max Hinder (?), Fanck, Itami, Sternberg, Hara 204
7.3   The *manji* fence 206
7.4   A close-up shot of Teruo 207

ACKNOWLEDGEMENTS

This book is the outcome of over a decade of study, trial and error, and trying to make sense of past events. I am thankful to the many people who gave their generous support during all these years.

First of all, I would like to express my deep gratitude to Isolde Standish and Christopher Gerteis for their continuous support, patient guidance and constructive critiques, far beyond their official supervisor roles. And the generous help I received from scholars and colleagues in the field and from various institutions surprised and humbled me. In particular I would like to thank: Tochigi Akira, Irie Yoshiro, Okada Hidenori, Daibō Masaki, Kamiya Makiko and Alo Joekalda of the National Film Archive Tokyo; their colleagues in the Filmmuseum München, Stefan Drößler and Gisela Pichler, for invaluable access to their resources; Matthias Fanck for providing me with material about his grandfather and for being open to questions. Wachi Yukiko of the Kawakita Memorial Film Institute gave invaluable support for more years than I dare think about. Also Bernd Martin, Okumura Masaru, Klaus Kanzog, Jan-Christopher Horak, Kobayashi Fujiko and the staff of Deutsches Filminstitut Frankfurt, Cinémathèque Suisse Genève and Tokyo Laboratory (Tōkyō Genzōjō) never hesitated to answer minute and seemingly random questions. Karl Sierek kindly provided incredible last-minute support. Finally, thank you to Horie Makoto of the NYK Maritime Museum Yokohama for steamship-sleuthing. I would also like to thank my editor at Bloomsbury, Katie Gallof, for her valuable advice and patience. And many kind thoughts go to the anonymous reviewers of the manuscript's various versions. Thank you for your positive comments, and I am particularly indebted to 'Reviewer Five's' suggestions for restructuring. It caused some sleepless nights but much improved the book.

I am grateful for the peace of mind provided by the Japan Research Centre at SOAS for the invaluable Kayoko Tsuda Research Bursary. This work was also partly supported by the Arts and Humanities Research Council as well as the Tokyo University of Foreign Studies' CAAS Program for Japan Studies in Global Context (sponsored by MEXT).

Of course, the project would have stalled at various points without the friendship, support and encouragement of people I am happy to call my friends and colleagues. My gratefulness in particular goes to the Heycocks who gave me a home for many years. You will always be in my heart. Also, big thank yous to Nakayama Muneharu, the Sugano family, Jennifer Coates, Irene Gonzalez, Lauri Kitsnik and Martyn Smith, and to my wonderful colleagues at TUFS, Tomotsune Tsutomu, Haruna Nobuo, Sen Raj Lakhi, Kimura Masami and Yukimatsu Hanae for their encouragement. Last but not least, many thanks to my amazing students, who inspired me with their inquisitiveness and humour, when having watched and thought about one film project for a decade made it look anything but exciting at times.

This book is dedicated to my husband for his unwavering support during a (very) long intellectual and personal journey and through moves across continents.

NOTE ON SOURCES AND TRANSLATION

This book is about a joint film project that resulted in different versions, attributed to two different directors (Fanck and Itami), and released under different titles in Japan and in Germany. The use of the title *Atarashiki tsuchi* (*New Earth*) in Japan for both versions and *Die Tochter des Samurai* (*Samurai's Daughter*) for the German director Fanck's edition as it was released in Germany proved problematic in terms of clarity. I have decided to use *Samurai's Daughter* for Fanck's version in its German context. When referring to the project as such as it took place in Japan, I use *New Earth*, distinguishing if necessary between 'Fanck's version' (FV) and 'Itami's version' (IV). In Chapter 7, which compares the version by each director, Fanck's version is labelled *Samurai's Daughter* and Itami's *New Earth*, in order to avoid the ad nauseam repetition of 'version'.

Much of the publicity material on the project from the time of its production and release was found in microfiche form in the National Film Institute Frankfurt, the Newspaper Archive Dortmund, Germany, and first and foremost in fifteen scrapbooks compiled by the production company Tōwa Shōji between 1935 and 1937. These include advertisement material, notes, press releases, event programmes and an overwhelming number of newspaper and magazine clippings, concerned directly or peripherally with the production of *New Earth*. While being an incredible archive, the age and quality of the prints sometimes render the stamped or handwritten publication dates, newspaper titles or parts of the texts illegible, and page numbers or other information on the cut-outs are often missing. Also, the pseudonyms used by critics and reviewers proved a challenge – could not be clarified: 'Q', writing for the *Asahi Shinbun*, for example, is Tsumura Hideo; the critic for *Der Bildwart*, Hans Pander, wrote as 'H.P.'. Some other authors could not be identified. I did my best to supplement necessary details, but some references had to remain incomplete at this stage.

For Japanese personal names, I have used the Japanese order of surname and given name; one exception is Japanese-born, Hollywood actor Sessue Hayakawa. I have excluded the macrons, indicating long vowels, from well-known place names such as Kyoto, Osaka and Tokyo.

Translations are my own unless otherwise stated.

An earlier version of Chapter 1 was published as 'Early transcontinental film relations: Japan, Germany and the compromises of co-production, 1926–1933', *Historical Journal of Film, Radio and Television*, 37 (2), (2017): 174–202.

Parts of Chapter 5 were previously published in 'Fräulein Setsuko Hara: Constructing an international film star in nationalist contexts', *Journal of Japanese and Korean Cinema*, 6 (1), (2014): 4–22.

TIMELINE OF RELATED CINEMATIC AND POLITICAL EVENTS

11.11.1918. The First World War ends.

17.12.1919. *Harakiri* released in Berlin.

1923–24. Kawakita Nagamasa studies in Germany.

01.06.1926. *Bushido* premieres in Japan.

09.05.1927. *Bushido* premieres in Germany.

10.10.1928. Tōwa Shōji Ltd. is established.

1928. Nikkatsu negotiates with Stietencron in Berlin.

November 1928. Stietencron visits Nikkatsu and selects *Music Teacher*.

March 1929. Kawakita brings *Music Teacher*, *Big City*, *Bonfire* and *Samimaro* to Berlin (likely also *Tragedy of a Marriage* and *Diary of Chuji's Travels*).

May 1929. Ufa releases *Shadows of the Yoshiwara*.

August 1929. Stietencron returns to Japan, negotiates with Shōchiku.

1930. *Eternal Heart* screened in Berlin as *Yakichi the Woodcutter*.

1930–31. Berlin: Kishi Kōichi, Wilhelm Furtwängler and Wilhelm Solf discuss the use of film for cultural rejuvenation in Europe.

1931. Kishi establishes Kishi Puro.

01.03.1931. Japanese army marches into Manchuria.

1932. *Nippon* premieres in Berlin.

1932. Kishi returns to Berlin, Ufa produces *Kagami*.

30.01.1933. Hitler is appointed Reich chancellor of Germany.

24.03.1933. Japan declares to leave the League of Nations.

October 1933. *Kagami* premieres in Berlin.

14.10.1933. Germany declares to leave the League of Nations.

20.03.1934. Hayashi Bunzaburō informs Tōwa about Fanck's wish to make a film in Japan.

1935. Shōchiku produces *The Lion Dance* for export.

Spring/Summer 1935. Hata Toyokichi of Tōhō travels to Europe and buys several new productions.

10.06.1935. Ribbentrop and Ōshima negotiate about a defensive alliance.

22.06.1935. Kawakita Nagamasa leaves for Berlin.

03.07.1935. Kawakita Nagamasa arrives in Berlin and meets Fanck in the evening.

03.08.1935. Kawakita Kashiko arrives in Berlin.

10.08.1935. Fanck and Kawakita sign the contract.

TIMELINE OF RELATED CINEMATIC AND POLITICAL EVENTS   xvii

	17.09.1935. First concrete talk between Hack and Ōshima.
	October 1935. Ōshima's first draft treaty.
	November 1935: Rumours about negotiations leak to the international press.
11.11.1935. Fanck informs Kawakita about his party's leaving from Marseilles on 3 January.	
	27.11.1935. Hitler-Ribbentrop talk: Definite decision for an anti-communist agreement between Japan and Germany.
08.02.1936. Fanck's party of eleven arrives in Kobe.	
09.02.1936. Fanck visits Nikkatsu in Kyoto and sees Hara on set of *Kōchiyama Sōchun*.	
10.02.1936. The team goes to Tokyo, settles in Mampei Hotel. Fanck starts working on the script.	
	26.02.1936. February 26 Incident in Tokyo.
04.04.1936. Team sets up base in Kyoto. Fanck continues working on the script, assisted by Itami.	
01.07.1936. Script is completed, cast and crew decided on.	
	August 1936. Olympic Summer Games in Berlin.
08.08.1936. Kosugi and Ichikawa leave for new assignment.	
25.08.1936. Kosugi returns for final location shootings (climax) in Kamikōchi.	

10.09.1936. Predicted completion of shooting, to be followed by editing and soundtrack.

15.10.1936. Predicted release on 'world stages'.

25.11.1936. Anti-Comintern Pact signed in Berlin.

17.12.1937. Fanck and Ōtani sign a contract regarding *New Earth*'s release in Shōchiku's S.Y. chain.

01.02.1937. *New Earth* (IV) premieres in Manchukuo.

03.02.1937. *New Earth* (IV) premieres in Tokyo.

11.02.1937. Itami's version replaced by Fanck's.

12.02.1937. Fanck leaves for Germany.

10.03.1937. Hara, Kumagai and the Kawakitas leave for Berlin.

23.03.1937. *The Samurai's Daughter* premieres in Berlin.

26.03.1937. Hara's party arrives in Berlin.

15.04.1937. Reception at the Japanese embassy.

Late May 1937: The Japanese party leaves for Paris, New York, Los Angeles.

July 1937. Hack is arrested in Germany.

07.07.1937: Marco-Polo Bridge Incident.

12.07.1937: The group leaves for Japan.

28.07.1937. Hara is welcomed back in Japan.

Introduction

The foreigners stayed at the Kamikōchi Hotel, and the Japanese at the Shimizuya Ryōkan. They rose at four to prepare for the ascent. It took two and a half hours to arrive at the shooting location on the summit. They arrived there around eight. The sky was clear and they began preparing the shooting in high spirits. Yet, when they were about to begin, clouds started to emerge. All stopped. The group of ten stared at the sky and waited . . . . But . . . Yakedake's summit is only clear for about two or three hours in the morning. They couldn't help but wait until the next day. They retraced the way they had so painstakingly come up. . . . Therefore, a bright day was a special cause for joy. Then the mountain showed a mysterious transfiguration. On set, always-gentle Fanck displayed an almost frightening vigour and greed. Like a beast, he circled the summit in order to seize each and every changing vista of the mountain.

(KAWAKITA 1936B: 66)

One October evening in 1936, Kawakita Kashiko reminisced over her diary and remembered a tumultuous year. In February, German film director Arnold Fanck and his team had arrived in Japan to make a jointly produced film with Tōwa Shōji, the film import–export and production company owned by her and her husband, Kawakita Nagamasa. The 'great efforts and hardships' that Kashiko anticipated in her entry for 5 January would eventually result in a 'great film' (Kawakita 1936b: 66) that would keep attracting attention, but in a different sense than its participants could have imagined. The crew returned from shooting the climax on Mount Yakedake in the scorching heat of August of 1936 (Figure 0.1), and Kawakita noted their tans and weight loss: 'Their trousers were far too loose. Yet, the film they brought back was all the more splendid' (Kawakita 1936b: 66).

Fanck was an internationally renowned specialist for films set in hard-to-access mountainous regions, and Japan provided an ideal environment in

FIGURE 0.1 *The film's climax, shot on an active volcano in the Northern Japan Alps.*

which to play out his strengths. Kawakita looked forward to the premiere in Berlin's grand Gloria Palast theatre on 15 November. The Tokyo premiere, however, would take place first, so that 'this first Japanese film to advance into the world with the label "Made in Japan" affixed to it will premiere in Japan prior to all other countries' (Kawakita 1936b: 67). Despite allusions to 'difficulties' in the project, her outlook as published in the film magazine *Eiga no tomo* was positive: the film's title, *New Earth* (*Atarashiki tsuchi*), expressed the new experience of the internationalization of Japanese film and the hope that this new field would bear rich harvest in the future (Kawakita 1936b: 67). When the film eventually premiered – later as predicted – on 3 February 1937, it was on a scale befitting the high hopes attached to it (Figure 0.2). The event in Tokyo's exclusive Teikoku Gekijō (Imperial Theatre) was opened by the president of the Society for International Cultural Relations (*Kokusai Bunka Shinkōkai*), Kabayama Aisuke, and attended by a large number of eminent Japanese and foreign guests, including diplomats from Germany, England, the United States, Italy and other countries as well as, unprecedented for a public film screening, members of the Imperial Family. Extensively reported by the press, this was the culmination of almost two years of preparation and strenuous work, and it seemed as if *New Earth* would fulfil Kawakita's expectations and open new ground for the aspiring Japanese film industry.

FIGURE 0.2 *'Announcing [our] true values to the world: Japan's greatest and finest masterpiece!'*

And indeed, in the field of Japanese and German cultural–political relations, the project is well-known; perhaps notorious. This interest, however, is not due to a beneficial effect on the film business but a consequence of historical hindsight and a second meaning of its title, the *New Earth*. The film's final scene sees the two young protagonists married and with a baby boy in the vast fields of Japan's puppet state Manchukuo (Manchuria), the establishment of which in 1932 had caused much international furore. In August 1936, when the film's shooting was well underway, the Japanese cabinet approved the plan 'Millions to Manchuria' (*Japan Weekly Chronicle* 1936: 27). One million Japanese farming households were to be settled in Manchuria within twenty years, each household being provided with 20 hectares of farmland, almost twenty times the average in Japan (Kiernan 2007: 463). A government pamphlet announced the need of a 'superior race well-trained in agricultural techniques to guide the backward Chinese farmers in the field' (Young 1998: 321–2). *New Earth*'s protagonist Yamato Teruo (played by Kosugi Isamu), who is shown working the vast Manchurian field with a modern Komatsu tractor, corresponds to this ideal (Figure 0.3).

Adopted as a future son-in-law into a wealthy family, he returns to Japan after eight years of agricultural studies abroad. In a previous scene he had

FIGURE 0.3 *Teruo driving a Komatsu tractor.*

told his Western companion Gerda Storm (Ruth Eweler) about Japan's 'enormous task of developing that backward country', visualized by shots of antiquated farming methods. The discourse is corroborated further by shots of narrow paddy fields and the words of Teruo's birth father (Takagi Eiji) in a later scene: 'Today, we are too many for this small piece of land. We are too many, my son Teruo.' This motif clearly referenced Japanese official discourse concerning its westwards expansion, but given the fact that film was scripted and directed by a German director, it also strongly calls into mind the notion of *Volk ohne Raum* (people without space), justifying Germany's drive to the East.

This nationalistic aspect that seemingly perverts the film's international objective provides the premiere's second background. Not quite three months before, on 25 November 1936, Germany and Japan had signed the Anti-Comintern Pact, their first military agreement in the lead-up to the formation of the Axis. Thus, the fact of German–Japanese cooperation came to the fore, both in diplomatic and *New Earth*–related discourse. In December 1936, the *Asahi Shinbun* labelled the film's scheduled simultaneous releases in Tokyo and Berlin on 1 February a 'Japanese-German Pact of the Silver Screen' (*nichidoku ginmaku kyōtei*), an obvious reference to the 'Japanese-German Anticommunist Pact' (*nichidoku bōkyō kyōtei*) (*Asahi Shinbun* 18.12.1936: 2). In the film's final scene, set in Manchukuo, a Japanese farmer guards the young settler family, and in fulfilment of his duty he is looking westwards. The staging here confirms the lines spoken in a previous scene by Yamato Iwao, the dignified patriarch of Teruo's adoptive family, played by former Hollywood screen idol Sessue Hayakawa: he reassures Gerda, a young German journalist and Teruo's friend, that the Japanese people are keeping watch and will fight 'storms' from the West, a more than implicit allusion to the military pact's covert direction against the Soviet Union.

At the Berlin premiere on 23 March, Dr Joseph Goebbels, Reich minister of public enlightenment and propaganda, and Heinrich Himmler, *Reichsführer* SS and chief of police, were among the high-ranking government officials and members of the Japanese embassy that filled the cinema. Ambassador Mushanokōji Kintomo, who had signed the pact in Berlin, was present as a matter of course. The film's German release title *Die Tochter des Samurai* (Samurai's Daughter), refers to the female lead role, Yamato Mitsuko, Teruo's fiancée, played by a very young Hara Setsuko, Ozu Yasujirō's later muse and grande dame of Japanese cinema's post-war golden age. Producing a link between current ideological discourses in Germany and Japan, Iwao, Mitsuko's father, also explains to Gerda that Japan is built on the (rock-) solid foundation of the family, the 'highest notion' of which is the Imperial Family: 'Our Japan . . . is our Imperial Family. Our Imperial family . . . is Japan' (Figure 0.4).

FIGURE 0.4 *Yamato Iwao explaining the principles of the family state to Gerda Storm.*

In his writings on the film, Director Fanck presented his representation of the concept of the 'family state' (*kazoku kokka*), which utilized the image of the family to delineate duties and rights on all levels of society and to firmly position the emperor as the father of the nation (Morris-Suzuki 2015: 94–5), as the key for a German audience to understand the Japanese mentality, due to an emotional correspondence to the *Führerprinzip* (leader principle). 'Adolf Hitler is Germany and Germany is Adolf Hitler', as 'Deputy to the Führer' Rudolf Hess pronounced in 1934 (Taylor and Shaw 1997: 335). 'Our Führer – is Germany. Germany – is our Führer', writes Fanck in 1938 (90–1).[1] The production's award by Goebbels's ministry as 'valuable in terms of national policy and artistic merit' was disseminated in Japan by the press and in trade magazines. German reporters found links to the new ally in the film's focus on Japanese bravery, the protagonist's reconversion to his

---

[1]The 'leader principle' was the National Socialist Party's ideological basis: following Social Darwinism, only the most able personality was destined to 'lead' and therefore his will was paramount. Completely opposed to democratic and human right principles, this construct promoted a pyramid-shaped hierarchical society of top-down command and obedience (on the origins and details see Welch 1999: 80–1).

traditional Japanese roots and his wish to work for the advancement of his native country in the 'new earth' of Manchukuo.

Taking these motifs and associated ideologies into consideration, it is hardly surprising that the project is today mainly mentioned with regard to political propaganda inherent in the film's message and in the very fact that these two countries made this film together at that point in time. But given the dismissal of the film as predictable propaganda with little artistic value, it is still curious how often it is mentioned in scholarly works across disciplines, including studies of historical–cultural relations between Germany and Japan, encyclopaedic entries on the participants, and accounts of Japanese films of the wartime period.[2] And in line with German reports on the premiere that celebrated the film as Director Fanck's achievement, subsequent studies argue that the film, written and directed by a German, aimed at corroborating German expansionist discourse by looking for new soil in the East. Marginalizing the production as German propaganda played out on Japanese soil by a 'thoroughly Nazified Dr Fanck' (Anderson and Richie 1982: 92), this nationalized focus cannot comprehend what was an ambitious, international project from its very beginning. In fact, such narratives, in disregarding the endeavour's complexities, tend to repeat the straightforward account Kawakita Kashiko gave in the running up to the film's highly anticipated release. Reading between the lines, however, Kawakita's description of the location shooting, with the Japanese and Germans staying at different inns, hints at a schism behind the facade of binational collaboration. She also did not make public the breakdown of cooperation between Fanck and his Japanese co-director, Itami Mansaku.

---

[2]The project is regularly mentioned in general histories of Japanese film, contextualized with burgeoning nationalism (e.g. in High 2003: 534; Iwamoto 2004; NHK 1986; Satō 1997: 79–86, 419–21; Sharp 2011: 49–51; Yamamoto 2004). The coming into stardom of one of Japan's iconic actresses, Hara Setsuko, has been considered *New Earth*'s most significant result in Japan (e.g. by Satō 1995: 395). Scholarship also takes it up either with regard to Fanck's persona and his relation to National–Socialist ideology and/or concerning German appropriations of an image of Japan (see Bieber 2014; Hack 1996: 251–63; High 2003: 150; Leims 1990; Maltarich 2005; Manvell 1974: 355; Weinstein 2014). Until very recently, Janine Hansen's in-depth examination of the project and analysis of Fanck's version was the only monograph on *New Earth* (1997a; for abbreviated articles, also in English, see Hansen 1997b, 2001 and 2007). While this book was underway, two further monographs dealing with or mentioning the project came out: Sierek's study (2018, written in German, like Hansen's) considers *New Earth* in context with a larger study of Kawakita Nagamasa's involvement in German and Japanese political circles and wartime regimes. Segawa's book in Japanese aims at a nuanced approach, considering motivations alternative to exclusively political ones (2017). His more sympathetic narrative confirms that a certain temporal and perhaps spatial distance is needed in order to open up the field of enquiry further, beyond dichotomous interpretations. In this respect, his is a very welcome contribution, to which this study adds a more comprehensive angle that considers personal, aesthetic, industrial and cultural continuities, with an emphasis on the film project's place within the participants' public personas and careers.

The two directors eventually each made his own version, both titled *New Earth* for the Japanese release.³

The breakdown of cooperation, which makes the undertaking such a 'famous episode in film history' (Irie 1996: 12), is attributed to Itami's resistance to the political motifs in Fanck's script: 'Fanck, however, would have none of it [Itami's alternative script] and insisted that his first real German-Japanese collaboration have a clear, pro-Fascist political message. Fanck won out' (High 2003: 161). Hansen's thorough examination of the project, in much the same vein, examines how Fanck intentionally placed National–Socialist propaganda into the film (1997a). However, she also brings the project out of the most blatant political context, in concluding that Kawakita and Fanck made this film not with direct governmental involvement as was usually assumed, but in 'anticipatory obedience' towards the powers that be (1997a: 124). But by eventually attributing the film project itself to Kawakita and the problematic content to Fanck, she maintains a nationalized dichotomy. Germany, personified by Fanck, is positioned as an active perpetrator of political propaganda – Nazi Germany's foremost director' (Yomota 2000: 36) – and Japan, in the person of Itami – a representative of former, more liberal times – as a victim. Kawakita appears as an industrious but somewhat naive pursuer of intercultural understanding and international recognition for Japanese film (Yomota 2000: 49; Tsuji and Shimizu 1987: 34–9).⁴ The perpetrator–victim narrative at work here is problematic, as it reverberates with post-war narratives of war guilt and responsibility. As Yamamoto shows, for instance, discussions of Itami as a victim of this film-making ordeal echo – and perhaps corroborate – similar discourses on a national level (2004). This nationalized narrative with its emphasis on the (ab-)use of culture for politics, and with Germany as personified in Director Fanck being the focus of attention, is caused by two interrelated factors.

First, the film is persistently contextualized with the Second World War, as for instance, indicated by the entry's cross-reference to 'war and film, ties with Germany' in Sharp's *Historical Dictionary of Japanese Cinema* (2011: 278). Similarly, Anderson and Richie establish a causal relationship between political developments and the film project, which is as straightforward as chronologically incorrect, and repeated in subsequent studies: 'Political co-productions officially began in 1936, just after both Japan and Germany had signed their Anti-Communist Pact' (Anderson and Richie 1982: 148;

---

³The use of different release titles for Fanck's edition in Germany and Japan proved problematic in terms of clarity. I use *Samurai's Daughter* for Fanck's version in its German context. When referring to the project as such as it took place in Japan, I use *New Earth*, distinguishing if necessary between 'Fanck's version' (FV) and 'Itami's version' (IV).

⁴Sierek's recent study on Kawakita's involvement in *New Earth*, his work with the German Ufa and his links to politics, with an emphasis on his Chinese connections, provides an interesting intervention in this discourse (2018).

see also Hirano 2001: 226; Shutsū and Nagata 2008: 56; Yamamoto 2004: 68). While various studies mention previous efforts to launch Japanese films into international markets as *New Earth*'s background (NHK 1986: 11; Yamamoto 2004; Segawa 2017), the eventual temporal framework for discussions remains 'war time'. References to the film as the 'first German-Japanese co-production' (e.g. Hansen 2007: 189) buy into the publicity campaign by the producers and distributors and confirm the notion of a beginning of (political) collaborations, containing it in a time bubble. These approaches cannot account for the industrial, stylistic and narrative continuities visible in the project that hint towards an interplay of diverse forces and agendas at work.

Second, Director Fanck was very visible in the project. The Japanese press hailed him as a famous director, German publications celebrated his achievement and Fanck made the most out of this opportunity. He published prolifically on the film and his impressions on Japan, made various follow-up short films and kept pushing until his death for his *Samurai's Daughter* to be broadcast by the German television. Fanck's authorship of the script, his prominence in the project and the ready availability of this version on DVD strengthen his position. Conversely, Itami's comments on the project are sparse; very often the film he made based on Fanck's script is not even considered entirely his, and his version had been kept closely guarded. In recent years, the grip seems to have loosened somewhat, but detailed (and costly) research viewings are only possible at the National Film Archive in Tokyo.

Here, the limiting effect of the 'propaganda' label becomes tangible: when the Japanese national broadcaster NHK showed Itami's film in the 1980s and introduced it as an example of 'cooperation with the war', Kawakita Kashiko banned further public screenings, because 'of course we were against the war, and we tried to do our best under the circumstances'.[5] Her decision severely restricted the possibility of engaging in depth with both films. This situation results in a neglect of the Japanese interests in the project. Various elements of the film, however, clearly resonate with discourses occurring in Japanese at the time. *New Earth*'s aesthetics and thematic concerns remind one much of the posters, pamphlets and travel brochures displayed in the National Museum of Modern Art Tokyo's 2016 exhibition *Visit Japan: Tourism Promotion in the 1920s and 1930s* (*Yōkoso Nihon e: 1920-30 nendai no tsūrizumu to dezain*, 9 January to 28 February 2016). South Manchurian Railway (Minami Manshū tetsudō; Mantetsu) trains, such as the iconic Asia Express shown in the film, and steamers, such as the one with which Teruo and Gerda (and the German film team) arrived in Japan, travelled to and through the colonies, thus discursively and visibly making them a part of Japan (Figures 0.5 and 0.6). The exhibition's

---

[5] Author's conversations with the Kawakita Memorial Film Institute.

FIGURE 0.5 *The Asia Express.*

FIGURE 0.6 *The protagonists arriving on a steamship.*

title, similarly, compresses the various countries controlled by the Japanese empire within 'Japan' (Nihon),[6] an ideology that in 1936 made it possible for *New Earth*'s newly-weds, Mitsuko and Teruo, to begin their own family and future in Manchukuo.

Teruo's conversion from a cosmopolitan intellectual to a Japanese model farmer echoes Davis's observation that the '1930s saw the movie screen take on the didactic function of awakening cosmopolitan Japanese to the glories of their own culture' (1996: 45). Finally, considering that the project took place in Japan, was mostly financed by the Japanese side and used a predominantly Japanese crew and cast, the focus on Germany is myopic. Mizuno succinctly summarizes the intricate tension between German and Japanese ideological motifs on a political level: 'The story faithfully reflected Nazi cultural policy and Japanese colonial and paternal desire projected onto Asia' (2009: 12). This binational co-production, however, was also aimed at international audiences. It is necessary to distinguish between the aim of film export, personal motives, politico-ideological concerns and an exercise in intercultural understanding, as these notions have become intertwined in the discourse.

This multiplicity becomes manifest in the vast amount of material produced by the project. Not only do we deal with four editions of the film itself – Itami's film, the release editions of Fanck's film for Japan and for Germany, a subsequently censored German version, not even taking into account three German re-releases (1943, 1959 and 2001) – but also comments on and recollections of the project by the participants, by film critics, advertising departments and distribution companies, intellectuals, journalists and so on. The Kawakitas and Tōwa Shōji's press department carefully collected close to any print material that was produced between 1935 and 1937 in context with *New Earth*, filling over fifteen scrapbooks with an estimated three thousand clippings, leaflets, programmes, notes and so on. This excessive discourse then becomes a topic of interest in itself. What was at stake that necessitated such effort? It is the vastness of the material, which makes palpable over a temporal distance of more than eighty years the attention and energy expended in the project (Figure 0.7). And a time when the introduction of sound had made a film's 'nationality' audible and dubbing had become the standard in Germany from 1933 – also because foreign-language films were seen as threatening both national culture and identity (Blinn 2008: 12–13) – *New Earth* being polyglot, with the actors speaking German or English and Japanese, appears innovative and ambitious. These

---

[6]The exhibition title was chosen consciously, well aware of its implications and contradictions, in order to avoid negative associations with the contested issue of colonialism and the feared, resulting decrease in domestic visitors. Interestingly, it did not call forth any negative reactions by Japan's neighbouring countries.

FIGURE 0.7 *The film team's commemorative picture on completion.*

unacknowledged high hopes associated with – and eventually disappointed by – *New Earth* inspired the reopening of its history in this book.

Propaganda and aspirations

When one looks closely at the project, it appears to be more than 'Fanck's Nazi propaganda in Far Eastern disguise' (Hansen 2001: 195). Gerow reminds us that a reflective history that links historical conditions and events to film contents fails to address the fact that the conjunctive points themselves are subject to continuous negotiations regarding 'meaning and influence' (2010: 4, 26). 'We must be careful of how our desires shape our vision of this film, for they can commit a violence against the text' and shape the analytical tools towards an anticipated outcome (2010: 5). Hindsight that remains unacknowledged can violate the text it is imposed upon. Is it possible that previous approaches to *Samurai's Daughter/New Earth* reflect present desires for distinct demarcation lines within the timeframe under consideration?

The project took place not only across national borders but also at temporal thresholds. In Japan as in Germany, the years 1936 and 1937 marked political turning points: the attempted coup d'état in Tokyo in February 1936, Hitler's announcement of preparations for war at the

Nuremberg Rally in September 1936, the signing of the Anti-Comintern Pact in November 1936 and the beginning of the Second Sino-Japanese War in July 1937. In both countries the state increasingly tightened its control over the media in an effort to mobilize public support. Kracauer's 1947 *From Caligari to Hitler*, a work frequently referred to in discussions of *New Earth*, initiated the post-war examination of 'propaganda' in German films (Kracauer 2004 [1947]; Hansen 2001: 187; High 2003: 150; Yomota 2000: 40). 'If, as their different arguments imply, the German nation is haunted by its cinema screen, and the films are haunted by German history, then their books are themselves haunted by the history that came after the films'. This argument, made by Elsaesser regarding the 'master narrative' in Kracauer's and Lotte Eisner's readings of 'proto-Nazi sentiments' in Weimar cinema, applies to a large degree to interpretations of *New Earth*, with its position as a watershed (Eisner 1973; Elsaesser 2000: 4). Consequently, Hansen's analysis 'is concerned foremost with the aspects of propaganda within the film, the adaptation of which also plays a role within the context of the political background' (1997a: 3). But 'the adaptation of propaganda' can play a role only in this context; the effectiveness of propaganda can only be measured at the audience level, and readings of films depend on the context of reception, rather than on films containing a transcendental meaning. It is for this reason that parts of *New Earth* could reappear in the 'anti-Japanese propaganda films' *This Was Japan* (1945 Wright), *Know Your Enemy: Japan* (1945 Capra) and *My Japan* (1945, produced by the U.S. Treasury Department, War Finance Division) in order to rally popular support in the last stages of the war against the Axis and to boost the sale of war bonds. The label of propaganda also holds the danger of obliterating the project's contradictory moments. As Kramer argues, to hold on to the misleadingly transcendental term 'propaganda' means to hold on to 'the myth of the deceived *Volk*' that has become obsolete in the historical debate (2009: 98). In the Japanese context, Fanck's co-director Itami Mansaku revealed this 'deception' as a myth already in 1946 (1961 [1946]a: 212).

While the theory of total manipulation by the state in wartime Japan and Germany has undergone a paradigm shift in favour of examinations of social interactions in the context of wartime mobilization and of audience reaction to the output of these processes,[7] these developments have been slow to impact on interpretations of *New Earth* as an international collaboration that addressed multiple problems and aspirations. The notion of 'propaganda' cannot be dismissed, but it must be re-situated from being the endpoint of examination to becoming an object of inquiry. All cultural

---

[7]The political use of film in Japan has been treated among others by Baskett 2008; Davis 1996; Furukawa 2003; High 2003; Hori 2017; Iwamoto 2004; Salomon 2011; Standish 2000; Wada-Marciano 2008. For the German context see Aldinger 2005; Hoffmann 1996; Kanzog 1994; Kettler 2011; Loiperdinger 2004; Moeller 2000; Welch 2001; Witte 1993.

products are influenced by – and in turn influence – ideological traits of the wider society they originate in, but it is individuals who choose, initiate and produce these motifs. The question then becomes one of intention:

> The maker of a picture or other historical artefact is a man addressing a problem of which his product is a finished and concrete solution. To understand it we try to reconstruct both the specific problem it was designed to solve and the specific circumstances out of which he was addressing it. (Baxandall 1985: 14–15; cited in Kirihara 1992: 160)

The project was supposed to address at least three concerns for the various parties involved: first, the successful export of Japanese film as evident from the support the project received on multiple levels; second, the authentic representation of Japan and the underlying idea that it is possible to discern a ('the') specific, authoritative Japanese authenticity and to translate and disseminate this quality cinematically, filtered through the foreign director's aesthetic sensibilities; third, the participants' positioning within their specific contexts of career and life, complicated by the endeavour's transnational environment. The interplay with political discourses and the propagandistic motifs appears symptomatic of a power struggle, rather than mono-causal for the project. And this struggle, I argue, was first and foremost concerned with the notion of authenticity, interpreted and instrumentalized according to the participants' individual agendas, and complicated by the unspoken endeavour of cultural translation.

Authenticity as a task and a problem

The ideal of authenticity underlay the project's very inception: producing a film that, for the first time, showed Japan to the world 'as it really is', while at the same time being economically viable. During the production period, the authentic depiction of Japan featured strongly in advertising campaigns, but it became the apple of discord between the directors as well as in the eventual critical reception in Japan. Authenticity and commodification are two entities whose reconciliation poses a general problem 'faced by publicists and "sellers of the genuine"' (Lindholm 2008: 61). Fanck was known in both Germany and Japan for his emphasis on the 'real', but he had to resort to adding narrative contours to his quasi-documentary adventure films to make them economically successful. Itami, in turn, took up the matter of authenticity and commodification with regard to Japanese film export in his thoughts on 'Film and national characteristics', in which he derided *New Earth* as a 'mongrel' that succeeded in neither category (1961 [1944]: 178). Within the project, Itami was regarded as closer to the 'authentic' than Fanck by virtue of being an 'insider'. He was supposed to help Fanck represent an authentic image of Japan and the Japanese and to 'correct' the foreigner's mistakes in this regard. Consequently, after the clash, we would expect Itami's version to be noticeably closer than Fanck's to what Lindholm, in his discussion of the cultural currency of authenticity, names the 'really real' (2008: 1). But it is difficult to determine what the really real 'really' is: The lived reality of Japan in 1936? But whose and according to whom?

> [Itami] wanted to represent Japan abroad, stressing all its modern, European achievements, such as imposing railway bridges, modern electric trains, modern skyscrapers, but avoiding old Japanese customs or ways of life. This was the opposite of the image of Japan as I wanted to show it and which accounted for its charm. (Fanck 1973: 342)

Divergent notions of authenticity are immediately visible in credit titles' backgrounds: Fanck's images are painted in gouache in a naïve Japonesque style. The collage of Mount Fuji, houses within a misty mountainscape, lanterns, fire braziers and branches full of cherry blossoms, calls to mind 'picture-postcard shots' and remains firmly within the realm of 'Old Japan' (Figure 0.8). This kind of authentication by ancientness is repeated in the music that exclusively uses traditional instruments and is then replaced by

FIGURE 0.8 *Impressions of 'Japan' superimposed in Fanck's credit sequence.*

parts from composer Yamada Kōsaku's fusion of Japanese traditional music and Western orchestration in his *Sinfonia 'Inno Meiji'* (*Kōkyōkyoku 'Meiji shōka'*) (1921).

Itami superimposes the credits over an astonishingly 'real' miniature model of Japan, with a smoking volcano at the centre, and a part of occupied Korea in the upper left corner (the same shot appears in Fanck's version, following the credit titles, in a birds-eye approach). The musical score provides a spatial marker through its slightly 'Japanese' style but switches into a contemporary orchestral piece, upbeat and indistinguishable from 'Hollywood' or 'European' film music as soon as the title *New Earth* appears, first in alphabet and then in Japanese characters (Figure 0.9).

Fanck considered the two films to be as different as the directors' diverging views on what to represent and how to do so (Fanck 1973: 343). He called Itami's version a 'bad film', far removed from his own subject matter (Fanck 1973: 351–2). Seen from a distance, however, *Samurai's Daughter* and *New Earth* seem quite similar in the general plot line and other aspects, as might be expected from two films made from the same script. The 'modern, European achievements' appear in both films, as do more traditional aspects. There are, however, divergences, and those made by Itami within the restricted environment described earlier bear all the more significance. Fanck's

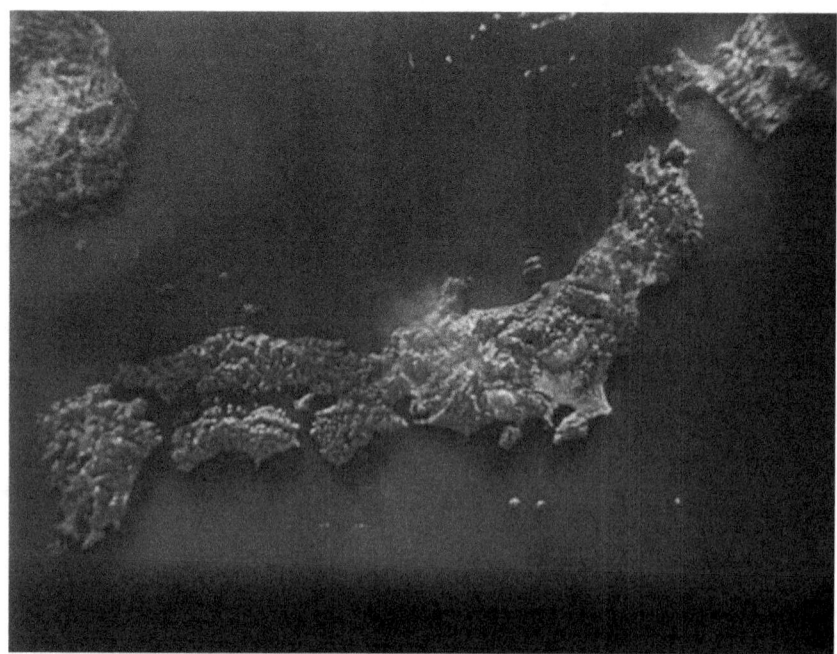

FIGURE 0.9 *The miniature model of Japan.*

comments indicate that the changes were quite distinctive to the participants, given their emotional and artistic investment. Both directors operated outside of their respective genres and comfort zones, and this discomfort was primarily due to the project's inherent focus on the 'really real'.

Authenticity as an intellectual concept is very often connected to power struggles. Its application to the determination of hierarchies – of artistic quality, for example – hints towards the power positions at stake. In this process, 'certain forms, styles, performers, regions, or ethnic groups are selected over others. Authenticity often validates a certain tradition, genre . . . and/or individual/s with a rationale for receiving government funding or being included in textbooks' (Terada 2007: 1). In the case of *New Earth*, 'cultural traits' that could be disseminated internationally were of value. Drawing on 'traditions', invented or not, was of course not an unfamiliar tactic either in Germany or in Japan at the time and indeed, '[e]very modern government appropriates indigenous aesthetic productions in order to give itself an aura of legitimacy, continuity, and embodied reality' (Lindholm 2008: 98). Whether or not there are actually traits that are somehow specific to and make unique a certain group of people, this idea is questionable when it comes to the constructed large community that is the modern nation-state (Anderson 1993; Hobsbawm and Ranger 1993).

On the other hand, as evident from the strong reactions to *New Earth* in Japan, regardless of the ontological status of such a quality, many feel strongly about it. Assuming that authenticity is not an intrinsic quality of a work of art, for instance, it seems nevertheless instructive to take seriously the emotional investment in discussions of what is authentic and what is not and start to think of the authentic as a sensory experience. As Hospers has argued regarding 'the esthetic' in the arts, 'Much confusion results from the failure to remember that "the esthetic" refers to a kind of *attitude* rather than the *object* toward which the attitude is taken' (1976 [1946]: 7). This problem with the use of 'object-language' rather than 'experience-language' (defining a tune as melancholic instead of stating that it makes one feel melancholy) (1976 [1946]: 14) shifts the focus to the perceiver, rather than the object itself, as is the case with a medium's propagandistic content. Moreover, the attitude towards an object as 'esthetic' or 'authentic' depends on and can change with the perceiver's context. It is interesting to note that a Japanese student in Berlin did not comment at all on the authenticity of the Japan represented in *Samurai's Daughter* when he saw it soon after its German release: 'The plot is boring, but the shots are beautiful' (Yamaguchi 2002: 6–7). Someone finds something authentic or not, and sometimes authenticity is not an issue at all. Moore, looking at the perceivers' reaction, asks who rather than what is being authenticated in a performance (2002) and thus closes the circle to Terada's cautioning about the power play at work when judging a performer or a performance as to the presence or absence of 'authenticity' (2007).

The issue of authenticity, however, becomes more complex and contested in transnational contexts, such as *New Earth*, because of the noxious character of the outsider/insider dichotomy and concerns about national prestige. When placing the project within its international context and its specific timeframe, it would be myopic to ignore the unequal power relations regarding the presentation of selves or others between Japan and the West. Fanck, as well as the Japanese producers, clearly aimed at explaining Japan to the West. This even becomes manifest in the film in the character of the German journalist Gerda Storm, who collects information about Japanese customs in order to introduce them to her prospective German readership (Figure 0.10).

Rather than 'explanation', the concept of 'cultural translation' – the understanding of culture as a text, the translation of which requires knowledge of both cultures – emerged in the field of social anthropology in the 1950s (Asad 2010: 10) and is helpful to understand the positions and choices available to those involved in *New Earth*. The cultural translator faces the same choices as the translator of literature: to 'domesticate' the texts, minimizing its strangeness and make it transparent and fluent for its target readers, or to intentionally keep aspects of 'foreignness', that is, to 'foreignize the text' and retain the cultural gap. Both have their specific

FIGURE 0.10 *Journalist Gerda capturing Japan.*

usage scenarios, but since, as we will see, *New Earth* was based on the assumption that 'Japanese film' and in extension 'Japan' was too strange to be understood by foreign audiences, and Fanck was invited to make the strange familiar, the former strategy was the obvious choice. Two factors complicated this unacknowledged translation project: As Asad shows via the difference between anthropological and linguistic translation, 'whereas the latter is immediately faced with a specific piece of discourse produced within the society studied . . . the former must construct the discourse as a cultural text in terms of meanings *implicit* in a range of practices' (Asad 2010: 24; emphasis in the original). Fanck was required contractually to construct his own text, based on his translation of his own observations, and then translate it again, this time into an audiovisual signal. Second, as all translations, *New Earth* was a perpetrator of violence in terms of 'the reconstitution of the foreign text in accordance with values, beliefs and representations that pre-exist it in the target language, always configured in hierarchies of dominance and marginality, always determining the production, circulation and reception of texts' (Venuti 2010: 68). As we will see, these hierarchies engendered the project itself, but they also configured the power positions of its participants in terms of whose opinion was valued and became visible in the film, as well as the interpretations of the way Japan was represented. Kirihara's suggestion to consider 'the author not as an object but as a network of forces organized from prior events' (1992: 24) therefore can be extended, remembering that past experiences and anticipations of the future impact present actions. This approach then not only locates the individual within contexts but, in introducing the issue of power in its insistence on influential forces rather than intentions, also points towards the intertextuality of 'the author'.

Clearly, 'culture is a sort of theatre where various political and ideological causes engage each other' (Said 1993: xiv), but personal and industrial motifs are just as central. And, as the engagement occurs at the levels of production, distribution and consumption, the reception of the cultural product *New Earth* was and is equally diverse. As an event, *New Earth* puts into the spotlight the tendency to take labels for granted, in particular regarding a period, delineated from the 1930s to 1945, that still leaves us puzzled by its personal motifs and societal movements. Yet its inherent multifacetedness – historical, national, cultural, industrial and personal – also accounts for the challenges one faces when opening it up for discussion.

Approaching contested terrains

Reconsidering the project's two dimensions, the actual, past event and subsequent scholarly and popular discourses demand an approach that combines various types of 'explanation' (Thompson and Bordwell 2003: 5):

biographical history, industrial history, social/cultural/political history and aesthetic history, merging into an analysis of the surrounding discourses and of the two films – as historical cultural artefacts – that grew out of and simultaneously contributed to them.

And if writing (film-)history is constructing a narrative, it seems instructive to look in more detail at the dramatis personae of these stories (White 1987). While there were various persons involved, such as former Hollywood star Sessue Hayakawa, Tsuburaya Eiji, who would go on to create one of the most iconic creatures of the century, Godzilla (*Gojira*, 1954, Honda) the Kawakitas and composer Yamada Kōsaku, to name but a few, the discourse on *New Earth* was and is to a large degree focused on its two directors. Itami and Fanck are usually portrayed as diametrically opposed: 'Fanck, a very capable filmmaker in his own right, was apparently a true Nazi. Itami was a subtle artist, a man of enormous literary talent as well as a master of psychological portrayal in cinema' (High 2003: 150). This assessment denies Fanck artistry and subtlety, traits negated by Nazism. As a preliminary observation, the two directors coming together in the project display similarities as well as differences. Fanck held a doctorate in geology, while Itami was educated to the middle school level. While both came to film from other visual arts (painting and photography), Itami was more literary and interested in his characters and Fanck more visual in his style. Both were opinionated and published copious articles related to film and politics throughout their careers. Ufa feared Fanck's letters of complaint (High 2003: 51), and Itami's insistent character earned him the unflattering nickname *Goteman* (*goteru*: to complain constantly; *man*: 'thousand'; a play on his first name, Mansaku) (Sugimoto 2005 [1934]: 110). Both were heavily involved in their films and established new genres and generic conventions in nationally specific genres: *jidaigeki* and *Bergfilm* (mountain film). While discussions of the film often take Fanck's professional background into consideration, not much is revealed about Itami beyond the fact that he was a top director at J.O. Studios when he was assigned to *New Earth*.[8] This lopsidedness prevents a comprehensive understanding of the film project as such and of the complexities of the time in which it took place. Without pre-empting the (predominantly) post-war problematizing of the film and its participants, in order to understand how they approached, filmed and finalized their two versions of the film, each in his own facilitating and constraining framework, it is also necessary to examine their respective positions within this binational undertaking.

I will approach this cinematic undertaking from various angles, and the book's first half, comprising Chapters 1 to 3, is strongly historiographical,

---

[8]Anderson and Richie 1982: 149; Baskett 2008: 128; Bieber 2009: 359; Hansen, 1997a; Yomota 2000: 35.

precisely to offer an in-depth rereading of predominantly historico-political interpretations. How did this 'famous episode' (Irie 1996: 12), or 'pathetic incident' (High 2003: 150), depending on one's point of view, come to pass in the first place? As history is made by people, the participants' past experiences and anticipations of the future shaped their present actions and interactions in the production of *New Earth*. Hence, Chapter 1 reinserts the project into an ongoing process of negotiating a national image of Japan on international cinema screens and focuses on previous cinematic relationships between Germany and Japan. A push towards the export of Japanese films in 1929 illustrates the importance ascribed to international recognition on industrial as well as cultural–ideological levels. Three German–Japanese co-productions with various degrees of relative Japanese participation show that *New Earth* was embedded in a series of related undertakings, also in terms of visual and thematic motifs, and all three already carry *New Earth*'s concern for the proper depiction of an 'authentic' Japan.

Chapter 2 then traces the production history of this subsequent binational co-production in detail, drawing on the extensive resources and documentation by the production company and the participants. The focus here is on the people involved, the changes of the film's titles and content and the shift from what looked to be an ambitious but well-planned, straightforward project, to a narrative riddled with inconsistencies and frictions behind the camera. Even after the two grandly advertised premieres in Tokyo and Berlin that brought their own conflicts that belie the idea of harmonious cinematic and political cooperation, the Japanese side harboured high expectations towards the film's international success or, instead, towards an international career of the seventeen-year-old lead actress, Hara Setsuko. Tracing *New Earth* and the Japanese party's way from Japan, over Germany and France to the United States, the chapter also touches on how the film became entangled in political developments.

Taking the political aspect as a springboard, Chapter 3 puts into perspective the prevailing, post hoc, ergo propter hoc conflation of the project and the conclusion of the Anti-Comintern Pact. By expanding on three possible backgrounds brought forward by Hansen (1997a), I will also give more attention to the Japanese side's motivations for embarking on this costly venture. An examination of the order of events establishes a lack of a causal, politically determined relationship between film and military agreement, and therefore the interactions of the film project and political developments leave an impression of intersections, interdependencies and instrumentalization, rather than a unilinear chain of cause and effect. Considering history writing as an ongoing process that is always subject to new findings, Chapters 2 and 3 thus build on the alternative context for the project to emerge, discussed in Chapter 1, and offers one possible alternative interpretation of past events.

Authenticity played a prominent role in the production as well as in political propaganda and nationalist discourses, and it was a means to power as it concerns the project *New Earth*. The film produced certain truths about Japan. Equally, certain truths about Japan produced the films. Japan became the object of both German and Japanese power/knowledge relations. Chapter 4 expands on the status of authenticity in the directors' personas and approaches to film and as a power factor in transnational, quasi-ethnographic encounters such as underlying the film project. The Japanese contract partners and the Japanese discourse played a concrete, constitutive role in the inception and production of the image of Japan presented in the film. Regardless of Fanck's objectives, invariably he engaged with the Japanese reality and filtered and interpreted it through his changing frame of mind. The relative proportions of the three components – the original input, the pre-existing frame of mind and local discourse – vary from case to case. And so do the images created of the encountered reality, which are finally instrumentalized at the level of consumption and exhibition (Orbach 2008: 117). This image creation happened as a purpose-driven process of audiovisual, cultural translation, and, as Asad points out, all 'good translation seeks to reproduce the structure of an alien discourse with the translator's own language' (2010: 21). Fanck's crystal-clear, moving images of landscapes and easily comprehensive stories motivated his invitation into the project, as his cinematic language was seen to promise a successful reception. This 'own' language, however, changed from 'Western' to German within the politically charged discourse, and instrumentalization already happened at the level of production, as Fanck – not necessarily always consciously but thoroughly – domesticated aspects of the Japanese discourse that resembled the German ones. The very possibility of this domestication to occur is grounded in the participants' and in particular Fanck and Itami's positioning within the project. These were determined by the relationship between cultural insiders/outsiders and 'the authentic' and coming to understand 'the status of those who are charged with saying what counts as true' (Foucault 1980: 31) helps to understand not only their respective roles in the project but also the divergent reception of the film(s) in Germany and Japan as well as the differences in their respective takes on contemporary Japanese reality.

As examined in Chapter 5, when it came to the films' reception, German critics mostly took the represented image of Japan for granted, also because it was never discussed as anything else but the real Japan as seen and filmed through perceptive, scientific German eyes and with the latest camera technology. In Japan, however, the situation was different, not least because both versions of the film circulated and thus inevitably sparked comparison. At the same time, and significantly, *New Earth*, while maintaining the problem of 'inequality based in power on which languages are being transformed and received', also breaks the general rule that 'the meaning inscribed by the anthropologist cannot normally be contested by the members of the original society' (Asad 2010: 24). The interested Japanese public had ample access to the films, articles and reviews, and they judged all aspects of the film against a standard of truth about Japan; however, due to the aforementioned inequality, their contestation did not matter to the foreign representing and receiving side. A second point of interest is that, faced with the outsider's gaze, Japan no longer appeared as the most natural thing in the world. In the Japanese reception of the stars in the film and of the represented landscapes, the politically charged nature of and misleading claims regarding authenticity come into the open. The question then changes towards what was represented and received as 'true' and whose interests were served.

The cultural and the political go hand in hand, and concentrating on Fanck and Itami's respective directorial and editorial choices for their versions, Chapter 6 compares the films with authenticity as the primary discursive framework, but keeping in mind its meaning within the current nationalist ideologies in both countries. Starting from the proclamation that Itami used entirely different footage from Fanck's, this chapter examines the processes of making two rather different films out of partially common raw material and within a restrictive framework. Discussing examples from the two versions' mise-en-scène, editing, dialogue and music, I will discuss Itami's changes from Fanck's script and what they can tell us about the divergent understandings behind the camera of what this film project was supposed to achieve.

New Earth's multiple levels pose various questions of how to approach film history and the people involved, a matter taken up in Chapter 7. Itami's curious discursive absence from the project, as well as his post-war persona, has had a strong impact on interpretations of his role in the project and, as Yamamoto demonstrates, these interpretations are extended to Japan as a whole (2004). However, the prevalent victim narrative goes against the grain of what Itami stood for during his lifetime. Fanck, in turn, is at the centre of most considerations of the film's propagandistic nature, and his persona has been connected to pro- and proto-fascist sentiments; the chapter engages with his public persona and discusses alternative motivations for the co-production as well as its impact on his career. Reinserting the films into the directors' careers and personas questions the victim–perpetrator narrative and reveals the importance of the notion of authenticity within their interactions, and 'propaganda' as a means to an end. The quest for an authentic Japaneseness brought forth both textual and extra-textual motifs that authenticated the persons concerned and the discourses addressed. At the same time, *New Earth* impacted actual people, our readings of their personas and, in extension, part of our interpretation of the sliver of time within which it occurred.

In the project, the power to represent and the question of what to represent played crucial roles and led to points of conflict and struggle, rather than the calm surface of film co-production evoked by Kawakita Kashiko in 1936. Yet, in questioning and expanding on previous approaches, I do not intend to substitute one 'truth' for another. The very heterogeneity and vastness of material makes such a conclusion impossible. As Gerow has shown in his study of the ambivalent politics in Kinugasa's *A Page of Madness* (Kurutta ichipeiji, 1926), approaching such complex networks of agendas as were also at play in *New Earth* is, quite consequently, 'in many ways about the complication of boundaries' (2008: 86). Itami wrote in 1946, 'once an intellectual problem becomes connected to human behaviour, it changes into an intricate complex of intentions and emotions' (1961 [1946]: 209). When it comes to human interaction in an international and politically charged context, and the cultural products growing out of converging strands, temptingly straightforward accounts do not necessarily offer the best explanation of events. *New Earth* provides the opportunity to delve into one such event and to investigate the power play in transnational encounters and representation, the volatility of subject positions, how subtle twists change interpretations that are nevertheless context-dependent, and the need for sensitivity towards fluctuations, contradictions and continuities, as they are all part of the story.

1

Film export and international (mis-)understanding

The cinematograph is international in the deep sense of being universally human.

(MORECK 1929: 40–1)

Kurosawa's *Rashomon* (Rashōmon, 1950) winning the Golden Lion at the 1951 Venice Film Festival is often considered to be the pivotal point for Japanese film export (Iwasaki 1961: 1; Nygren 2007; Yomota 2000). This approach, however, tends to see pre-war efforts to realize the dream of export as isolated, eccentric events. *New Earth* originates in this dream, and looking behind its representation as 'the first' brings into focus the largely neglected area of previous contacts. About fifteen years before *New Earth*'s grand premieres in Tokyo and Berlin, its producer Kawakita Nagamasa experienced the joys and woes of a foreign language student in a rural part of northern Germany. While not unfriendly, the small town's population was as curious as uninformed about their guest's exotic home country in the Far East (Kawakita N. 1988: 5–7). A pivotal moment was his visit to a performance of Puccini's *Madame Butterfly* in Hamburg. He was looking forward to familiar sights, but everything he 'saw on the stage – sets, costume, make-up, acting – [were] all so far removed from things Japanese and unbearable to look at' (Kawakita N. 1988: 7). Kawakita started thinking about ways to 'let the West know who we really are in terms of emotions, customs, manners and culture', and he also wanted for Japan to learn from the 'rationality' of Western life and culture. Film appeared to him as the appropriate means for such cultural cross-fertilization because of its popularity and because 'even if people could not travel very far in those days, motion pictures could' (Kawakita N. 1988: 7). His recognition would lead to a lifelong career dedicated to cultural exchange through film, a mission that his later wife Kashiko kept pursuing after his death. More immediately, however, it was one of the main factors behind the co-production with Arnold Fanck of *New Earth*, hailed as 'the first German–Japanese co-produced film'.

This label, in connoting a beginning of collaboration, fits in well with the political situation that developed during the production period. And therefore, it has remained firmly in place and disguises the project's embeddedness in an ongoing discourse on cultural representation, international recognition and authenticity. For the Japanese producers, promoters and commentators, however, the word 'first' attached to 'German–Japanese film' or to 'Japanese international film' not only expressed the anticipated success of Japanese film exports, but it also triggered flashbacks to earlier attempts that had been both unsuccessful enterprises and inadequate representations of their country. The inequality that was felt on a cultural level – foreign productions, after all, were very popular in Japan – found its mirror image in unpleasant political realities: the Triple Intervention of 1895 forcing Japan to recede the Liaodong peninsula to China, the rejection of indemnity demands against Russia despite the victory in the war of 1904–05, the denial of influence in China after having fought German colonial forces in the First World War, the rejection of Japan's proposed 'racial equality clause' by the League of Nations in 1919 and the United States' 1924 'Exclusion Act' prohibiting further immigration from Japan (see Krebs 2009; Young 1998). The question of Japan's place in the modern world concerned political and cultural power, as both were seen as reflections of – or at least heavily impacting – one another. Therefore, the national image became a matter of great concern, on the cinema screen and in the international arena. Before this background, *New Earth*'s label as 'the first co-production' emerges as nothing more, and nothing less, than a marketing tactic. The film also inherited thematic and stylistic similarities from a series of related undertakings that were concerned with an authentic representation of Japan and intertwined with the question of international recognition.

In 1928 Japan was the largest producer of films per year (Richie 2001: 44) and could have satisfied the local demand by local productions. But foreign films also enjoyed great popularity, with Hollywood films accounting for the vast majority of imported films, followed by German films in a distant second place.[1] On the other hand, very few Japanese films were exhibited

---

[1] Import statistics for 1933 exemplify the dominance of the American market share: USA 256, Germany 15, France 2, Great Britain 2, Soviet Union 4, Italy 1 (Foreign Affairs Association of Japan 1934: 1014–5). Comprehensive statistics regarding 1931–61, including the number of cinemas, audience numbers and releases of Japanese and foreign film are found in Furukawa (2003: 20; see also Kirihara 1992: 41–7).

in the West,[2] and consequently, the 'dream of export' was directed towards Western markets as yet another means to prove national equality, after having emerged victorious out of three international wars and successfully pursuing modernization and industrialization. A case in point is the discourse on *A Page of Madness*: Film critic Iwasaki Akira praised it as 'the first international film made in Japan' and 'the first film-like film born in Japan' (cited in Gerow 2001: 23). To others it represented 'the first stage in ascending to leadership in the world market', reflecting a growing confidence in the Japanese film industry (Gerow 2008: 57), but also the perception that exportable films were a step on an evolutionary ladder of cinematic proficiency. The quest for recognition by the outside world was coupled with issues of power: the power to represent Japan and Japanese cinema – truthfully and successfully – on international screens and markets. Power was also implied in the question of which 'Japan' was represented in such a work.

The Japanese film world was far more knowledgeable about the foreign film industry than vice versa, and they closely observed the trend to produce films about 'Japan', especially with regard to the representation of their country: *The Cheat* (1915, DeMille), with Japan-born actors Sessue Hayakawa and Tsuru Aoki, seriously damaged Hayakawa's reputation (Miyao 2007): he was criticized as a 'traitor', and this 'national disgrace film' (*kokujoku eiga*) – a term that would come up again and again in this discourse – was never released in Japan (Bernardi 2001: 1, 23; Yomota 2000: 33). Later, unsuccessful Japanese efforts to put their films on Western screens, such as *Nippon* (1932, Koch), which will be discussed in this chapter, were also labelled a 'national disgrace' because of their twofold failure to succeed commercially and to convey an authentic image of Japan (Honma 1933; *Yomiuri Shinbun* 24.07.1935). Matters of national image and film export were intermingled with the notion of national esteem:

> Though handicapped by imperfect equipment these studios [Nippon Katsudo Kaisha, Tokyo, Shochiku Cinema Kaisha, Tokyo, Teikoku Cinema Engei Kaisha, Cinema Kaisha] are producing picture plays almost as good as in other countries, only they have not attained the exportable stage, chiefly because films of Japan produced abroad, despite their absurd representation of Japanese manner and custom, are acceptable to ignorant spectators. Pictures made in Japan are much better than 'La Bataille' [*The Danger Line*, 1923, Édouard Émile Violet] with Sessue Hayakawa, a Japanese picture player who has risen to notoriety abroad. (Foreign Affairs Association of Japan 1926: 324)

---

[2]Intra-Asian film trade relations had been established as early as 1903 with the import of Japanese films and the – more successful – screenings of re-exported films in Thailand and Malay (Baskett 2008).

Germany – where Hayakawa and his films were also well known – had its own tradition of cinematically interpreting Japan.[3] One of the earliest films documents *The March of the Japanese Second Army to the Battle of Liaoyang* in 1904 (Das 2. Kaiserlich-Japanische Regiment auf dem Weg nach Liaoyang, 1904, Greenbaum). Various geisha-themed works followed in rapid succession, and the fascinating custom of ritual suicide was displayed in two films titled *Harakiri*, by Harry Piel in 1913, and just after the First World War by Fritz Lang in 1919. The strained Japanese–German post-war relations – following a sense of betrayal after Japan's declaration of war and the taking over of German concessions in China (Horne and Austin 1998: 402–3) – were not left unacknowledged. One critic of Lang's *Harakiri* asserts that the land of cherry blossoms 'despite all that and all that can rest assured of German sympathy' (Flüggen 1920: 2). This sympathy, however, had less to do with cautious political reconciliation than with the appeal of exotic images. The film – somewhat predictably – based on *Madame Butterfly* was shot in Hamburg's famous Hagenbeck zoo. 'Ethnographic counsellor' Heinrich Umlauff's 'rich ethnographic expert knowledge' and his museum's 'extensive exotic collection', which was used for set dressings, props and costumes, authenticated its representation of Japan (*Der Film* 1919; *Erste Internationale Filmzeitung* 17.08.1918; see also Thode-Arora 1992: 149). For German film to once more 'take up the fight' against foreign competitors after the destructions of the First World War, the contemporary taste for the exotic was a fruitful field (B 1919: 19).

The producers cleverly combined the public demand for exotic subjects with the educational claim of using expert knowledge to authentically represent 'foreign people and their manners and customs' (L. B. 1919). 'Ethnographer' Umlauff added to the production value, and Lang himself had likely visited Japan on his world tour in 1910 (McGilligan 2013 [1997]: 32), an impression reflected in the nightclub *Yoshiwara* in his epic *Metropolis* (1926). For *Harakiri*, a critic claimed, Lang 'successfully studied the idiosyncrasies, the temper, of this foreign yellow race that is highly cultured but maintains age-old customs and manners' (B. 1919: 19). Authenticity loomed large in the film's evaluation, and the splendid costumes and props were unanimously praised. One critic, however, pointed out that 'almost all, even beautiful Lil [Dagover], were lacking typical Japanese appearance and bearing' (P. 1919: 40). But still, O-Take-San's (Dagover) childlike nature, graceful daintiness and courage 'in the face of death' were received as the archetype of Japanese womanhood (B. 1919; L. B. 1919; Flüggen 1920). The critics used a fixed image of Japan in German representational traditions as a point of reference. Almost twenty years later, these archetypes had not

---

[3]On the historical cultural relationship between both countries see Bieber 2014; Hack 1996; Kreiner 1984; Leims 1990; Maltarich 2005; Martin, ed. 1995; NHK 1987; Schuster 1988.

changed much; the description of O-Take-San could also be that of Yamato Mitsuko, the 'samurai's daughter' in *New Earth*.

In the year of *Harakiri*'s release, then scriptwriter and film critic Mori Iwao (1899–1979) reviewed the Japanese image in Western films and 'was offended by the tendency to depict the Japanese as a semi-barbaric race with a propensity toward self-sacrifice – the most extreme expression of which was ritual suicide, a key ingredient in nearly all of these plots' (Bernardi 2001: 133). Closely connected to the notion of self-sacrifice was another attractive motif, *bushidō*.[4] The 'way of the warrior' had been made widely known in the West at the beginning of the century by Nitobe Inazō's westward-directed interpretation of *Bushido: The Soul of Japan* (1899), translated into German in 1901 (*Bushido: Die Seele Japans*).

Bushido

The label 'Japan's first international co-production' likely should be given to *Bushido: The Iron Law* (Bushido: Das eiserne Gesetz, 1926, Heiland and Kako), produced in Japan by German and Japanese film-makers (Ogawa 2005: 235). The German press initially referred to *Bushido* when reporting on *Samurai's Daughter* (Schu. 1937), only to adopt the advertising slogan 'the first German-Japanese co-production' shortly before the premiere.

During an extended journey through Japan, China and India between 1924 and 1926, German travel writer, director, producer and cameraman Karl Heiland (or Heinz Carl Heiland) co-directed *Bushido* with prolific Shōchiku Studios director Kako Zanmu. Heiland's preferred actors, Carl Tetting and Loo Holl, played alongside their Tōa Studios colleagues Okajima Tsuyako and Akashi Ushio, which contradicts the impression of an ad hoc undertaking. A *jidaigeki* (period film, set before the Meiji Restoration in 1868) 'full of oriental exotic traits such as *harakiri* or geisha' (National Film Center Tokyo 2005), *Bushido* tells the story of the introduction of firearms to Japan in the mid-sixteenth century; a young Portuguese sailor is washed ashore and becomes entangled in civil wars and two love stories. Three points of popular fascination (geisha, *harakiri*, *bushidō*) converge in this co-production. However, evidence suggests that both the original idea and the script were the work of a Tōa scriptwriter (*Yomiuri Shinbun* 24.05.1926); hence the Japanese influence was greater than apparent at first glance. The film was produced explicitly for export, capitalizing on the trend for films about Japan, while introducing 'bushidō and *chūkō* [loyalty and filial piety] to the world' (Tomita 2005: 70). The Japanese release of this 'joint

---

[4]On the modern development of a concept of *bushidō* and the quest for a unified national identity, see Benesch (2014).

product' was announced for 1 June 1926 (*Asahi Shinbun* 24.05.1926). It thus predates the 'first Japanese-American co-productions', which began in September with the establishment of the short-lived Bantsuma Tachibana Universal production company, a collaborative venture by film star Bando Tsumasaburō and Universal Picture's Japanese subsidiary (Howard 2010: 37). *Bushido* was attributed to Tōa, with Deutsch-Nordische Universal Film (DNFU) as the European distributor. In the German context, however, DNFU appears as producer and Tōa remains unmentioned (Pander 1927). The Japanese publicity thus claimed the product for the Japanese film industry, but also utilized the appeal of foreign participants. Wada-Marciano notes that 'filmmakers would sometimes falsely credit a film's narrative source to a foreign sounding author in order to give their film the imagined cachet of higher production values' (Wada-Marciano 2008: 36). Soga Masashi wrote and directed various films for Chiezō Production under the pseudonym Furitsu Rankyō, alluding to 'Fritz Lang' (*Lichtbild-Bühne* 1931). The nationally ambiguous 'James Maki' wrote modern films for Shōchiku; he was composed of Ozu Yasujirō, Fushimi Akira, Ikeda Tadao and Kitamura Komatsu (Standish 2005: 42). The 'modern' notion of international film collaborations and the announcement that the film had been 'honoured by being watched by the Imperial Family' in private further underlined *Bushido*'s prominent status (*Asahi Shinbun* 05.06.1926).

Germany also claimed the film for itself, while 'otherness' added interest to the production, too. With the conscious use of culture as a mediator for political reconciliation from the mid-1920s, German interest in Japanese culture was fuelled by theatre, literature and lectures (Hack 1996: 284). Japanese films, however, had yet to appear on public screens, and when *Bushido* premiered in Berlin on 9 May 1927, it was announced as 'the first original Japanese narrative drama' (*Kinematograph* 1927a; *Beba-Woche* 1926). Heiland introduced it as 'the first real Japanese film to be screened publicly in Germany' (cited in Pander 1927). But what 'real Japanese film' actually meant remains puzzling. Leaving his collaboration with Kako unmentioned, he explained that because 'the Japanese produce films only for their own taste', they are 'impossible for Western people' and *Bushido* should be seen as a compromise: 'The film shows Japan through European spectacles' (Pander 1927). One critic, however, criticized the discrepancy between the grandiose advertising, which promised something new and different, and the weak, meandering script, even allowing for the fact that a fire in the Afifa studios during the editing process had damaged the copy and delayed the premiere. The editing prevented close observation, disappointing his high expectations of a 'different school, a different race of actors', and without prior knowledge about the culture, the dance and battle scenes could not be made sense of (Pander 1927). The problems faced by Japanese films abroad question the assumption of silent cinema's relatively unproblematic border crossing: according to Williams, 'to make a "foreign" version of a film, you only had to put in new intertitles in a new target language. National barriers would definitively arrive only with (recorded) *speech*' (2002: 2). Yet, as seen here, this strategy was not necessarily successful at greater cultural distances: 'If the Japanese mentality makes it impossible to produce Japanese films catering to European tastes they should give up on this idea altogether' (Pander 1927). The method he rejects, of showing Japan through European spectacles, was the impetus for Kawakita and Fanck's project ten years later.

Compared to the discourse on *Harakiri*, the issue of authenticity had become more complex. Heiland proclaimed his film to be Japanese but simultaneously assumed an unspecified difference between representations made by an insider and those made by an outsider. Another reviewer of *Bushido* had more down-to-earth understanding of what an actual 'Japanese film' was, and wished to see 'one of the real Japanese films . . . that repeatedly have been shown successfully in Paris' (*Kinematograph* 1927b). *Street Juggler* (Machi no tejinashi, 1925, Murata) had been screened in the avant-garde venue Studio des Ursulines in 1926, followed by Gosho's *Musume* (Karakuri musume, 1927) (Howard 2010: 34–5). In Berlin, only a select audience had the chance to see *Street Juggler*, and there was appetite for more: 'Why don't we get to see Japanese films?' (*Film und Volk* 1928).

Nippon

Several 'real Japanese films' arrived in Berlin in 1929 through Kawakita. Following his impulse to use film for cultural exchange, and likely in order to gain a foothold in the industry, Kawakita had assisted German's major film producer and distributor Ufa (Universum Film AG) in exporting the first part of *Die Nibelungen* (Die Nibelungen: Siegfrieds Tod, 1924, Lang) to Japan where the influential *Kinema Junpō* magazine ranked it the fourth best film for 1925 (Tōhō Tōwa 1978: 235). With backing from his German friend Georg Eduard Freiherr von Stietencron, trader Otto Schacke and French financier André Germain, Kawakita established his trading company Tōwa Shōji Ltd on 10 October 1928 (Tsuji and Shimizu 1987: 34, Sierek 2018).[5] He began importing European films to Japan, while initially also making money from trading with sandpaper, ink and face cream (Tōhō Tōwa 1978: 236). Soon, however, the export of Japanese films became an important point on his agenda.

Director Kinugasa Teinosuke had taken his avant-garde *Crossroads* (Jūjiro, 1928) to the Soviet Union and then to France. On the occasion of a screening in Paris, resident Japanese artist Fujita Tsuguharu (aka Fujita

---

[5]For a detailed account of Kawakita's connections to Ufa, see Sierek (2018).

Tsuguji aka Léonard Tsuguharu Foujita) gave a talk about the Japanese cinema to the audience. Despite the film being stylistically and technically close to European productions, the goings-on on screen were met by utter bafflement 'owing to the fact that it revealed many points of difference in manners and customs and that its interpretations of the moral outlook upon life were entirely in conflict with those of the people there, it was at best an enigma to them, producing no appreciable effect beyond arousing their sense of curiosity' (Foujita 1937: 32). The film also came to Germany, where Ufa released it in May 1929, as *Shadows of the Yoshiwara* (Im Schatten des Yoshiwara), perhaps capitalizing on the erotic appeal of the eponymous 'temple of lust' in Lang's *Metropolis*, which had been released just a month before. Following the film's surprising, relative success, Tōwa concluded a distribution agreement with Ufa, including rights for performance in China (Kawakita N. 1988: 12).[6] Shōchiku's *gendaigeki* (*jidaigeki*'s counterpart: a 'contemporary film' set after the Meiji Restoration of 1868) *Eternal Heart* (Eien no kokoro, 1928, Sasaki) was screened in Berlin, titled *Yakichi the Woodcutter* (Yakichi der Holzfäller). The promotional pamphlet announced a 'genuine Japanese narrative film featuring the most famous East Asian actors', but misspelled the names of both lead actors ('Kinnyo [Kinuyo] Tanaka' and 'Yakichi [Yūkichi] Iwata') (*Illustrierter Film-Kurier* 1930) (Figure 1.1). Based on *Yakichi*, Fanck later planned to cast screen idol Tanaka Kinuyo for *New Earth*.

Kawakita also presented to Ufa one Nikkatsu film, *The Love-Mad Music Teacher* (Kyōren no onna shishō, 1926, Mizoguchi); three Shōchiku's silents: Ushihara's *gendaigeki*, *Big City: A Chapter on Labour* (Daitokai rōdō-hen, 1929); and the two *jidaigeki Bonfire* (Kagaribi, 1928, Hoshi) and *The Time of Tempei: Mysterious Thief Samimaro* (Tempei jidai: Kaitō Samimaro, 1928, Koishi). Ufa's culture film department would later assemble *Nippon* (1932) from parts of *Samimaro*, *Bonfire* and *Big City* (Honma 1933; Ushihara 1933a; Ushihara 1933b). *Nippon* preserves parts of films that are now lost, but, more importantly for our purpose, it also reveals 1929 as a watershed for export films and sheds some light on Kawakita's motivation for embarking on *New Earth*. Contrary to some accounts (Howard 2010: 43; NHK 1986: 6–16), Mizoguchi's *Love-Mad Music Teacher* was not used in *Nippon*, but tracing its way to Europe shows the industrial power plays revolving around film export: *Music Teacher* was selected to be 'Tōwa's first export film', and Kawakita took this film and the other productions mentioned earlier, to Europe in March 1929, coming back around May (Sasō 2005: 312). In the summer, Stietencron came to Japan and met with Shōchiku's president, Ōtani Takejirō, and the head of Kamata Studios, Kido

---

[6]Tōwa opened a Shanghai branch in 1930 but closed it two years later. When Ufa ended their contract in 1932, Kawakita concluded an agency deal with Tobis.

FIGURE 1.1 *German advertisement for* Yakichi the Woodcutter *aka* Eternal Heart.

Shirō, to arrange the establishment of a shared Berlin office for Tōwa and Shōchiku. The ensuing foundation of the Shōchiku European Distribution Company (*Shōchiku eiga ōshū haikyū kabushiki kaisha*) is referred to by Kawakita and the press, but remains unmentioned in Shōchiku's company history (Kawakita 1988: 11; *Yomiuri Shinbun* 29.06.1929; Shōchiku 1996).

Yet, Shōchiku's main rival Nikkatsu was 'one step ahead'; they had already negotiated with Stietencron in Berlin in 1928 (*Yomiuri Shinbun* 03.09.1929). Stietencron then visited Nikkatsu for test screenings in November 1928, and selected *Music Teacher* for a trial, which Kawakita then took to Berlin in spring (Kawakita and Satō 1991: 12). Stietencron's negotiations in Japan with Shōchiku happened only after this, in August 1929 (*Yomiuri Shinbun* 28.08.1929; Ushihara 1933a). With the presumably short-lived distribution company, the movements towards export to Europe were given an industrial foundation, and Shōchiku tried to position itself at the forefront of a potentially profitable undertaking. As shall become clear later, the export business with Germany proved less lucrative than was assumed in 1929, when the five Shōchiku films and Nikkatsu's *Tragedy of a Marriage* (Kekkon higeki, 1929, Higashibōjō) coming to Germany signalled Japanese film's 'advance into the world' (*Yomiuri Shinbun* 29.06.1929).[7]

Ufa eventually bought the three Shōchiku silents, and Carl Koch edited them into *Nippon*, a piece of sixty-two minutes, with added German intertitles, music and, 'oddly enough, synced Japanese dialogue' (Bordwell 2007). It has the appearance of one film, consisting of three acts, titled *Nippon: Love and Passion in Japan* (Nippon: Liebe und Leidenschaft in Japan), produced by 'Towa Shoji Berlin-Tokyo' with the participation of Shōchiku's 'most eminent actors' (Figure 1.2).

Shōchiku's prominence in the credit titles would, in the case of a successful release, have been a triumph over rival Nikkatsu. The plot constructed by Koch's editing, in the effort to promote Japan and its films abroad, corresponds to a critic's coupling of film export to emotional 'understanding': 'Human fate is the same everywhere [. . .] The cinematograph is international in the deep sense of being universally human' (Moreck 1929: 40–1). Using material from three films to offer a cross-cut through Japanese history, from Tempei (or Tenpyō, roughly corresponding to the Nara period) (*Samimaro*) over the Warring States period (*Bonfire*) to contemporary Japan (*Big City*), and to focus on a universal human emotion seems a fruitful implementation of this line of thought: love and passion through the centuries beneath Mount Fuji's timeless silhouette. Fanck in 1936 used a similar technique when he introduced the notion of love into Teruo and Mitsuko's arranged marriage to avoid alienating European sensibilities (Fanck 1938: 94–6).

Nippon as an undertaking is more complex than the piece of Orientalism – the West taking and rearranging fragments from the East according to its own agenda – that it appears to be at first glance. Tōwa and Shōchiku commissioned the editing and soundtrack (Honma 1933; Kawakita and Satō 1991: 39). Lagi Solf, B. Hayashi, Y. Yosano and F. Roeding are credited

---

[7]Kawakita also might have brought Nikkatsu's three-part series *Diary of Chuji's Travels* (Chūji tabi nikki, 1927, Itō) to Europe (Sasō 2005: 309).

FIGURE 1.2 *Credit titles in* Nippon.

as 'contributors'. Lagi (Sóoáemalelagi) Solf was the daughter of former German ambassador to Japan (1920–28), Wilhelm Solf (Hempenstall and Mochida 2005: 209–19). After Solf's death in 1936, his widow led the Solf-Kreis (Solf-circle), a meeting of anti-Nazi intellectuals. She and Lagi survived internment in a concentration camp (von Vietsch 1961: 337–8). 'Yosano Y.' likely refers to Yosano Yuzuru (1903–39), a nephew of the prominent writer couple Yosano Akiko and Yosano Tekkan (Hiroshi). Yosano was enrolled at Berlin's Friedrich Wilhelm University at the time, and was also active in the leftist, anti-imperialist 'Association of Revolutionary Asians' (*Die Vereinigung der revolutionären Asiaten*; *Kakumeiteki Asiajin Kyōkai*), which had been founded in Berlin following the Japanese occupation of Manchuria and denounced both Eastern expansionism and Western fascism (Hartmann 2003: 188; Katō 2005: 130). 'B. Hayashi' almost certainly refers to Hayashi Bunzaburō, Kawakita's contact in Berlin, who would later also play a role in the production of *New Earth*. *Nippon*'s editor Koch and his wife Lotte Reiniger[8] left Germany in 1933 because of political opposition (Schmidlechner 2011: 309). The composer of the film score, Hans Bullerian,

---

[8]Reiniger's ground-breaking silhouette animation film *Prince Achmed's Adventures* (Die Abenteuer des Prinzen Achmed, 1926) was among Kawakita's first imports and released in 1929 as *Akumeddo ōji no bōken* (Kawakita and Satō 1991: 20).

headed the Music Section of the *Kampfbund für deutsche Kultur* (KfdK; Fighting League for German Culture), the National Socialists' 'primary vehicle for cultural and artistic mobilization' (Steinweis 1991: 403), and subsequently led the Reich Music Chamber's department of composers in several major territories (Klee 2009: 79). The composition of staff and advisers, cooperating in the 'earnest desire to represent the real Japan to the world' (Ushihara 1933a), reflects the shifting, unstable and by no means unified cultural field. The film was presented to members of the Japanese embassy and influential Japanese residents in Berlin in September 1931, altered according to various requests, and released in May 1932 (Honma 1933; Kawakita 1968: 131). In using 'native experts' and Japanese advisers to introduce Japan and Japanese film to the world, *Nippon* is the prototype of Kawakita's concept for *New Earth*.

Following the credit titles that are superimposed on scenes of Japanese landscapes and traditional architecture, the first scene of *Nippon* presents a young Japanese woman in a kimono. She kneels on *tatami* mats in a Japanese-style room and bows before taking up the *shamisen*. The woman simultaneously introduces and represents a foreign world – a task later shared by *New Earth*'s female characters. The Orientalist representation of Japan in terms of traditional femininity, however, is undermined by the actual person (Figure 1.3). Yuasa Hatsue exemplifies the new social and indeed global mobility that some Japanese women were able to enjoy. She had come to Berlin with her violinist husband in 1922 to study music (*Yomiuri Shinbun* 15.07.1926) and participated in four German films between 1932 and 1934, always playing a Japanese singer. Her voice betrays her training in classical Western music, and her perfect black bob reminds one more of the quintessential flapper Louise Brooks than of Chō-chō-san, a role she successfully portrayed at the prestigious Salzburger Festspielhaus in 1930 (Salzburger Festspielhaus 1930). The story that her affair with her German instructor drove her husband into suicide by leaping out of window (*Yomiuri Shinbun* 15.07.1926) also has more in common with the idea of the modern girl's dangerous sexual transgressiveness (Silverberg 1991) than with received images of docile Japanese femininity.

In the film, however, these nuances are absent. Yuasa's song leads the audience into a foreign world: 'Life and love vanish, but you [Mount Fuji] remain in your glory, eternally'. Mount Fuji as the focal point of the exposition is another shared trait with *New Earth*. *New Earth*'s opening scene, which shows a miniature model of Japan being approached from above, was either created by director of special effects Tsuburaya Eiji, or by avant-garde artist Asano Mōfu, who is credited for the 'models' in *New Earth*. Incidentally, Godzilla's creator is credited (as Tsuburaya Eiichi) as the cinematographer for both *Samimaro* and *Bonfire*, providing yet another line of continuity. In *Nippon*, while the lyrics switch from Japanese to German, the frame changes from a medium close-up of Yuasa to the stylized image of

FIGURE 1.3 *Yuasa Hatsue as the 'singer' in* Nippon.

a scimitar-like sword that slowly morphs into a model of Japan seen from a bird's-eye perspective (Figure 1.4).

Following close-ups on the model of Honshū's mountainous landscape, the camera focuses on Mount Fuji. A cut to a long shot of the volcano leads from the model to the 'real world'. The prologue almost certainly was created during the production process in Berlin, but Fuji as a symbol of Japan was not only a trope of foreign or German representational traditions. In Japan itself the volcano had come to stand as a symbol for (the people of) Japan (Bernstein 2008: 63).

Old-fashioned motifs – or a 'recourse to tradition' – were ready at hand when the purpose was to represent 'Japaneseness', as also seen in subsequent Japanese films intended to present Japan to international audiences, including *New Earth*. At the same time, Japanese critics derided volcanoes, cherry blossoms and geisha as clichés, and condemned representations of Japan that drew on these icons as disgraceful misrepresentations of their modern reality. Responding to the accusation that *Nippon* was a 'national disgrace film' (Honma 1933), *Big City*'s director Ushihara makes a strong point related to the film's editing process and its choice of material: in the original films 'swordplay follows on swordplay, and even when the plot

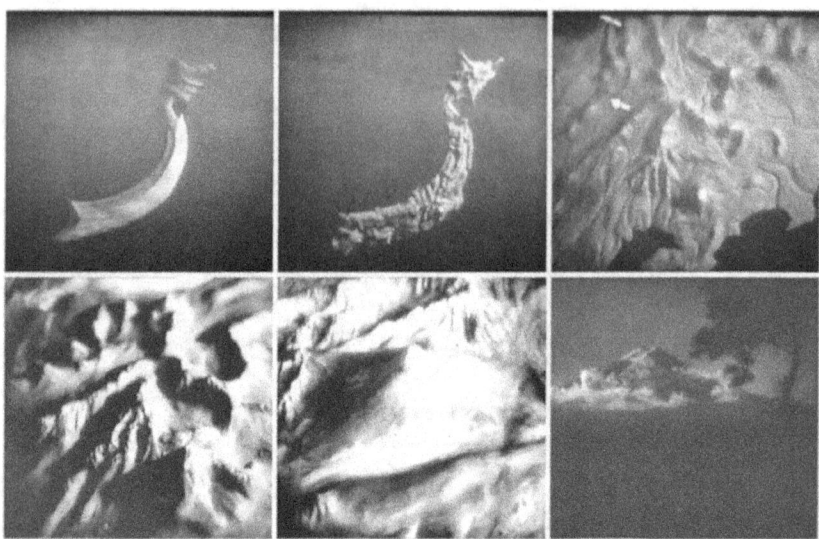

FIGURE 1.4 *Special effects in* Nippon.

[in *Nippon*] moves into contemporary Japan with material from *Big City*, the focus is again on strife' (Ushihara 1933b). And indeed, the eponymous hero in *Samimaro* rescues his lover from a corrupt Buddhist priest, *Bonfire*'s Kunitari goes on a killing spree after having been utterly betrayed by his lord and his fiancée, and in *Big City*, class struggle takes the forefront as the protagonist's technical innovation is stolen by a railway engineer. In this vein, a Berlin critic identified *Nippon* as a 'propaganda film' with the motive of improving Japan's international reputation that had suffered following the annexation of Manchuria, a suspicion later also voiced by an American reviewer of *New Earth*. To the critic of *Nippon*, the film seems to have been made exclusively to 'impress' the European audiences by showcasing Japan's 'ability to pick a fight' (*Acht-Uhr-Abendblatt* 1932; cited in NHK 1986: 11).

This was certainly not the image the production crew and advisers had aimed for, but a result of faulty translations of the material in terms of genre and language. Concerning genre, the original *Samimaro* and *Bonfire* fall into a new period of *jidaigeki* production. Both films display the new type of fast, more realistic swordplay that replaced the kabuki-style *tachimawari* of earlier periods (Spalding 1992: 137–9) (Figure 1.5).

The heroes contrast with their tough and stoic predecessors in terms of their new depth of character, which was corroborated by the *benshi*'s (film-explainer) stream-of-conscience narration during 'poignant scenes of the heroes' contemplative musings' (Standish 2005: 68–9). However, Koch underscored *Bonfire*'s dream sequence, with its superimpositions and

FIGURE 1.5 *Fast swordplay by Hayashi Chōjirō in* Samimaro.

strange camera angles, as well as various long takes of a pensive Kunitari with music; without narration, the hero is denied character development. *Nippon* thus represents him as almost mad in his drive for revenge. Shot-reverse-shots establish his point of view as he slays his former lord, his fiancée and her now-husband; a final cut closes up on his manic expression before the screen fades to black (Figure 1.6). As the German critic remarks, 'the samurai transformed Japan into a battleground because of their exaggerated notions of honour, tradition and revenge' (*Acht-Uhr-Abendblatt* 1932; cited in NHK 1986: 11).

Kunitari's mad laughter fades with the screen. The three original films were all silents, but in 1932, about three-quarters of German cinemas were equipped with sound technology (Pruys 2009: 146). It was crucial for the 'first genuine Japanese film' to appear up-to-date and to whet the appetite of the German distributors. One means to achieve this goal was to transform the silent material into a sound film. The Japanese dialogue was added in Berlin, and the German intertitles inserted following consultations with resident 'Japanese artists and film experts' (Ushihara 1933b). Using Japanese, rather than German dialogue, was an unusual choice. Dubbing would become the predominant German mode of film translation from 1933, but it was still regarded somewhat suspiciously. A critic for the *Berliner Tageblatt* argued

FIGURE 1.6 *The hero's manic laughter in* Bonfire.

that dubbing would not 'build bridges but create gulfs. We enjoyed silent films, knowing that we were facing a different world and that it might be beneficial to get to know this world. But dissonances between form and content, between inner substance and outer expression will emerge when the language of the film is no longer the language of its culture' (*Berliner Tageblatt* 10.6.1934; cited in *Weisse Wand* n.d.). On important raison d'être of *Nippon* was to convey an authentic impression of Japan, and the main argument for sound – and Japanese dialogue – was the addition of an additional layer of realism. The male roles seem to have been dubbed by native speakers, perhaps Yosano and Hayashi, but in the case of female roles, I favour the thought that one or several female roles were synched by Lagi Solf who had lived in Japan during her teenage years; but then the question remains why this task was not given to Yuasa. This strategy of dubbing into the 'source language' contributed much to the negative criticism: throughout the film, the style of speech is well-pronounced and modern. The contemporary *mō daijōbu da* when Samimaro, in the eighth century, reassures his lover that everything is 'ok now', sounded strange to Japanese speakers, as Ushihara pointed out (1933b). Moreover, the new Japanese dialogue still needed intertitles for its German target audience. But only about half of the dialogue is made intelligible in this way, and of those translations, many are partially wrong. Kunitari's fiancée tells him that she will wait for his return, but the intertitles read, 'What did my father want from you?' Her lips are moving but only a few lines are spoken. The obvious selectiveness of the dialogue highlights the film behind inherently constructed. When Kunitari later demands back a valuable sword from his lord's enemy, his threat 'I won't ask again! I'm going to take the sword by myself!' is rendered: 'I repeat my demand'. As the intertitles were inserted following the test screening (Ushihara 1933b), these discrepancies between spoken text and intertitles appear to be the result of the alterations asked for by the consultants. These 'translations' weaken negative notions of duplicity and violence: The fiancée's betrayal is nullified because she never promised to wait, and Kunitari courteously repeats his request instead of offering violence. And what is not translated remains utterly foreign: while Kunitari is reading a letter informing him of his lord's betrayal of his loyalty, he exclaims in short, monosyllabic shouts, and we cannot understand his behaviour until we see the letter's content. Quite consequently, a German columnist found the language 'unpleasant' with its 'many gutturals or hissing sounds' befitting 'the rage and belligerence as illustrated by [Japan's] blood-drenched history' (cited in NHK 1986: 15). Thus, his criticism remained firmly within an Orientalist discourse about exotic barbarianism, veiled under a modern, film-producing mask.

The second part, consisting of *Bonfire*, presents yet another editorial intervention into the material. The opening title reads 'From the time of knights, anno 1500'. Kunitari hides in the 'Yoshiwara', but in fact the entertainment district did not open for business until late 1718 (Seigle 1993: 24). The visual cues hint at his lover being a geisha; however, female geisha appeared in the Yoshiwara only from about 1760 (Seigle 1993: 172). It seems that *Bonfire* originally was set at least about two hundred years later than the Warring States period 'anno 1500', in the much more typical *jidaigeki* setting of the Tokugawa Period (1603–1868). Why did the expert advisers not correct this anachronism? In Europe the time of knights ended around 1500, and in Japan the warrior class was abolished in 1876, about fifty years before *Nippon* premiered in Berlin. The intertitle, first, utilized 'chivalry' as the smallest common denominator to build intellectual bridges and foster understanding. Second, putting the Japanese 'knights' into a far-away period shared by their German counterparts prevented Japan from appearing to be 'just out of the middle-ages'. However, the strategy was ineffective, as evidenced by the critical responses that, as we have seen, focused on the old-fashioned elements, rather than innovative techniques, for instance.

Nippon's third (missing) part features *gendaigeki* superstars Suzuki Denmei and Tanaka Kinuyo. In *Big City*, the new type of a 'goal-orientated hero' (Standish 2005: 39–40) pushes the development of railway technology, and the plot deals with the interconnected notions of class struggle and upward social mobility. *Big City* was criticized as the weakest part of the trilogy because it overtly reflected the film's motive of 'impressing us Europeans' by presenting Japan as equal to the West in terms of 'clothing, lifestyle, tempo and, most of all, technology' and for its portrayal of 'intrigues at the workplace and solidarity'. It could have been filmed anywhere in Germany; 'even the facial features of these Japanese are almost indistinguishable from Europeans' (*Acht-Uhr-Abendblatt* 1932; cited in NHK 1986: 11). Lacking difference, or perhaps too contradictory to received images of the 'always ancient East', this part of *Nippon* was dismissed as uninteresting.

Clearly, the cultural translation of 'Japan' for a German audience had failed. And the condemnation by Japanese travellers of *Nippon* as a 'national disgrace' (Howard 2010: 43) was yet another setback for those interested in the export of Japanese film and the Japanese image abroad. The Kawakitas, on a belated honeymoon journey, arrived in Berlin in July 1932. Upon their arrival at the train station, they were met by Hayashi and *Big City*'s director. Ushihara was on a tour through Europe and the United States to study sound technology at the time, and he had probably followed the release and reception of *Nippon*, together with Hayashi, who would later participate in *New Earth* as translator and supervisor for Fanck's version. The film had been received with ridicule, as might be expected when three unrelated films are combined in an attempt to foster 'understanding'. After the failures of *Yakichi the Woodcutter* and *Nippon*, the German distributor asked Kawakita to '[s]top bringing in Japanese films. We are troubled by the audience guffawing at people sitting on the floor with folded legs or eating with two sticks' (Kawakita and Satō 1991: 24–5). Despite Ushihara's urging to produce and export one film after another to introduce 'real Japan, the Japanese and the Japanese spirit' (1933b), the prospects for Japanese film on the German market looked bleak.

Kagami

Around the time of *Nippon*'s release, conditions in both countries regarding international understanding and national image construction were changing profoundly. 'The new politics of cultural isolationism and national expansionism [. . .] after 1933 would put an end to the ethos of collaboration' (Hake 2002: 47). Yet, in the years to come, the 'ethos of collaboration' played a prominent role between Japan and Germany, as well as for *New Earth*. The third German–Japanese co-production, *Kagami* resulted from cooperation between Ufa and a Japanese partner and initiator, Kishi Kōichi (1909–37). It premiered in Berlin in October 1933, and its production period and personal continuities with *Nippon* bridge the perceived historical break after Hitler's appointment to Reich

Chancellor on 30 January, the establishment of the Propaganda Ministry in March, and of the *Reichskulturkammer* (Reich Culture Chamber) in September 1933.

Kishi's activities as film director, actor and composer have been largely neglected in favour of his short but impressive international career in music (Kajino, Chōki and Gottschewski 2011; Mishima 2005). He first came to Europe in 1926 to complement his violin studies. During his second stay in Berlin (1930–31), discussions with conductor and composer Wilhelm Furtwängler and with Lagi Solf's father, Wilhelm Solf, led to the idea to use Eastern art to infuse new life into Europe's impoverished post-war cultural sphere, just as Japanese culture had influenced Western art at the turn of century (Mōri 2006: 153; von Vietsch 1961: 323–4). Yet Kishi was also concerned with what was 'Japanese' and what aspects of this Japaneseness should be presented to the West in order to rectify misrepresentations. In a familiar move, in 'order to introduce Japanese culture, he immersed himself into [all things] Japanese' (Botschaft von Japan 2009), a philosophy that is audible in his composition that expresses 'Japaneseness' in Western-style arrangements (Mehl 2014: 6–7). As with *New Earth* and its predecessors, making 'Japan' accessible to Western eyes and ears seemed to require Western spectacles or artistic sensibilities as a mediator, in any case some sort of target-oriented cultural translation. In Berlin at the turn of the decade, the group decided on film as the appropriate means for cultural enrichment and understanding, maybe inspired by Lagi Solf's participation in *Nippon*. In 1931, Kishi was back in Japan and founded the Kishi Scientific Film Research Institute (*Kishi Gakujutsu Eiga Kenkyū Sho*, *Kishi Puro*) with a group of artists and scientists who worked on various aspects of modern technology and mass aesthetics (Mōri 2006: 157–9; Nornes 2003: 137–47). Closely observing technological developments, they were concerned that Japan(ese film) fell behind, especially in comparison with America (Nakai 1951). They produced four short films: the 'cine-poem' *Poem of the Sea* (Umi no uta), the 'avant-garde film' *Ten-Minute Meditation* (Jippunkan no shisaku), *Third Opus* (Daisan sakuhin) and *Fourth Opus* (Daiyon sakuhin) (Nakai 1951; Mōri 2006: 160, 178–80). The latter two remained incomplete, as Kishi planned additional scenes shot in Berlin. *Poem of the Sea* and *Ten-Minute Meditation* premiered in Osaka and Kyoto in October 1932. Its use of colour was celebrated as an 'achievement of the Japanese film world' that was 'expected to surpass international film' (*Ōsaka Jiji Shinpō* 03.02.1933). Again, the link between the film industry and national self-confidence within an international framework becomes obvious.

Ufa's culture film department bought the incomplete *Third Opus* and *Fourth Opus* in order to turn it into a 'short culture film', the omnibus strategy being reminiscent of *Nippon*. Kishi acted as director and also wrote the musical score, and the new script was written by Ufa's Wilhelm Prager. They also shot additional scenes with *Nippon*'s Yuasa Hatsue and added

German voice-over narration. Although never marketed as such, the sixteen-minute short *Kagami* is a third German–Japanese co-production, written and directed by a Japanese, co-written by a German, using Japanese actors, a Japanese topic, Japanese and German locations, Kishi Puro and Ufa studios and crew.[9] Two months before the screening permission was granted, a new stipulation concerning 'foreign films' came into effect (*Kinematograph* 1933). Building on a Weimar Republic 'law regarding the exhibition of foreign films' ('Gesetz über die Vorführung ausländischer Bildstreifen', 15 July 1930), intended to protect the domestic market from a surge of foreign – mainly cheap American – films through quotas (Schiweck 2001: 21–2), Goebbels now used the stipulation to clearly define what a German film was. Previously, the participation of more than 75 per cent German passport holders made a film non-foreign, now all participants had to be of 'German origin' as well as nationality (Birett n.d.). Also according to all other points – production by Germans or a German company, set and location shooting in Germany, script and music by Germans – *Kagami* clearly was 'foreign' and thus subject to quota regulations. Only about three months after its establishment, the ministry aimed at 'Aryanizing' the film industry. The *Reichskulturkammergesetz* (Reich Culture Chamber Law), excluding Jews from all spheres of cultural life, passed on 22 September 1933, the same day that *Kagami*'s registration card was stamped (Film-Prüfstelle Berlin 1933). According to Mōri, the process of obtaining screening permission for *Kagami* was complicated by the participation of Jewish staff (2006: 205). While, characteristically for the arbitrary realpolitik at the time, the minister could disregard the regulations 'out of political or cultural considerations' (*Kinematograph* 1933), it was perhaps also before this background that Ufa announced it as 'our culture film', despite Kishi being named as producer, director and composer.

The word *kagami* (mirror) is left untranslated in the full title *Kagami: Traditions in the Japanese House* (*Traditionen im Hause des Japaners*). Throughout the film, explanatory text is spoken by the voice-over narrator Wilhelm Malten and by Yuasa. As she is credited as the only 'actress', the other scenes with actors (the rickshaw man, the father, the maid, cousin Teru, several Buddhist monks) must have been shot in Japan. Yuasa – as in *Nippon* she acts as the female representative of her country and a 'tour-guide' – is seated in a Japanese-style room and provides us with explanations concerning Japanese culture, handling various related objects, such as a mirror, or a tea set. Wearing hair ornaments in her chignon, a dark kimono and a brocade *obi*, she looks more 'authentically-traditional' than in *Nippon*. Malten's bodiless, omnipresent voice holds the traditional

---

[9] For a subsequent French version, the dialogue scenes were reshot with resident soprano Sekiya Toshiko (Mōri 2006: 215–16).

authority of the male, Western commentator, who describes and clarifies what is happening on the screen. Following the opening section, Yuasa looks straight at the camera and begins to speak: 'Kagami means mirror'. She explains the mirror's meaning in Japanese folklore, but also points out that the film itself is a mirror of 'traditions in a Japanese house'. The ensuing section of the film that deals with Tamaki Tarō's arrival back home from his studies in Europe is thus established as 'true', the veracity of the mirror image. Kishi plays Tarō, and the plot may also 'mirror' his experiences, travelling between Japan and Europe. Looking very much like official photographs of a well-dressed Kishi, Tarō steps out of a rickshaw wearing a three-piece Western suit, complete with fob and chain, a hat, and he carries a walking stick. In the next scene, he has already changed into a kimono. While his father pours him *sake* and they talk, the camera suddenly closes up to show Tarō grimacing and fidgeting, 'for in Europe he has forgotten the Japanese way of sitting'. This humorous shot clearly was inserted into the footage from Japan; the plain grey wall in the background is not consistent with the room's otherwise Japanese décor. Tarō's ensuing dream is presented in a remarkable experimental montage sequence that reflects the Osaka group's experimental work and was praised as 'excellent' by German critics (*Lichtbild-Bühne* 1933). It conveys the confused, disjointed and often verbally inexplicable impressions of returning 'home' after a long stay abroad. Several images are layered on the close-up of Tarō's sleeping face in a series of simultaneous superimpositions: 'Home' is represented by a smiling Japanese woman in serene surrounding and by small dishes of food, appearing as if by magic one after the other on round trays placed on *tatami* mats. The 'outside' is mostly presented as urban, industrial, modern; yet fragmented and made odd through film technique, such as camera movements, canted camera angles and fish eye lenses. In *New Earth*, Mitsuko has a similar 'dream' that also presents past events and using eye-catching editing techniques, including various types of wipes and superimpositions (Figure 1.7). The visuals of Tarō's 'fantastic dream', mixing the strange and the familiar, also parallel *New Earth*'s scene of Teruo's experience in a bar, a clash of two worlds symbolized by *sake* and Western cocktails, *shamisen* and jazz music (Figure 1.8).

Tarō and Teruo share the 're-entry shock' caused by the impact of culture that should be one's own but feels strange after a long absence. The focus in both films is on the way they have changed during their time away and how the change impacts their return. The psychological discussion in cultural representation of the 'loneliness of the returning wanderer [between] cultures', is a modern development, and this motif is prominent in semi-autobiographical works by writers such as Natsume Sōseki and Mori Ōgai, or in Inoue Yasushi's historical novels (Mrugalla 2002). *Kagami*, therefore, was embedded in a well-established Japanese discourse, as would be *New Earth*. The motif was not yet present in Fanck's earliest

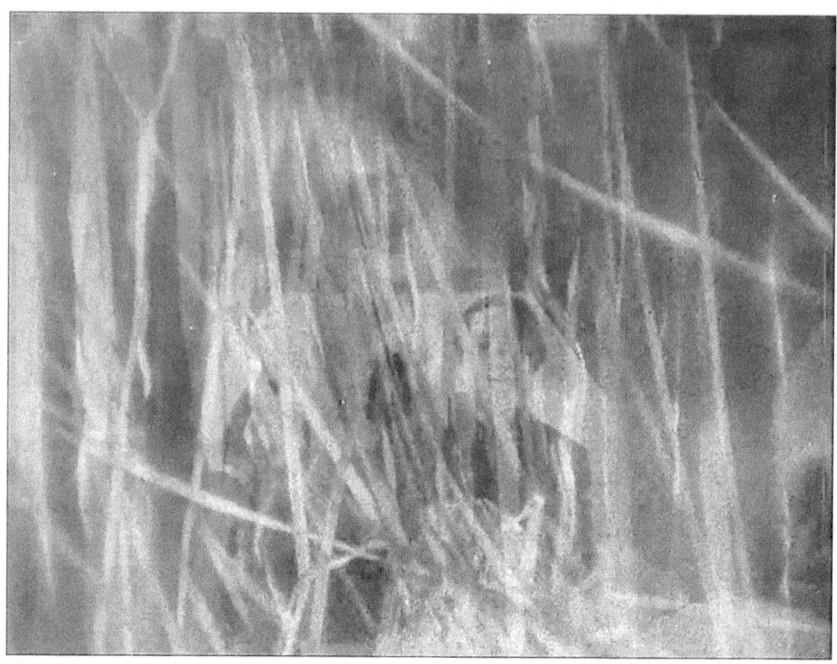

FIGURE 1.7 *Mitsuko's dream of Teruo leaving on a ship.*

FIGURE 1.8 *Teruo torn between East and West.*

ideas about a young factory worker who eventually settles in Manchuria or Korea (1935), while the 'existential conflict' upon re-entry (1935: 8) is very pronounced in the final product, which hints at the Japanese impact on the script, as well as *Kagami*'s legacy.

As a short film with an almost purely didactic intention, *Kagami* gives less reel time for dramatic development than *New Earth*. For Tarō, the problem is easily resolved through the dream sequence. The subsequent scene presents an introduction to the tea ceremony, using mostly long takes and close-ups of objects. Shots of Tarō and his 'pretty cousin Teru' – the woman in his memories – enjoying tea signify that he has resettled into his surroundings. Neither way of life is vilified in this film. However, following the tea ceremony, the homecoming motif is dropped and the narrative abruptly – and curiously – turns to customs for the anniversary of a death in the family, completely unrelated to the previous plot and characters. A group of Buddhist priests leaves a temple: their procession to the family home and back is accompanied by Malten's narration:

> Lined up militarily behind one another, they often march for many hours. Without a word, continuously pondering spiritual problems . . . . In the military order that determines their entire way of life, the monks embark on their way home. Silent and pensive, as they came. From ancient times, we have known Japan as a nation of fighters and soldiers. No wonder that even Buddha's spiritual warriors grow up in strict subordination and keep up severe discipline. Their wooden sandals clatter rhythmically over the grey stones of Old-Japan today, as did those of their valiant ancestors more than thousand years ago.

Malten's tone of voice becomes brisk and the music, through the use of trumpets and drums, becomes military. The sudden stressing of belligerence and martial spirit and the nation as a whole neither fits the visuals nor makes diegetic sense. A quick fade-in then reveals a large regiment of soldiers marching through an East Asian town, followed by a cut to soldiers, bayonets shouldered, marching through roads lined with people. A cut to the monks and Malten's text finally links soldiers and priests, evoking a syncretism of religion and military obedience. The roots of this constellation in an ancient, unchanging Oriental tradition contribute to the powerful image.

The conflation of monks and soldiers seems to be a later decision in the production. As Kishi's original idea had been to present the Hōryūji temple as a meaningful and aesthetic artefact (Mōri 2006: 157–9), related footage came to Germany with him. Yet editing it together with scenes of military prowess appears to be a product of the very context of this editing process: as the monks' feet walk away and the screen fades to black, an interpretation along the lines of Germans walking towards a new future based in ancient traditions suggests itself. Indeed, one reviewer saw the film as a 'wake-up call for the Germanic people to remember their origins' (*Film-Kurier* n.d.; cited in Mōri 2006: 207). As Leims points out, the stressing of commonalities rather than differences – as in *Kagami* and later in *New Earth* – can work as a 'backwards-stabilization' of the ego through recognition of the same in the other (1990: 455). Fanck and others moved within a framework originating in a Western representational tradition dependent on 'the Other', albeit in a specific German vernacular of inwardly directed, 'deep', Orientalism (Pollock 1993). As in Said's original analysis, however, the representer places himself in a position of power with regard to knowledge about the other. The announcement of a screening of *Kagami* explains that Kishi 'will attest to what he has been taught by German music and German film' (*Pamphlet: Japanischer Abend* 29.02.1934). Japan is positioned as the gifted pupil of German achievements, despite the ground-breaking film-aesthetic work having been done at Kishi Puro. By pointing out the discrepancy perceived in the film between an externally 'quite modern country' and the manners and customs, internally 'bound to old traditions' (*Lichtbild-Bühne* 1933), the trope of modern form and traditional content (or essence) is maintained, regardless of the film's avant-garde elements. '*Kagami* shows us ancient culture and the mysterious, traditional customs of the Japanese' (*Filmwoche* 20.03.1935).

However, taking the film's international production background seriously, we must also think about the questions this scene might have answered in a transnational context. After the international controversies regarding its annexation of Manchukuo, Japan declared its intention to leave the League of Nations in March 1933. Germany was still ambiguous concerning its affiliations in the Far East but followed the Japanese example only four days after *Kagami*'s release. In 1932, an anonymous pamphlet had publicized *Reflections on the Manchurian Question: By an East-Asian German* (*Betrachtungen zur Mandschureifrage. Von einem Ostasien-Deutschen*). The writer was Friedrich Wilhelm Hack, who accompanied *New Earth*'s German production team to Japan, disguised as producer but in fact as a secret negotiator for the Anti-Comintern Pact. Hack's work for the South Manchurian Railway's East Asian economy bureau (1912–14) made him 'an expert' on Manchurian-related topics. His knowledge of Japan – gained during his time as a prisoner of war in Tsingtao and in Japan until his return to Germany in 1921 – made him an 'East-Asian German'. Following the military aggression in Manchuria in 1931, Hack lobbied against anti-Japanese sentiments in Berlin. He organized press conferences that helped to transform the German journalist's attitude; 'incorrect reports [*sic*] were stopped and the antipathy towards Japan suddenly disappeared' (Hack 1996: 113–22). Less than a month before *Kagami*'s premiere, Solf and Hack wrote an appeal for the enrolment of members on the German–Japanese Society's behalf:

On the occasion of a reception, hosted by the DJG on 27.10.1933 in honour of Count Tokugawa [Iesato], the count testified for Japan's friendly attitude towards Germany. Inter alia he said 'I may assure you that of all the nations, there is none that understands you as well and that observes your national movement with as much sympathy as the Japanese'. (cited in Hack 1996: 133–5)

Although an actual military alliance was a future matter, the forging of goodwill on both sides was highly topical. Some Japanese in Germany shared an initial and long-lasting attraction to the radical changes. And Japan, too, took measures to raise sympathy and approval for their actions in Manchukuo. *The Japan Yearbook* of 1933 dedicated twenty-one pages to 'The Manchurian Incident', pointing out the need for self-defence against Chinese hostilities as well as for the creation of peace and order in the region, if necessary by 'armed immigrants' (Foreign Affairs Association of Japan 1933). Like the footage of Japan's early exploits in North China inserted into Ushihara's otherwise not markedly militarist *Marching On* (aka The Army Advances, Shingun, 1930) (Drew 2003 [1996]; see also Standish 2005: 44, 98), *Kagami*'s strange final act in hindsight leaves a disconcerting aftertaste. It displays a concern with Japan's military prowess in a world that is treating her somewhat unfairly. It also reverberates with the commonalities of the *zeitgeist* in both countries.

In 1934, Kishi suggested the establishment of a binational film production company to Ufa, with the Japanese government contributing 1 million Reichsmark. The board was not interested, as the Japanese market did not promise to be very profitable (Hansen 2007: 187). Unperturbed, Kishi planned to create an international market for domestically produced films through his new 'International Film Inc.' (*Kokusai Eiga Kabushikigaisha*) on his return to Japan in 1935. Very much within the trend discussed so far, the first item on Kishi's list for his company's activities also sums up the concept for *New Earth*: 'To produce [narrative] films in Japan, using foreign directors, cameramen and famous foreign stars together with Japanese actors and to create an appropriate script' (Môri 2006: 283–4). Also around 1935, the state began to increase its influence over the film industry and film export, coming to perceive film as a potent means for moral education and for influencing opinion, internally and externally (Freiberg 2000). Shôchiku's short documentary about the renowned *kabuki* actor Kikugoro VI performing the *The Lion Dance* (Kagami jishi, 1935), directed by Ozu Yasujirô, was made explicitly for export (Yamamoto 2004: 71). Some footage found its way into a 1930s German short film *The Land of Cherry Blossoms* (Das Land der Kirschblüte, 1930s). The remark 'as filmed by a German crew' is obviously only partially true in the best case, but again demonstrates the power position to be obtained through the depiction of exotic others. The

Ministry of Education was likely involved in the production of *The Lion Dance* (Richie 1974: 221), but there is evidence that the film was also made in cooperation with – or even commissioned by – the Society for International Cultural Relations (*Kokusai Bunka Shinkōkai*) (Shibasaki 2011: 31–2). The society – a forerunner of the Japan Foundation – had been established under the auspices of Prince Konoe Fumimaro in 1934 with the objective of promoting Japanese culture overseas, and would play an instrumental role in the production and domestic exhibition of *New Earth*. The establishment of various 'Film Associations' reflects the state's growing interest in film: in 1935, the semi-governmental, conservative Greater Japan Film Association (*Dai Nippon Eiga Kyōkai*) grew out of a committee created by the Home Ministry of Internal Affairs to define the direction for further film regulations, drawing inspiration from the infamous German Film Law of 1934 (Standish 2005: 139). Composed of high-level politicians and members of the film industry, their mission statement called for high-standard productions: 'There is a danger that films introducing Japan overseas can give the wrong impression of Japan, and damage the reputation of Japan. It is impossible to rely on private companies alone to project a pure and superior image of Japan abroad' (Freiberg 2000: n.p.). The International Film Association of Japan (*Kokusai Eiga Kyōkai*) was founded in September 1935, under the Foreign Ministry's auspices, also with the intent of exporting an accurate national image on film:

> The various countries of the world are perhaps aware that our country is proud of her old civilization of two thousand six hundred years and is at the same time showing brilliantly swift progress in modern civilization, but it is a matter for regret that, due to the peculiar character of our language, customs, etc., the opportunity of having them made accurately known in foreign countries are [sic] lacking. With regard to the motion pictures of Japan, too, notwithstanding [sic] they can be compared with those of other countries so far as skill and efficiency of production is concerned, it is exceedingly regrettable that for the same reason the opportunities of having them presented and enjoyed in foreign countries are lacking. (Kokusai Eiga Kyōkai 1937; cited in Hu 2010: 59)

Kawakita and Fanck had signed their contract one month earlier. Kishi, on the other hand, stopped his film-related projects, perhaps because he was warned off the 'dog-eat-dog' Japanese film world, perhaps because of ill health (Nakai 1951). He died on 17 November 1937.

As we have seen with these three German–Japanese co-productions and the contexts from which they emerged, film export was linked to Japan's assertion of a powerful position in a newly developing world order. Contemporary discourse did not try to set Japanese cinema apart as a separate national cinema, but aspired to make it 'the same' as others, while at the same time conveying an authentic national image. As Morris-Suzuki points out, 'The global frame creates a uniform showcase in which national distinctiveness can be all the more easily exhibited to public view' (1997: 2). In this sense, we have observed a movement from German representations of Japan to films produced in Japan with German and Japanese participants and finally to Japanese films with German participation. International co-productions are a means to produce a joint film project that 'either of the co-producers alone would find difficult to achieve in any other way' (Enrich 2005: 2). The undertakings examined here, on the Japanese side, aimed at overcoming market barriers based on representational issues. The Japanese participants wished to utilize their contract partners' expertise, their name-value and the foreign 'gaze' to successfully and truthfully represent Japan. Consequently, *New Earth* appears as the fourth German–Japanese co-production, following *Bushido*, *Nippon* and *Kagami*, all three of which involved producers from Japan and Germany: *Bushido* was produced by Tōa/DNFU, *Nippon* by Tōwa Shōji/Ufa and *Kagami* by Kishi Puro/Ufa. These forerunners contradict *New Earth*'s label as the first co-production, putting into spotlight the actual use of the phrase in the film's discursive environments. Moreover, they were produced in accord with certain sets of expectations, formats and motifs that fed into *New Earth*'s production, reception, narrative and style. *Bushido* already attempted to show the 'real' Japan through a foreign lens but remained ambiguous about the foreign representer's status within this framework. *Nippon*, in which Kawakita was heavily involved, displays a conscious tweaking of the material towards the target audience and the construction of similarities between both countries. The notion of returning home and being 'Japanese', finally, is prefigured in *Kagami*, as is the addition of politically relevant motifs. Other common tropes are a female representer/representative, Japan being introduced as a miniature from a bird's-eye view, and fragmented 'dream sequences'. All the predecessors were also concerned with 'authenticity', from the ethnographic power of the props used in *Harakiri* to Heiland's claim to represent the 'real Japan', *Nippon*'s cross-cut through Japanese history, and Kishi's didactic endeavour to explain Japanese traditions. The international 'misapprehensions' about Japan to be corrected, however, slowly shifted from the 'Madame Butterfly image' to include political concerns, such as Japanese intentions in Manchukuo and China. *New Earth* inherited the mission of rectifying all kinds of foreign perceptions, political as well as cultural.

Yet, there were also purely economic reasons for producing a successful Japanese 'international film': Kawakita Kashiko refers to a 'shock' inflicted on Tōwa by the 'Tōhō block' (Tōhō Tōwa 1978: 264). Tōhō, originating in the Tokyo Takarazuka Theatre Company, emerged as a major competitor in the film world in 1935. It suddenly branched out into European film imports as temporary attractions 'to supply its growing collection of theatres until it could bring its own sound film studios up to an acceptable level of production' (Kirihara 1992: 46–7). Hata Toyokichi of Tōhō preceded Kawakita in travelling to Europe that year and acquired the rights for about ten new productions (Tōhō Tōwa 1978: 264; Kunisaki 2006: 141). Tōhō's founder, Kobayashi Ichizō, arrived in Germany in October 1935, during an 'observation tour' to Europe and America (*Film-Kurier* 1935b; *Yomiuri Shinbun* 07.06.1936). Like Tōwa, Tōhō also bought French films, such as *Verdun* (Verdun, souvenirs d'histoire, 1931, Poirier) (*Lichtbild-Bühne* 1935a). With the decreasing market share for European imports, this competition gave Tōwa cause for concern. Kawakita then 'rushed' to Europe, and it was during his stay that he concluded the contract with Fanck (Kawakita and Satō 1991: 39). The plan to diversify Tōwa's range of activities and to embark on film production could well have been propelled by these forces.

The difficulties encountered during the production of *New Earth*, attributed by Fanck and the Kawakitas to its being a 'first' and thus explained by their lack of experience (Fanck 1938; Kawakita and Satō 1991), rather appear to be due to increased pressure within changing political and industrial environments. To be 'first' can be both a marketing device and an excuse. *New Earth* was not the 'first-ever Japanese-German collaboration' (Nogami 2006: 237), but it was the first – and last – to be so highly proclaimed and supported at a governmental level, and followed by the press in both countries to such an extent. Furthermore, it occurred at a time when the eyes of the world increasingly came to rest on Germany and Japan as they moved towards international isolation and then into a binational alliance with the Anti-Comintern Pact. While the military agreement impacted on the production by facilitating, influencing, changing and impeding it, the long background story of attempts to bring Japan onto German (and international) screens also left its mark. Finally, another legacy carried over into *New Earth* is its label applied by some as a nationally disgraceful *kokujoku eiga* (e.g. Takada 1937). After the long production period, the large amount of money spent, and the feverish press and advertising campaigns, this verdict must have been a disappointment for those behind the production, and one they could not have anticipated in 1935, as they set out – once again – to make Japan's first, proper export film.

2

Producing *New Earth*

People, stories, inconsistencies

> *Completion is planned for 10 September 1936. Following the editing and soundtrack work, the film will appear on the world's screens by mid-October. The final outcome is yet unknown, but the Japanese-German team's frenetic efforts over two years, from planning stage to completion, will be felt in the finished product.*
>
> (KAWAKITA 1936A)

A relatively straightforward account

Reading Kawakita Kashiko's mid-production article in *Eiga no tomo*, the project appears to be a rather straightforward affair, albeit not without its difficulties (Kawakita 1936a). Her piece is the most immediate account of its background and progress as they were presented to the cinephile readership in Japan before the highly advertised and anticipated release. Reading it into the previously established context of film export and international understanding provides a first impression of who joined or left the project, when and why, keeping in mind, however, the veiled frictions and developments in the course of the film's production, distribution and exhibition as well as in the political climate.

On 3 July 1935, Kawakita Nagamasa arrived in Berlin – in pursuit of Tōwa's competitor Tōhō – and met Fanck on the same evening to discuss an 'interesting project' (*Film-Kurier* 1935a). On 10 August, with Kashiko now in Berlin as well, they signed a contract about the production of a film, to be directed by Fanck in Japan, using Japanese actors. Fanck was known in

Japan – and internationally – for his mountain films (*Bergfilme*). Despite his reputation as the 'father of mountain films', he was not the first person to make a film on or about a mountain: British climber Frank Ormiston-Smith recorded his *Ascent of the Mont Blanc: 15,781 Feet High* in 1902, followed by subsequent films commissioned by the Tyrolean Tourism Bureau and targeted at British and German tourists (Köck n.d.). But it was Fanck who established and perfected the genre, with a dedicated production company and a school of cameramen. Berg- und Sportfilm GmbH Freiburg (BSF) was founded by Fanck and other mountain and film enthusiasts in 1920. Prolific in other genres as well, they also produced over twenty short films and films commissioned for sport events, tourism and book launches as well as animated films (Fanck 2009: 31; see also Appendix 3). After falling into financial difficulties BFS was bought by producer Henry Sokal in 1925, and in 1928 was integrated into Ufa. The 'Freiburg school' includes well-known names such as Hans Ertl, Sepp Allgeier, Hans Schneeberger, Walter Riml and Richard Angst. The group constantly invented and perfected techniques and technology for the *Bergfilm*'s specific requirements and difficulties (difficult terrains, extreme temperatures, natural light), and established a set of idiosyncratic aesthetics: they brought the camera out of the studio, up to high altitudes and into deep crevices, blending documentary and narrative (Figure 2.1).

These films use dynamic moving shots, for example, by fixing cameras on the ski boots of the cameramen, all of whom were experienced sportsmen. The development of unusually long focal length lenses facilitated effective

FIGURE 2.1 *Cameraman Sepp Allgeier on location (ca. 1930).*

use of high contrast, backlighting, the contrast of light and shadow and frequent cutting between extreme close-ups and long panoramic shots. The simple plot – often a love triangle – merely serves to propel the narrative forwards to yet another spectacular landscape (Elsaesser 1994: 25). Natural forces play a dominant role, and the human protagonist's inner state is expressed through pastoral scenes, accumulating clouds, raging snowstorms and avalanches. Huge amounts of landscape shots 'in all sorts of moods' were brought down from the mountains, and Fanck edited the most beautiful or extraordinary images into the plot so 'as to fit with the human action', using his collage-like 'free cutting' technique (Fanck 1976: 4; Weigel 1976: 31–2). These idiosyncrasies made 'Fanck films', such as *Mountain of Destiny* (Berg des Schicksals, 1924), tremendously successful. Their look-and-feel, fundamentally different from the aesthetics of studio-made Ufa productions, introduced alpine landscapes and sports to urban audiences cooped up in grim cities ridden by unemployment and inflation. Fanck's images were governed by a natural scientist's search for exactness paired with a still photographer's ideal of truthful representation, yet deeply grounded in the 'iconography of romantic painters, evoking the impetus of artists like Caspar David Friedrich. . . . The cinematic medium becomes a vehicle to simulate unmediated experience, a modern means of restoring pre-modern wonder and enchantment' (Rentschler 1990: 147).

However, in order to secure a steady flow of income for further projects, Fanck increasingly had to consider more mainstream audiences and give his mountain epics 'narrative contours' (Rentschler 1990: 142). *The Holy Mountain* (Der heilige Berg, 1926) is an example of this stylistic shift, as well as the beginning of a critical crossfire. Fanck was – and is – not easy to place; he polarizes opinions: 'People get upset about him. Dr Fanck is not praised but loved, not criticized but attacked. Evaluations of his work not only contradict one another, but also themselves' (Balázs 1984 [1931]). It is also here that the dichotomous definition of Fanck as a director gifted with a great visual style but lacking in narrative sophistication and the ability to direct actors started. Kracauer, in his review of *The Holy Mountain*, distinguished the 'wonderfully accomplished' photography from the plot, a 'gigantic composition of body cult phantasies, sun-moronism and cosmic babbling', and in 1947 he still applauded the landscape shots while denouncing the narrative elements (Bogner 1999: 29). Nevertheless, the success of 'Dr Fanck' films, in particular *White Hell of Piz Palu* (Die weiße Hölle vom Piz Palü) (1929), notably with G. W. Pabst taking over the dramaturgy and directing of actors, brought him international recognition and led to his German–American co-production with Universal Studios, *SOS Iceberg* (SOS Eisberg), a spectacular adventure film set in Greenland, in 1933. His film on the Olympic Winter Games, *The White Stadium* (Das weiße Stadion, 1928), was one of the first films Kawakita imported to Japan, followed in quick succession by his other mountain and ski films

(*Yomiuri Shinbun* 28.12.1935). From the vantage point of 1935, his films, precisely because of their strong visuals and simple plot, seemed ideal for an attempt at traversing national and cultural borders. A second, important factor was their stress on authenticity, due to location shooting, the crew's experience in mountain sports, their use of high-tech equipment and finally Fanck's doctorate in geology. This was just what the Japanese producers were aiming for in their endeavour and added to Fanck's name value in Japan; yet, as in Germany, his limitations as a director were known: 'Fanck is the only person in the world able to make nature's great feelings and sensations come alive [but] is neither a master of narrative films nor famous for depicting a national character' (*Yomiuri Shinbun* 28.12.1935). A further trait of his style would not prove amenable to the project: Fanck's early films were unscripted, and his later works were improvised to a large degree. *New Earth*, however, had to be entirely scripted, following the Japanese producers' request.

For Tōwa, this was their first venture as a production company; the second Japanese contract partner was Ōsawa Yoshio, head of J.O. (Jenkins-Ōsawa) Studios. They fixed in the contract that the Japanese partners would pay for all costs incurred in Japan and during the return journey, that Tōwa Shōji's distribution rights for the finished product excluded the German-speaking markets and that Fanck had to bear the cost of travel to Japan by a party of eight and their wages, as well as to provide the necessary equipment, including a much-admired and discussed Zeiss zoom lens and raw film stock (Tōhō Tōwa 1978: 264–6; Fanck 1973: 329). In 1935, U.S. imports supplied 78 per cent of the domestic demand, supplemented by the newly established Fuji Shashin Film K. K. and British and German suppliers (Kirihara 1992: 49). For *New Earth*, however, the stock was delivered by the Indian branch of the German Agfa, and Ōsawa happened to be Agfa's representative in Japan (Hirano 1992: 207).[1] Directly after finalizing the contract with Fanck, Kawakita left for Japan and worked out the details with Ōsawa and Kabayama Aisuke, the president of the Society for International Cultural Relations (Kawakita 1936a). With Kabayama, like Wilhelm Solf, a strong advocate of strengthening international ties through cultural exchange (Auslin 2011: 158), Kawakita had secured yet another solid backing, both financially and in terms of political and personal connections. Kawakita,

---

[1]Agfa was part of the infamous IG Farben conglomerate of pharmaceutical and chemical companies, established in 1925. Bayer, which the Kawakitas visited later during their 1937 stay in Germany, was also a member. While before 1933, no member of management was in support of the National Socialist Party and the right wing attacked IG Farben as an 'international capitalist Jewish company' (Bäumler 1988: 277); in 1933 it provided 'the largest single contribution' to the NSDAP's election campaign (Borkin 1978: 71). After the war, the management level faced the Nuremberg trials, for war crimes, such as utilizing slave labour and for providing the poison gas Zyklon B to Auschwitz concentration camp (Borkin 1978: 71).

Ōsawa and Kabayama embarked on the highly publicized venture of producing 'Japan's first international film' that would fulfil a threefold objective: to represent Japan truthfully to the world, to do so in a cinematic language that foreigners would understand and thus to push Japanese film onto the international scene.

In November, following a telegraph by Fanck announcing their departure date, 'Kabayama at once went to the Railway ministry, foreign ministry and military department and acquired their agreement of support for this plan, then Ōsawa and Kawakita publicized the plan with the backing of the Dai Nippon Eiga Kyōkai [Greater Japan Film Association], Nikkatsu, Shōchiku and P.C.L. [Photo Chemical Laboratory Film Studios]' (Kawakita 1936a). P.C.L., a new, small but very modern production company, was not only proficient with the still relatively new sound technology, it already had some experience with international co-productions, too, having made a film with two Burmese film-makers, *The Japanese Girl* (Nihon musume aka Japan Yin Thwe, Nyi Pu) in 1935, albeit on a more modest scale (*Hōchi Shinbun* 15.02.1936: n.p.).

The archives of the Kawakita Memorial Film Institute hold a statement of purpose 'regarding the invitation of the Dr Fanck group' ('Fanku hakase ikkō' 1937). It confirms the project's purpose as to fulfil the 'Japanese film industry's long-harboured desire of film exports' by inviting the world-renowned German director to make an 'international-style Japanese film' (*kokusaiteki nihon eiga*). The International Film Association under the Foreign Ministry's Cultural Affairs Division, the Society for International Cultural Relations and the International Tourism Bureau promised their support, demonstrating the concern regarding the promotion of Japan in the international arena. Shōchiku's managing director Kido Shirō, his counterpart at Nikkatsu, Matsukata Otohiko, who was also a board member of the Dai Nippon Eiga Kyōkai and P.C.L. founder Uemura Yasuji agreed to act as advisers. Ōsawa, Kawakita and Kabayama Chūji (Aisuke's son and J.O. board member) are listed as the inviting party and project representatives. This composition of people hints at the scale and status envisaged by the project's participants. Kabayama had studied in the United States and Germany, his son Chūji as well as Ōsawa were Princeton alumni and Matsukata had been to the United States in 1934 for a personal talk with his Harvard peer Theodore Roosevelt about binational relationships following the diplomatic disturbances after the annexation of Manchuria (*Princeton Alumni Weekly* 1927; Reischauer 1986: 269–71). Kawakita had lived and studied in China, while Uemura had studied photographic chemistry in Germany. These were all people genuinely interested in cultural exchange due to their international backgrounds, with many of them belonging to the 'finance-aristocracy' (*Film-Kurier* 1935b), a highly influential and affluent layer of society.

The German party left Marseilles in early January 1936 on the *Suwa Maru* (*Asahi Shinbun* 13.11.1935; Kawakita 1936a). On board were Fanck, his wife Elisabeth, their two-year-old son Hans, Hack as 'financial adviser and manager', assistant director Walter Tjaden, editor Alice Ludwig, cameraman Walter Riml, production assistant Karl Buchholz, actress Ruth Eweler, journalist Hans-Walter Betz and secretary Minna Rueck. They were accompanied by translator and 'mediator' Hayashi Bunzaburō, who had participated in one of the previous co-productions, *Kagami*, and had also helped translate *Girls in Uniform* (Mädchen in Uniform, Seifuku no shojo, 1931, Leontine Sagan and Carl Froelich), which Kawakita Kashiko had liked and brought back to Japan in 1932 to high acclaim. Star cameraman Richard Angst and Hannes (Hans) Staudinger were currently in Indonesia, shooting for the Dutch-German ethnographic feature film *Head Hunters of Borneo* (Die Kopfjäger von Borneo, 1936, von Plessen) and would join the team later. According to Fanck, the ship's departure from Marseille had been delayed for four days by a technical defect; the Propaganda Ministry rejected his request for financial help for hotel expenses, whereas his Japanese contract partners promptly sent him a generous amount (Fanck 1973: 329–30). In 1973, Fanck attributes this indifference to Goebbels's 'anti-Japanese attitude', an assessment contradicted by a certain admiration expressed in Goebbels's Japan-related diary-entries during this period (Goebbels 1987: 102, 146, 154), but Fanck approaching the ministry for help seems to speak for some early political involvement. On 8 February, all arrived safely in Kōbe and toured film studios in Kyoto the following day, before moving on to Tokyo. After setting up headquarters in the Mampei Hotel, Fanck began working on his script. The contract obliged him to write the script after his arrival in Japan to ensure an authentic representation of Japan based on first-hand experience (Kawakita 1936b; Fanck 1973: 329), but likely also to enable to producers to keep an eye on and if necessary intervene into the script, due to Fanck's aforementioned reputation as a relatively ungifted scriptwriter. This provision also necessitated the establishment of Fanck's own production company, Dr. Arnold Fanck-Film Berlin-Tokyo. When Fanck wrote about his new Japanese project in July 1935, he quarrelled with the film industry's reluctance to back a film financially without an existing script (Fanck 1935). This was due to a great part to the German government's clampdown on the industry, as from 1934 'film treatments' had to be submitted to the Reich Film director (Welch 2001: 14) – in other words, pre-production censorship had been put into place, a condition that Fanck could not fulfil. While he was working on the script in Tokyo, troops entered the Mampei Hotel (Fanck 1973: 331; Kawakita and Satō 1991: 40–1), an event that illustrates similarities between Germany and Japan in terms of political trends: the pre-production phase in Tokyo coincided with a major step on Japan's road towards ultra-militarism – a group of young

FIGURE 2.2 *Gerda and Teruo watch troops marching through Tokyo.*

army officers attacked and assassinated various political leaders in the 'February 26 Incident' (*ni ni roku jiken*), which put Tokyo under martial law for three days. Chiba even claims that a scene in the film of marching troops seen from a hotel roof was influenced by the incident (Chiba 1987: 9) (Figure 2.2). In fact, the visual and acoustic emphasis on their 'marching in step' also reminds strongly of the similar scene in *Kagami*.

Fanck also studied films selected for him by his Japanese partners and formed a concept of 'Japanese film' that he could work with or against. All eighteen feature films were recent successful productions, and most of them were *gendaigeki* (Appendix 1). Naruse's *Wife! Be Like a Rose* (Tsuma yo bara no yō ni, 1935) was likely the first Tōhō film that made its way to American screens, hence, its relevance to the planned export film. Fanck also saw short films by the International Tourism Bureau and ten documentary films by Tsukamoto Kōji (Kawakita 1936a). Tsukamoto's *Mount Zao* (Zaō san, 1935) won several international awards for its successful presentation of the Japanese mountains 'through Japanese eyes' to an international audience in 1936, while the production of *New Earth* was still underway (Saito 2007; Kattelle 2003: 245). The surviving shots appear quite similar to Fanck's style, in the dramatic impact of backlighting, for example. As several of Fanck's films had been previously imported by Kawakita, a stylistic influence on

FIGURE 2.3 *Members of the crew during a location shoot (names and place unclear).*

his colleague is possible. A contemporary review of *Mount Zao* also bears a striking resemblance to evaluations of Fanck's works; despite the simple, almost non-existent plot, 'just people skiing down a mountain', the film is 'surprisingly exciting, beautiful and enjoyable' (Soda 2007). Meanwhile, crew members scouted for suitable locations. The *Asahi Shinbun* reported on the cameramen Buchholz, Riml, Tjaden, Hoshi and Ueda shooting the snow-monster-like, frost-covered trees that were the stars of *Mount Zao*; the Germans now in turn used Japanese input to make their own films (*Asahi Shinbun* 29.02.1936; *Asahi Shinbun* 15.03.1936). Tsuburaya, who would also work on the ambitious screen processing for *New Earth*, accompanied at least a part of the footage-hunting exhibition (Yanagizawa 2014: 69) (Figure 2.3).[2] The Tourism Bureau planned to use the resulting films showing 'the beauty of Japan's winter sports through Fanck's senses' in order to introduce Japan as a skiing location and to promote the 'still infantile Japanese mountain-film [genre]' (*Yomiuri Shinbun* 28.12.1935).

---

[2]Titles mentioned for these films are *The Conquest of Mount Zao* (Zaō seifuku), *The History of Skiing in Japan* (Nihon sukī hattatsu shi) and *Zao: Silver Frenzy* (Zaō: shirogane no rappu), an homage to Fanck's ski comedy *White Frenzy* (Der weiße Rausch (1931), which had been released in Japan as *Shirogane no rappu*.

It appears that, for unclear reasons, the footage was never assembled; the further fate remains unclear (Yanagizawa 2014).

In any case, the selection of films shown to Fanck makes it clear that the Japanese side planned to combine Fanck's internationally acclaimed skill of depicting nature with the qualities of the best domestic narrative films.

During his previous international co-production with Universal Studios, *SOS Iceberg*, Fanck had felt 'alienated' because of his lack of English (Weigel 1976: 23). Thus, again having to deal with an unknown language, unfamiliar conditions and the task to represent the 'real Japan' (*hontō no nihon*), he asked for a Japanese co-director. His partners introduced him to Japan's 'top ten directors' regardless of studio lines: Saeki Kiyoshi, Ozu Yasujirō, Shimazu Yasujirō, Yamanaka Sadao, Naruse Mikio, Gosho Heinosuke, Shimizu Hiroshi, Itami Mansaku, Kinugasa Heinosuke and Uchida Tomu (*Nippon Hyōron* 18.02.1937). Fanck eventually decided on a specialist writer and director of 'cheerful period dramas' (*meirō jidaigeki*), Itami Mansaku, after having seen his *Chuji Makes a Name for Himself* (Chūji uridasu, 1935) and *Frivolous Servant* (Kimagure kaja, 1935).

Along with Yamanaka Sadao and Inagaki Hiroshi, Itami (born Ikeuchi Yoshitoyo) represented a new generation of film-makers who broke established norms of *jidaigeki* (period drama), one of the two 'mega-genres' of Japanese film – the other one being *gendaigeki* (contemporary films, set after the Meiji Restoration of 1868). His school friend and mentor Itō Daisuke (1898–1981), by 1925, had become a director at Nikkatsu's Taishōgun Studios. Itō set a new benchmark for *jidaigeki* with *Diary of Chuji's Travels* (Chūji tabi nikki, 1927), one of the films Kawakita and von Stietencron selected for export to Europe. Starring superstar Ōkōchi Denjirō, with an anarchist plot, Itō's characteristic dynamic action (his nickname, after all, was 'Idō Daisuki', 'Really Loves Movement') and new camera technology, the film became wildly popular. When prominent actor Kataoka Chiezō (born Ueki Masayoshi, 1903–83) set up his independent production company, Chiezō Productions (Chie Puro), in the spring of 1928, Itō recommended Itami as a scriptwriter and assistant director (Ishiwari, Maruo and Tani 2005: 24). As increasing state pressure and censorship were slowly leading to a decline of Itō's leftist 'tendency' (*keikō*) films with their nihilistic heroes, he advised the studio to opt for 'bright humour' instead (Abel 2012: 3; Yoshimoto 2000: 22). Itami's first script for Chie Puro, *Peace on Earth* (Tenka taiheki, 1928, Inagaki), consequently deviated from generic conventions by humorously depicting a master-less samurai's tough rather than glamorous life (Kishi 1953: 197–8). Itami moved up the ranks to director in just four months, an almost incredible feat within the tightly structured Japanese film industry and soon became the leading director and scriptwriter of Chie Puro's 'antithetical' *jidaigeki* productions (Yamane 1997: 77). With Kitagawa Fuyuhiko as the spearhead, many film critics praised Itami's works for incorporating a 'plain and lucid spirit' until then not inherent in Japanese film (Kishi 1974: 37). Itami observed modern individual and societal trends and translated them cinematically into premodern chronotopes; hence their denomination as 'contemporary dramas wearing a topknot' (*mage o tsuketa gendaigeki*) (Hirano 2001: 214). He then put a critical spotlight on these currents by utilizing satire's political potential. Itami's and his colleague Inagaki Hiroshi's personal discontent with Japan's militarist turn, for instance, as argued by Yoshida, is the origin of the 'pacifist' protagonist Date Mondo in *Wandering Gambler* (Hōrō zanmai) in 1928: the film's subversiveness lies in Mondo's refusal to use violence for any reason other than to protect his family (2006: 116–17). Itami left Chie Puro in May 1934 and joined the Shōchiku subsidiary Shinkō Kinema. His first film at Shinkō – and Itami's first proper talkie – *Chūji Makes a Name for Himself*, however, was taxing: a typhoon destroyed the set and the company's brand-new Tsuchihashi sound system did not perform well. After the film there were rumours that he had handed in his notice (Saeki 1987: 160–1; *Yomiuri Shinbun* 11.03.1935). In March 1936, while still contracted to Shinkō, Itami began shooting *Akanishi Kakita* for Chie and Nikkatsu, and Fanck came to meet Itami and Kataoka on set. Their initial discussions appear quite amicably, with Fanck admiring Kataoka's make-up as Akanishi, praising Itami's directing and the three of them going out for drinks and discussions (*Mainichi Shinbun* 25.03.1936). However, after Itami had read Fanck's draft for the script, his 'manager' at Shinkō, Morita, told the press in advance of negotiations with J.O.'s Ōsawa that Itami would be interested in collaborating with Fanck on a mountain film, but not on a 'film drama' (*geki eiga*) (*Nippon Kinema* 26.03.1936). He clearly doubted Fanck's capabilities to make a film that so strongly diverted from the genre he was famous for. Itami made his participation in the scriptwriting process a precondition for his participation and composed a light-hearted story about Japanese children (Kawakita 1966). Fanck rejected this alternative and negotiations dragged on, also because Itami was busy finishing *Akanishi Kakita* and already had a tentative offer from Daiichi Eiga for his next film, *Dōshi no hitobito* (Comrades), after his contract with Shinkō expired on 15 April ('Tanaka Kinuyo o zessan' 26.03.1936; *Tokyo-tō* 28.03.1936). The film was based on a 1923 play by Yamamoto Yūzō (1887–1974), a dramatist and popular writer, who spoke out publicly against censorship policies (Miller 2009: 142–3). Set during the end of the Tokugawa Period, it deals with warriors of the Satsuma clan sacrificing of their comrades in the hope to safe their own lives, thus betraying the very ideals they claim to protect (Yamamoto 1979 [1923]). The censors halted the production in the aftermath of the February 26 Incident (*Tokyo-tō* [28.03.1936], to which the story's message indeed offered a critical comment. Itami agreed to join J.O. to work on the German–Japanese film – now suddenly titled *Sacred Rice* (Seinaru kome) – exclusively until its completion in August, collaborating with

Fanck on the overdue completion of the script and the casting (*Mainichi Shinbun* 02.04.1936). Clearly, Kawakita's statement about Itami's 'ready consent' was a publicity tactic, but he eventually joined the production out of concern for the international reputation of Japanese film (Itami 1961 [1937]: 245; Kawakita 1936a).

In terms of cast, Fanck had brought with him Ruth Eweler,[3] in her first main role, and selected his Japanese actors based on the films shown to him. Kosugi Isamu, one of Japan's top actors at that time, was cast for the male lead on the basis of his performance in *Theatre of Life* (Jinsei gekijō, 1936, Uchida). Immediately after his arrival, Fanck had visited J.O.'s Kyoto set for Yamanaka Sadao's *jidaigeki The Priest of Darkness* (Kōchiyama Sōshun, 1936) and 'especially liked Hara Setsuko', a young actress with 'modern looks' (Kawakita 1936a; *Yokohama Bōeki Shinbun* 28.06.1935). Fanck's later, often-repeated claim that he requested Hara Setsuko for the Japanese female lead role because the Shōchiku star Tanaka Kinuyo would not appear attractive to Western audiences is at odds with contemporary reports about Tanaka participating in the film (Fanck 1973: 340). In fact, negotiations failed due to J.O.'s association with Shōchiku's rival Nikkatsu (*Asahi Shinbun* 18.04.1936; Satō 1995: 394), and the coveted role fell to Hara, generating much attention by the press (*Asahi Shinbun* 13.05.1936). With the borrowing of Takagi Eiji, Nakamura Kichiji and Ichikawa Haruyo from Nikkatsu, and of Hanabusa Yuriko from P.C.L. and the addition of former Hollywood star of the silent era, Sessue Hayakawa, the cast was complete. Cameramen Angst and Staudinger arrived in Japan on 24 March (Tōhō Towa 1978: 266), and on 4 April the team moved into Ōsawa's Kyoto residence (Chiba 1987: 10). Fanck wrote and revised the script 'with Itami's assistance' by the end of June (Kawakita 1936a). Angst and his crew had already begun to shoot parts on Mt. Fuji and Miyajima. Shooting on set began on 4 July (Figure 2.4) and was reported by Kawakita as 'almost finished' on 10 August, when Kosugi and Ichikawa left for a Nikkatsu production.

The final shooting on location on Miyajima and Mt. Asama took place during August and was to be completed by 10 September, followed by the final stages of editing and adding the soundtrack. Judging from Kawakita's estimate, the project would end more or less within the German team's originally contracted six-month stay in Japan. But it did not, and the prolonged production time brings into focus concealed conflicts on set as well as political developments that impacted the film's narrative and discursive position.

---

[3] Eweler's career never took off: 'Ironically, those films in which she played a main role, never passed National Socialist censorship' ('Ruth Eweler' 1999); this assessment clearly ignores *Samurai's Daughter*.

FIGURE 2.4 *Shooting a 'Hotel Europe' scene (J.O. Studios).*

Inconsistencies and frictions

Kawakita's account, published roughly two weeks before the film's anticipated release in mid-October, disguises internal controversies. Itami and Fanck were unable to cooperate, and too many discrepancies in opinion regarding the representation of Japanese life resulted in a tense atmosphere on set. As Itami wrote, 'in my opinion, Dr Fanck has not learned that much about Japan' (Itami 1936). Antithetically to Itami's style, Fanck scripted a *gendaigeki* with premodern mannerisms that could not have appealed to Itami. There are also indications that Itami's idiosyncratic take on things was a factor in his joining of the project – contradicting the idea that Fanck had selected Itami freely. In an article following the release of *New Earth*, Nishimura contrasted works like Itami's *Frivolous Servant* (Kimagure kaja, 1935) and Kimura Sotoji's extensively censored *Youth Across the River* (Kawamukō no seishun, 1933), 'perhaps the last *keikō* film' (Satō 2008: 45), with films by 'Ushihara, Suzuki and Tsukamoto' (Nishimura 1937). Suzuki Shigeyoshi made short propaganda films for the Army Department and because of these films and 'the influence of the army that had supported Suzuki's work', Nishimura argues, Fanck's film 'took a distinctive shape [that] apparently was not to the taste of Tōwa Shōji's film department. . . . Eventually, Itami Mansaku was selected by the awakening conscience of the persons concerned at J.O.' (Nishimura 1937). According to this version of events, Itami was assigned to prevent the film from becoming yet another 'national disgrace film', like *Contemporary Japan*, and perhaps to curb the army's influence. This a posteriori version of event is difficult to ascertain, but strikingly Itami himself never refers directly to political matters with regard to *New Earth*. The first issue he brought up as problematic about his potential cooperation – and the one he would continue commenting on – are Fanck's shortcomings as a director of people. As Fanck, perhaps conceding to Itami's opinion, had planned to concentrate on the landscape and location shootings and to entrust Itami with directing the actors, Itami's influence on the script appears rather significant at first glance. During his collaboration, the title was fixed as *New Earth* (Atarashiki tsuchi), and the film was to become a 'film drama', the genre Itami was more adept in (*Mainichi Shinbun* 02.04.1936). Rather consequently, the finished script was attributed to Itami as its original author (*gensaku*) (*Ōsaka Mainichi Shinbun* 03.08.1936)

Shooting on set began in early July and according to Fanck's original idea to leave the actors to Itami (*Eiga Mainichi Shinbun* 07.07.1936). It did not take long for their cooperation to fall apart, and the reason appears to be a clash between two very strong characters. Fanck began interfering in Itami's work on the actor scenes, and Itami objected to his representation of life in Japan. What exactly the issues were, and how Itami dealt with them in his version will be discussed in the following chapters. In order not to jeopardize the high-profile project, Kawakita eventually decided to 'let each have his own version, making two negatives. It was a costly undertaking. . . . It was rumored at one point that this co-production would result in bankruptcy for both Tōwa and J. Ōsawa & Co.' (Kawakita N. 1988: 20). On 22 July 1936, the split in terms of directors between the different language versions was announced – albeit without any allusion to a conflict – and the completion date postponed to September (*Nippon Kinema* 22.07.1936). Angst recalls strenuous double shifts, almost every scene of Fanck's script was shot twice, with the same actors and at the same locations, directed by Fanck in the morning and then by Itami in the evening (NHK 1986: 130). The aforesaid impression of what happened behind the camera is further corroborated by an almost-post-production article, published in December 1936, which could have proven very problematic for Tōwa's advertising campaign (Sawamura 1936: 10). The threatening potential is indicated by somebody at Tōwa having underlined with pencil two 'scandalous' statements, purportedly made by Itami to the article's writer Sawamura Tsutomu and journalist Kitagawa Fuyuhiko. Itami does away with the story that he was responsible for the script: 'Well, yes, I wrote one, but mine wasn't used. That was the one written by Fanck and translated into Japanese' (Sawamura 1936: 10). This statement is trustworthy, given the resemblance of the eventual story with Fanck's initially announced topic and title *People Without Space*, and his later-voiced suspicion that his work had been translated incorrectly in parts (Fanck 1938: 8). Significantly, Itami had a similar problem regarding translation. First, he constantly had to 'culturally translate' Fanck's directions for the Japanese actors. Itami repeatedly states that Fanck did not understand (how to work with and direct) people, and the language and culture gaps seem to have been pronounced. Second, not all translators on set were equally skilled, and – together with Fanck insisting on his own point of view – Itami felt it was pointless to even try and argue about issues regarding the representation of Japan they disagreed on (Fanck 1938: 8). He also predicted very bad critical responses, even more so to Fanck's version: 'The critics will consider this a poor film! As for the Japanese version, I did my best for it not to become completely ridiculous, but the Fanck version is entirely due to this specification, and it is really absurd (*jitsu ni kokkei desu yo*)' (Sawamura 1936: 10). Surprisingly, given the penchant for gossip observable in the press coverage at the time, this tantalizing information did not feature prominently, if at all, in the context of the premiere. It is also noticeable that, if these passages really came from Itami verbatim, the political dimension does not feature, even after the successful and public conclusion of the military pact in the previous month.

Although I assume that it was for scheduling reasons, rather than deep-seated animosities, even the musical score was performed by two different orchestras and used a slightly different compilation of music (Daibō 2010: 15–16; see Appendix 1). The composer responsible for *New Earth*, Yamada Kōsaku (1886–1965), greatly added to the production's high profile. Yamada had studied music in Japan and Germany, and was the first Japanese to compose a symphony and to gain international recognition as a conductor and composer, as well as the founder of Japan's first symphonic orchestra (Galliano 2002: 44–8; Gōto 2014).[4] His fame abroad and his successful integration of Western and Japanese musical styles made him very suitable for *New Earth* as a film directed at international markets. Furthermore, Yamada had written film music before and also worked on a previous international co-production *Big Tokyo* (Daitōkyō, 1933), a joint effort between renowned Soviet film-maker Vladimir Shneiderov and the Tokyo Asahi Shinbun. In many ways, *Big Tokyo* as a project carries an eerie resemblance to *New Earth*. Incepted as a (documentary) film about contemporary, modern Japan, it was eagerly followed by the press but eventually dismissed as – once again – merely exposing the foreign representer's lack of knowledge

---

[4]Japan's first classical composer was likely Kōda Nobu (1870–1946); her pupil Taki Rentarō (1879–1903) is seen as the first notable Western-style composer. Kōda also taught Yamada at the Tokyo Music School (Tōkyō ongaku gakkō) before he left for Berlin.

and understanding (Fedorova 2014: 104). Yamada, however, considered the footage he was shown as an impressively realistic image of Japan, and was enthusiastic to go to Moscow to direct the music for *Big Tokyo*. His ambitious plans for the film's soundscape, however, were met with relative disinterest, both in Moscow and in Japan when the film was released. As Fedorova demonstrates, the film needed popular music for the Soviet audience, whereas the Japanese audience demanded an 'authentic sound image of Japan', and thus two release versions were made (Fedorova 2014: 118). Soviet concerns over Japanese activities in Manchuria ideologically charged the production and reception: 'The ideological battle over the film's sound, however, left no winners. Their inability to compromise resulted in the creation of two imperfect film versions, both of which were quickly forgotten in the history of cinema' (122). *New Earth*, on the other hand, keeps generating discourses about the relationship between film and politics, but the 'ideological battle' over authenticity resulted in a split end product as well. With both films resulting from this Japanese–German co-production being titled *New Earth* (*Atarashiki tsuchi*) for their release in Japan, eventually Itami's version would be known as *Itami han*, 'the international version' (*kokusai han*) or 'the Japanese-English version' (*nichi'ei han*), and Fanck's was called *Fanku han*, or 'the Japanese-German version' (*nichi doku han*).

The split left the distribution rights as per the original contract untouched. The German side still held the rights for those markets interested in a German–Japanese language version. Unwilling to sponsor the film directly, distributor Terra had nevertheless loaned Fanck 100,000 Reichmarks against security and distributed his version as *Samurai's Daughter* (Die Tochter des Samurai) (Fanck 1973: 329). For 'worldwide distribution' by Kawakita and J.O., an English version was required in any case. The production of different language versions was not unusual for films aimed at varied audiences (see Wahl 2008). The non-German language versions of Fanck's *SOS Iceberg* (SOS Eisberg, 1932) and *Eternal Dream* (Der ewige Traum; Rêve éternel, 1934), for instance, were directed by American and French colleagues, Tay Garnett and Henri Chomette (René Clair's brother). P.C.L.'s Burmese–Japanese co-production had used Burmese subtitles for scenes with English or Japanese dialogue and Japanese subtitles for Burmese and English lines (Ferguson 2018: 278). The idea to pursue a similar path with this new project seems logical, but it deviates from Fanck's original vision: because of the 'one hundred per cent Japanese' topic, it would be 'absurd to make "versions" in which the Japanese suddenly speak German or English. What is spoken must be comprehensible without the actual words, but through the simple plot, the unambiguous situation and the clear mimic expression' (Fanck 1935). Fanck aimed at using the conventions of silent film, drawing on the concept of film as a transcendental visual art and on the relatively unproblematic border-crossing of silent films. However, as we have seen with previous attempts, in the case of Japanese film this strategy had proved unsuccessful. Moreover, sound had already changed aesthetic sensibilities and conventions and was requisite to successful export. As seen with *Nippon*, 'authentic' languages were seen to ensure an authentic look-and-feel of the end product. In Japan, early reports announced that Eweler was going to perform in English as well as in German (Uchida 1936; *Yomiuri Shinbun* 25.01.1936). When the team reached Tokyo on 10 February 1936, newspapers had reported on three different versions: two German–Japanese versions (one for release in Japan with Japanese subtitles for German dialogue and another for release in Germany with German subtitles for Japanese dialogue) and an English-language version (*Yomiuri Shinbun* 10.02.1936). Eventually the project resulted in the German–Japanese version(s) by Fanck and the Japanese–English version(s) by Itami, each with the subtitles necessary for each target country. The foreigners mostly speak German or English and the Japanese characters speak German or English to their foreign conversation partners, apart from two lengthy dialogue scenes: the priest Ikkan Oshō's speech to Teruo about the need to abolish individualism, and Kanda Kōsaku's talk about Japan having become too small to feed its many people, and the work in the small fields being too hard. Fanck here used German voice-over for his anticipated target market, due to their importance to the narrative, whereas Itami dispensed with this stressing of the message and merely used English subtitles for the Japanese dialogue.

Originally, the project, in all its language versions, was intended to be the product of one director. Fanck never considers Itami's version outside the Japanese domestic market and merely alludes to a planned American version, which never transpired because it 'proved impossible to get an American co-director' (Fanck 1938: 89).

The participants felt the 'difficulties of a co-production . . . keenly' (Kawakita N. 1988: 21) and the problems contributed to the extraordinarily long production period. Rumours in the film world circulated around difficult negotiations about actors, such as Tanaka Kinuyo, but there is evidence that the delayed start of shooting on set, that is, with actors and according to a script, was caused by conflict about the representation of Japan in Fanck's first draft (*Nippon Kinema* 10.07.1936). Too much of a 'Japan seen through foreign eyes', it was 'far removed from the premise of introducing the real Japan to the world', and so the script had to be revised several times (*Nippon Kinema* 10.07.1936). Yet, even this article does not relate the true state of two discrete films being made, rather than merely different language versions. An article mistakenly reported on Fanck returning to Germany in early November, but sound editing continued to late January (*Yomiuri Shinbun* 03.11.1936). The involuntary extension resulted in the project running into financial difficulties. The originally planned for production costs of 450,000 yen swelled to about 750,000 yen, including a vast amount of film stock valued at 100,000 yen (Kawakita and Satō

1991: 42; Mizumachi 1937; *Shanhai Nippō* 04.06.1937a). Even the initially announced 450,000 yen amounted to roughly ten times that of a regular feature film; in fact it equalled the gross of Shōchiku's successful tragedy *A Love in Heaven* (Tengoku ni musubu koi, 1932, Gosho), which was produced for only 5,000 yen (*Lichtbild-Bühne* 1935b; S-k. 1937). Japanese commentators, not unreasonably, argued that with equal funding a 'genuine' Japanese production on an entirely new level could have been made (Hansen 1997a: 67). One such attempt occurred during the production of *New Earth*; artist Fujita Tsuguharu and director Suzuki Shigeyoshi jointly directed the *Contemporary Japan* (Gendai Nippon) series, also to be distributed by Tōwa Shōji and with Yamada Kōsaku's involvement. The Home Ministry (*Naimushō*) commissioned and spent 500,000 yen on this project, similar to *New Earth* in terms of time and money (*Yomiuri Shinbun* 08.04.1937). The part titled *On Children* (Kodomo no maki) premiered in April 1937, but once more failed to achieve the wished-for authentic image. It was criticized as a 'national disgrace film' for its depictions of ritual suicide and children playing with swords (*Yomiuri Shinbun* 08.04.1937):

> [*New Earth*] was followed by 'Picturesque Japan', produced with the aid of Tsuguji Fujita, the noted painter, and 'Glimpses of New Japan' by Shigeyoshi Suzuki [*Gendai Nippon* consists of both productions]. The former was a highly artistic production, but because it was unconventional both in technique and the subjects treated, the picture was criticized as conveying an inadequate picture of Japan. (Foreign Affairs Association of Japan 1939: 904)

In the light of the enormous cost and reputation at stake, non-completion of *New Earth* would have been a disaster: for Fanck, it would have meant having to pay back the loan from Terra, and, for the Japanese partners, the loss of their substantial investment and, perhaps, reputation (Fanck 1938: 7; Fanck 1973: 329, 345; Kawakita 1968: 267). In contrast to Fanck's account, according to an early announcement of the co-production in Japan, the 'Fanck Film Studios' (*Fanku eiga satsueijo*) had been set up in order to divert the high risk of this costly production from Tōwa Shōji and J.O., with Kawakita and Ōsawa 'merely' assuming personal responsibility (*Nippon* January 1936). Whose version of events regarding Fanck's new company holds the most truth is difficult to ascertain, a characteristic that runs through the story of the production, and this also concerns the important question of where the money actually came from. Investing, after all, signals investment into a cause, and we will turn to the question of further stakeholders later. In any case, an excellent end- and box office result was crucial, but the problems during the production also complicated the matter of distribution. No distributor was initially willing to shoulder the necessary deposit of 100,000 yen (*Shanhai Nippō* 04.06.1937a).

FIGURE 2.5 *Announcement of the nationwide release in Shōchiku SY chain theatres.*

Negotiations reached a deadlock, but eventually the Shōchiku tycoons Ōtani and Shirai stepped in and assumed the financial risk (*Shanhai Nippō* 04.06.1937a). In December 1936, two months after the originally planned release date, Ōtani and Fanck signed a contract regarding Shōchiku's countrywide release of 'Fanck's film' in their SY chain theatres (*Asahi Shinbun* 18.12.1936) (Figure 2.5). This is a significant change from earlier plans that continuously had announced Nikkatsu as the exhibitor (e.g. *Kokumin Shinbun* 17.05.1936).[5]

From 1929 Nikkatsu's financial situation had worsened, while Shōchiku was on the rise, and during the time of *New Earth*'s production and release, Nikkatsu increased its debt rather than making profit (Miyao 2013: 58–9). 'In October 1936, Otani . . . personally undertook Nikkatsu's 2,500,000-yen debt to Chiba Bank and took charge of the company' (Miyao 2013: 59). Shōchiku taking control of this high-profile film may be seen within the same context. Ōtani and Fanck also agreed on the simultaneous release of 'Fanck's film' in Tokyo and Berlin on 1 February 1937.

Unprecedented and uneasy premieres

Eventually, the Tokyo premiere took place on 3 February and 'on a scale unprecedented in film history' (Ebisaka 2004: 47), but Fanck proceeded to the stage only after Ambassador von Dirksen cautioned him about a diplomatic *éclat* in front of the distinguished audience (Fanck 1973: 352). Kabayama had introduced the film as '*The New Earth*, which has just been completed under the expert direction of Dr. Fanck with German and Japanese collaborators' (*Japan Times* 04.02.1937: n.p.). Yet, the film shown that evening was Itami's version, and Fanck claims to have been ignorant about this until the very last minute (Fanck 1973: 352). Even following the split, Fanck anticipated the release of 'his film' and hoped for a favourable reception by Japanese audiences (Aoyama 1936; Fanck 1937a). Itami merely commented that he 'would not have dreamed of the German version being screened in Japan' (Itami 1961 [1937]: 246). The story goes that, with support from Kabayama and the German embassy, Itami's film was replaced by Fanck's after one week (Hansen 1997a: 56). But the release schedule had been announced already at the end of January: 'In the first week, the Japanese-English version will be released nationwide, including Dairen and Hōten, followed by the Japanese-German version in the second week'

---

[5]From 1935, J.O. and P.C.L. were controlled by Kobayashi Ichizō and became part of his new Tōhō chain in 1936 (Anderson and Richie 1982: 82–5). Due to Kobayashi's distribution agreement with Nikkatsu, and 'project adviser' Matsukata being the company's president, this scheme seems a logical consequence of the production's set-up.

(*Nippon Kinema* January 1936). The premiere was special, and Itami is very much absent from its detailed programme and advertisement material, apart from being listed, as usual, as co-director ('Premiere of the New Earth' 03.02.1937) (Figure 2.6).

In the light of Kabayama's speech and the advertisements, Fanck's consternation is believable. But why was Itami's version chosen for the event? With the rising international mistrust after the conclusion of

FIGURE 2.6 *Itami's absence from the premiere programme's cover.*

the military agreement and the various ambassadors and envoys in the audience, Kabayama perhaps thought it prudent to use the Itami version to avoid reference to a Japanese–German friendship. In his letter of reply to Fanck's complaint Kabayama testifies to substantial differences between the two version, and retrospectively considered Fanck's the better one, after he had seen it in a private screening after the premiere (Kabayama 1937). He, however, argued that, initially ignorant about these differences, he and the Society chose Itami's film due to its use of English as a lingua franca for the international guests. Finally, the most pragmatic explanation, which also explains Itami's 'absence', is by Soyama Naomori, who was concerned with the production of the release prints for in J.O. Studios Kyoto: Fanck's twenty-two-reel film was just not ready, even by seven o'clock in the morning (1937: 113). The studio even considered sending the finished portion to Tokyo by airplane, but eventually they had to use Itami's version. This explanation clashes with Kabayama's reply to Fanck, but the fact remains that the two verifiable, contemporaneous sources dealing with the reason for the 'premiere swap' do not posit the political aspect that is later assumed more or less automatically.

Following the premiere and general release, the fact that they had seen a version made by Itami that differed from Fanck's in more ways than merely the languages used, only dawned to the audience after the fact and became a hotly discussed topic. In retrospect, this strategy can even be seen as a clever marketing tactic, as people now wanted to see the 'real', grandiosely advertised film that showed the beauty of Japan through the eyes of the famous master of mountain film. And, indeed, Shōchiku advertised the release of Fanck's version just like that. Without losing a word about Itami's film, they argued that Fanck's version, having been intended for the German market, had just been finished and turned out just too wonderful to not show it in Japan, too. They urged every film fan to 'come, see and compare!' (Shōchiku 10.02.1937). Curiosity explains the great box office success, despite increasingly negative, disappointed reviews. The critics, unavoidably comparing the two films, generally preferred the 'Fanck version' for its grandiose landscape photography, but in over half of the reviews and comments, the representation of Japanese life was almost as harshly criticized as Itami's. The matter of two images of 'real Japan', shown through the eyes of a foreigner and through the eyes of a compatriot, moved the discourse away from the mere question of film export, and towards the question of what constitutes an authentic national image and what an adequate cultural translation could be. But despite the ambivalent reception, for the film people involved, the issue of international film kept its momentum, and various follow-up projects were discussed. Fanck was even invited to Prince Takamatsu's residence and asked to make further collaborative films and to return to build up an export film industry in Japan (*Hōchi Shinbun* 12.02.1937; cited in Fanck 1973: 354). Before he left Japan on the *Chichibu*

Maru via America on 12 February he and Hara participated in a broadcast to Germany. Fanck spoke about 'the hardships of the year of production and his fondness for Japan'; Hara announced – in German – that she would be 'coming over soon' to make another film (*Asahi Shinbun* 12.02.1937; *Asahi Shinbun* 13.02.1937).

The German premiere was anticipated in Japan with great interest, fuelled less by the issue of political cooperation, but all the more by the promise of the successful launch of Japan and its films on the world's screens, and of having in international film star of their very own. The title for the German release was *Samurai's Daughter* (Die Tochter des Samurai). Fanck perhaps aimed at tapping into the success of Etsu Inagaki Sugimoto's novel *A Daughter of the Samurai* (1925), released in Germany in 1935 as *Die Tochter der Samurai*, by using (almost) the same title (Hansen 1997a: 24). At least, he (and/or the distribution company) utilized the exotic attraction of Eastern warriors and exotic femininity. And, indeed, Hara was the film's one almost unanimously positively received feature. On 10 March, an 'unprecedented crowd' of fans sent her off to the Berlin premiere from Tokyo Station (*Asahi Shinbun* 11.03.1937). Her brother-in-law, film director Kumagai Hisatora, accompanied her as a 'chaperone' (Kida 2010: 98), but he also held professional ambitions of his own, planning 'two co-productions with a German company' (Adachi-Rabe 2002: 168). The Kawakitas pursued a threefold purpose: to sell the international version, to negotiate further co-productions or contracts, and to establish Hara on international screens. The party of four journeyed via Manchukuo, where Itami's version had already premiered on 1 February. Hara and Kumagai gave radio interviews in Shinkyō and Harbin, and on 17 March the group boarded the Trans-Siberian Railway (Tōhō Tōwa 1978: 267) (Figure 2.7).

As planned, they arrived in Berlin on 26 March, the day of the gala premiere in the Gloria Palast theatre (*Berliner Lokalanzeiger* 27.03.1937; Hara 1937b). However, as in Tokyo, the event did not go smoothly for those intimately involved in the project: history repeated itself: unbeknownst to them, the gala premiere, at which Hara was supposed to appear on stage in a beautiful kimono and address the audience in German, had taken place three days earlier. 'Due to Easter, all businesses are closed until the 29th and all dignitaries are on holiday. Therefore, the pre-release . . . was suddenly advanced to the evening of the 23rd'; the location had been changed to the Capitol am Zoo theatre (Kawakita 1937; see also Herzberg 1937) (Figure 2.8). Despite several official receptions and press attention after their arrival, this lapse in planning – or indifference to the invited guests' sensibilities – speaks volumes about the importance this cinematic collaboration held in German political circles. Still, in order not to vex binational relations, Goebbels instructed the press to report on the premiere in grand style, 'as it had been in Japan' (Toepser-Ziegert and Bohrmann

FIGURE 2.7 *From the Kawakitas' photo album: Sightseeing in Manchukuo and on the Trans-Siberian Railway.*

1984: 244). The German–Japanese Society (DJG), naturally taking an interest in these relations and with Hack at its helm, had organized the premiere and an evening reception at the Fellowship of German Artists club (*Kameradschaft der deutschen Künstler*), which had been founded in 1931 as the 'Association of National-Socialist Stage and Film Artists' (Fanck 1973: 361; Knopp 2003: 240).

During the reception, Fanck and Hack did not receive the attention from Goebbels they had expected, and the minister was not impressed by the many speeches and much 'palaver' (Fanck 1973: 361; Goebbels 1987: 89). In accord with many viewers, then and now, he considered the film visually stunning, but 'unbearably lengthy' and in need of rigorous cutting. But it was nevertheless awarded the high rating of 'politically and artistically valuable' in the system of 'positive censorship' established in 1933 (Kreimeier 1999: 257). In order to be exhibited without special permission films now needed a rating, which only about 30 per cent of the 1,094 German productions shown between 1933 and 1945 received (Kreimeier 1999: 254). A 'politically and artistically valuable' film such as *Samurai's Daughter* benefited from reductions of the entertainment tax, which in turn made it attractive for

> Die
> Deutsch-Japanische Gesellschaft
> beehrt sich, in Verbindung mit den Direktionen der
> UFA und der TERRA
> zu der Uraufführung des
> deutsch-japanischen Gemeinschaftsfilms
> Die Tochter des Samurai
> im
> CAPITOL am ZOO
> ergebenst einzuladen
>
> Dienstag, den 23. März
> abends 6 Uhr
>
> Diese Einladung ist streng persönlich. Sie gilt nur in Verbindung mit beiliegenden numerierten Karten und zu der darauf bezeichneten Vorstellung. Im Falle der Nichtbenutzung wird höflichst um Rückgabe der Karten gebeten

FIGURE 2.8 *Invitation to the premiere on 23 March, 6.00 pm, issued by the German–Japanese Society, Ufa and Terra.*

exhibitors as well as producers who received a bonus of the profits (Welch 2001: 15–17). The minister had also predetermined the reviews of *Samurai's Daughter* in terms of tone and information to be included, such as the rating, and the avoidance of negative remarks about alien customs (Toepser-Ziegert and Bohrmann 1984: 238–46). Goebbels specifically instructed the press not to mention the existence of a higher rating that the film was *not* awarded (Toepser-Ziegert and Bohrmann 1984). Consequently, Hara reported back to Japan on the film's success and that it had received the 'highest rating' (Hara 1937b), and Fanck presented the film and his own 'mission fulfilment' in a similar light (Fanck 1938). This, again, was a marketing ruse for an expensive but problematic film: the Kawakitas collected articles and reports in Germany, as they had in Japan, and reports on the film's second-tier rating are filed next to an article on 'Dr Goebbels's reform of the rating system' ('*Auszeichnung für deutsche Filme: Neuregelung der Prädikatsverteilung durch Dr. Goebbels*'), which clearly explains the five-tier system. Fanck was equally involved in advertising his film, and collected and published (mostly positive) snippets from the German reviews in 1938 (Fanck 1938: 15–80). Regardless of his obvious self-interest in his publication, it remains unclear how much *zeitgeist*, opportunism, indifference, ideological conviction or genuine enthusiasm these articles reflect, and some writers left the rating unmentioned or did not comment on the plot's politico-ideological aspects (Hansen 1997a: 80).

In Germany, the existence of a second version became known publicly only after the Tokyo premiere, via an article by the *Frankfurter Zeitung*'s foreign correspondent Lily Abegg and an interesting example of implicit criticism by left-wing film critic Iwasaki Akira (Abegg 1937; Iwasaki 1937). A Tokyo Imperial University graduate in German literature, Iwasaki had been involved with the Proletarian Film Movement (Purokino) of the 1920s, and also with the import of German expressionist films to Japan (Makino 2001: 32–3). In 1934, he had warned his readers about how the German state control had qualitatively ruined the film industry, which had 'plummeted into an abyss from which it may never again rise' (High 2003: 70). In a little-known turn of events, Iwasaki was the correspondent for the German film magazine *Der Film* when *New Earth* was released in Japan. Iwasaki explained to his German readers that Itami's version had premiered on 3 February:

> The messages of success transmitted to Germany regarding this premiere therefore are not connected to Fanck's work. The Japanese press also passed judgements on this version that were less than flattering. Dr. Fanck was of course in no way responsible for this version. Because the name Fanck, however, was mentioned in relation to this version, it nevertheless broke box office records in Japan. (Iwasaki 1937)

Iwasaki's account is vague about the actual reception. His wording questions the 'success messages' in the light of the 'less than flattering' reviews, and his comments on the positive reception of Fanck's version are followed by his own more or less veiled opinion: 'The newspapers declared in unison that this Fanck film at least rates as an exemplary export film. . . . Even if there is room for objections regarding its conceptual content, it depicts Japanese life and Japanese people far more interestingly than Itami['s version]' (Iwasaki

1937). After his arrival back in Germany, Fanck gave several interviews, in which he sometimes mentions the existence of a 'Japanese version' from a 'Japanese director', but stresses that his own version had been received and praised as being 'much more Japanese' than the other one (Oberhauser 1937). Furthermore, 'in this film, we are of course interested in what is as authentically Japanese as possible. The Japanese director was attracted to European aspects' (Oberhauser 1937). Itami had been absent from the Tokyo premiere and, according to Yomota, declined Fanck's invitation to the German one for health reasons (Yomota 2000: 51–2). In the programme for the event, the film is described as 'Terra's Dr Arnold Fanck film' and Itami's name is missing from the cast and crew list. The German discourse designated the film as a product of 'Fanck's Japan expedition' (Schu. 1937), even after 1938, when Fanck acknowledged Itami in his booklet on the production (Fanck 1938: 8–9).

In terms of monetary results, the three-week run of first Itami's and then Fanck's film broke box office records in Japan (Kawakita 1973a: 49). In the first two weeks, 242,753 people saw them in Shōchiku's three major Tokyo cinemas alone (Musashino kan, Teikoku gekijō and Taishō kan) (*Eiga Engeki Naihō* 25.02.1937). Fanck version's long run of two weeks was followed by a five-day screening in the Kabukiza from 26 February for a cheap fixed entrance fee of 50 yen, as suggested by Ōtani (*Eiga Engeki Naihō* 1937); the theatre was filled beyond capacity each day (Tōhō Tōwa 1978: 268). Due to the somewhat surprising lack of a structured reporting system until 1940, German audience numbers remain unclear. Japanese reports on the film's success abroad claimed that it attracted 6 million people in 2,600 cinemas (*Asahi Shinbun* 20.05.1937; cited in Hansen 1997a: 60). Yet, one of the Third Reich's greatest cinematic successes, the similarly rated *The Great Love* (Die große Liebe, 1942, Hansen) boasted audience numbers of 27 million. In Japan, Kinugasa's Shōchiku All Star production *The Summer Battle of Osaka* (Ōsaka natsu no jin, 1937) had broken the box office record in April (Ebisaka 2004: 47). *New Earth* never made it onto the *Kinema Junpō*'s 'Best Ten' list, neither as a foreign nor as a Japanese production. But as seen from the box office results, the film by no means was 'a failure from all points of view' and an expensive fiasco (Anderson and Richie 1982: 149; likewise, Manvell 1974: 355; Rhodes 1976: 250). Hansen rightly identifies the desire for the 'film's signal lack of success' as originating in another desire, namely the authors' wish to demonstrate the audience's rejection of the 'propaganda piece' (1997a: 57).

Apart from the high attendance numbers and media coverage, what did the project effect in terms of the dream of export, national prestige and further collaboration? Not only had the Japanese party journeyed for fourteen days only to realize that they had missed the premiere 'for the convenience of Hitler and other high dignitaries' (Tōhō Tōwa 1978: 268), but furthermore:

Terra Film AG is not much good at advertising; somehow, they are not very interested, despite having had Fanck make the film in Japan for a year. Therefore, Kawakita spoke to Terra, and, although late, placed large-scale announcements in the newspapers' evening edition of 26 March and the morning edition of 27 March. (Hara 1937a)

On that evening, which Hitler did not attend after all, Hara greeted the audience for the first time. Despite the disappointing lack of concern for the film from the German side, Kawakita's group – accompanied by Fanck – met various high officials during their stay in Germany. Goebbels mentions an 'interesting discussion with Japanese director Kawakide [sic] and Dr Fanck' during a dinner in the Japanese embassy on 15 April (Goebbels 1987: 114). The minister spoke 'pleasantly' to Hara, who thought him small in stature but strong-spirited in face (Hara 1937c). Yomota attributes Hara's star persona becoming the wartime 'goddess of Japanese militarism' and Kumagai's turning into an ultra-nationalist[6] to her involvement in the production and her and Kumagai's exposure to strong nationalism in Germany (2000: 83, 51–8). This point is visually confirmed by a frame from a photograph taken that evening that shows Hara and the figurehead of fascist propaganda, Goebbels, standing close together. The original photograph, however, a group shot of Eweler, Goebbels, Hara, Fanck and Mushakōji standing in front of a mirror in the Japanese embassy, emphasizes the very multifacetedness of interests and objectives interwoven in the production and in the group of people gathered in the Japanese embassy (Hara 1937c).

The following day the Japanese party resumed the nationwide promotion tour for *Samurai's Daughter*. While Leipzig, for 'the first time in film history . . . organized a reception on the occasion of a film premiere and the visit of a film artist' (*Film-Kurier* 1937a), Hara indicates a discrepancy between the grandiose representation of her tour and her own perception. Often, the film had already run for a while and had lost its novelty, so she performed in front of only a few people and felt lonely and homesick (1937c). Still, Kawakita determinedly pursued his goal of further film-related cooperation (Figure 2.9). In an article published in *Film-Kurier* shortly after the premiere, he uses the new political situation as a means to opening doors, flattering German self-perception by praising the high artistic quality of German productions following the industry's restructuring after the National–Socialist seizure of power.

According to Kawakita, the Japanese film world aspired to a similar involvement of the state; in this sense Germany is seen as a model, just as *Samurai's Daughter* is a model and an initiator of further, fruitful ties

---

[6]After the war, Kumagai was the only film director to be temporarily suspended from the film industry as a war criminal 'class B'.

FIGURE 2.9 *The Kawakitas 'in front of Cologne Cathedral' (1937).*

with Germany and a positive development for the Japanese industry through cooperation (Kawakita N. 1937a). Such public statements strongly contrast with Kashiko's later account of their impression: 'With the Nazis' tyranny and the persecution of the Jews, German film headed down the road towards suicide' (Kawakita and Satō 1991: 33). Clearly, interpretations of situations depend on the context of these statements, a tendency that is very pronounced with regard to *New Earth* as an historical event within a highly loaded time frame.

The next co-production Fanck told the German press about, a feature-length documentary film chronicling Japan's rise to power after the Meiji Restoration in just *Seventy Years* (Siebzig Jahre), was never heard of again (Oberhauser 1937). Nor did Kawakita's potential follow-up project, *The Diplomat's Daughter* (Die Tochter des Diplomaten; Gaikōkan no musume), with Hara in the leading role, co-directed by Fanck, Kumagai and Italian director Carmine Gallone, proceed beyond the early planning stage. The title and plot indicate the attempt to build on *Samurai's Daughter*: The Japanese ambassador's daughter (Hara) is courted by four (!) Berlin beaus. Out of homesickness, she returns to her fiancé in Japan (*Asahi Shinbun* 28.03.1937b). A link between Italy's joining the Anti-Comintern Pact six months later on 6 November 1937 and three directors from Germany, Japan and Italy working together is not corroborated by contemporaneous evidence; *Der Film* had reported extensively on *Samurai's Daughter* but did not publish anything about her sibling. Reports on composer Yamada Kōsaku travelling to Berlin to work again with Fanck on a 'Hara Setsuko film' are perhaps overstating the affair, as Yamada's journey is better explained with him having been invited as a guest director for the Berlin Philharmonic Orchestra (*Asahi Shinbun* 11.04.1937; Galliano 2002: 49–50). In a repetition of the clash between Itami and Fanck, Kumagai says he rejected the project due to controversies about the script, later characterizing it as a 'mish-mash of idealism and opportunism. . . . By that time, I was a fire-breathing Japan-ist and so I ended up tossing aside the contract and storming out' (Iida 1976: 151; cited in High 2003: 228). In any case, Hara did not participate in a second international co-production.

Kawakita had also begun to negotiate with film producer Tobis regarding a monopoly on the import of Tobis films (Hara 1937c). However, known or unbeknown to him, Tobis had already signed a contract with Ogasawara Takeo and Kida Zenso of Kokkō Film shortly before (*Film-Kurier* 1937b). The subsequent establishment of Cocco-Tobis-Nippon (C.T.N) secured the 'sale of a significant number of Tobis films to Japan', a beneficial arrangement for the German film industry (S-k. 1937). *Der Film* contrasted Kawakita's more 'production-oriented' company with C.T.N.'s distribution business model (*Der Film* 1937a). Since Tōwa's main line of business was film imports, this new rival on the German market would have given Kawakita enough cause for concern, but C.T.N. also anticipated his plan for subsequent co-productions modelled on the method for *New Earth*. Kida announced C.T.N.'s objective as 'to produce Japanese films fit for the world market, in cooperation with the best artistic and technical talents from Germany' and to set up a top-notch film studio in Japan (S-k. 1937). While Kawakita succeeded in securing a contract with Ufa for the import of culture films – the culture film department being headed by Nicholas Kauffman who had also been involved in the production of *Nippon* – and later brought Leni Riefenstahl's controversial Olympia films to Japan to great acclaim (see also Sierek 2018),[7] *New Earth*'s immediate follow-up project included none of this story's main protagonists: C.T.N. re-invited much-praised cameraman Angst to Japan to make a film about Japan's fishing industry, *Typhoon* (Taifun) (*Der Film* 1937b). *Typhoon* was to be tailored for an international market, featuring a 'universally comprehensible and interesting plot' and an exclusively Japanese cast (*Der Film* 1937b). Japanese reports noted that

---

[7] It won the *Kinema Junpō*'s prestigious first (for *Olympia Part 1: Festival of Nations* [Fest der Völker], 1938) and fifth places (*Olympia Part 2. Festival of Beauty* [Fest der Schönheit], 1938) for foreign films of 1940.

after the criticism that *New Earth* was boring, this project would have great entertainment value (*Asahi Shinbun* 01.08.1937). *Typhoon* was abandoned, but Angst – and composer Yamada – participated in a promotional ski film for the eventually cancelled 1940 Olympic Winter Games *The Oath of the People* (Kokumin no chikai, Das Heilige Ziel, 1938, Nomura Hiromasa). After the spin-off documentary, *Album of Snowy Mountains* (Yukiyama no arubamu; Album der Schneeberge, 1939), Angst stayed on in Japan to film and edit a Tōhō semi-documentary on the war in China, *The Comrade's Song* (Senyū no uta, Das Lied des Kameraden, 1939).

As for *New Earth*'s 'international release', reports that Kawakita sold the film in thirteen European countries were flawed by obvious marketing and damage-control strategies (*Asahi Shinbun* 20.05.1937). It was Fanck who sold the film quite profitably to Romania, Bulgaria, Yugoslavia, Czechoslovakia, Poland, the Baltic States, Finland, Sweden, Norway, Holland and Austria (Deutsche Filmexport GmbH 1936–38). This list significantly excluded France and England, where Kawakita planned to sell Itami's 'international version'. Following screenings, various official receptions and visits to film studios throughout Germany, the Japanese party left Berlin in late May for Paris, where *La Fille du Samouraï* was screened at a private theatre, and a French–Japanese co-production was discussed (*La Cinématographie Francaise* 1937; Turquan 1937). The promotion of the film's international version and of Hara as a prospective international star continued in New York and Hollywood (Figure 2.10).

FIGURE 2.10 *Kawakita Kashiko and Hara Setsuko in Central Park.*

But despite sporadic reports of sales and re-editing (e.g. *Asahi Shinbun* 04.05.1937), the reactions were generally negative. The poor quality of the soundtrack and the cast's spoken English – surprising in the case of former Hollywood star, albeit of the silent screen, Hayakawa – certainly also would have necessitated a re-dubbing. Kawakita, however, attributed the rejection solely to the negative international reception of the Anti-Comintern Pact and to strong anti-German sentiments (Tōhō Tōwa 1978: 71). He entrusted the distribution in the United States to 'Mr B. of M. Company' (Tōhō Tōwa 1978: 67), specifically because the 'Modern Film Corporation', unlike most major American film companies, was not dependent on 'Jewish capital' (Kawakita N. 1937b). Since 1933, many talents had left Germany because of the persecution of Jewish members of the film world, and exported German productions were boycotted in many countries by a 'Jewish lobby' (Welch 2001: 23–4, 73). Hence, Kawakita in New York also vehemently denied a 'political angle' in context with the foundation of C.T.N. (*Variety* 1937a). Still, although the trade press reported on Modern Film acquiring the American rights (Variety 1937b), *New Earth* was never publicly released in the United States, and Hara's launch as a star on an international scale ultimately failed. After she was recalled to her new studio, Tōhō, the party's return journey coincided with the Marco-Polo Bridge Incident (Lugouqiao Incident) of 7 July 1937. The battle between Japanese and Chinese troops southwest of Beijing marks the beginning of the Second Sino-Japanese War and thus of the Second World War in Asia. When the group arrived in Yokohama, they had come back to a country at war.

The very heterogeneity of the parties involved and of their motives mapped out so far point to the lack of the commonly assumed direct political motivation for these films. However, politics and culture interact and their mutual instrumentalization intensified during the production and took up speed in accordance with the tightening of binational relations and the deterioration of international ones. Ribbentrop's negotiator Hack, the most obvious interface between Fanck and politics, also provides an interesting hint regarding the issue of Fanck and a conscious, ideologically inspired and politically determined background for *New Earth*: building his niche within the discourse on Japanese–German military and political and cultural alliances in his booklet about *Samurai's Daughter* in 1938, Fanck explicitly thanks 'Dr Hack, former vice-consul in Japan, for his guidance' (1938: 7). Not only is there no evidence that Hack was ever an official member of the German diplomatic service, but when Fanck published his booklet, Hack had already been arrested and left Germany after his release (Bundesarchiv Berlin 2012). Despite having been awarded an order for his work for the Reich in connection with the Anti-Comintern Pact, Hack was 'persona non grata in Germany' in 1937 (Spang 2003: 15–16). The inaccurate use of 'vice-consul' and the evocation of a close connection with Hack in a political context are interesting blunders on the part of title-conscious Dr Fanck that question the extent of his knowledge of the actual background politics. Yet, this does not necessarily rule out the possibility that the state supported the film financially, or politically, once the moment became opportune and Fanck was ready to make the most of it.

3

A pact of the silver screen

> Samurai's Daughter *embodies the common world views ways of new Germany and old Japan.*
> (MECKLENBURGER TAGEBLATT 10.7.1937; CITED IN FANCK 1938: 63)

> *As the importance of Japan's position in international political affairs has increased, with the conclusion of the German-Japanese Anti-Comintern pact as a turning point, there is a need to introduce to overseas countries life in Japan as it really is. . . . The first picture to meet this need was Dr Arnold Fanck's 'New Earth', of which an English and a German version were made and exported to America and Europe.*
> (FOREIGN AFFAIRS ASSOCIATION OF JAPAN 1939: 904)

In 1939, the Foreign Affairs Association of Japan (*Nihon Gaiji Kyōkai*) posits the authentic representation of contemporary Japan as a paramount feature of *New Earth*, contextualized within political developments. Both countries' militarist turns had complicated their international standings, increased their isolation and contributed to the conclusion of the Anti-Comintern Pact, which is presented here as a 'turning point' for Japan's move towards an international position of power. *New Earth* and the pact had become part of a common discourse. Many studies therefore assert that the film was made *because* of the pact (e.g. Anderson and Richie 1982: 148). Yet, previous efforts to introduce Japanese film internationally, the film's long production time and the very heterogeneity of its participants challenge interpretations of the preceding political agreement as the sole cause of the subsequent release of the film.

Furthermore, such unilinear readings are based not only in the parallel political developments but also in the public personas of the two directors tasked with representing Japan's authentic image. As much as Fanck's pre-war reputation as a geologist and 'master of mountain film' was used to categorize, promote and evaluate the film in 1936/1937, his post-war image as 'Nazi Germany's appointed director' is featured in recent discussions (Yomota 2000: 301). The implications of this tendency to take labels for granted are perhaps most obvious in the linking of Fanck to his 'beautiful disciple' Leni Riefenstahl, another controversial figure in film history, and Propaganda Minister Josef Goebbels: 'For *SOS Iceberg* (1933), Fanck was praised by Goebbels as a "true Nazi"' (Yomota 2000: 35; see also Klee 2009: 132). The evoking of the notorious minister to categorize Fanck fits into the general picture, but it is flawed by words missing from the source consulted (albeit indicated by ellipses in the 1987 edition of Goebbels's diaries). A newer transcription (2006) shows that the object of praise – 'a nice guy and a true Nazi' – during a visit to Fanck's Berlin residence on 4 June 1933 was not Fanck but skier-cum-actor-cum-cameraman Guzzi Lantschner (Goebbels 2006a: 214). The issue at hand here is not by whom, when and according to which criteria the label of 'a true Nazi' can be applied to somebody, and what, exactly, Goebbels might have meant by it on that occasion. It is more important to note that this label is easy to adopt and fill with meanings that then dominate approaches to the text.

In order to understand the context in which *New Earth* was examined and evaluated, it is necessary to understand the mountain film as firmly associated with Fanck's persona and as contested terrain in film studies. Although there were other directors working in the genre, most notably Luis Trenker and to a lesser extent Leni Riefenstahl, Fanck remains its principal exponent, not least through self-proclamation. Kracauer, and later Sontag, considered the genre as expressing an explosive mixture of proto-fascist sentiments of *ubermensch*-ism, irrationality and fatalism, which paved the way for these sentiments to become manifest in the Reich (Kracauer 2004 [1947]: 111, 257; Sontag 1987 [1975]). Although Fanck's persona has thus spurred discussions in the re-evaluation of German film and its people under National Socialism,[1] these re-evaluations still have to be applied to *New Earth*.[2] By finding similarities between the film's opening scene, featuring the birds-eye view of Japan, and the opening scene of

---

[1] Bogner 1999; Brandlmeier 2008; Giesen 2008; Horak 1997a; Kirchmann 2005; Rentschler 1990; Steiner Daviau 2002; Weigel 1976.
[2] Segawa, whose study temporally overlaps with mine, is the notable exception in that he appreciates Fanck's complex positions in the German film world and within *New Earth*'s production environment (2017).

Riefenstahl's *Triumph of the Will* (Triumph des Willens, 1935), in which Hitler's plane descends through the clouds, Baskett evokes the ongoing discussion about the relationship between Fanck's and Riefenstahl's cloud images and the meaning of clouds in fascist imagery (Baskett 2008: 129). Beginning with Kracauer in 1947, these instances have been identified as either foretelling or representing Nazi sentiments. While Kracauer visually confirms his argument by juxtaposing two frames depicting clouds, Fanck's *Storms over Mont Blanc* and *Triumph of the Will*, Kirchmann analyses Fanck's clouds as visual techniques for the graphic impact of the frame and expressions of his fascination with constant change in nature, rather than expressive of a 'Hitler cult' (Kracauer 1984: 271; Kirchmann 2005: 117, 129). And in fact, the opening shot of *New Earth* resembles nothing more than the opening shot of *Nippon*, confirming the project's embeddedness in a backstory of German–Japanese film collaborations. Hake also locates ideologically problematic points rather in the later films by Trenker and others with their 'apotheosis of physical beauty and strength in the figure of the solitary hero' (Hake 2002: 43). For Horak, the ultimate resignation and passivity of Fanck's heroes in the face of nature and their own limited human power is, in fact, contrary to National–Socialist megalomaniac belief in the power of action (1997a: 51; likewise, Loewy 1999: 6; Jung 2013: 244). Powers, on the other hand, argues that the pre-Nazi sublime lies in the 'combination of physical flawlessness and the blind celebration of danger' of the pre-Nazi *Bergfilm* heroes (2007). This polarized discourse is due to the historical specificity of Fanck's work, which straddles a threshold between the aesthetics of the Republic and the aesthetics of the Third Reich, a stylistic blend of the beautiful and the sublime (Rentschler 1990: 154). It is precisely because Fanck tapped into the partially shared discourse of two ideological systems that his films resonated with representatives of a variety of ideological and political positions, 'indicating common needs and shared desires that crossed party lines' (Rentschler 1990: 145). 'Fanck films' were connected to both völkisch and communist revolutions. And although the second option was not established, it is nevertheless instructive to see that it was possible to think of such a connection with regard to the contested genre of *Bergfilm*.

Itami, on the other hand, is known for a genre that became increasingly contested as Japan moved towards militarism, because it, in turn, contested some of the ideological traits connected to this development. The films he and his colleagues, most notably Inagaki Hiroshi and Yamanaka Sadao, made at Chie Puro and elsewhere were at the time labelled 'new' period films (*shin jidaieiga*), and particular Itami's scripts and films were known as outstanding examples of the *nansensu* (nonsense) variety. *Nansensu shin jidaieiga*, which ridicule received images of the past, are often seen as a 'vestige of Taishō liberalism' that necessarily clashed with the burgeoning state ideology of imperialist militarism, but for Yoshida, Itami's and his peers' breaking of the conventions of classical as well as 'leftist' *jidaigeki* was due to a general 'crisis of representation' in the early 1930s, as the rhetoric of the national polity (*kokutai*) was in crisis (2006: 111–14). *Emergency Era Japan* (Hijōji Nippon, 1933, Kondō), for instance, portrayed the clash of Western and Japanese values, with War Minister General Araki admonishing idle pleasure-seekers to return to a Japanese way of life. As the distinction between *jidaigeki* and *gendaigeki* was instrumental in defining the nation vis-à-vis the Other, Yoshida concludes that these genres were in crisis as well (2006: 109–15). The old rhetoric no longer made sense of the experienced reality and, hence, a new form of representation had to be found (2006.: 115).

But not only did these *shin jidaieiga* address contemporary concerns and sensibilities, they also actively disrupted by negation received images of the past that were increasingly used to legitimize current ideologies. A case in point is Itami usually avoiding the glorification of the hero through the stylistic conventions of the final battle scene or sword fights in general by ridiculing their conventions, as in *Peerless Patriot* (Kokushi musō, 1932), or by making them happen off-screen, as in *Akanishi Kakita* (1936). Unsurprisingly, his heroes therefore deviate from the samurai archetype. *Peerless Patriot*, in a sarcastic wordplay on 'in the gallant days of chivalry' (*bushidō hanayaka narishi koro*) is set 'in the excessive days of chivalry' (*bushidō hanayaka sugishi koro*). The story of an impostor of humble origins (played by Katakoka), impersonating a famed swordfighter addresses issues of authenticity, origin and historical veracity, which Yoshida identifies as the 'major thematic concerns' of the mid-1930s (2006: 77–8). In *Akanishi Kakita*, an adaptation of Shiga Naoya's novel, Itami again challenged expectations about the past and the glorified samurai cast, but also about the story itself (McDonald 2000: 21–6). Contrary to the open-ended novel, visually unattractive but kind Kakita finds love and gains the upper hand in the plot, eventually uncovering the conspiracy. The samurai who made fun of him become the comic target, and the anti-hero prevails. For Barrett, his triumph 'even questions by implication the authority of Japan's political and military leaders of the 1930s, for they adhere to old samurai values, particularly their prerogative to rule as the superior class. Thus, the comic target in *Akanishi Kakita* is ultimately the values of society at large' (Barrett 1992: 214–15). Today, the film is considered probably 'the best satire of the samurai class', but at the time critical voices questioned the veracity of its portrayal of the past and its treatment of the original novel (Barrett 1992; *Asahi Shinbun* 10.06.1936). While the censors clamped down on such films in favour of canonical images of the past, Itami kept speaking – or rather writing – out against the government's actions and incompetence: In 'My wish for the end of war' (*Sensō chūshi o nozomu*, 1943), he condemned all further war efforts as hopeless, cruel struggles, driven forward by a regime incapable of reacting to the true state of affairs (Itami 1961 [1943]). The essay 'The question of those responsible for the war' ('*Sensō sekininsha no mondai*'), which he wrote in 1946 to immediately address the topical issues of wartime guilt and individual responsibility, likely cemented his public persona as understood today. He wrote this piece in response to the Association of Independent Filmmakers (*Jiyū Eigajin Renmei*) drawing up a list of 'war criminals in the film industry':

> Many people would think that the distinction between deceivers and deceived was clear, but this is an illusion. . . . I think that probably all Japanese were absorbed in this process and deceived and were deceived by each other. . . . Even though being deceived means to be victimized by the dishonest, no dictionary defines the ones deceived as being honest. People who mistakenly think that they are released from all responsibilities and unconditionally belong to the side of justice, just by saying they have been deceived, must reconsider . . . . The saying: 'To apologize for a lack of insight' clearly denotes the concept of judging ignorance as a sin. In short, being deceived is also a form of crime and by no means something to be proud of. (Itami 1961 [1943]: 210)

Itami's cooperation in *New Earth*, which has been articulated as unity with Axis powers' military agreements, does not fit into his image as a moralist. His participation is therefore either omitted or treated sympathetically. For Yamamoto, however, Itami's retrospective 'deification as a "conscientious member of the intelligentsia"', and the associated psychological denial of Itami's participation in this 'national policy film', is problematic, as it reverberates the 'victimization' of Japan as a whole (2004: 80). While this narrative on a micro level positively established Itami's reputation, on a macro level, it re-narrated Japan as a victim of circumstances (2004: 92). Taking Yamamoto's argument further, perversely, Itami became incorporated into the very victim myth he wrote against in 1946. With regard to *New Earth*, however, Itami was as constitutive of the event as Fanck, in particular because the split into two versions was due to his opposition. Yet, he was less visible, partly due to the advertising campaign that celebrated Fanck, Itami's own restraint regarding *New Earth*,[3] and, conversely, Fanck's copious comments on the project far beyond 1937.

It is for these reasons that *New Earth* has been discussed exclusively with regard to its political context and scrutinized for Fanck's propagandistic intentions. However, in light of the previously discussed multiplicity of motives, the entanglement in politics of the film and its participants appears

---

[3]Itami (1936; 1961 [1937], 1961 [1944]; *Yomiuri Shinbun* 20.04.1937b). This list is not necessarily conclusive, but based on newspaper and magazine articles located during archival research as well as the edited collections of Itami's writings published posthumously.

subsequent rather than determining, and therefore the political backgrounds and contexts are worth reevaluating.

If Fanck, from the inception of the project, pursued the production of a 'commemoration film for the conclusion of the Japanese-German Anti-Comintern Pact' (*Yamato Nippō* 21.02.1937: n.p.), he knew about the negotiations far earlier than most politicians. The one conceivable source of such insider knowledge is the somewhat mysterious figure of Friedrich Wilhelm Hack. As secret emissary for Hitler's then-foreign affairs adviser, Joachim von Ribbentrop, Hack facilitated pre-negotiations between Ribbentrop, military attaché Ōshima and head of military intelligence (*Abwehr*) Canaris in early 1935 (Boyd 1981: 317–18). He entered Japan as the production's 'manager', soon disappearing from the public eye for negotiations about the pact (Nishimura 1937). While the NHK argues that Hack, out of political considerations, delivered the impetus for the production, Fanck's participation and the project's political content, Hansen refutes a direct commission by either government as 'improbable, as the cultural-political relations were characterized by mutual distrust and economic interests' (NHK 1986: 101–6; Hansen 1997a: 48). This characterization could as well apply to *New Earth*, when one looks behind the facade of binational collaboration. Hansen acknowledges the possibility of some influence from political circles on the film's content, but does not develop this line of thought further (NHK 1986: 101–6; Hansen 1997a: 48). The 'Anti-Comintern' motif in its historical specificity, however, must be distinguished from the other ideologically tinged tropes. Looking back at the project in a booklet that was published in 1938, Fanck wrote that the 'obvious Anti-Comintern tendency' was not intended from the beginning but developed out of the input he received during his stay (89). This statement acknowledges the premiere's highly politicized context but also hints at changes occurring during the production process that question the one-way road from military agreement to binational film project.

On 25 November 1936, Ribbentrop and the Japanese ambassador, Mushakōji Kintomo, signed the Anti-Comintern Pact in Berlin. The binational agreement was officially directed against the perceived threat of the disintegration of states posed by the Communist International (Comintern). The pact's actual orientation against the Soviet Union – each signatory nation guaranteeing strict neutrality in the case of the other nation becoming involved in war with the Soviet Union – in its supplementary protocol was to remain secret and was denied by the German press in reactions to foreign reports (Goebbels 1987: 264). The fact of the negotiations, however, had been leaked early on to Molotow and subsequently the international press by Soviet spy activity in Japan (Mund 2006: 187–9). Despite the secrecy and the international repercussions, many historians agree that the pact today appears as 'a temporary stratagem that had sprung from military thinking much rather than being the first step on the way to a solid military alliance'

(Martin 1995: 221). Japan interpreted the pact as an alliance against the Soviet Union and a chance to strengthen their hold on Manchuria. Prime Minister Hirota was careful to stress that this alliance 'should obviously not be considered as in any way approving Germany's domestic policies' (Ohata 1976: 36). For Hitler, it was 'nothing more than a propaganda means to let the world know about National Socialist Germany's claim to worldwide power' (Martin 1995: 221). As with *New Earth*, it is unclear which side initiated the negotiations, and both sides pursued individual, and not necessarily reconcilable, objectives.

And even after the signing and despite Hitler's appreciation of Japan's geostrategic position, military strength and anti-communist leaning, Germany had not yet clearly sided with Japan (Bieber 2009: 367). There were strong military and industrial ties with China, with profitable contracts regarding the import of important raw materials, and the export of arms, equipment and German military advisers to support the Kuomintang (Sommer 1962: 63). This explains why in July 1937, when Japan initiated total war against China – to 'contain communism' – and demanded German help in compliance with the pact, the Foreign Office's reply was lukewarm, emphasizing 'Germany's "strict neutrality" in the Far Eastern Conflict' (Fox 1982: 233). This reply echoes the equally 'lukewarm' response to Chinese complaints regarding *New Earth* and *Samurai's Daughter*. On the day of the gala premiere and only shortly before Tobis concluded their agreement with Kokkō, members of the 'Kuomintang committee in Germany and the assembly of Chinese physicists and chemists in Berlin' visited the Tobis studios in Berlin. This visit was represented as a 'confirmation of the friendship between Germany and China' as Germany's Chinese friends convinced themselves of the 'careful consideration of their national interests in Tobis productions' (*Film-Kurier* 1937c). In early May 1937, the Chinese embassy in Germany demanded either *Samurai's Daughter*'s final scene in Manchukuo be cut or that screenings stop immediately. The Propaganda Ministry ordered Terra to cut the intertitles referring to the puppet state, so as not to offend Chinese national sentiments (Hansen 2001: 194), and it appears that several shots of typically Manchurian landscapes were edited out as well, but the diegetic references to Manchukuo and the spatial setting were still glaringly obvious, as was the political context of Japan's expansionist endeavour (Figure 3.1).[4]

The screening in June of an uncut version of *New Earth* in Shanghai's international settlement led to 'indignation' about what was seen

---

[4]The premiere version for Berlin was 120 minutes, the one available on DVD today is 106 minutes; this difference in running time is due to the cutting of the Manchukuo-related scenes in 1937 and Fanck's voluntary 'de-politization' of the film for its rerelease in 1958. It is impossible, however, to ascertain where more political scenes could have been included before.

FIGURE 3.1 *The map of 'Manchuria'* (Mandschurei).

as propaganda for Japanese expansionist policies (*Yomiuri Shinbun* 06.06.1937). Intellectuals reacted violently against the film, as perhaps could or should have anticipated by its producers, in particular by Kawakita with his personal and professional connections to the country. The scenes in Manchuria were regarded as an affront, and demands for the cutting of relevant parts became a diplomatic affair (*Shanhai Nippō* 04.06.1937b). The film was, unsurprisingly, considered as an instance of Japanese propaganda, and Kawakita as its mouthpiece (Fu 2003: 95–100).[5] A second cause of Chinese anger was the interpretation of *New Earth* as an attempt to outdo the successful American–Chinese co-production *The Good Earth*, based on Pearl S. Buck's novel, that had premiered in the United States only few days before *New Earth*'s Tokyo release (Bieber 2009: 365). Political concerns and cinematic representation became discursively intertwined. And, in politics and film, all participants followed their own agendas.

The fact that this film project occurred within a period characterized by nationalism, war and crimes against humanity influences retrospective discussions by its participants and by scholars, resulting in controversial accounts: Who initiated it? Who paid for it? Did the German government

---

[5]On Kawakita's subsequent involvement in the Shanghai film industry and politics under Japanese occupation, see Fu 2003 and Zhang 2004: 87–9.

send Fanck to Japan to make a propaganda film for the Anti-Comintern Pact? None of the participants later wished to be connected with 'fascist'[6] regimes and their political use of culture. Kawakita was temporarily suspended from the film industry as a war criminal class B, for having made wartime films in China and for *New Earth*.[7] Fanck's *Samurai's Daughter* and *A German Robinson* (Ein Robinson, 1939) were banned in Germany by the occupation forces, and his career ended. Still, neither the Kawakitas nor Fanck publicly disavowed the production after 1945 and wrote about it on various occasions (Fanck 1973; Kawakita 1966; Kawakita 1968; Kawakita 1973a, b; Kawakita and Satō 1991; Kawakita N. 1955; Kawakita N. 1988). The point, however, is how they wrote about it, and how they distributed responsibility for the project as well as its political and cultural ramifications. In order to understand the relation of the film to political developments, it is necessary to reconsider the film's timeline in context with the planning stages for the pact. Hansen discerns three different background stories, with the project being initiated by Kawakita, by Fanck or by the German government (1997a: 46–61). In fact, these are three different viewpoints on the same event, with different spatial and temporal timeframes and range of story information, so to speak. Supplemented with additional information, their contradictions can be brought into a 'plausible' synthesis, but not necessarily into a causal chain of events.

The first version hinges on Fanck's statement in his autobiography that Kawakita approached him on behalf of the Japanese Culture Ministry to make a film on Japan 'especially for export', since the Japanese 'knew that their films could not be understood in the West. A German director was more suitable than an American one, because the Germans are more empathic towards foreign people' (Fanck 1973: 329). During the production and until around the time of release in Germany, everything points towards the Japanese side initiating the project and inviting the German team. After his return from Japan, cameraman Angst told a reporter that the reason for the project was to film Japan through European spectacles and to learn from Western film-making techniques (*Bremer Zeitung* 28.02.1937). And still in 1938, Fanck presents Kawakita as a 'farsighted and energetic initiator who, due to his long-standing connections to Germany and his superb knowledge of the German language, was the only one who could initiate such a cooperative venture and create the necessary networks in Japan' (Fanck 1938: 83–4). These portraits coincide with Kawakita's recollections

---

[6]The applicability of the term 'fascist' for the Japanese case is contested and has been discussed by Payne (1995: 328–37; see also Tansman 2009a, b).
[7]Kawakita's Japanese contract partner for *New Earth*, Ōsawa Yoshio, later became a member of the Tōhō Studio's board of directors. After the war, he was classified as a 'war criminal class B' due to Tōhō's extensive production of propaganda films and suspended from 1947 to 1950 (Mizuno 2009: 13).

published in 1988: he wished to promote the export of Japanese film by using a 'well-known foreign director' (20). Fanck's reputation in Japan through his mountain films and preceding international co-production, *SOS Iceberg* with Universal, made him suitable for the undertaking (20). Kawakita Kashiko's 1936 article relates that 'on 20 September 1934, Hayashi Bunzaburō informed Tōwa about Fanck's inclinations to come to Japan to make a film' (1936a: 94). This fit her husband's plans, and so both parties came together readily.

Fanck, in 1938, writes that it had been his 'artist's dream' to produce a film about Japan (83), perhaps influenced by Hayashi's link to *Nippon* in 1932, and certainly by Johannes (Hannes) Schneider's earlier sojourn in Japan. Schneider was an Austrian ski ace, who had also acted in ten of Fanck's mountain films. The films and his work as ski instructor for international guests in Austria had made him famous in Japan, and in 1930 he had been invited to teach his Arlberg technique of skiing. As Fanck told the Japanese press in 1936, Schneider's photographs and stories of Japan's mountains had whetted his appetite to point the camera on those sights (*Ōsaka Mainichi Shinbun* 09.02.1936). The early date of Kawakita's article prevents an interpretation that shifts the blame for 'wartime collaboration' onto the German side. In both accounts so far, the political dimension plays no role.

Thirdly, in the late 1980s, Fanck's widow recalled an 'acquaintance in the Foreign Office' approaching Fanck with the idea to 'make a film for German-Japanese friendship', which seemed a solution to the family's financial problems (NHK 1986: 125). This acquaintance, according to the NHK, was Friedrich Wilhelm Hack, who was not a member of the ministry, but Ribbentrop's secret negotiator for the Anti-Comintern Pact (NHK 1986: 125). And, indeed, in 1938 Fanck explicitly thanks Goebbels and now-foreign minister Ribbentrop for their support of the project (7). Ribbentrop had nothing to do with the film industry, but had been instrumental in the conclusion of the military agreement. Goebbels, on the other hand, was heavily involved in all things film related. It is interesting to note, however, that Goebbels himself never brought *Samurai's Daughter* into context with the pact, neither in his instructions to the press nor in his diary. This in stark contrast, for instance, to his contextualization of Abe's *Burning Sky* (Moyuru ōzora, 1940). When it was screened in Toku Bälz's 'Germanified' version as *Nippon's Wild Eagles* (Nippons wilde Adler) in Berlin in 1942 to mark the military alliance, Goebbels's diary entry focuses on Japan as a close ally (Goebbels 2006c: 457–8). This version of events emphasizes political objectives behind the production of *New Earth*. Chiba – albeit based on unnamed and unverified recollections – states, 'Following the completion of *SOS Iceberg*, Fanck looked for the next venture and, on the German Foreign Office's suggestion, embarked on a German-Japanese co-production' (1987: 8). In the autumn of 1934, according to Chiba, he sounded out Hayashi about a joint project. Although these dates concur with Kawakita Kashiko's article, the implied causal chain from German plans for political rapprochement to the film project is problematic. A direct involvement by the German Foreign Office is unlikely since Ribbentrop and Ōshima used Hack specifically to circumvent the traditionally sinophile ministry (NHK 1986: 9). A message from Ribbentrop to Hack, dated 28 January 1936, explicitly states, 'Do not speak to [Ambassador] Dirksen' (*Hack Documents*). Even if Chiba means Ribbentrop's section, set up in August 1934, the temporal sequence he suggests begins too early, as the initial Ōshima-Ribbentrop meetings mediated by Hack occurred only in the spring of 1935 (Boyd 1981: 317–18). Concrete talks did not begin before September, and Ōshima's draft treaty dates from early October 1935 (Tajima 2009; *Hack Documents*). The definite decision for an anti-communist agreement between Japan and Germany was made in a talk between Hitler and Ribbentrop on 27 November 1935 (Martin and Kuß 2003: 445). To arrange an expensive film project on this scale in response to political dealings before concrete negotiations had even begun is unlikely. It is, however, entirely possible to give subsequent financial support to such a project, in the light of developments that caused it to be seen as relevant to political objectives.

The NHK's interview with Sakai Naoe, secretary to the naval attaché in Berlin, helps to delineate two different strands of objectives. He divorces the initial idea of a film to represent Japan through a foreign director's sensibilities from the immediate political sphere. At the time, Sakai acted as the German–Japanese Society's interim managing director. He shared this role with Hack, who had played a part in the dismissal from office of its Jewish president, Professor Wilhelm Haas, in 1933 (Hack 1996: 106). Sakai told Hack 'his idea' (the description of which bears striking resemblances to Kawakita's line of thought), and Hack contacted Fanck and approached Kawakita through Tōwa's (here unnamed) Berlin representative (NHK 1986: 83–4). Leaving aside the question of Sakai as originator of the idea and the unverifiable nature of his recollections, the impetus for Kawakita's and Fanck's coming together came from Hack. However, this does not necessitate the far-reaching, political and ideological objectives usually assumed. The fact that Hack, as the society's president, was involved in a project related to binational relations is unsurprising. Taking this scenario as a basis, the other accounts begin to lose some of their contradictions: Hayashi (the Berlin representative) – who had been involved in *Nippon* and had connections to the film world and Fanck via Ufa – informed Tōwa about the idea; Kawakita discussed the matter with his partners and contacted Fanck. The political dimension enters Sakai's account with Hack's visit to Goebbels – prior to contracting Hayashi – and Goebbels's 'promise to support the project with 100,000 Reichsmark' (NHK 1986: 83–4). Hansen could not find evidence for this transaction, but announcements of the project in Japan confirm this element of Sakai's story: 'the German government contributed about 300,000 Yen [213,000 Reichsmark] to the project' (Hansen 1997a: 35; *Asahi Shinbun* 13.11.1935). The amount from Goebbels and Terra's loan to Fanck of 100,000 Reichsmark roughly add up to this sum. Whatever the reasons for Goebbels's support, it was not much of an investment for a promising full-length film. If successful, the project would have brought an interesting film onto German screens for a fraction of the average production costs of a feature-length film in Germany in 1937 of 537,000 Reichsmark (Kreimeier 2002: 228).[8] If financial investments are markers of ulterior motives, this sum does not signify an overwhelming interest.

Even though 1934 is too early for the pact to be the concrete incentive, Hack's involvement in the film project and the covert political negotiations is a common link. He accompanied Fanck to a dinner with the Kawakitas on 3 August 1935 and was introduced to Kawakita Kashiko as a 'producer' (NHK 1986: 85–6). In a meeting on 19 October, Ōshima asked Hack to wait with his arrangements for travelling to Japan for the outcome of talks with Lt Col Wakamatsu Tadaichi (*Hack Documents*). However, the film project is first mentioned in Hack's documents in November, more than three months after Fanck and Kawakita concluded the contract: 'His travel is explained in terms of business, with meetings regarding the German–Japanese film, especially with various Japanese governmental authorities, as well as with negotiations regarding planes, plane parts, instruments and machines, especially with the army and navy' (NHK 1986: 85–6). Hack had liaised between Heinkel, a major German aircraft designer impeded by the Versailles Treaty, and the Japanese navy from 1923 (Sander-Nagashima 2006: 44). This justification would have allowed Hack easy and unsuspicious access to all persons potentially concerned with the pact. On 11 November, Fanck informed Kawakita that they would leave from Marseilles on 3 January (Kawakita 1936a). It is unclear, whether Hack's schedule determined that of the team, and the degree to which Fanck was informed about the precise nature of Hack's plans. Kawakita's claim that she knew nothing about Hack's activities in Japan is probably determined by hindsight. Hack's disappearance in March 1936, two weeks after his arrival in Japan, did not go unnoticed; on 27 November 1936, immediately after the conclusion of the pact, newspapers reported on his suspected dealings. His entering the country disguised as part of the crew, his movements and activities within Japan entirely apart from the film team and his return

---

[8]This figure is the apex of production costs spiralling out of control in 1937, posing a serious threat to the German industry, especially in context of the decreasing export revenue (Kreimeier 2002: 228). Mühl-Benninghaus gives a slightly lower number for 1936 of 420,000 to 470,000 RM (1989: 327).

FIGURE 3.2 *Reception at the Mainichi Shinbun Office (8 February 1936): Hack is the first person from the right.*

to Germany in August 1937 are noted and contextualized with his role as secret negotiator ('Hisokani fukumen no tateyakusha' 27.11.1936). The same article also features an interview with the Kawakitas, in which they state that they understood Hack as an expert in things Japanese, who suddenly seemed very busy with his own affairs ('Hisokani fukumen no tateyakusha' 27.11.1936). It is unlikely that the Kawakitas did not, at least, wonder about his behaviour (Figure 3.2).

In any case, political developments began to instrumentalize the film project, influencing its organization, travel planning and the eventual production of two competing films, thus impacting on the image of the project itself, on and off the screen.

Only a week before the team's arrival in Japan, Ambassador Dirksen contacted the German Foreign Office to request instructions on whether or not to support the making of a film called *People Without Space* that would receive financial support from a (non-specified) Japanese government office (Hansen 1997a: 49). 'General support' was recommended, without any allusion to political cooperation. One year later, after the dramatic change of official political relationships, Dirksen reported on the film's 'considerable success' that was 'sure to impact positively on German-Japanese relations' ('Bericht der Botschaft Tokyo' 19.2.1937; cited in Bieber 2009: 365). The Japanese government's dealings with the project also reveal divergent interests, splits and manoeuvring. 'Tōwa Shōji, the Foreign Ministry, the Railroad Ministry, the Tourism Bureau, the Society for International Cultural Relations ... all endeavour and prepare to show Japan to the world' (*Asahi Shinbun* 13.11.1935). Like their German counterpart, the Foreign Ministry was excluded intentionally from Anti-Comintern matters. Ōshima regarded the Foreign Ministries of both countries as too conservative, and the Japanese army as having more actual influence in diplomatic matters (NHK 1986: 29). While the Ōshima-Ribbentrop talks were discussed in army circles in late 1935, the first real chance for the alliance came after the February 26 Incident. New prime minister Hirota and foreign minister Arita stood close to the army and were strongly anti-Soviet (Krebs 1994). Therefore, the Foreign Ministry had promised support for the film project before they first heard about the negotiations in late January (Krebs 1994: 98). Incidentally, on the scheduled day of the crew's arrival in Kōbe, the pact was discussed as a point on the governmental agenda for the first time in a meeting of army and navy representatives at the Foreign Ministry (Krebs 1994: 98). From 4 April 1936, the Foreign Ministry under Arita led the negotiations (Krebs 1994: 109). The Home Ministry was also instructed to deal favourably with the production (Hansen 1997a: 49–50). Fanck, however, refers to the police's strict surveillance. The 'strange blossoms sprouting' from the 'Japanese fear of espionage' (Fanck 1938: 103) impeded the project and disrupted the image of smooth cooperation between 'kindred' nations. Fanck had to present his script to 'each ministry' for examination (Fanck 1973: 339). Hansen considers this statement to be unlikely, as laws for pre-censorship were not in place before October 1939 (Hansen 1997a: 48), but the project's unusual circumstances meant that there were no precedents. They also had to request the approval of local authorities before shooting on location (Fanck 1938: 103–4). Fanck retrospectively quarrels with the prohibition of filming steelworks as examples of Japanese heavy industry (Fanck 1938), and the police stopped shooting in a silk factory in order to prevent scenes of 'dishonourable' places (Hansen 1997a: 50). Since the ministry was aware of Fanck's work for the German counterintelligence in the First World War (he examined strategic photographs for manipulations) and also suspected a connection to the Propaganda Ministry (Hansen 1997a: 50), their concern was not only about Japan's cinematic image abroad but also about industrial and political espionage. Scenes of 'steel casting, rolling and forging' (Fanck 1938: 104) and of a silk factory are, however, included in both versions. It is likely that those scenes were re-approved later, perhaps through Kabayama, who had previously acted on an executive level for Japan Steelworks (Nihonsei Kōsho) (*Kokuji Daijiten* n.d.) (Figures 3.3 and 3.4).

In terms of further governmental involvement, Fanck stated that the 'Japanese Culture Ministry [*Kultusministerium*] commissioned [him] to make a film, especially for export' via Kawakita, and supported the project in the background (1973: 329). Fanck refers to the 'Culture Ministry' several more times, for example, regarding an invitation to a 'geisha party' by the minister (1973: 332). The project, however, is not mentioned in the ministry's (albeit fragmented) archived documents, and film productions were the responsibility of the Home Ministry in any case (Hansen 1997a: 46). The Culture Ministry also remains unmentioned in contemporaneous publications, but Fanck's recollections are not therefore bogus: the Foreign Ministry's Culture division

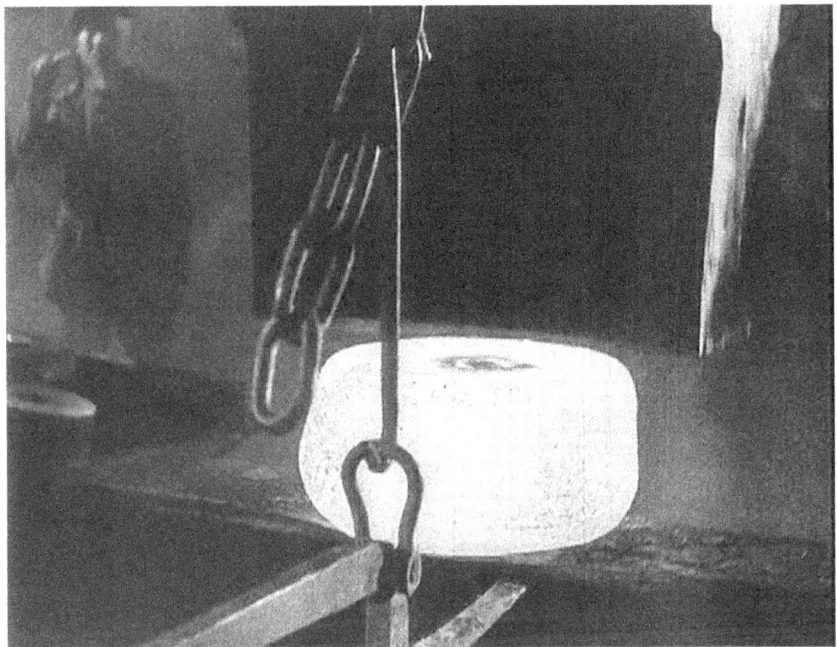

FIGURES 3.3 *Shots of steelworks*.

(*Gaimushō bunkabu*) was in charge of the *Kokusai Eiga Kyōkai* (International Film Association of Japan) and supported the export of films *Contemporary Japan* and *Picturesque Japan* with the considerable amount of 350,000 yen. The Foreign Ministry, as 'film director', supported the release of 'one *kokusaku* [national policy] film after the other' and also spent 15,000 yen on Fanck's film (*Asahi Shinbun* 27.08.1936b; *Shanhai Nippō* 04.06.1937a, n.p.). Finally, a newspaper article reports on Fanck and Hack visiting the Foreign Ministry soon after their arrival in Japan and discussing their plans with the head of the Culture Division, Okada Kenichi (*Tōkyō Jiji Shinpō* 13.02.1936). Fanck, across a language gap and a distance of over thirty years, confused the Foreign Ministry's Culture Division and the Ministry of Education, Science and Culture: *Monbushō* translates into German as *Kultusministerium* (Figure 3.5).

The Foreign and Military Ministries did support the project, both financially and by granting access to various locations despite a tense political environment (Kawakita 1936a; *Asahi Shinbun* 27.08.1936a). The Foreign Ministry's role slowly changed. Starting out as producer of *nihon shōkai* films to introduce Japan to the world, it was now the 'director' of *kokusaku* (national policy) films, as well as the authority negotiating the Anti-Comintern Pact. The international release of the *kokusaku* films

FIGURE 3.4 *Shot of a silk factory.*

FIGURE 3.5 *The 'geisha party'? Fanck, Hack, Eweler, Elisabeth Fanck, Kawakita, others unknown.*

supported by the ministry, *Contemporary Japan* and *New Earth*, was heralded as the launch of Japanese 'international' (*kokusai*) films (*Asahi Shinbun* 27.08.1936b). The issue of representing an authentic Japan within a universally understood, international format harks back to the long-held 'dream of export' and perceived foreign misrepresentations. In the light of international reactions to Japan's foreign politics, however, the topic had also taken on a new meaning: the correction of a distorted image of Japan abroad became a political matter. The international, *kokusai*, image, as transported by film, was now a national policy, *kokusaku* (Yamamoto 2004: 71).

Political, personal, industrial and cultural interests converged in the project, and some were similar or connected to those that resulted in the Anti-Comintern Pact. At this specific temporal juncture, both events became related. The political discourse in both countries instrumentalized not only the represented image of Japan, but also the film project as an instance of successful German–Japanese collaboration. But in the light of the frictions during the production and the 'cooperation' ending up in two versions of the same film, the project serves, after all, as a metaphor for Japanese–German wartime relations as a 'hollow alliance' (Meskill 1966) between 'reluctant allies' (Krug 2001). At the same time, the film project and its participants stood in constant discourse with and also utilized the political discourse.

The script for *New Earth* went through many stages, with Fanck writing about 'Shinto' while still in Germany, the idea for the plot being about a young Japanese farmer who has to emigrate to Korea or Manchukuo due to the scarcity of land, in order to secure a livelihood for him and 'his girl'; 'when this *new land* is threatened, the mighty Japanese state with its army and navy protects its children' (Fanck 1935; my emphasis). At some point during the team's journey to Japan, the title switched from *Shinto* to *People Without Space*, the topic being presumably very similar. Once arrived in Japan, however, Fanck stated that he did not want to make a film on this topic any longer and wished to consult with Japanese writers and intellectuals; the reporter's question of whether this had to do with international sensitivities after Hitler's demands for a redistribution of the colonies remained unanswered (*Ōsaka Nichinichi Shinbun* 09.02.1936). On 4 February, four days before the team's arrival in Japan, Hitler had demanded the return of two former German colonies from Britain; Germany would relinquish these territories in exchange for 'Eastern Europe' (Graichen and Gründer 2005: 410–5). The Japanese reporter contextualized his question with the 'increasing situation in narrow Germany', rather than with the very similar discourse in Japan (*Ōsaka Nichinichi Shinbun* 09.02.1936). Ironically, as Fanck wrote in 1935, expansion – west- or eastwards – was a discourse common to both countries, and suitable for evoking the international understanding that was the project's ultimate aim. Hack, however, in a rare interview about the project shortly before his disappearing from the scene and in his alleged role as 'manager', stated that 'people without space' was too serious a topic (*Teito Nichinichi Shinbun* 09.02.1936). The aim was to deepen international understanding about Japan, and therefore two or three alternative scripts would be prepared and the most suitable one selected in cooperation with the Tourism Bureau (*Teito Nichinichi Shinbun* 09.02.1936). It is difficult to ascertain how much politically based caution, wishes regarding a specific image of Japan and/or insights into what kinds of films the target audiences would be interested in were behind these changes of mind – and by whom – but in the following weeks, the titles and presumably topics fluctuated: *Sei no kome* (*Sacred Rice*), *Heiliges Nippon* (*Sacred Nippon*), *Ostwind-Westwind* (*Eastwind-Westwind*), *Tapfere kleine Mitsuko* (*Brave Little Mitsuko*) were announced in film magazines in Japan and Germany. Kawakita Kashiko and popular playwright and poet Kume Masao were among those working with Fanck on the script, before Itami joined (*Ōsaka Nichinichi Shinbun* 24.03.1936).

The definitive script remains lost. What Hansen describes as 'the first published draft' appeared in the Japanese film magazine *Serupan*, albeit quite belatedly in November 1936 (Hansen 1997a: 13). It is rather an early account of Fanck's thoughts on what to represent, the reasons for his choices and how to realize them. Hansen concludes that the film is basically congruent with the draft in terms 'of the plot and the propaganda content' (Hansen 1997a: 13). However, the draft is substantially different: in it, the protagonist works in a modern arms factory following his 're-conversion'. The final scene in Manchukuo imagines him in an agricultural research institute, rather than as a regular farmer, before the grand finale, staged with the help of the Japanese army and showcasing large numbers of tanks, marching soldiers and planes, so as to impress the West (Hansen 1997a: 13). Moreover, Teruo has not been adopted but merely betrothed since childhood; his bride, who works in a factory, reminds one of factory worker Hideko, his sister in the eventual film. From this brief account, it becomes clear that despite the various changes, the original idea for the film based on internationally topical, political discourses remained more or less intact, the eventual title *New Earth* even echoes the phrasing Fanck had used in his 1935 article. Furthermore, despite Hack's pre-production involvement, the pact is neither mentioned in Fanck's early ideas for the film nor in Itami's criticism of the original script (Fanck 1935; Itami 1936), but it was with the progression of Hack's negotiations, that the film's content as scripted by Fanck changed from 'People Without Space' to include an 'obvious Anti-Comintern tendency' (Fanck 1938: 89), which would make the film topical and valuable – politically and therefore career-wise – upon its release.

Hack, however, subsequently was arrested in Germany, overtly for his illegal homosexuality, in fact for his laxness with classified information in

Japan that ended up in Soviet hands (Spang 2003: 15–16). The source of this intelligence was Richard Sorge, a Soviet military intelligence officer who worked undercover as a hard-drinking, womanizing and more-than-convinced National Socialist German journalist in Japan (Prange, Goldstein and Dillon 1985). Sorge had not only befriended military attaché Eugen Ott, but it appears that Hack also confided in him fairly soon after his arrival. In March, Ott had informed his friend Sorge of information he received from the General Staff headquarters of the Japanese army that 'some talk is going on in Germany between Ōshima and Ribbentrop through Admiral Canaris. Neither I nor Dirksen know anything about it. This talk must be something important and may be a negotiation for an alliance between the two countries' (Prange, Goldstein and Dillon 1985: 238). Dirksen, apparently, had vaguely known about the Ōshima-Ribbentrop talks from December 1935, but now he and Ott endeavoured to gather more information, and provided Sorge with this information (Prange, Goldstein and Dillon 1985: 241). Hack, in turn, spoke about his mission rather openly to Ott, once he learned that the attaché already knew about the talks, and later even told Sorge about Soviet agents having spied on Ribbentrop, Canaris and Ōshima in Berlin and him therefore serving as a secret emissary so as to prevent any Soviet detection (Prange, Goldstein and Dillon 1985: 242). It seems conceivable that Hack, after initial caution and maybe over a drink, advised Fanck to make his film so that would be welcome in the newly emerging political context.

The hypothesis that this 'hot topic' evolved in accordance with political developments is supported by the delay experienced by the production. Apart from pragmatic, technical and interpersonal difficulties, a delay out of twofold political considerations – the insertion of relevant motifs and an opportune timing vis-à-vis the Anti-Comintern Pact – seems plausible. Hitler gave his first approval of the pact in August 1936, and Ribbentrop most likely informed Hack at once, but negotiations about the secret supplementary protocol continued until October (Mund 2006: 104). Goebbels's diary entry of 21 October relates that Hitler 'yesterday . . . signed a contract with Japan. Pact against Bolshevism. Its publication in three weeks' time will change the entire situation . . . Ribbentrop toddles off with his authorization' (Goebbels 1987: 219). By then, Fanck's anticipated German audience, if not supplanted, had been supplemented by the Propaganda Ministry. The depiction of topical political currents in a satisfactory way would bring a coveted state award and secure further assignments. The 'Anti-Comintern tendency' is missing from Itami's version, which seems to hint that Fanck held information unknown to his colleague and not included in the common script, or that Itami deliberately omitted this motif. In this context it is interesting to note that Hack mentions a conversation with Goebbels regarding the opportunities for film-making in Japan only shortly before the conclusion of the pact, on 15 November 1936, and therefore almost at the end of the film's production (*Hack Documents*).⁹ In Japan, the film's release came to be advertised as 'Japanese-German pact of the silver screen' (*Asahi Shinbun* 18.12.1936). Similarly, Kawakita used the notion of German–Japanese friendship and cooperation in the context of his negotiations regarding further co-productions in spring 1937: 'There are, of course, always rather big obstacles in the way of co-productions, but I am sure that we can overcome them with the help of our German friends' (Kawakita N. 1937a). On 25 November 1937, an entire evening in the Hibiya Eiga Gekijō Theatre was dedicated to the Anti-Comintern Pact's first anniversary (*Yomiuri Shinbun* 24.11.1937). The three national flags heading the advertisement signify Italy's accession. The special programme contained two selected short films dealing with the pact and the preservation of world peace by the three associated countries: *Anti-Communist Crusaders* (Bōkyō jūjigun; presenting each country's armed forces) and *Advancing Italy* (Yakushin Itari; describing life in Italy).¹⁰ The two feature films shown were *I was Jack Mortimer* (Ich war Jack Mortimer; Namae no nai eiga, 1935, Froelich) and *Samurai no musume* (*Samurai's Daughter* aka *New Earth*).

Located at a temporal threshold, the project was driven by multiple objectives throughout and Kawakita's future problems with this 'export film', caused by political developments during its conception, could not have been anticipated at that time. Nor could he have foreseen the increased public attention to political cooperation between Japan and Germany when he embarked on making a Japanese export film. Turning the lens backwards to 1934–35, subject matters such as the Anti-Comintern Pact, as Fanck says, 'had not yet been accomplished', were 'not even talked about in public', at the most 'could be discerned to draw near' (1938: 83), and were as yet unjudged in relation to eventual disastrous outcomes. Kawakita as well as the various ministries and associations involved in the costly and chancy film production later on used the film and the political developments to their advantage, but when the project was in its planning and early stages, politics played a role only insofar as a point can be made for culture as the third pillar of foreign politics. The notions of film export, international understanding and national prestige had been intermingled almost since the birth of cinema, with each factor taking relative centre stage depending

---

⁹Hack compiled and wrote these documents after 1946, perhaps for a planned autobiography. While Hack dates the event as late 1935, a gala dinner at Hitler's residence with the members of the Japanese embassy and the 'Nazi big wigs' Hitler, Goebbels, Himmler, Ribbentrop and so on present, Professor Bernd Martin of Freiburg University (who holds the *Hack Documents*) considers this date unlikely, as there is no evidence of such a grand event in late 1935, but that the set-up points towards Hitler's reception on the evening of 15 November 1936, in context of the signing of the pact.

¹⁰*Anti-Communist Crusaders* appears to have been produced by various Japanese newspaper companies; I found no further information on *Advancing Italy*.

on the cultural–political environment. *New Earth* occurred at a watershed where national prestige was slowly but surely taking the upper hand, to the eventual detriment of the other two issues. Yet, it clearly originated in the dream of export and in the idea to portray an authentic cinematic image of Japan, which would lead to an adequate understanding by international audience, in a 'language that even foreigners could understand', which would open up markets to Japanese films and thus doubly increase national prestige. To invite a foreign director for this exercise in cultural translation was not the ground-breaking idea as which it was sold, but based in a history of binational co-production. Yet, as with all translations, the project brought to the fore questions of original and rendition, of personal skills, of individual agendas. All of these formed the eventual text, and on both the producing and receiving sides, the issue of what is authentic and what is not was related to individual or collective power positions in unstable sociopolitical contexts.

4

The politics of authenticity

Representing others, recognizing selves

After 1936, however, real efforts were made to express a national essence. The military-led government needed to define 'Japaneseness' since its expansionist politics . . . depended upon the durability of the imperial Japanese aura. This led to a state-sanctioned ideology of Japanese identity and the necessary resulting mystique. The search for this amalgam of characteristics had been going on for some time. It had continued beneath the liberality of the prewar period and lurked under modernism. Now, however, with war both as reason and excuse, there was new need for an agreed-upon 'Japaneseness'.

(RICHIE 2001: 100)

Fanck always aimed for the symbolic and Itami for the real. This is a very interesting aspect of the production.

(HAYASHI 1936)

Due to the common script, both *New Earth* and *Samurai's Daughter* contain motifs pertaining to political propaganda, certainly more pronounced in Fanck's version, but the intention to 'propagate' appropriate characteristics of this Japan abroad needs also to be seen in the history of efforts to correct perceived 'misrepresentations', which reveals the notion of propaganda as not necessarily the polar opposite of the authentic. What is 'really real' can be understood as propaganda; the intention to somehow influence public opinion remains the same. Fanck's statement that the venture was designed 'to represent Japan and its people's mentality in a way Europeans could understand' (1997 [1937]: 181) confirms the Japanese interests in the production. The contractual provision for Fanck to write the script in Japan was intended to ensure 'authenticity' in the end product. At the same time, the target-oriented representation of Japan demanded from the project also brings to the fore the notion of cultural translation, of how to render one culture for another. And contrary to accusations of inauthenticity, blamed on Fanck's political and Orientalist eye, these motifs did not always spring entirely from German ideologies or were alien to the Japanese context.

The motif of Mitsuko's intended suicide by throwing herself into the volcano crater, for instance, has called forth criticism as belonging in the realm of Hollywood 'South Sea adventures' rather than Japanese reality (Hansen 1997a: 22). Assistant director Tjaden, however, in an interview about the project, mentioned several suicide instances of young lovers throwing themselves into volcanoes (Schu. 1937): the 'lovers' suicide rage of 1932-1933' was a series of 944 copycat suicides kindled by sensationalist media coverage, including plays, radio dramas, ballads and the Shōchiku film *A Love in Heaven*. A young couple, unable to marry because of class differences, threw themselves into the Sakatayama volcano and left a suicide note directed 'to the whole nation' (High 2003: 27). The motif, therefore, is not inauthentic but suicide being one of the main tropes of German representational traditions regarding Japan, it also guaranteed pulling power at the box office and, on a discursive level, reinforced preconceived images of Japan (see Orbach 2008: 117–18). By depicting a woman determined to commit suicide, Fanck drew from the Orientalist attraction exerted by the very 'Madame Butterfly kitsch' he had dismissed earlier (Fanck 1935), but with a twist: here a Japanese man comes back to Japan with a Western woman, which compels 'his' Japanese woman to kill herself. Mitsuko's decision also makes way for Teruo to 'live for Japan and die for Japan' in the Manchurian project. 'Self-sacrifice for people and nation' had been introduced to Fanck under the label of 'Shinto' in a talk by military attaché Ōshima on 'Japanese state philosophy' in Berlin, which explains his earliest idea for the film's title, 'Shinto' (Fanck 1935), and in 1938, Hara's brother-in-law, Kumagai, used the contemporary subject of 'voluntary death in service to the nation' in his 'spiritist film' *The Abe Clan* (Abe ichizoku, 1938) (High 2003: 227–8). Second, the suicide motif stressed the Japanese martial spirit: Teruo had rejected Mitsuko because he considered her to be soft and spoilt and hence useless for his plan to settle in Manchukuo. Her 'steely' determination on the mountain convinces him (and the audience) of the opposite. His own

FIGURE 4.1 *Teruo proving himself on the volcano.*

physical dexterity and endurance also stand in an impressive contrast to the previous impression of a suit-clad cosmopolitan (Figure 4.1).

As the project fell apart, Fanck went on to tailor his version of Japan specifically to the needs of his – by then – German audience. He explained his purpose-driven 'condensation' of selected aspects of the real Japan into what some called stereotypes but what he took to be archetypes: 'Everything else I could leave aside [. . .] by virtue of the artistic freedom to choose and create from the infinity of the real only what occurred to me, as the creative artist, as fit for choosing and creating for my own people' (1938: 92). Still assuming that one of his aims was to show Japan 'as it really is' and to make the strange familiar, drawing on things that are 'almost the same here' might appear to have been a feasible strategy. Moreover, finding familiar patterns in a foreign setting, for the representer, is often a first stage of engaging with his environment. This, in turn, makes the foreign and the domestic patterns appear to be even more authentic. If some of these patterns coincide with topical 'propaganda', such as 'people without space', they might have been chosen, nonetheless, for their authenticity and familiarity rather than for the dissemination of domestic propaganda. How best to sympathetically explain Japanese expansion into Manchukuo to a general audience? By resorting to a similar topic in Germany. It is precisely the resemblance of discourses or motifs in the source and target cultures that can complicate endeavours in cultural translation as well as their interpretations or readings. Venuti's warning about the dangers of (cultural) translation certainly applies here, in particular, to Fanck's version:

> The aim of translation is to bring back a cultural other as the same, the recognizable, even the familiar; and this aim always risks a wholesale domestication of the foreign text, often in highly self-conscious projects, where translation serves an imperialist appropriation of foreign cultures for domestic agendas, cultural, economic, political. (2010: 68)

In this vein, the conveying of 'bravery' abroad as a defining Japanese national characteristic has been interpreted as expressive of Fanck's worldview: 'Fanck . . . wants to illustrate the unpredictable and destructive Japanese natural environment that educated its inhabitants towards stalwart courage' (Hansen 1997a: 28). Yet, we cannot disavow the Japanese impact on the project, and indeed, this part of the plot was 'ordered' almost literally by the head of the *Asahi Shinbun*'s news department, Ueda, during a round-table discussion in February 1936: 'Natural catastrophes, earthquakes for instance, are common in Japan. Despite such calamities, the Japanese bravely paved their way and built today's Japan. I hope you won't fail to stress this point in your film, apart from Japan's beauty' (*Fanck Documents* 1936). Teruo's first line of dialogue in the film quotes Ueda almost verbatim, but reflects Fanck's double agenda of depicting 'the authentic Japan' for his Japanese sponsors and of finding and projecting 'things of value' for German audiences – and for his own career: Ueda's 'despite' becomes a 'because' in Teruo's speech, which thus links climate and landscape to national characteristics: 'The Japanese people have been trained to be brave by this country's natural forces. By the many earthquakes, volcanoes, typhoons' (see also Chapter 6). Philosopher Watsuji Tetsurō's (1889–1960) book *Fūdo: ningen gakuteki kōsatsu (Climate: An Anthropological Consideration*, 1935) had just been published, and its connecting of the Japanese people and the nation, Japan, as a single, natural habitat was thus highly topical. Watsuji drew on Japanese classics and studies on Shinto, in particular by Motoori Noringa (1730–1801), but he was also much intrigued by German philosophers, such as Heidegger, to whose theory on *Being and Time (Sein und Zeit* 1927) he added the dimension of 'Space' (Morris-Suzuki 2015: 56–8). *Fūdo* (wind-earth) comprises the concepts of 'landscape', 'climate' or 'environment' and, in Watsuji's theory, determines cultural and social characteristics of the people living therein: Monsoon, desert and grassland environments foster relaxed, aggressive and rationalist attitudes towards nature, respectively (Morris-Suzuki 2015: 57). Japan's uniqueness – and here is the link to nationalist, exclusionist discourse – stems from its *fūdo* combining monsoon and grassland aspects resulting in the dualistic nature of passion and calm that, strikingly, *New Earth* attributes to the Japanese: at the Yamato house,

Gerda worries about Mitsuko's frame of mind in the light of Teruo's refusal to marry her and consults the German/English tutor:

> **Gerda:** It is hard to believe, that such a quiet person like her . . .
> **Tutor:** You might not believe it, but like the men of this volcanic country, there is something volcanic in the temperament of the women, too.[1]

Of course, a similar theoretical strand had a long tradition in Western philosophy, legitimizing imperialist aggression since antiquity (Isaac 2006), and later bolstering racialized thinking and hierarchies of domination and submission.[2] The belief in an environmentally determined inequality (and the very existence of the 'races') thus is closely related to antisemitism, eugenics and National–Socialist 'raciology' (*Rassenlehre*), equally ascribing certain, inherent characteristics to the various people of the world. In short, the idea of a specific national character, the representation of which was foremost on the project's agenda, was familiar in both contexts, Japan and Germany, but with different implications that challenged a successful translation, cultural and cinematic. A similar observation applies to one of the other main topics, Teruo being torn between East and West in the film's first act. The second act resolves the conflict through his re-becoming his authentic, Japanese self; a return to his roots, quite literally in his father's paddy field. Importantly, however, the narrative breaks down the clash between East and West into one between the common good and individual desires. Teruo's desire to be free (from his engagement to Mitsuko) hinders his re-assimilation into the Japanese society he, after all, wishes to serve. Consequently, Gerda tells him that he must 'abandon your individual wishes'.

> **Teruo:** What – my individual freedom?
> **Gerda:** In this matter, you have no right to individual freedom.
> **Teruo:** I always have that! That's just what I've learned in your Europe!
> **Gerda:** Then you've just learned something wrong! ('Learned it in the wrong way' [Itami's version])

Later, a lecture by his former teacher, a Buddhist priest, convinces Teruo to return to the fold. Fanck chose to dub these lines into German, in order to make the message unambiguous – for his German audience:

> **Priest:** You, as a sole individual, are not so important, for you are only a small link in the long chain of your ancestors. But even the smallest

---

[1] This is a direct quote from the English–Japanese version; the German lines say the same.
[2] On the genealogy, of climate determinism and its relationship to racial theory (including Montesquieu, Kant Hegel, Huntington, Heidegger) see Stehr and von Storch (2010: 11–17).

link is the bearer of the whole chain, and thus responsible to the whole that was before him, and responsible for that which follows, which is passed on from his blood. And again, this blood is only a drop, flowing by in the eternal stream of the life of your people, to whom you owe everything.

The uncanny resemblance to the introduction of the pseudo-history textbook targeted at the paramilitary SS (*Schutzstaffel*, Protection Squadron), *Der Weg zum Reich* (The Road to the Reich, 1942), certainly is no coincidence. 'Today, we know that we are but one link in the chain of our ancestors' blood stream, which comes from eternity and must go to eternity. It is every generation's greatest duty to prevent this blood stream from vanishing' (Reichsführer SS 1942: 1). The metaphors of blood, links in a chain, unbroken ancestry and so on were part of the National–Socialist discourse – rather than the Japanese one, despite some resemblances – and had been mobilized for two main aims: to exclude others, in particular Jews, from society, as even seen in a speech given at a local sport club after the dismissal of its Jewish former head, in line with the 'Aryan Paragraph' (*Arierparagraph*) for Public Servants passed on 7 April 1933: 'The individual is not the measure of all things. Man, as an individual, is nothing. Man only means something and is worth something within the organic community, when he is one link of this community. . . . We are all but one link in the chain of our ancestral line, and we must pass on this heritage (genes, *Erbgut*); we are one link on the long chain of fate of our ancestors and descendants' (Pfeiffer and Wahlig 2012: 154–5). These lines not only stress a society based on 'bloodlines', which does not really apply to Teruo's identity crisis in the film, but, in the first part, expresses the National–Socialist cultural critique of liberalism and individualism as one of the Weimar Republic's main evils (Pfeiffer and Wahlig 2012: 154–5). In the new order, or rather in the 'natural order of things', to which society was now to return, the individual is always bound to a specific role of service or office in the group from which he or she draws 'worth'. And it is here that the priest's speech and the film's plotline tap into a shared ideology, albeit violated and reconstituted 'in accordance with values, beliefs and representations that pre-exist it in the target language' (Venuti 1995: 18), that is, in the German discourse.

Teruo experiences the classic tension of being (*sein*) as an individual or being as part of a group, as also theorized by Heidegger in *Being and Time*, and elaborated on by Watsuji in his *Rinrigaku* (*Ethics*, first published in 1931 and consequently re-edited and re-published several times [Sakai 1991: fn.2]). Watsuji criticized an overemphasis on the individual in Western (and Heideggerian) thought,[3] and posited human beings as 'in-between':

---

[3] See Sakai's insightful article on Watsuji's engagement with Heidegger and his development of a different 'philosophical anthropology as ethics with a comprehension of social praxis' (1991).

man does not exist in isolation but is nevertheless different from society, and it is precisely within this tension that personhood comes into being. The concept of the human being as deeply social thus defines individuality as the failure to identify oneself 'with the designated subject position' within the totality (Sakai 1991: 173). And consequently, the return to one's authentic self, 'living to the true great self by denying one' small self' (Hall 1949: 134; cited in Morris-Suzuki 2015: 117) demands the negation of individuality, self-sacrifice. And, 'the highest and most encompassing of finite totality should be found in the nation-state, where its communality consists not of associations but of individual citizens, so that the individual citizen participates directly in the whole' (*Rinrigaku* [1937]; cited in Sakai 1991: 179). Not only does this line of thought – in tandem with the concept of *fūdo* – support nationalism through this specific image of the national community, from the family as the smallest unit to the state, it also mirrors *New Earth*'s major plot line, which was not extant in Fanck's first ideas for the film (1935). The strong message that Teruo returns to his authentic – archetypically Japanese as Fanck would put it – self by 'giving up his individual freedom' is rooted in both German and Japanese nationalist ideology. Gerda telling him that he 'learned something wrong' negates Weimar and supposed Western/American liberalism in one swing. In the light of my argument, however, that much of the representational power struggle circled around the very notion of authenticity, the change in Gerda's lines in Itami's English–Japanese version appears significant: 'You have learned it the wrong way' comments on the concept's application, not its validity, and indicates Itami's resistance to the German and simultaneously to the nationalist definition of what constitutes authentic Japaneseness.

In order to convey these meanings of what he saw and planned to convey, Fanck chose, as Hayashi states, symbolism, whereas Itami aimed for realism (1936); both, however, claimed to represent something authentic. Itami, in his foreword, even introduced the film as a translation of Japan by a foreigner, prompting his audience to read it not as the 'original' but as a 'translation'. A translation, however, 'communicates not so much the foreign text as the translator's interpretation, and the translator must be sufficiently expert and innovative to interpret the linguistic and cultural differences that constitute that text' (Venuti 2013: 111). The Japanese producers inviting Fanck was to a large degree based on the idea that his specific style and ability to capture the 'real' were conducive to the truthful interpretation of Japan. However, while 'domestication' can be a valid choice, it is a matter of degree, and at some point, the focus on the target audience obliterates aspects of the original. Divergent aims, different levels of expertness towards the text, and the power positions within the project, however, resulted in the eventual split and the layers of meaning inherent in both versions.

Capturing the real?

When about two-thirds of the film were finished, Hayashi reported on the state of the production, evoking the image of the J.O. Studios' set bustling with activity and the hardship of operating heavy equipment in the summer heat. Without making public the breakdown of cooperation, he mentions some issues, particularly related to Fanck's peculiarities as a director: because the script *still* was not finished, there was 'rather big-scale improvising on set. It is hard to imagine the completed film . . . but . . . the author cannot help but wonder if it will not resemble a picture scroll *(emaki)*' (Hayashi 1936). Fanck had not overcome his reluctance towards an entirely scripted film, which made the entire endeavour chaotic, but also the idea of a certain 'flexibility' with regard to political developments and associated topics in the film becomes quite clear here. As Hayashi continues, *New Earth* is a film consisting of various 'topics' and of 'nature', rather than a regular narrative, conflict-driven film. Hence, already in mid-1936 there is concern about the plot, and about whether it will become a slide show of beautiful, but spatially unrelated footage from all corners of Japan and aspects of 'Japanese' life (Hayashi 1936). While Fanck, according to Hayashi, tried to make something symbolic, Itami tried to make something real. This schism ascribed to their directing style, however, goes beyond *New Earth* and touches on the two directors' idiosyncrasies with regard to the notion of authenticity. In their works, both are concerned with this quality, but their ways of approaching it displays fundamental differences in understanding that explain the unpleasantness of their cooperation.

Despite being one of the most prominent directors and scriptwriters in the genre, Itami was very critical towards *jidaigeki*, and this is related to his pondering regarding the authenticity depicted in and demanded by these films: 'Scriptwriters and producers turning their backs on aspects of the rich present surrounding them and producing stories about a far-away past that they have neither seen nor lived in, combined with the gleeful reception by readers or audiences, is indicative of a unique disposition' (Itami 1961 [1933]: 25–6). This judgement points out conflicting ideological currents. According to Itami, 'a certain stratum of society who love our native country Japan's pure manners, customs and way of life' rejected *gendaigeki*, which depicts 'cafés, dance halls and bad girls' as indicative of the superficial imitation of foreign countries, in favour of *jidaigeki*, which they considered to be closer to 'the real Japan' (Itami 1961 [1933]: 30). However, since these period films were made by contemporary people, they unavoidably reflected current social conditions (Itami 1961 [1933]: 30). Historical accuracy is necessarily void from this point of view, and the same can be said for the sought-after authenticity. Yet, due to a conservative desire for a 'pure' history, relatively untouched by foreign influences, depicted in these films that were set before the Meiji Restoration and the 'opening' of Japan to the West, at the beginning of Itami's career *jidaigeki* were all the rage, and thus '[I] wrote several scripts that caricatured [these] murder films. . . . People happily called these "*nansensu*" . . . Secretly, [I] thought that the label *nansensu* should not be applied' (Itami 1997 [1933]: 34). He did not agree with the meaning transmitted by the media as superficial, meaningless fun, because, in fact, *nansensu* is significant due to its subversive potential (Silverberg 2007: 231; Itami 1961 [1931]: 8). *Nansensu* makes no claims; it does not try to convert or convince. In its insistence on nothing it is inoffensive to everyone. And precisely because of this lack of seriousness and respect, Itami sees *nansensu* as a 'dangerous concept'. People laugh only about those they do not respect; in former times 'one wasn't allowed to laugh in front of people of higher status' (Itami 1961 [1931]: 11). *Shin jidaieiga* and *nansensu* are the first step for disrupting the 'wrong things' asserted by former *jidaigeki*, in particular 'foolish heroism' and 'all sorts of unpleasant mannerisms' (Itami 1961 [1931]: 16). Yet, '[J]ust like we have come from a time that claimed mistaken things to a time that claims nothing at all, let's move from a time that claims nothing at all to one that claims the right things'. And in an afterthought Itami adds, 'if our path will be unobstructed' (Itami 1961 [1931]). His anachronistic use of Mendelssohn's *Wedding March* and Chopin's *Raindrop Prelude* in *Akanishi Kakita* (1936) – dealing with the 1671 strife for power within the Date clan – reflects the contemporary cultural repertoire and simultaneously challenges the idea of the very possibility of representing a mirror image of the past. A scene in *Peerless Patriot* (Kokushi musō, 1932) in which the impostor Nise (Kataoka Chiezō) almost persuades the real Ise no Kami (Takase Minoru) that he, Nise, actually is the 'real thing', is preceded by the intertitle *Mental Test* (*mentaru tesuto*), an English loanword, displayed next to a 'pondering' cartoon stick figure reminiscent of Disney aesthetics. 'Inauthentic' for the period depicted but authentic for the period of production, these instances break the cinematic illusion of an ideal past and redirect perceptions to the present. On being asked in 1934 why he joined predominantly *gendaigeki*-oriented Shinkō Kinema, Itami replied that for him 'there is no such thing as *gendaigeki* or *jidaigeki*' (Kishi 1953: 198).

Fanck also based much of his (self-)image and his style on the notion of the 'real'. His scientifically authenticating academic title appeared in every 'Dr Fanck Film', whose images were governed by a natural scientist's search for exactness paired with a still photographer's ideal of truthful representation (Elsaesser 1994: 392). He attributed his growing up, from an asthmatic child in an industrial town to a healthy outdoor sportsman, to his education at a Swiss boarding school, which toughened its pupils through outdoor activities, and his youth spent climbing and skiing in the Black Forest (Fanck 1973). This background provided the basis for his subsequent career in the physically demanding and skilled work of making mountain films. Many of Fanck's films therefore contain instructions on skiing and climbing and all, in their depiction of heroic struggles, emphatically provoke a 'proper' appreciation of what was valuable for him and what he thought valuable for society (Fanck 1973: 118, 315; Weigel 1976: 34). This integral part of his persona even featured prominently in newspaper reports that introduced him during his early days in Japan. The 'real' and 'authentic' in Fanck's work takes a more physical, didactic and value-laden position than in Itami's stance.

The following introduction for *The Holy Mountain* demonstrates the prominent part taken by the 'really real' (Lindholm 2008: 1):

> The sportsmen participating in *The Holy Mountain* ask the audience not to think of their performances as photographic tricks, to which they would never lend themselves. All shooting on location really took place in the mountains, in fact in the most beautiful parts of the Alps, taking one and a half years. The big ski race was performed by German, Norwegian and Austrian master skiers. The manuscript of this story set in the mountains . . . originates in the real experiences of a life led in the high mountains for twenty years.

Then-actress Leni Riefenstahl was buried by a planned avalanche during shooting to make her reactions more authentic, Fanck fell into a glacier during *Storms over Mont Blanc* (Figure 4.2), numerous strenuous ascents and descents of the volcano in the climactic mountain-rescue sequence completely exhausted Hara Setsuko, and she and Kosugi almost burned their sock-clad feet on the volcanic rocks before the team provided them with asbestos sandals (Riefenstahl 1994: 89–90; Chiba 1995; Fanck 1973: 225, 364).

In *New Earth*, Fanck applied his usual techniques to produce an authentic image of Japan, just as his previous films had provided of mountain sports, and just as he had been invited to do, but within entirely foreign circumstances. For the first time, he was overtly involved in politics, and he was also supposed to produce an image of a country he did not know much about, as opposed to European Alps. Furthermore, he was also put into the position of a cultural interpreter of this strange country, the translator's 'crucial role of cultural go-between' (Venuti 2013: 109), without the necessary deep knowledge of one of the two cultures concerned. Although he had Japanese advisers and a co-director, his headstrong nature and status within the project got the better of him in the end. Both directors struggled with and pursued authenticity in their work, but Fanck's positivist stance within a context of changing values and ideologies on the threshold between Weimar and the Reich and Itami's approach that was based on the negation of the values attached to the notion in representations of the national past were necessarily opposite. When Itami found himself in the position to produce *the* authentic image of Japan for external projection, in interplay with Fanck's vision, he was faced with an assertive representational rhetoric. If the 'national essence' or 'Japanese spirit' that Fanck set out to capture

FIGURE 4.2 *Location shooting for* Storms over Mont Blanc: *Left to right: Hans Schneeberger, Leni Riefenstahl, Richard Angst, Sepp Allgeier, Arnold Fanck.*

(Aoyama 1936: 90), and consequently assert, was indeed one of 'the wrong things' Itami had endeavoured to break with in his *nansensu* films, the subsequent clash appears unavoidable. Fanck fails to take into consideration the subjective nature of his (expressionist) endeavour and claims to arrive at a universal truth, authenticated by his status as an artist. Itami challenges this point of view and negates Hayashi's positive spin on the conflict: 'In Dr Fanck's script we do not feel the Japanese of today, but of one generation ago. This is not a question of symbol or reality' (1936). Yet, as becomes clear from the two final products, Itami was not able to turn the narrative around, which is due to his position in this project of revealing others to selves, in the case of Fanck, or selves to others, in the case of Itami.

Ethnographic endeavours and encounters

So far, the framework of (cultural) translation has been helpful in opening the view on the choices made, consciously and unconsciously, by the two directors with a view towards their target audiences and to see how Fanck did not necessarily always misunderstand 'Japan' or Itami's input but also specifically chose and 'domesticated' certain topics. And indeed, the opposite option, 'foreignization', despite his claim to 'look for beneficial ideals' to enrich the German discourse, would not have been feasible within the narrow, racially hierarchical configuration of knowledge-power. With the concept of cultural translation to arise almost twenty years later (Asad 2019: 10) and because of the unequal representational power of the West and the rest of the world, it seems fruitful to expand our focus through another, already well-established film genre that represented others to others: despite *New Earth* being a completely scripted narrative film, current discussions about knowledge production through ethnographic or documentary films are helpful for clarifying the power issues at work in the project. This is because in both countries, the film was read not merely as fiction but as a supposedly true image of Japan. In the extreme, this led to Japanese opposition to, and German acceptance of, its authenticity. If documentary film in its most generous definition is 'filmmaking that [claims] a special relationship to reality' (Nornes 2003: 1), the truth claims made or refuted by the project's participants and reviewers make it obvious that the line between fiction and non-fiction is blurry in this co-production. The showcasing of architecture and landscape and the liberal use of close-ups on interesting objects, for example, Mitsuko's tea set when she performs *chadō*, are indistinguishable from techniques used in ethnographic film. That scene in particular reminds one of the tea ceremony in the forerunner *Kagami*. Indeed, if 'ethnographicness' is often not a matter of kind but of degree in a film's constitutive processes (intention, event and reaction) (Banks 1992: 117, 127), the two speakers' presences and their authoritative narration move *Kagami* towards explanatory non-fiction:

> **Narrator Malten:** The props are of simple, elegant shapes. The water container. The smokeless brazier. A tea caddy. Porcelain bowl, bamboo brushes and spoons are usually family heirlooms.

In *New Earth* the camera's gaze replaces the narrator's voice, enhanced by twenty-one exchangeable lenses with extremely high aperture and focal lengths (Figure 4.3). Fanck had commissioned the much-commented-on technology in Germany especially for the project, and they permitted an even closer scrutiny of the foreign country (*Asahi Shinbun* 13.11.1935; Fanck 1973: 140).

In that it aimed for the real, the original, the authentic, 'Dr Fanck's Japan expedition' (Schu. 1937), shared several traits of the ethnographical endeavour of entering unknown 'inside' spaces and making them accurately known. The camera technology contributed to this endeavour, as it allowed for even sharper, clearer images than the Freiburg School was known for anyway; shots of lovely landscapes, bubbling lava, vast desolate mountain ranges, as well as of urban buildings, private houses or factories convey a feeling of 'being there' due to their crystal-clear, seemingly distortion-free quality, regardless of spatial (and temporal) distance. Technology

FIGURE 4.3 *Angst operating the telephoto lens.*

clearly links to content; according to the contract, Fanck was to write his script only after a period of observation in Japan that would guarantee the 'authenticity' of the end product. His extended stay in Japan was also crucial for his power position in Germany. As Geertz points out, the issue 'of having, one way or another, truly "been there"' underlines the representer's authority in terms of the truth-value of his or her representation (Geertz 1988: 4–5). Pre-, mid- and post-production reports in film magazines clearly established that Fanck had 'been there'. Apart from his characteristic style, signifying auteurial presence and, of course, his signature, he does not appear in the film itself (as in some examples of self-reflexive ethnographic films). However, Fanck subsequently edited and released a short (culture-narrative) film, *Little Hans* (Hänschen Klein, 1938). We follow the adventures of his small son on the ship that 'delivers little Hans to his father waiting in Japan', as the male voice-over explains. The final scene shows Hans toddling towards a Japanese house set within a large garden. Fanck steps out onto the veranda and sits down to begin writing. Hans walks into the frame and his father picks him up and carries him inside:

> **Fanck**: Well, if that isn't my Hänschen! Where did you spring from, you little rascal? Were you looking for papa? Look, Hänschen, your papa has to make a great film here [*close-up on rushes lying on the tatami mats*]: *Samurai's Daughter*. Now you can help him nicely. [*Hans picks up a rush and waves it around while the screen fades to black.*]

There is no doubt that Fanck 'had been' in Japan and that he was the one who made the film. Not only do we see him 'there', writing the script, we also see him collecting the material as manifest in the rushes. As in a museum, these physical artefacts proclaim their authenticity; 'they were collected while he-was-there' (Lidchi 1997: 171). In 1938, however, this 'evidence' is provided less in order to authorize the material but to situate Fanck as both author and authority. This stressing of authority and knowledge-power may also be seen with Fanck's booklet on *Samurai's Daughter*, self-published in 1938, the same year he began making his last film on a grand scale (*A German Robinson*). Ethnographic or documentary films in the reflexive mode may use forewords – either written or spoken – that address the audience and situate the author and his or her work, and thus giving it a preferred reading. Fanck had used this technique before to stress the quality of authenticity in *The Holy Mountain*. In the project *New Earth*, however, it was Itami who resorts to addressing his audience through opening titles. The text, crucially, is in Japanese and thus aimed at Japanese recipients. By emphasizing that *New Earth* is but 'a foreigner's dream of Japan' from the very first scene, Itami also aimed at predetermining the Japanese audience's decoding of the film as mediated and authored by someone other than himself. The criticism of *New Earth*, however, was nevertheless mostly directed against Itami, who 'misrepresented' Japan despite being Japanese (e.g. Uchida 1937; cited in Irie 1996: 12). His insider's position was too strong to be disregarded amid demands for the truthful representations that an insider was supposed to provide.

The existence of cultural differences was a primary assumption, and a clear dividing line was set from the beginning between the German and the Japanese points of view vis-à-vis Japan. With the German position privileged in the project, Itami's status was complicated. The hierarchical dichotomy at work in discourses about an original and an adaptation traditionally privileges the original. Here, however, we deal with two originals (Japan and Fanck's script) and two adaptations: the image of Japan in the film – pointed out by Itami as 'one subjective version of reality' – and Itami's adaptation of Fanck's script. Itami, being Japanese, was regarded as closer to the original, but he had to manage with adaptations. In projects that involve revealing 'one society to another' – such as *New Earth* – as Trinh shows, the relationship and the situatedness of the outsider and the insider must be considered carefully (1994: 133). In this project, Fanck was situated as the invited outsider, Itami as the insider who, due to his privileged understanding of the society to be represented, was to counsel and to correct mistakes in understanding. In effect, Itami was to contribute to the outsider's power position through his inside knowledge and to 'authenticate' the outsider's representation (1994: 136). The dichotomies of outsider/insider and objective/subjective that make up such a relationship are also clearly visible. Fanck's doctoral title was used repeatedly by himself and by the press, highlighting his background in the natural sciences and corroborating his objectivity. As is also typical for such a relationship, Fanck – in Trinh's phrasing – took away the gift he had bestowed on Itami, namely to co-direct, as soon as Itami 'trespass[ed] on his preserves' (1994: 136), that is, when he rejected co-directing according to Fanck's vision. During the shooting of the climax scenes on Mount Yakedake, the crew had spent the nights halfway up in a mountain hut, 'but *kichōmen* (methodical) Itami returned to the valley every night' (Kawakita 1936b). Reading between the lines, tubercular Itami preferred to 'scramble up and down those rocks eighteen times' to staying with the film team. Eventually, Itami's insights were dismissed by both sides, Fanck rejecting his input and the majority of his Japanese audience criticizing his output. The notion that nothing 'can be more authentically "other" than an otherness by the other him/herself' (1994: 136) explains why Fanck retrospectively acknowledged Itami's contribution to the German version, at a time (1938), it should be noted, when his own star and hence his own power position within German film discourse were in decline.

The politics of cultural identity played a prominent part in the project *New Earth*, not only in Fanck's representation of 'Japan' but clearly, even more so, in Japan itself, because of the historical controversies surrounding its very representation. We are dealing with issues of recognition and misrecognition throughout the project, from its beginning to its reception. During a round-table discussion following the German team's arrival, director Kinugasa Teinosuke urged: 'I believe European audiences, who have their own ideas about Japan, will not be happy with a film that only shows its exterior' (*Fanck Documents* 1936). The idea of some intrinsic quality was central to the project, and Fanck declared that the authentic depiction of the Japanese spirit was his aim (*Fanck Documents* 1936; *Yomiuri Shinbun* 09.02.1936). Misrepresentation by the 'insider' Itami then not only evoked the fear of misrecognition abroad but also questioned a unified, essential national identity, clearly identifiable and representable by each member of the nation. Nevertheless, Itami's input is obvious in one scene, which serves as an example of the insurmountable differences between them (Fanck 1938: 115–16). In the first interior scene, the Kanda house, Fanck planned to have Teruo's mother receive and read the telegram announcing her son's return. Itami objected, insisting that this did not reflect Japanese customs and that she should give it to her husband to read. For Fanck, this would have made her look like a maidservant and thus render the situation incomprehensible for the foreign audience. Torn between his insight that Itami was right about Japanese customs and his understanding of himself as mediator and translator of Japan, Fanck suggested shooting the scene twice, with the mother standing by her husband and reading the telegram for his own version. Itami stayed adamant. Fanck subscribed to the Japanese mise-en-scène, but then 'dissolved the scene into single shots' so that the mother returning to her original place next to the rice mortar was left out and her position in the following sequence of cuts between her husband reading and her listening remained ambiguous (Fanck 1938: 115–16). However, in both versions, she gives the telegram to her husband, walks towards the mortar, looking over her shoulder, and the subsequent shot-reverse-shots between the father and mother are the same. Despite labelling the solution a compromise that he came up with, he dismissed Itami's opinion. Fanck is clear in that the European 'partner', due to his superior knowledge of what appeals to European audiences, 'must have the highest authority when it comes to making decisions' about what of Japan to present and how to represent it (1938: 117). The Western representational authority by virtue of its knowledge-power is upheld to the detriment of the knowledge and agendas of the represented insiders. This not only concerned Itami but the Japanese producers as well. The idea of a universally appealing export film made by Fanck was futile because of his aspirations towards success in the German market.[4]

In the German discourse, as represented by the politically aligned press, the authenticity of 'Japan' in *Samurai's Daughter* – that lacked Itami's pre-positioning of the film as a translation – remained unquestioned; and the 'really real' was further corroborated by Hara Setsuko's personal appearance in German theatres, looking just like Mitsuko. Moreover, the mediation through and for European eyes facilitated the feeling of familiarity. 'Authentic' images appeared so because they had been recognized and chosen for their resemblance to German discourses, which were then (re-)authenticated when they returned to Germany. Despite earlier announcements that the project would show the 'real Japan' to the world, it seems fair to say that eventually Fanck neither contradicted nor added to any conventional knowledge of Japan, whether grounded in facts or in myth. Goebbels's assessment that the film 'provides a good insight into Japanese thoughts and actions' is repeated by German scholar Eduard Spranger, who, in contrast to Goebbels, had some experience in the country (Goebbels 2006b: 89–90). Writing from Japan, he urged a friend to go and see the film: '[It is] contested. But a lot [of it] spares me written descriptions' (Spranger 1937: 4). Spranger's remark that the film was not unequivocally approved of shows that the authenticity of the represented Japan was not readily accepted in the country itself. When it occurred to the majority of Japanese critics that both films disappointed their expectations, but that the foreigner Fanck displayed a better understanding of Japan than the Japanese Itami (e.g. Inui 1937a; Mizumachi 1937), Japaneseness became an externalized object to examine and discuss. Judging from the

---

[4]Kawakita Nagamasa, in the spirit of *fūdo*, attributed the failed export attempts of *New Earth* to the culturally specific cinematic preferences of various Western nations: the 'Germanic tribe' likes nature/landscape films, but 'Latin tribes' prefer realistic topics. Consequently, a subsequent film aimed at France, Spain or Italy should be more 'artistic', and the director an artist, not a natural scientist like Fanck (1937b).

adverse reactions and the production's financial problems, spectators and distributors were 'not paying to be reminded that identity is unstable and contingent' (Lindholm 2008: 47); they were paying to see a foreigner's view of Japan and invariably compared the authenticity of Itami's and Fanck's respective representations.

Things typically Japanese

The Japanese discourse on *New Earth* evolved into discourse on *Japan*, unsurprising in the light of the project's claim to capture just this elusive notion, to facilitate the recognition of selves, at a time when the search for and fixing of the national essence was high on the agenda. A phrase frequently used in the discourse surrounding the films is 'things typically Japanese' (*nihontekina mono*), for example, in Inui's eponymous four-part series on *New Earth* (Inui 1937a–d). The categorizing of things as 'typically' or intrinsically Japanese is a precondition for drawing borders in transnational contexts. It is also a way of reasserting cultural identity vis-à-vis a (Western) counterpart, claiming cultural ownership of the 'things' represented, and adjudicating the authenticity of their representation. Even Itami's most ardent supporter, Kitagawa Fuyuhiko, sought recourse to the national context in his defence: 'Itami's version is in fact a sabotage of Fanck's *New Earth*. It is a passive protest. Itami, having done such a thing as a Japanese citizen, is a distinguished patriot full of perseverance, sacrifice, courage' (Kitagawa 1937). Kitagawa turns around the arguments, maintaining that in an extradiegetic way Itami has fulfilled the task of serving Japan's national interest in an international context. The matter had become both personal and political. Even journalist and social critic Hasegawa Nyozekan (1875–1969), author of *Critique of Japanese Fascism* (*Nihon fashizumu hihan*, 1932, banned from publication) had to work through his 'discovery' of nationalist sentiments after watching Fanck's version (Barshay 1988: 124–7).

The notion of self-discovery is closely connected to the outside gaze; the German Gerda explaining 'Japaneseness' to Teruo evoked strong reactions in Hasegawa. However, he noted with distress that his anger towards this film was just as 'un-Japanese' as he considered the represented image. Japaneseness, for Hasegawa, was defined by openness and tolerance, a willingness to learn from talented people, regardless of their origins. The critic eventually had to attribute his emotional reaction to his nationalist sentiments, which he himself found confusing, given his decidedly liberal ideology (Barshay 1988: 124–7). The reception of *New Earth* in Japan points to the complexity of the intellectual discourse and its interplay with political and ideological developments at the time. Shortly after publishing an article on this reception, Marxist economist and socialist thinker Sakisaka Itsurō

(1897–1985) was imprisoned for two years because of his political stance. Sakisaka saw problems he discerned in Japan's society reflected in the film's reception: 'Rather than going with the flow of new social developments, [they] experience a profound feeling of "Japan" through an attachment to the old' (1937). The similarity to Itami's argument about the reasons for the proliferation of period films is striking. The idea that *New Earth* is located in a time of competing currents of thought, intensified by its transnational character, is underlined by these articles that go beyond mere film reviews to discuss the interplay between representation, reception and authenticity. Reflections in Japan on *New Earth* regarding the authenticity of the star personas and the authenticity of the represented landscapes show how contested and sensitive a subject 'authentic Japan' was, in particular with regard to the anticipated foreign audience's gaze on this cinematically rendered Japan. While it was clear and a matter of great curiosity that Japan would be shown adequately for the very first time, and through foreign eyes, the fact that this involved a translation process remained unacknowledged regarding Fanck's version at least. This is due to the 'translator's invisibility', to borrow Venuti's phrasing (1995):

> Publishers, copy editors, reviewers have trained us, in effect, to value translations with the utmost fluency, an easy readability that makes them appear untranslated, giving the illusory impression that we are reading the original. We typically become aware of the translation only when we run across a bump on its surface, an unfamiliar word, an error in usage, a confused meaning that may seem unintentionally comical. (Venuti 2013: 210)

An audiovisual translation, such as *New Earth*, involves not 'only' words but images and sounds, relations of space and time, all translated, captured, staged and edited. Thus, the film provided even more opportunities for the audience to encounter 'bumps' that reveal the film as not the original and therefore give rise to questions regarding the true nature of the original and its relationship to its translated image.

5

International stars and national landscapes

Authentic star personas?

> *The more he becomes Japanese again, the more we like Isamu Kosugi.*
> (*FILM-KURIER* 24.3.1937; CITED IN FANCK 1938: 72)

The Japanese critics judged *New Earth* against its adherence to a standard of truth about Japan, but, in the outsider's gaze, Japan no longer appeared as the most natural thing in the world: 'The actors are all suitable; however, Kosugi Isamu with his looks, won't he appear to foreign people backwards and rustic rather than Japanese?' (*Sanyō Shinbun* 06.03.1937) (Figure 5.1). Other reviews denied Kosugi's eyes the 'glimmer of intellect' (Hansen 1997a: 74–5). These critical voices were directed at the actor himself, not necessarily at his role in *New Earth*.

Kosugi was one of the top *gendaigeki* actors at that time, prominent for his roles in left-leaning films, such as Uchida Tomu's *Living Doll* (Ikeru ningyō, 1929), 'one of the first and most famous "tendency films"' and that had secured the fourth place in the *Kinema Junpō*'s best ten of 1929 (Shutsū and Nagata 2008: 90). Likewise, *Theatre of Life*, in which Fanck had 'discovered' Kosugi, was highly acclaimed. Voted actor of the year in 1930, he played the main character in *Mister Japan* (Misutā Nippon, 1931, Murata Minoru), and there was no question as to his 'authenticity' as a Japanese in the domestic market, when border crossing and the representation to the outside were not issues. As with his other actors, Fanck had opted for those who represented – to him – some essential Japanese trait, and Kosugi's powerful build made

FIGURE 5.1 *Kosugi as a thoughtful Teruo.*

him appear ideal for the image of Japanese masculinity Fanck wished to project. He was drawn to Kosugi's 'roughness and unpretentiousness' in *Theatre of Life*. In *New Earth*, one article stresses, Kosugi wore no stage make-up (Aoyama 1936: 91). He showed his 'true' face as *the* Japanese man as Fanck saw him, and as his Japanese audiences so far had accepted him naturally, but suddenly, his national identity was far from self-evident. Kosugi also had been reported as having become good friends with Fanck, and the representation of their relationship conformed more to the image of two friendly nations than the undertaking itself (Hazumi 1936b; Fanck 1938: 6). However, a subsequent article sarcastically commented on Kosugi having become a 'connoisseur' (*tsū*) through his work with the Germans. He was quoted as criticizing the crew by referring to Fanck's techniques while shooting his next film *Writings on Love and Marriage* (Renai to kekkon no sho, 1936, Abe) (*Yomiuri Shinbun* 25.08.1936). In a way, this repeated his role in *New Earth*: a Japanese, heavily influenced by German ways, disparages Japanese practices.

Yet, despite the criticisms regarding his 'Japaneseness', Kosugi remained popular within a purely domestic context: together with Yamada Isuzu and Kawamura Reikichi, he was on a list of three to be voted 'Best Actor of 1937' by the Directors' Guild (*Yomiuri Shinbun* 27.04.1937). This selection did not mention *New Earth*; rather, Kosugi was recommended for his performance in *Theatre of Life* and for his long-time contribution to Japanese film. Later, he starred in Tasaka Tomotaka's humanist *A Pebble by the Wayside* (Robō no ishi, 1938) and the director's other signature films, *Five Scouts* (Gonin no sekkōhei, 1938) and *Mud and Soldiers* (Tsuchi to heitai, 1939). While *Five Scouts,* especially, is often mentioned for its humanist depiction of soldiers and the visual absence of the enemy, the two later films are nevertheless interpreted as 'spiritual preparation' for war (Satō 1982: 102–3). Given the previous criticism of Kosugi as un-Japanese, his roles as model military leaders in *Five Scouts* and *Mud and Soldiers* underline the context-dependency of such evaluations. Körber-Abe argues that these films cast 'average types' instead of 'superheroes' as the protagonists in order to facilitate spectator identification (2010: 44). The 'average-type' protagonist brought the events on the screen closer to home and thus made them more relevant. In this sense, Kosugi again stood for the average Japanese man, but his 'authenticity' was not questioned because the films did not cross borders. Kosugi also played the main role in Uchida's highly acclaimed adaptation of Nagatsuka's novel *Earth* (Tsuchi, 1910). The eponymous film was released in 1939, when the Film Law had tightened censorship considerably, but it displayed a surprisingly sharp criticism of social conditions in its depiction of the struggles of a poor farming community in Northern Japan (*Kinema Junpō*'s top film of 1939). '*Earth*'s freedom from the overt patriotic flourishes so common in wartime films', as pointed out by Sallitt (2010), seems to imply a direct line to Uchida's previous left-leaning films. But it is almost impossible to refrain from wondering if the casting of Kosugi as the main character, Kaji, was a reference to *New Earth* and if it was intended to contrast the paradisiac farming conditions enjoyed by Teruo in Manchukuo with Kaji's predicaments. Indeed, according to Watts, *Earth*'s 'final triumphant scene of a farmer tilling his new field was made into a poster and co-opted by propagandists recruiting settlers to Manchuria' (2001). The referential link to both the cinematic and the physical *New Earth* serves to illustrate the various ways in which the discursive currents were appropriated and that the issue with *New Earth* was precisely the supposed co-production with another nation and the concern of misrecognition abroad.

The presence of the other male protagonist, Sessue Hayakawa, in the project remained disproportionally uncommented on. Abroad, he had denoted *the* Japanese man for several decades, but his portrayal of Japanese masculinity, notably with regard to the 'national disgrace film' *The Cheat* (1915, DeMille) was heavily criticized in Japan itself (Miyao 2007). In *New Earth*, his part (Yamato Iwao) embodies both an 'old samurai' and a 'new Japanese', hence an all-compassing national identity (Figure 5.2).

At this time, Hayakawa was struggling to add the notion of authentic Japaneseness to his persona in order to find a foothold in the industry, his career in the United States having declined. However, paradoxically,

FIGURE 5.2 *Promotional picture of Hayakawa as Yamato Iwao.*

New Earth was presented as a chance for him to revive his international career in Germany or France rather than solidifying his status in Japan (Hayakawa 1936). Fanck and Hayakawa's cultural translations of a Japanese patriarch did not convince in Japan and, subsequently, Sakisaka referred to Hayakawa's French films *Yoshiwara* (1937, Ophüls) and *La Bataille* when he labelled *New Earth* as yet another instance of the misrepresentation of Japan (Sakisaka 1937).

The female protagonists were also selected for their 'archetypical' qualities and both succeeded in manifesting a national authenticity in the

FIGURE 5.3 *Promotional picture of Eweler.*

film. In 1933, Ruth Eweler had been described as an 'ideal German type' and 'the most beautiful blonde' in a beauty pageant organized by an American hair care company, an event that led to her film career (*Gartenlaube* 1933) (Figure 5.3).

However, public interest in Eweler was limited, both in Japan and Germany; many German reviewers, for example, merely commented on her 'blondness' (see the selection of reviews in Fanck 1938). Hara Setsuko emerged as the real star of the project. In fact, Hara's role in *New Earth* was so powerful that it shaped her star persona and the meaning she brought to her roles for a long time (Haukamp 2014).

Although it was not Hara's first leading role, *New Earth* today appears as the beginning of her career (e.g. Takahashi 2012), and Fanck's discovery of one of Japan's most iconic actresses (*Yomiuri Shinbun* 08.01.1954) is one of the film's selling points today. In *New Earth*, she appears as the epitome of Japanese femininity. Fanck had conceptualized her role as Mitsuko as the archetypical Japanese woman, not only a character but a motif: Mitsuko is a 'ladylike Japanese girl' and a strong but 'submissive Japanese woman' (Fanck, cited in Aoyama 1936: 90). When Fanck cast this relative newcomer for the main role in 1936, the notion of authenticity was a central issue: 'There was nobody more suitable than Hara for depicting the profile of the Japanese girl as I saw it' (Fanck cited in *Sutā* 1937), and it continued to underscore Hara's star persona until – probably even after – her official retirement in 1963: 'When talking about an actress fulfilling the concept of the "beautiful Japanese woman" there is no one but Hara Setsuko' (Yomota 2000: 313). Unlike Kosugi, her 'Japaneseness' was never questioned (Figure 5.4).

As Satō argues, Hara being 'acknowledged as a representative Japanese woman by a famous European director made her the subject of much attention at a time that was torn between the two extremes of worshipping the West and nationalism' (1995: 395). And indeed, writing about the hardships of shooting on location, a Japanese reporter notes contentedly that 'the Japanese Hara Setsuko does not lose out to [Fanck's mountain film actress] Leni Riefenstahl' (Hazumi 1936a). Later, newspapers reported on Hara's success in Germany and pointedly contrasted it with 'Eweler's disgrace'. Itami and Kosugi defended her, blaming myopia for her inability to follow directions and criticizing Fanck's directing (*Yomiuri Shinbun* 20.04.1937b). Eweler did not shine in the film, yet, reports about her 'strict banning from [domestic and foreign] screens' because of her failure are powerful but bogus (*Yomiuri Shinbun* 20.04.1937a; *Yomiuri Shinbun* 20.04.1937b). Immediately after *New Earth*, she appeared in the German–Czech co-production *Ground for Divorce* (Der Scheidungsgrund, 1937, Lamac), and continued her career until 1943. The blowing up of a story with little substance exemplifies the way in which the undertaking was magnified in the media and, more importantly, shifted the blame for the project's failure to a single person: 'Eweler stands alone, crying, and before her very eyes and in her own country, Hara receives flowers' (*Yomiuri Shinbun* 20.04.1937a). In the international context, Hara's star persona became a projection space for national pride; a process that simultaneously depended on and contributed to the quality of authentic Japaneseness in her star persona.

This quality emerged only as a result of *New Earth*. Previously, her 'modern' aspects had predetermined her roles. She debuted as a *gendaigeki* actress at Nikkatsu's Tamagawa studios in 1935, in the leading role of

FIGURE 5.4 *Production snapshot of Hara.*

Taguchi Tetsu's teen love story *Do Not Hesitate, Young Folks* (*Tamerau nakare wakōdo yo*). With this film, Aida Masae acquired her stage name Hara Setsuko, based on her character's name. The *Yokohama Trade Newspaper* described her as a tall, 'modern beauty', her modern aspect underlined by a photograph of her in a sharp, tailored suit (*Yokohama Bōeki Shinbun* 28.06.1935). In subsequent contemporary dramas, Hara played the roles of schoolgirls and younger sisters. As a member of the second generation of Japanese actresses – Irie Takako and Tanaka Kinuyo being part of the first – she represented many young girls of the time: her high school pursued a policy of providing its pupils with a 'mixture of Confucian-style *ryōsai kenbo*-ism' and a 'vocational education, responding to [the requirements of modern] life' (Chiba 1987: 19). *Ryōsai kenbo* denotes the doctrine of the 'good wife and wise mother' that defined the social ideal of woman in the Meiji Period and was revived during the war. Seen from this angle, Fanck's casting choice when he looked for someone 'authentic' was not a misjudgement. A certain ambiguity in terms of being both 'a modern beauty' and a 'canonical Japanese girl' played a decisive role. Fanck saw Hara on the set of her first *jidaigeki* film, *Priest of Darkness* (Kōchiyama Sōshun, 1936, Yamanaka), but he finalized his decision to cast her only after a meeting to which she brought a 'modern photo' on the magazine cover of *Modan Nippon* (1935). *New Earth* reflects this combination, specifically in the scenes of Mitsuko's education, which echo Hara's own high school experience. On her way to becoming the perfect bride, she practises using a sewing machine, doing the tea ceremony, swimming, gymnastics, rowing, *ikebana* and so on. But what appeared 'really real' to Fanck, and what others approved of in the subsequent discourse, is manifest in the film's exposition scene introducing Mitsuko, which conveys a 'purely Japanese' – untainted by Western influences – visual impression.

The narrative increasingly turns towards the traditional Japanese lifestyle. Mitsuko's father warns her not to wear a Western dress when welcoming Teruo – a cultural prescriptionist nuance that is, significantly, missing from Itami's version – and in the second half of the film she is always in a kimono and in 'typically Japanese' surroundings. Photographs of a European-style kitchen which Mitsuko shows to Gerda were not included in Fanck's final edited version (Figure 5.5), and the Yamato house appears as a picture of 'Old Japan' (Figure 5.6).

Japan finds its extension in the Manchurian field in the final scene, and Hara's status as a farmer's wife and young mother, wearing a farmer's *kasuri*-patterned kimono, signifies the 'authentic Japanese' feminine qualities as promoted through the *ryōsai kenbo* doctrine.

The defining moment of Hara's authentic Japaneseness came in March 1937, when she travelled to Germany to attend the premiere. Her journey was a much-publicized event. The image of Japan as projected by Fanck's film in Germany could not have been better 'authenticated' than by the eponymous 'daughter of the samurai' appearing on stage in her beautiful kimono. Simultaneously, this event authenticated Hara's star persona. Along with the film, she was exported as the archetypical Japanese girl whom Fanck had constructed. Prior to her journey she had declared that she was going to wear a kimono while in Germany but for convenience would wear Western-style clothes (*yōfuku*) on the Trans-Siberian Railway (*Kyōto Nisshutsu Shinbun* 08.03.1937). The strong, affirmative phrasing used in the article signals something more than a simple choice of fashion. The kimono is significant because it is part of a dichotomous pair: Japanese clothes (*wafuku*) and Western clothes (*yōfuku*). Given the various kinds of Japanese clothes, the term *kimono* (lit. 'object of wear') appears when

FIGURE 5.5 *A production still of the modern kitchen in the Yamato house.*

FIGURE 5.6 *The set of the 'Yamato house'.*

the choice is between *wafuku* and *yōfuku*, and that choice is often political (Dalby 2001: 67, 126). Hara's physical presence in a kimono transported the 'aura of legitimacy, continuity, and embodied reality' that is ideologically bolstered by indigenous productions (Lindholm 2008: 98). The responsibility for standing for what is authentic and hence representative of one's nation frequently falls to women, who in this discourse become 'the figure of tradition within modernity' (Vlossak 2010; Duara 2003: 131). This function is signified by their wearing national dress, while men, associated with advancement, are likely to leave tradition behind and join the global army of suits. To (re-)present Japan was part of Hara's role, and the kimono was integral to this undertaking. Despite frequent references to Hara's wearing a kimono in various articles, there is never an explanation given for her choice of clothing. It was simply anathema that she might present herself abroad as a modern girl (*moga*), 'the symbol of all that was non-Japanese' when the *ryōsai kenbo* was being revived as 'authentically Japanese' (Duara 2003: 137). Fanck aimed at representing Mitsuko as an archetype, like the German 'ideal girl' (*risō shojo*). Anticipating his German audience, Fanck states, 'It would be wonderful if Mitsuko, played by Hara, was [perceived as] the "Japanese Gretchen"' (*Sutā* 1937). Sweet and simple 'German Gretchen' of Goethe's *Faust* (1908) had become a synonym for 'typical German woman', but she was, crucially, antithetical to the *neue Frau* (new woman), and as much of a conservative backlash as the new *ryōsai kenbo* was to the *moga*. It is therefore not surprising that a rare exception to the unequivocal praise of Hara was articulated by a feminist writer, Ichikawa Haruko, who points out that the portrayal of Mitsuko is an anachronism, a setback to the achievements made by women in the preceding decades (Ichikawa 1937). On the visual level, the way that Mitsuko is first presented walking in the garden exemplifies the issue: the film is specifically set in the 'today' of 1936 (as indicated by the official stamp on the telegraph sent to Teruo by his adoptive father: 'Tokyo, 10 April 1936') and her premodern hairstyle alone is startling enough for an 'everyday scene in contemporary Japan' (Figure 5.7). Her elaborate coiffure, in comparison to the simple chignon worn by Teruo's factory-worker sister Hideko, or by Yuasa in *Kagami*, hints at an agenda behind this representation: Fanck later nostalgically contrasted Mitsuko's two hairstyles; the 'artful Japanese updo [and] the plain European hairstyle. That, by the way, became dominant amongst the youth even then' (1973: 343).

Aware of the anachronism in his representation, Fanck consciously used it in order to convey his image – and dream – of Japan. Itami's criticism of the film as a *hama mono* (thing from Yokohama) comes straight to the point (1961 [1944]: 178). The abbreviation of 'Yokohama mono' denotes often overly decorated, gaudy Japanese products made exclusively for export. The exposition scene of Mitsuko appears as a moving version of a *Yokohama shashin*, photographs that were produced around the turn of the century,

FIGURE 5.7 *The first shot of Mitsuko.*

by both foreign and Japanese artist, specifically tailored to foreign tastes and aesthetic sensibilities (Satow 2006: 51): 'They flit among the flowers in their multi-hued attire, radiant human butterflies, making the scene at once a living picture and a poem' (Enami ca 1905). This caption for such a photograph, picturing young women in kimono, almost perfectly captures the mood of 'Mitsuko in the Garden', apart from *New Earth* being black and white, rather than 'multi-hued'. Mitsuko corresponds to a 'foreigner's dream of Japan', one that had been 'recorded' by foreign and Japanese cameras for over forty years and, by 1936, had become a representational tradition. In his initial thoughts on the project Fanck paradoxically draws back on precisely the 'Madam Butterfly' theme he claimed to avoid. He elaborates on the well-known and well-documented 'erotic attractiveness' of Japanese women for the 'white man', considering it 'foolish' to refrain from this 'erotic moment' by using a run-of-the-mill European actress (Fanck 1935).[1] This 'foolishness' refers to audience attraction, and it is also clear which preconceptions Fanck brought with him to Japan. These were fuelled and maintained by (Orientalist) representational traditions that

---

[1] This part is missing from the published article. The manuscript (Ausführungen über des Projekt eines japanischen Films) is part of Fanck's estate (Film Museum Munich).

often – with or without an erotic moment – focus on women as national icons and stress traditional aspects that signify authenticity. Consequently, while in its Japanese context Fanck's version was also titled *New Earth*, with its own implications, the release titles for the European markets refer to the samurai's daughter. Clearly, Mitsuko (and Hara Setsuko) had become the icon of the undertaking.

The project's international aspect, however, played a crucial role in the increasingly nationalist discourse. Japanese cinema had to be seen as equal to that of other film producing countries, parity signified by its own international star. The power assigned to Hara's star persona through her international travel corroborated the national narrative: 'She became an international person of the silver screen through *New Earth*' (*Kokumin Shinbun* 02.04.1937). This 'power factor', however, leads to a seeming conundrum in the construction of her star persona as the authentic 'beautiful Japanese woman'. If women were, indeed, a repository of tradition, how did Japanese discourse reconcile this with the image of an international film star – Hara was labelled 'the world's darling' (*sekai no koibito*) – travelling the world in pursuit of a professional career? Dyer defines the star image as 'a complex configuration of visual, verbal and aural signs' that 'function crucially in relation to contradictions within and between ideologies, which they seek variously to "manage" or "resolve"' (2007: 38). Consequently, the image is fluid enough to change with the discursive environment. Roach's performance-centred analysis locates the star's attraction in 'the power of apparently effortless embodiment of contradictory qualities simultaneously' (2007: 8). It is this balance that attracts attention and is able to fulfil the desire for an apparent unity of discourse; in this case a unified, authentic national identity. Especially in the context of her journey to Germany, the press attention signifies Hara as one of Roach's 'abnormally interesting people' (2007: 1): we are given the insight into her supposedly 'private life' that is typical for media representations and constructions of stars, for example, a 'love scandal' with short distance runner Yasawa and her brother-in-law Kumagai's public defence of her, or 'five snapshots' of Hara's 'everyday activities' in Berlin (*Kokumin Shinbun* 11.03.1937; *Asahi Shinbun* 27.04.1937). The 'breathless spectatorship' inherent to star status (Roach 2007: 8) was directed at her embodiment of 'the modern' and 'the traditional', her 'non-Japanese' exotically Western beauty and 'pure, canonical Japaneseness'. Hara waved goodbye to her fans at Tokyo Station in a Western-style suit, but she is wearing a kimono when she is welcomed back in July 1937 (*Asahi Shinbun* 13.03.1937; *Yomiuri Shinbun* 29.07.1937). It is from her strengthened position as an internationally travelled actress that she states, 'I definitely felt that Japanese culture is in no way inferior to that of any other country' (*Yomiuri Shinbun* 29.07.1937). Hara's body combined international aspirations and national narratives without sacrificing the notion of authenticity.

Like the style of dress worn by the samurai's daughter over the course of the film, the media discourse on the film changed. It had become a vehicle for both a star and a nation. Fanck had imagined 'a pretty, brave samurai's daughter, living within and harmonizing with Japan's beautiful and scary landscape. This girl as a *symbol* of this landscape [. . .]' (cited in Aoyama 1936: 90–1). The connection of the landscape, national cinema and the imagined and represented nation itself has been amply discussed;[2] and notions of a national landscape and a national cinema are central to expressing the essential difference and unified uniqueness of a culture.

The authenticity of landscapes

Not only mountains, but also the Yamato spirit.

(FANCK'S PLANS FOR THE FILM, IN *YOMIURI SHINBUN* 09.02.1936)

Fanck's primary concerns always were the landscape and his 'optical vision', and he needed little character development or plot to leave enough screen time for his 'grandiose pictorial motifs' (1973: 218–19). The Japanese side, however, was greatly concerned to include the human aspect in order to 'correct' previous misrepresentations and to foster international understanding. Hence, Japanese articles usually refer to a film about Japan – meaning its 'character' – made before the beautiful backdrop of Japanese scenery (e.g. *Yomiuri Shinbun* 21.01.1936). But they had invited an enthusiastic expert on mountain scenery, and despite Fanck's concessions to the plan and his effort to come up with the script for a narrative film, his 'inner mountain photographer' took over: in February 1936, before the script was even written, Fanck sent two Japanese cameramen up Mount Asama to capture footage of an eruption, regardless of plot. They lived in a hut until mid-July, when the long-awaited eruption finally occurred (Fanck 1973: 345); their footage was then edited into the exhibition scene as well as the climactic rescue scene on Mount Yakedake (Figure 5.8).

Landscape shots and collage-like sequences of beauty spots take up a large proportion of *New Earth*'s screen time. Itami, preferring the portrayal of human characters, was irritated by Fanck's spending a disproportionate amount of time on landscape shooting (Saeki 1987: 163).

Nature as basic element determines the human character and thus the specific culture. . . . The film begins with a volcanic eruption, followed by an earthquake. Fanck here wants to illustrate the unpredictable and

---

[2] For example, by O'Reagan 2002; Wollen 1972: 94–8; Satow 2006.

destructive Japanese natural environment that educated its inhabitants towards stalwart courage, as he has Teruo say. (Hansen 1997a: 28)

This use of landscape seamlessly fits into interpretations of Fanck's aesthetics as close to National–Socialist ideological emphasis on (irrational) human acts of bravery in the face of natural forces (Powers 2007). Considering the film and the use of landscape within it as expressive of Fanck's worldview only, however, relegates the Japanese partners to mere extras. Discourses connecting natural and national characteristics were found in Japan as well, most prominently in Watsuji Tetsurō's influential *Fūdo* (1935), which conceptualizes thought systems and societies as bound by space and climate (Berque 1992). In a round-table discussion shortly after the German team's arrival, the head of the *Asahi Shinbun*'s news section urged Fanck to stress the occurrence of natural catastrophes, 'such as earthquakes' and the bravery that enabled the Japanese to 'build today's Japan' (Ueda, in *Fanck Documents* 1936). This is almost exactly how Teruo introduces Japan to Gerda, following the earthquake scene at the Kanda's house (see Chapter 6). Fanck therefore in fact followed Japanese requests in this regard, and later wrote about his task to evoke mutual understanding by creating 'a cross-section . . . of Japanese culture and the landscape determining this culture'

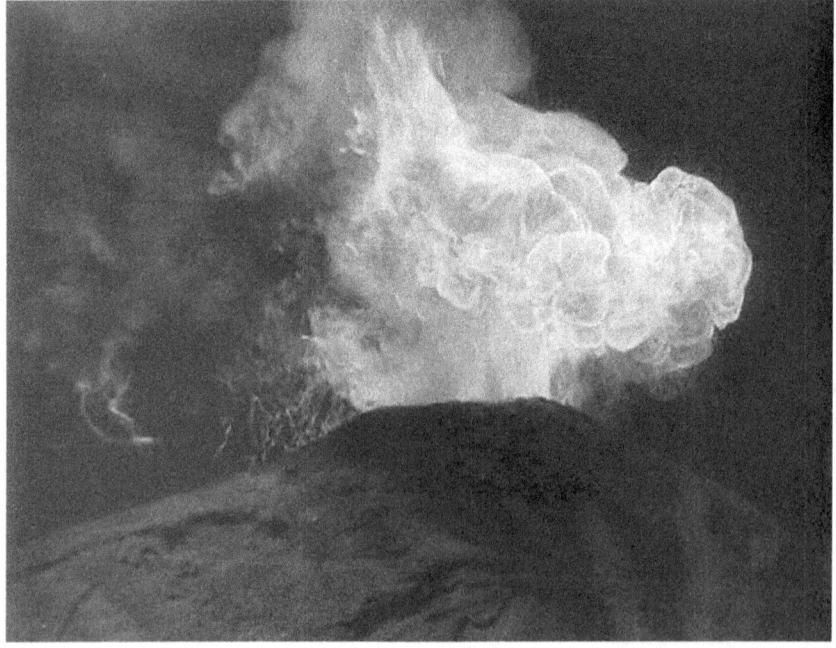

FIGURE 5.8 *Mount Asama erupting.*

(1938: 90). The landscape is perceived to be expressive of a community's idiosyncratic 'quality' and to provide its natural boundaries. Film being an audiovisual medium, Fanck's task of cultural translation consequently involved the landscape and, equally consequently, the authenticity of landscapes, comprising cityscapes, rural vistas and colonial spaces, became a topic of concern in *New Earth*'s critical reception in Japan.

Urban

On Gerda and Teruo's arrival in Tokyo, the German journalist is astonished by the tall, modern buildings and the ubiquity of flashing neon signs. On their drive to the hotel, the cutting between Gerda looking out of the car's window and the sights of 'Tokyo by night' establishes the audience's point of view (Figure 5.9). We see through Gerda' eyes and perhaps share her amazement at the sights of the metropolitan capital.

Gerda: I never imagined Tokyo to be like this.

Fanck here aimed at conveying and possibly evoking an authentic emotional response and, at the same time, at presenting Tokyo 'as it really is'. However, in order to fulfil his objective of giving audiences a positive first impression of Japan (Fanck 1938: 90–1), he fabricates a twist and shows us Tokyo by night – because Fanck himself had not imagined Tokyo to 'be like this'.

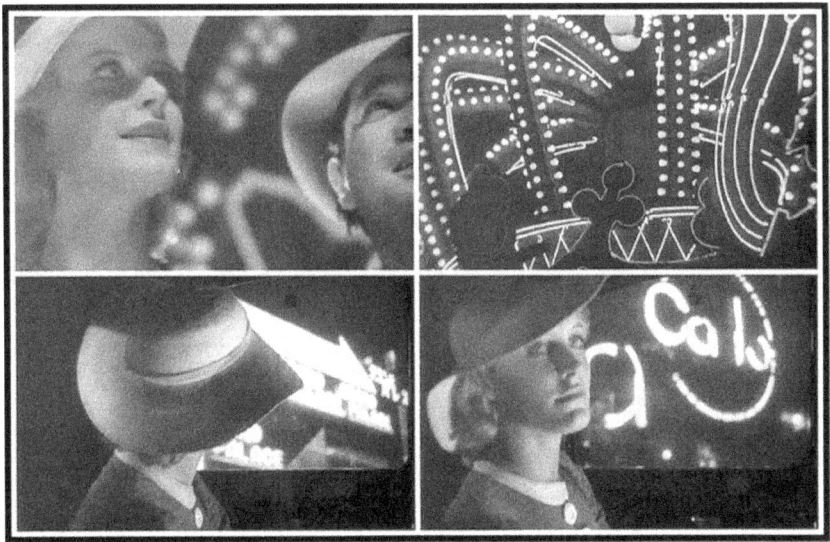

FIGURE 5.9 *Tokyo by night*.

When one travels through a Japanese town for the first time, one is no doubt disappointed. I too felt there is nothing uglier than a big city in Japan. . . . I saw telephone pole after telephone pole, electric line after electric line [and for] whichever Westerner is invited and comes to Japan, this completely destroys the fairy-tale image. (Fanck 1937b)

He was, however, impressed by Tokyo's modern architecture and chose representational tactics that exclusively show 'positive aspects' of the reality surrounding him. Fanck's impression, when he saw Tokyo for the first time, is replicated by Gerda's gaze and comments. Taken together with the earlier shots of heavy industry sites, it is not the case therefore that Fanck focused his representation entirely on 'traditional' aspects, or 'Old Japan'. A later, fast montage sequence mostly of ultra-modern buildings, churches and temples in warped angles recalls Fanck's expressionist style of filming vertical landscapes and underlines his admiration for the modern aspects: the factory girl Hideko, standing for modern Japan, shows her farmer father around Tokyo, asking him: 'Isn't this great (*subarashī deshō*)?' (Figure 5.10).

The same scene in Itami's version comprises streetcar tracks, overhead electricity wires, bicycles and rickshaws and thus depicts an authentically

FIGURE 5.10 *Hideko and Kanda in modern Tokyo.*

mundane experience of the metropolis. In Fanck's version, however, Teruo's explanation of the surprising cityscape authenticates the contemporary Western perception of Japan as double-faced or, in a more positive sense, as a 'country of side-by-sidedness', of old and new, Japanese and Western (Schalek 1925):

Teruo [FV]: We've got two faces. One old and one young!

The film's narrative and iconography do not allow for syncretism, the 'old' underlies the 'young', thus being represented as the authentic essence: Teruo's words are visually enforced by two superimposed shots of a blinking neon sign and a 'typically Japanese' looking theatre front, decorated with lanterns and wood block prints, the dissolve literally underscoring the 'young' with the 'old' (looking) (Figure 5.11).

The lively tune accompanying the following sequence, almost one-minute-long, of tall modern buildings and more neon signs seen through the car window stops as they enter the lobby of their hotel, suggestively named 'Hotel Europe'. The piece of music – characterized by a woman's high-pitched, warbling voice, a chorus, a male singer using a traditional

FIGURE 5.11 *The old underscoring the new.*

style, all accompanied by traditional instruments such as flutes or drums – seems to corroborate my previous statement about the old underscoring the young regarding the iconography of modern Tokyo. However, this particular song is a very interesting instance of varying notions of authenticity: it sounds strange and hence 'traditional' to foreign ears and likely to overseas audiences. The tune is not one of Yamada Kōsaku's compositions,[3] and the use of this specific piece, *Tōkyō ondo*, in a scene showcasing modern Tokyo is extremely fitting and, in that sense, 'authentic'. In 1933, the *Tōkyō ondo* was a craze in Tokyo and beyond (Seidensticker 1990: 36–7). The genre is based on the *bon odori*, a group circle dance usually performed during the summer festivals in honour of the ancestors: a 'kind of collective Japanese folk dance and song with indigenous rhythm emphasized by response refrain sung in chorus, *ondo* was reinvigorated with a new melody and lyrics in traditional style performed with basically Western orchestration which featured traditional drums and *samisen*' (Mitsui 1997: 161). Sung by Kouta Katsutarō, 'the first nationally famous folk-singing geisha', and Mishima Issei, who was famed for his traditional vocal style, *Tōkyō ondo* is – crucially – a 'new folk song' (*shin min'yō*), explained by Hughes as 'new pieces in a folksy mood' (2008: 230; see also Hughes 2007: 293). In 1932, Nakayama Shinpei had composed its forerunner, *Marunouchi ondo*, with lyrics by Saijō Yaso, on commission to praise the modern attractions of Tokyo's Marunouchi shopping district. When it was expanded in 1933 to encompass all of Tokyo, over 1.2. million copies were sold, a prime instance of modern mass culture and consumerism (Lancashire 2011: 63). Lyricist Saijō worked with Yamada on Fanck's *New Earth*, which may explain the tune's appearance in the film. For unaccustomed foreign ears the traditional elements overwhelm the modern, but the Japanese audiences certainly recognized the big hit of a few years earlier.

Nevertheless, in this collage-like sequence signifying Tokyo's modernity, Fanck took a crucial visual misstep. In terms of an authentic, that is, a 'truthful' representation of Tokyo, it is unfortunate that Gerda's first POV shot is of a large, blinking neon sign of the Hanshin Electric Railway (Hanshin Densha) linking Osaka and Kobe and the world's first railway terminal department store Mikasaya, all located at Umeda Station in Osaka (Figure 5.12).

---

[3]For Fanck's heavy intervention into the musical score, cutting out four of Yamada's five new compositions, see Daibō (2010: 17). In *Big Tokyo*, the Soviet side replaced Yamada's compositions for urban scenes with the popular *Tokyo March* (Tōkyō kōshinkyoku) (Fedorova 2014: 116). Daibō cites Yamada's outrage and desperation after discovering that one of his songs in *New Earth* had been changed in favour of *Tokyo March* (2010: 17). I assume that this episode concerns *Tokyo ondo* and solicited this strong emphatic reaction from Yamada because of his previous experience.

FIGURE 5.12 *Hanshin Railway and Misakaya in Tokyo?*

Furthermore, the aforementioned superimposition of the 'young' and the 'old' uses the same shot and one of a theatre advertising Shōchiku 'family drama' (*katei geki*) that was located in Osaka's Nakaza district. After 1923, Shōchiku had capitalized on their prime location in urban – and intrinsically 'modern' Tokyo – to use shots of the city in their films and audiences throughout the country formed expectations and standards about the cinematic use of shots of Tokyo's modern, urban space (Wada-Marciano 2008: 18). Consequently, shots of 'Tokyo' that included an iconic scene from Osaka violated established cultural codes of Japanese cinema, and the spectators' acquired knowledge and sensibility about the use of the cityscape reacted to this inconsistency in what was supposed to finally show Japan as it 'really is'. As also alluded to in the foreword to his version, one of Itami's functions in the project was to correct Fanck's geographical inconsistencies: 'As for the Japanese version, I did my best for it not to become completely ridiculous' (Itami; cited by Sawamura 1936: 10; Yamamoto 2004: 78). And, indeed, he replaced the 'Hanshin Densha' shots with shots of the bar 'Moulin Rouge', which was actually located in Shibuya. This replacement and the vehemence with which this scene in Fanck's version was criticized by Japanese commentators (see Hansen 1997a: 21) are indicative of the high sensibility to matters of geographical authenticity.

Rural

New Earth, like many of Fanck's earlier works, and like numerous contemporaneous Japanese productions, uses a dichotomy of the city and the country as a narrative-driving device. After Teruo experiences a collage of 'things typically Japanese', such as a lovely landscape in spring, a sumo match, a Noh performance, and the encounter with the priest in the temple grounds, he returns to his 'authentic self' in the countryside, walking towards Mt Fuji and wearing a kimono for the first time in the film (Figure 5.13).

For scenes signifying the countryside, Fanck connected footage from famous spots such as Kyoto's Heian Jingu temple or Miyajima, which would look beautiful to foreign audiences, but, again, alienated the Japanese (Satō 1991: 266). The Yamato residence with its sprawling 'garden' is a geographically incoherent collage of beautiful vistas that remind one once more of the 'Yokohama photographs' of 'Old Japan'. But what is interpreted as a lack of understanding, or just arrogant carelessness, must be reconsidered within the project's specific framework. Nostalgia for an 'authentic' landscape, 'untainted by civilization' is a global phenomenon: Satow argues that the Japanese photographers' fondness for 'Yokohama photography' and the construction of a specific

FIGURE 5.13 *Teruo returns to his roots.*

type of Japaneseness was driven by nostalgia as well as by 'internalizing the gaze of the guest' (2006: 51). The film's visual style also reminds one of the Tourism Bureau's short films that Fanck had been shown. When their *Autumn in Japan* was screened in Germany in 1935, the audiences saw a 'car trip through the Fuji National Park, the rice harvest, etc., beautiful landscapes, attractive motifs and a musical score adapted to European style' (*Film-Kurier* 1936). This description is not unlike the scenes in Fanck's version. He had also used the same technique in many of his films to achieve the visual style for which he was famous, and the joining of disconnected scenes was not criticized as a distortion of the actual Alpine landscape, neither in Germany nor in Japan. In his *Izu Dancer* (Koi no hana saku: Izu no odoriko, 1933), Gosho Heinosuke delivered a collage of different rural locations in order to present the imagined nostalgic landscape of perfection (Wada-Marciano 2008: 29). There is no indication that this was understood as the film-makers' lack of understanding. In the early production stages of *New Earth*, the arrangement of scenic shots 'in a way that disregards geographical logic' is not necessarily regarded negatively; the 'geographical artificiality' must be forgiven because, for Fanck, 'there is just too much great scenery in Japan' (Hayashi 1936). Simultaneously indulging the invited guest and confirming the striking beauty of the Japanese landscape, Hayashi was not critical of the fragmentation and assemblage of landscape at this point. The problem arose later, after the film's release, compounded by the extensive media coverage on the production that enabled Japanese spectators to see the inherent constructedness of 'Japan'. Fanck's much-praised landscape shots tap into the discourse of yearning for the 'beautiful Japanese scenery' but were interpreted within the context of presenting Japan to the outside.

Moreover, Fanck was not intimate with the vernacular discourse on modernity that incorporated the city dwellers' culturally specific need for nostalgic rural spaces. Both of Mizoguchi's 'hometown' (*furusato*) themed films, *A Song of Hometown* (Furusato no uta, 1925) and *Hometown* (Fujiwara Yoshie no furusato, 1930), used the dichotomy of city/country, addressing 'the power of nostalgia' (Wada-Marciano 2008: 143). Washburn, contrasting *Hometown* and the 1985 film *Fire Festival* (Himatsuri, Yanagimachi Mitsuo), points out that in 1930 the 'pure Japanese space and time' suggested by images of nature and the rural village in *Hometown* in principle still provided 'the imagined space of an *authentic* Japan' to come 'home' to (2001: 29; my emphasis). In *New Earth*, Teruo's future lies in Manchuria, but he completes his spiritual homecoming in his father's rice field. The 'Japanese spirit' (*yamato damashī*) that Fanck set out to represent is bound to 'Old Japan', signified by *furusato*, as it was in coeval Japanese productions. However, the creation of a nostalgic space for a Japanese audience was not on Fanck's agenda. He made an export film, eventually for German audiences who would not find a nostalgic space in Japan. Despite subsequent conflations of the aesthetics in Fanck's films with German nationalism, the landscape in his films works on a different level. Often, the landscape is used as an establishing shot in films fitting the framework of 'national cinema'. In Fanck's film, the Alps frequently take on this role, but being multinational they represent an experiential sphere rather than a nation. The mountains do not stand for 'Germany', but for the preferred 'country' of the country/city dichotomy and hence these films are closer to Japanese *furusato* films than one might assume. The Japanese countryside, however, was too exotic and too embedded in previous representational traditions to work on such a level. The Japanese rural landscape as an essentialist, timeless space in effect reinstalled Orientalist notions of Japan as pure and beautiful, at odds with the industrialized and militarized reality of the mid-1930s, although the representation of that aspect was also part of Fanck's effort. For the Japanese audience, however, it proved impossible to be absorbed in the film because of the various irritations described earlier. The film was announced and judged as a representation of contemporary Japan, blurring lines between fiction and documentary. These scenes, inadvertently, made obvious the film-making process, so that the inherent constructedness of the cinematic landscape – consciously framed and constructed according to an agenda – became obvious and subject to criticism.

With the audience's critical awareness and the subsequent discourse on authentic Japaneseness, Japan no longer seemed to be 'the most obvious thing in the world' (Brecht 1964: 71). The feeling of discomfort with how Japan looked *from* the outside was then, in turn, projected *to* the outside. It was feared that a distorted representation would lead to a distorted understanding. But, arguably, most foreign audiences would neither notice nor care that the volcano seen from the Yamato house was filmed by Fanck before the background of the island Miyajima and then again in front of Kirishima, the islands being several hundred kilometres apart (Hansen 1997a: 54). In Fanck's cultural translation of the Japanese landscape for its target audience, this landscape just looked beautiful and impressive, as intended. It is unlikely that this would have led to a fundamental international misunderstanding of the Japanese or of Japan, but the discussion within the overall context of international isolation and burgeoning nationalism was extrapolated on Japan's status in the world and on how it was treated by foreigners. What kind of liberties did they take? What kind of power statement did the distorting fragmentation of the Japanese landscape make in a project among 'equals'? Who held the ultimate power over the authenticity of what is represented? As with the various previous attempts at film export, it was comparatively easy to point out what is 'not Japan' in the versions of reality by both foreigners and Japanese. But what Japan actually *was* in 1936 and 1937 and how to project this supposed single, authentic image to the outside was a far more difficult question, also with regard to the issue of colonial expansionism.

Colonial

'In 1936, the Hirota cabinet adopted Manchurian colonization as one of the pillars of national policy' (Young 1998: 352). Manchukuo, the location of the film's final scene and resolution to one of its crises, was a major factor in Japan's increasingly tense international position. With the victory in the Russo-Japanese War (1904–05), Japan had acquired Russia's lease of the Kwangtung territory and the South Manchurian Railway ('Mantetsu') and its railway zone as well as mining concessions. The region in northeastern China was considered important because of its supply of industrial raw material, its agricultural resources, its potential as a destination for emigration and for its geostrategic position vis à vis Russia (Young 1998: 25–35). After decades of increasing industrial investment, and informal and indirect control of the area through Mantetsu and the Kwangtung Army, in September 1931 the Mukden Incident, a minor bomb explosion on a Mantetsu railway track, gave the Kwangtung army, who had fabricated the very incident, the pretext to finally occupy Manchuria (Young 1998: 40–1). In February 1932, Japan declared the state of Manchukuo independent from China, and following China's appeal, the League of Nations Commission of Enquiry, headed by Lord Lytton, investigated the situation. In August, while the Japanese government waited for international recognition of its 'puppet state', parliament passed a pilot emigration plan providing for the funding of between 500 and 1,000 households. The year 1932 saw the 'publication of 107 scholarly articles on Japanese resettlement in Manchuria' as a solution for population pressure and demographic change in the rural areas (Kiernan 2007: 470). In February 1933, forty-two nations, including Germany, voted for the Lytton Commission's recommendation of an independent government under Chinese leadership (McClain 2002: 417–19). Japan refused to acknowledge the report and announced their withdrawal from the League in March. Germany followed in October (Wendt 2000: 110).

New Earth explains Japan's mission, as a 'great civilizing nation', to bring order and progress into backward China, authenticating this discourse by visual representation of intensive construction work (Figure 5.14), newly erected 'model cities' and railway lines. Teruo's explanation of Manchukuo as a plentiful land that 'could feed many more people if it was just being cultivated properly' strongly reminds one of Japanese delegate Matsuoka Yōsuke's defence of Japan's actions as her 'desire and duty' to 'assist Manchukuo to her feet', presented to the League of Nations in 1933 (cited in McClain 2002: 419).

The authenticity of Manchukuo as a third, colonial landscape, however, remains curiously unquestioned. Baskett points out a Japanese interpretation of these scenes that considers Manchukuo in the film actually to mean Germany's 'new order', ascribing German domestic ideological discourses to the representation of emigration to the continent as a solution for Japan's

FIGURE 5.14 *Helping Manchukuo to her feet through construction.*

'overpopulation' (2008: 129–30). Fanck actually planned to use this topic because of its 'metaphorical similarity to the German situation' (1935: 5), tapping into both German and Japanese discourses on military expansion. Expansionist ideologies might have appeared 'authentic' to Fanck because he recognized the discourse from his own cultural background. At the same time, as he already anticipated in 1935 – with a focus on achieving financial backing – the Manchukuo storyline authenticated domestic German discourse on 'living space' (Fanck 1935). But despite the relative lack of comment in Japan as pointed out by Baskett (2008: 130), the film project, nevertheless, corroborated Japan's imperial endeavour and orientalist gaze on other landscapes on an extra-textual level. The film was released in Manchukuo three days earlier than in Japan and its record-breaking box office success was attributed to the film's depiction of the 'pioneers' and soldiers in 'Paradise Manchuria' (*rakudo manshū*) ('*Atarashiki tsuchi* Manshūkuo de mo daijū' 24.02.1937). On their way to Berlin, Hara's party travelled via Dairen (Dalian), Mukden (Shenyang) and Shinkyō (Changchun) to Harbin (Heilongjiang), where they boarded the Trans-Siberian Railway's Trans-Manchurian leg (Hara 1937b). The very possibility of this route and Hara's reported presence at screenings and talks authenticated the discourse on Manchukuo as a legitimate extension of Japan. An explicit link between the film and the advance into Manchukuo was made, for example, in July 1937, when a newspaper article on fifty-two 'members of the Manchurian Industrial Spearhead Immigration Group' leaving for Manchuria's 'new earth' (*Manshū no 'atarashiki tsuchi' e*) clearly alluded to the film *New Earth* through the use of quotation marks in the title (*Asahi Shinbun* 02.07.1937).

Indeed, *New Earth* is well embedded into Manchuria-related media coverage: starting with the 'war fever' following the 'incident' of 1931, radio news, newspapers, theatre plays, novels, magazines and films swam with the discursive tides of a 'total empire', backed by the interrelated fields of culture, politics, economy and society (Young 1998: 55–114). Yamada Kōsaku, the world-renowned conductor and composer working on *New Earth*, in 1932 had provided the musical score for Mizoguchi's film *The Dawn of Manchuria and Mongoli*a (Manmo kenkoku no reimei) and, in 1933, composed the first draft of Manchukuo's national anthem (*Dai Manshūkuo Kokka*) (which was replaced soon after; Daibō 2010: 27). From early 1935, well before Fanck and Kawakita signed their contract, Sessue Hayakawa – *New Earth*'s Yamato Iwao – toured Japanese settlements in Shanghai, Manchukuo and Korea. In an 'attempt to transform his star image into a nationalistic one', he announced his plan to make a film 'that would praise the efforts of the Japanese army and Japanese colonizers in Manchuria and Korea' (*Pyongyang Mainichi Shinbun* 20.04.1935: n.p.; cited in Miyao 2007: 268).

Manchukuo as a topic and a visual trope is employed twice in both versions of *New Earth*. Teruo's speech to Gerda about his wish to go to Manchukuo is accompanied by a sequence of shots from the area, and the final scene takes place in a large Manchurian field. The relative lack of comments about the authenticity of these scenes is a striking commonality in both Germany and in Japan, given four factors that should have engendered a discussion: the trope's topicality through binational trade agreements, Japan's emphasis on emigration, the heightened sensitivity toward authentic representations and Fanck's reputation as a recorder and specialist of the 'real'. Because of the extensive media coverage given to the project, this lacuna is surprising because the absence of corresponding articles clearly implies that Fanck and his team *had not been there*, despite the subsequent release of several related short films. This issue has hitherto remained undiscussed because the presence of the scenes fits well into the prevalent discourses about the film as a propaganda piece:

> On the occasion of the shooting of his feature film, Die Tochter des Samurai (1938) [sic], Fanck produced six short documentaries that he shot in Japan, China and Manchuria. These films dealt with the history, traditions and culture of the Japanese people. They took on a political undertone, for example, when they legitimized, under the guise of a *Kulturfilm*, the Japanese occupation of southern Manchuria in Winterreise

durch Südmandschurien (1938). Kaiserbauten in Fernost (1938) deals with the Chinese wall with the same emphasis as does Atlantik-Wall (1944) with the German bulwark along the coast of the North Sea. (Jung 2013: 244)

Apart from the questionable statement that Japanese tradition was portrayed in films dealing with occupied China and Manchuria, it is clear how Fanck's post-war reputation as a propagandist impacts on and naturalizes such assessments. Linking Fanck and the later, notorious, head of the Manchurian Motion Picture Company, Amakasu Masahiko, Culver even states that Amakasu 'directed the shooting in Manchukuo' (2013: 223). *Imperial Buildings in the Far East* (Kaiserbauten in Fernost, Berlin premiere, 28.07.1938) and *A Winter Journey Through Southern Manchuria* (Winterreise durch Südmandschurien, Berlin premiere, 10.11.1938) were commissioned by Ufa and Terra following Hitler's announcement of his plan to officially acknowledge Manchukuo in February 1938, and the establishment of embassies in August. The promised authentic representation of these landscapes by a German director known for his objectivity in turn authenticated Germany's overview of international developments as well as the power to represent these 'truthfully'. The subtitles and credits, *Shots Taken by the Fanck Expedition to Japan*, 'directed and produced by Arnold Fanck', lend authority to Fanck as the originator, a claim that is not justified.

The first visual instance of 'Manchukuo' in *New Earth* has a distinctly documentary look and feel about it. A main difference between *New Earth*'s two versions is that Itami's employs mostly rural sights, traditional architecture and people's everyday lives, whereas Fanck's version concentrates mainly on a development from 'old' to 'modern', that is, the 'Japanese achievements' in Manchukuo. The footage used in Itami's version reappears in Fanck's aforementioned short films; I assume, however, that the 'everyday' material in Itami's film was actually contained in Fanck's version as it was originally released in Japan and Germany. As mentioned before, offending scenes referring to Manchuria were subsequently cut following the Chinese embassy's complaint, which makes the available version fourteen minutes shorter than the lost premiere version. Hansen states that, as the plot seems to be complete, judging from the script, it is unclear which scenes were cut (and when) (1997a: 8), but it seems reasonable to assume that it were these scenes that obviously showed 'Manchuria'. However, one wonders how these shots found their way into Itami's version, Fanck's feature film and the two short films, when the team had *not* been there. The credit titles for the two shorts give a first hint, as they reveal the participation of the same cameramen, Hayakawa Ichirō and Hayashida Shigeo, and composer Kami Kyōsuke. They had also worked on a film that was released during Fanck's stay in Japan in the summer of 1936, distributed by Tōwa Shōji's culture film (*bunka eiga*) department. Unusual for a documentary film, it secured tenth place in the *Kinema Junpō*'s ranking for 1936. Directed by Akutagawa Kōzō, *Secluded Jehol* (Hikyō Nekka) 'tours the major cities in Nekka-shō (Rèhé Sheng) and visits the buildings, castles and Buddhist temples constructed during the early Qing Dynasty. It also shows the culture and lifestyle of Tibetan Buddhists, commonly known as Lamaists' (Koni Bideo 2005). Nekka (the Japanese reading for Rèhé or Jehol: 'Hot River') and its capital Chéngdé, a political centre of the Chinese empire in the eighteenth century, had been occupied by the Japanese in the spring of 1933 and annexed to Manchukuo (Inaga 2010: 99). *Secluded Jehol* was produced by the South Manchurian Railway Company (Mantetsu), which 'opened up' such secluded regions, physically by building railway lines (Young 1998: 244) and discursively by producing publicity material, such as the 'large scale propaganda films promoting national policy' and ethnographic documentaries directed by Akutagawa during his time as the head of Mantetsu's film-making unit (Nornes 2003: 58). While recent accounts stress the ethnographic quality of *Secluded Jehol* (High 2003: 267; Nornes 2003: 58), its release advertisement by its distributor, Tōwa Shōji, clearly frames it within 'classical' orientalizing strategies of visual penetration and occupation, and makes a strong case for Japanese engagement in the area: 'The camera reveals the secret region of scorching heat! Why? Nekka must be protected by the Japanese to the very last!' (*Asahi Shinbun* 30.06.1936). Likely through the connection to Tōwa, Fanck had received the footage as a 'present' (*Yomiuri Shinbun* 27.11.1936), early enough for it to be edited into both versions of *New Earth*. This interpretation is corroborated by editing assistant Nogami's recollection that Fanck's Askania camera and the famed zoom lenses eventually ended up in Akutagawa's hands (Kishi and Nogami 2012: 33). The equipment could have well been a 'present in return' for the footage.

The *Yomiuri Shinbun*'s article about Fanck's taking the material with him to Germany and editing his own version gravitates around the issue of 'export fever' for Japanese film, 'heightened by *New Earth*', and does not mention the objective of explaining national policy abroad (*Yomiuri Shinbun* 27.11.1936). Fanck's later proclamation of the footage as his own, made during his 'expedition' to Japan, is in breach of the agreement that allowed him to make his own edition. Other Mantetsu footage somehow found its way into Fanck's version as well: shots of the iconic Asia Express, Mantetsu's pride, and the aforementioned construction sites signified the ultra-modernity to be found and developed in Manchukuo's utopia. The train features heavily in Mantetsu films such as *A Journey Through Manchuria* (Manshū no tabi, 1937), as do the scenes of construction works seen in Fanck's film. The quality of some of these shots of the Manchurian landscape is so dissimilar from the crisp images the former photographer Fanck was known for – and that make the film very attractive visually –

FIGURE 5.15 *'Manchukuo'*.

that there is no question that they were not shot by his crew and with his equipment (Figure 5.15). Yet, no staff of Mantetsu's film division is credited in either Fanck's or Itami's version. While the Manchukuo in *New Earth* and the subsequent short films is authentic by virtue of geographic origin, it is inauthentic in the context of the production that stressed Fanck's direction and Richard Angst's camerawork.

The second appearance of Manchukuo presents us with the exact opposite in terms of authenticity (and optical quality). A cut from the small, 'old' fields of overpopulated Japan to the vast, fertile fields of Manchukuo authenticates the need to find 'new earth', which Teruo's biological father had just explained to the young couple. In Fanck's Manchukuo, Teruo drives the Komatsu tractor, the trailing plough breaking the dark, fertile soil, and a second farmer, also on a tractor, works the land in the background. A soldier guards the young couple and their fellow farmers. The far-away, flat horizon is characteristic of the represented Manchurian landscape, so different from the mountain backdrops of the Japanese landscape as represented in film (High 2003: 267) (Figure 5.16).

Modern technology underscores Teruo's use of his agricultural studies to benefit his country and simultaneously authenticates the Japanese rhetoric about taking advancement into a 'backward region', while also

FIGURE 5.16 *Manchukuo's large, fertile plains.*

resonating with similar German discourses regarding eastwards expansion (Kiernan 2007: 422–3). The visual emphasis on the tractor is also in line with the previously discussed Japanese representation of Manchukuo as 'ultra-modern'. However, taking these corresponding discourses into consideration, this is yet another instance of the film undermining what it was supposed to represent: these vast, fertile fields and advanced agricultural technologies that provided the rationale for leaving 'cramped' Japan were actually *in* Japan, and the soldier stood on a Japanese field. These scenes were shot – by *New Earth*'s production team – on the grounds of 'New Farm' (*Shinkō nōjō*), an agricultural centre established in 1932 for educating selected young people in creating new farmland from wild mountain forests (*Yomiuri Shinbun* 03.10.1990) (Figure 5.17).

Apart from the geographical subversion of the narrative, the representation of utopia is also as inauthentic as it was in Japanese propaganda:

> While the Japanese settlers in Manchuria were frantically trying to learn local cultivation practices from Chinese and Korean farmers, at home settlement propaganda was instructing Japanese farmers of the burning need to go to the new paradise to disseminate superior Japanese farm methods. (Young 1998: 371)

FIGURE 5.17 *The film team (including Fanck, Itami and Kawakita) on location. Cameraman Angst (second row, middle) is wearing a Kwantung army costume.*

Teruo is an unusual agricultural settler, indeed. As Yamato Iwao's adopted son, he would have inherited his (unknown) line of business and considerable wealth, and while émigrés to Manchukuo's urban centres were mainly 'white-collar' administrative staff, the new farmers had usually fled from the destitution in their villages (Young 1998: 45). Yet, on his modern tractor Teruo does precisely what settlement propaganda proclaimed, with the twist that he learned the technology abroad. Thus, in Fanck's target-oriented version, Japan's industrial development is credited to German teachers. The Manchurian subplot reminds us that authenticity is not a value in itself but a means to authenticate positions of power within a given discourse (Moore 2002). The Manchurian landscape in *New Earth* has multiple authors and serves to authenticate culturally specific discourses on territorial claims and technological advancement in two different contexts. In the German reception, the industrial development Japan brings to Manchukuo, therefore, originated in the West, authenticating knowledge about others and ultimately about the self. In its Japanese context, the 'Manchukuo' represented in the two scenes authenticated its image as an 'empire famed for the modernizing activities of Mantetsu and the martial spirits of the Kwantung army' (Young 1998: 51).

Already in Fanck's early vision of the project, following the initial talks with Kawakita and Hack, 'the colonies' were going to play a prominent role

(Fanck 1935). Hack provides the link to Mantetsu, his former employer. For Mantetsu, sharing power in the region with the Kwantung Army, the authorization of their actions was crucial, as evidenced by their advertising campaigns. It is significant in this respect that, during the production of *New Earth*, Mantetsu planned an eventually unrealized co-production of their own. Fanck explains that this was to be a 'film about Genghis Khan', showing 'how hordes from the Asian plains almost raided and conquered Europe; how they lethally threatened Japan; and how they failed, due to the combined forces of German and Polish knights and the bravery of Japanese samurai' (Fanck 1973: 350). It was supposed to rival the best Soviet films, featuring 'fifty-thousand Mongolian horsemen' and reconstructions of the siege engines used by Genghis Khan and Kublai Khan against the walls of Chinese strongholds. This plan emerged out of the same discursive strands that inspired Hayakawa's plan for a film about the Mongolian invasion and the kamikaze, another topic of national pride (Miyao 2007: 253). The first theme of this planned film – Genghis Khan's establishment and extension of the Mongolian Empire and Kublai Khan's two attempted invasions of Japan that were prevented by the 'divine winds' (*kamikaze*) sinking the hostile fleets (1274 and 1281) – echoes a main trope in Fanck's script for *New Earth*: a (Comintern) 'storm' from the middle of Asia breaking on Western and Eastern (Anti-Comintern) rocks. The second motif, the sieges of Chinese strongholds, together with planned landscape shots in the frontier region between China and Manchukuo (i.e. Rèhé), points towards conquest rather than defence. The annexation of Rèhé took place within 'Operation Nekka' (*Nekka sakusen*, 1933) or, in Chinese, the 'Defence of the Great Wall'. The Great Wall became Manchukuo's southern frontier and a point of tension regarding further expansion into northern China (Young 1998: 144). In 1924, Christian pastor Oyabe Zenichirō had published his bestselling book, *Genghis Khan is Minamoto Yoshitsune* (*Jingisu Kan wa Minamoto Yoshitsune nari*), which claimed that the famous general of the twelfth century fled to Mongolia, where he 'became' Temujin, the later Genghis Khan (Inaga 2007: 58–61, 2010: 104–5). The Genghis legend provided the historical precedence of an Asian empire, created and ruled over by a 'Japanese'. When Mantetsu approached Fanck concerning the Genghis Khan film, the legend was part of the militarist-expansionist discourse, and the camels seen in Itami's *New Earth* (taken from *Forbidden Jehol*) and Fanck's shorts, originating in Mantetsu footage, were a popular trope of colonialist imagination, 'full of political connotations' concerning Inner Asia (Inaga 2007: 57). And so was Mantetsu's plan to use film technology to authenticate 'ancient' Japanese claims in the region.

The motifs discussed earlier – Kosugi as 'the Japanese man', Hara as 'the Japanese woman' and the Japanese landscape – converge in an article about the authentic representation of today's Japan in *New Earth*'s two versions: the piece discusses a scene of Teruo and Mitsuko hiking up Mount

Asama (*Yomiuri Shinbun* 06.08.1936): for the 'Japanese version', they *of course* (*mochiron*) wear dashing hiking clothes, whereas for the export versions, which must exude a 'Japanese feeling', they were 'somehow made to wear Japanese-style clothing', in fact highly formal clothing decorated with a family crest (*monpuku*). There is indeed a scene, exclusive to Itami's version, in which Mitsuko looks at a photograph and remembers a happy day with Teruo in the mountains, and they are wearing Western-style hiking clothes. In neither edition do they wear *monpuku* while ascending a mountain, but Itami's version contains a shot showing Teruo and Mitsuko after their wedding, walking down a country road in formal clothing. In any case, the article demonstrates the importance and variance in the views of authenticity in *New Earth*'s critical appraisal: Western-style hiking clothes are considered to be 'natural' for a Japanese audience, whereas a sort of (Self-)Orientalizing seems to be the obvious choice for bringing across a 'Japanese feeling' to the overseas versions and for maintaining an exclusionist sense of national identity vis-à-vis the Other. The article concludes that the two actors dressed in *monpuku* look as if they are on a *michiyuki*: in kabuki or puppet play (*jōruri*), the *michiyuki* (lit. road travel) usually occurs towards the end, hastening the narrative towards its conclusion, often one of the death and rebirth of two doomed lovers. In Noh, *michiyuki* is more literally a (poetic) journey along famous places, the names of which evoked certain associations connected with the play's narrative (Nakanishi 1985; Wells 2002). To the article's author, referring to theatrical conventions, the mise-en-scène looks staged and stylized instead of natural, but this is justified by the need to look 'Japanese' for overseas audiences. The split between 'authentic for us' and 'authentic for them' remains undiscussed.

Itami, however, found too many 'dreams of Japan' in Fanck's script and style of directing and eventually exploded the idea of a co-production by directing his own version, in which he is credited as director following Arnold Fanck. Yet, he had his reservations about the film, and his foreword – between the credits and the first scene – addresses Japanese spectators and positions the film as a foreigner's dream of the Japan 'he came to love' and as one, subjective version of reality (see epigraph at the beginning of book). Temporally close to the release of both films, a journalist asked the important question of why did Itami think it necessary to make his own version (Inui 1937a). The answer is found in the changes he made to specific scenes. These instances of Itami's deviation from Fanck's script show which problems regarding the overseas-directed representation of Japan he wished to address by his intervention.

6

Itami's version of Fanck's dream

Itami's version is lifeless. He merely corrected things that appeared strange to Japanese audiences.

(NHK 1986: 127)

The one who gained an unexpected profit is Fanck. If it wasn't for Itami's 'bad' version [. . .] the German version of New Earth *is clearly inferior to Fanck's usual work. The crude editing does not meet even half of the expectations of people who know* Storm Over Mont Blanc *[. . .].*

(KITAGAWA 1937)

Facing devastating criticism of his film, Itami also countered accusations that it had been edited *entirely* from Fanck's 'NG [no good] shots', material that Fanck rejected, as absurd, but conceded that he used some of Fanck's footage (Itami 1961 [1937]: 245). The idea that the 'Japanese' version was made from the 'waste' of the German edition indicates that it was perceived as inferior, reflecting Japan's distrust of the West: Japan gets the short end of the political and cinematic stick internationally. On the other hand, leaving the material level of the actual footage and coming back to the authenticity of 'Tokyo': where Teruo's sister admires Tokyo's modern buildings in Fanck's film, in Itami's version she and her father merely cross a road with the overhead electricity lines that Fanck rejected as unattractive and detrimental to his vision of Japan as tailored to his target audience. Fanck, on the other hand, was suspicious that Itami changed the script in order to represent 'modern Japan' only (1938: 8). The matter at hand, however, was not one of modern versus non-modern, but one of Fanck's understanding of Japan as well as the image he wished to convey, both issues being partly intertwined in this process of audiovisual cultural translation.

Although Itami's geographical corrections did present a more 'authentic' image of Japan, less irritating for Japanese audiences, the film was intended ultimately for export. The problems associated with the idea of making a Japanese film that would be successful overseas or, taking the argument full circle, a Japanese film that would *first and foremost* be successful overseas resonate with Itami's later arguments against films made for foreign audiences. If films are 'just' excellent, he argues, they have a good chance of also being successful elsewhere, if the 'cultural fence' allows (Itami 1961 [1944]). Itami attempted to come as close to making a 'good film' as possible in the restrictive framework he found himself in, as can be discerned from his statement regarding his impact on the eventual result: 'if anything, it could be said that it is perhaps due to me if the cast's acting is not entirely weird. "Acting", as it relates to Fanck, really is unnatural and odd' (Sawamura 1936: 11). In a translated interview from the early stages of their cooperation, found in Fanck's collection, Itami confirms that he was supposed to conduct most of the directing in order to guarantee the film's narrative and visual authenticity (Itami 1936). Yet, due to the cultural and linguistic gaps, he was not only concerned about his ability to direct according to Fanck's vision but also doubted the possibility to voice his dissent when necessary: Fanck explicitly encouraged Itami to give his opinion but 'not to contradict [him] but to be of use for the script' (Itami 1936). Fanck had 'not yet understood much about Japan' (Itami 1936), and Itami already seemed quite discouraged regarding the enterprise. Contrasting their comments on the project, he was more concerned with cinematic quality and, accordingly, with topics that 'work' in a film, whereas Fanck looked for topics he wished to tackle and convey. Aimed at providing a cross-cut through Japanese contemporary society, similar to what had been attempted in *Nippon* (1932) with regard to 'Japaneseness' as expressed through national history, Fanck's overloading of the film with multiple plots digressed from his characteristically simple story lines and went beyond his scriptwriting skills.

Itami, more skilled in dramaturgical matters, criticized the lack of a straightforward plot (Itami 1936), perhaps also caused by the various changes and interventions into the writing process. He identified 'four or five basic ideas' in the script that he considered unsuitable, while not denying their general 'validity' in the Japanese context. The 'family system', for example, seemed too complex a topic to treat properly in a 'culture-narrative film'. The motif of 'bravery and samurai blood' resonated with Itami as he had dealt with them in his iconoclastic *jidaigeki* films, but the conflation of the two terms in traditionalizing discourses had different implications for the two directors. Itami had staged contemporary sensibilities in *jidaigeki*-times to criticize – not characterize – aspects of contemporary Japan, whereas Fanck was turning this strategy around. Although Itami diplomatically does 'not negate the bravery of the Japanese and samurai blood', he is uncomfortable with using these notions to explain modern Japan, as they threatened yet another anachronistic reading of 'Japan' by foreign viewers (Itami 1936).[1] The most clearly developed motif, he points out, is 'people without space', in terms of 'returning to the soil and honest, rural labour' (Itami 1936). At first glance, even the mentioning of this topic as interesting contradicts Itami's anti-militarist reputation, but regardless of any personal stance, his explanation remains firmly dramaturgical. He also stressed the 'unnaturalness' of Teruo's family situation[2] and was uncomfortable with the stark contrast between the Yamatos' wealth and the Kandas' poverty and with their daughter Hideko's role as a factory girl (Itami 1936). Fanck, maybe in response to Itami, describes Hideko as a 'young girl of today's generation', too proud to let herself be kept by her brother's rich, adoptive family. He constructed Hideko and Mitsuko as two ideal types: 'modern' and 'traditional but adapting to today's requirements' (*Illustrierter Film-Kurier* 1937). Clearly Itami's take on contemporary Japanese society and his recommendation to concentrate on only one main topic would have benefited the film and may have prevented it from turning into a 'picture book' of Japan, also saving it from Goebbels's accusations of 'unbearable' length and loose plot. However, all these motifs remained in the script, and they are also part of Itami's *New Earth*.[3] The question is if and, if so, how he tackled the problems he had identified.

The German release's title *Samurai's Daughter* carries very different connotations from the title of the Fanck's version for Japan and Itami's Japanese–English title *New Earth*. When Mitsuko learns about Teruo's rejection of their betrothal and starts crying silently, her father Iwao admonishes her: 'Mitsuko, aren't you a samurai's daughter (*samurai no musume*)?' This line, significantly, is missing from Itami's version, but in a previous scene in which Iwao and Mitsuko are on their way to meet Teruo. Mitsuko frets over her piano lessons: as in Fanck's version, she says, 'I should have practiced more. The women abroad must be all very good at it!' Fanck then cuts to the next scene, but Itami has Iwao counter her inferiority complex: 'Don't worry. You are a Japanese girl (*nippon no musume*), and you know everything you need to know.' Given Itami's stance towards 'samurai'-related discourses, this

---

[1] One specific example of such readings is the German instrumentalization of the samurai discourse. Reichsführer SS Heinrich Himmler's introduction to Heinz Corazza's book *The Samurai: Honourable and Faithful Knights of the Empire* appropriates traits of 'samurai culture to the SS as a German elite group' (Corazza 1937; see Orbach 2008).

[2] Here and in the earlier drafts, 'Teruo' is named 'Torao'. One possible reason for the change is the semantic closeness of 'Teruo' ('radiant male') to 'Mitsuko' ('shining female'). This nuance certainly did not come from Fanck.

[3] As this chapter is concerned with a comparison of the two versions, in order to avoid a constant repetition of 'Fanck's version' and 'Itami's version', *Samurai's Daughter* and *New Earth* are used instead in some places.

change in dialogue appears significant, and a potential counter against the German title and the associated distortions of contemporary Japan. Yet, as seen in his critical thoughts about the social role of *jidaigeki* (Chapter 3), for Itami, 'samurai bravery' not only was anachronistic, but in the domestic context this anachronism also was related to the heightening militarist discourse that appropriated the samurai image for its purpose.

In both films, Gerda and Teruo talk on the Hotel Europe's rooftop terrace about the necessity of 'marching in step' instead of insisting on one's individual will, reinforced by shots of marching soldiers in the street below. Both versions were shot in slightly different corners of the terrace and in *New Earth*, Gerda looking at the soldiers, states, 'They keep in step very well. In such unity lies Japan's power.' In *Samurai's Daughter* it is Teruo who makes the connection between Japanese achievements and the military after Gerda's nudging him towards this conclusion. Itami here avoided the Japanese character corroborating the ideology behind mass mobilization. This interpretation is corroborated by a change in the dialogue. As the atmosphere on set soured, Fanck became as weary about the endeavour as Itami. He suspected deliberate mistranslations from the German into the Japanese, but Hayashi's translations of the dialogue are correct; judging from other translated texts related to the project, mistranslations were likely due to insufficient skill rather than a deliberate distortion of meaning (Fanck 1938: 8; Hansen 1997a: 40). However, the translation of the German–Japanese into the English–Japanese version is a different matter, and there are a few changes that subtly impact on the message, and to me, indeed, appear deliberate, as with Mitsuko being called a 'daughter of Japan' rather than a 'samurai's daughter' in Itami's version. In the aforementioned rooftop scene, for instance, Gerda lectures Teruo about his reluctance to marry Mitsuko and thus fulfil the conditions of his adoption that, after all, enabled him to embark on his costly studies abroad. Fanck has her link his moral failure to the nation: 'No, my dear. One cannot just shirk one's country's customs so easily. It is not as easy as you think.' Itami, however, brings it down to the more personal level: 'You think that now you are independent and you can ignore your family customs. Oh no, you cannot run away from your duties so easily.' His way of dealing with Fanck's script in his own version was far more nuanced than is often assumed.

Politics of editing

The directors worked in separate editing rooms and according to their idiosyncratic styles. Itami, like Fanck, edited his film himself, but with changing assistants, although the sound editing was partly taken over by Alice Ludwig, who also worked on Fanck's version (Kishi and Nogami 2012: 32–3; Saeki 1987: 163). His emphasis on authenticity extended to his work on the soundtrack, and he always used synchronous recording on set and location, which facilitated the editing of the dialogue scenes as well as the eventual post-recording, while Fanck relied entirely on post-syncing (Kishi and Nogami 2012: 33). It must be pointed out, however, that the sound quality in some sections is very poor, partly due to the rather basic state of sound technology in Japan at the time, but particularly Itami's version. One of the reasons is the actors' poor English pronunciation, and it is unclear why this was not fixed in the post-syncing process. On the other hand, as pointed out by Irie, Itami's sound editing is a sophisticated play with the audiovisual senses: for instance, the 'score accompanying Mitsuko's nightmare sequence becomes the sound of a steam engine and collides with the image of the ship appearing on screen' (1996). Visually, Fanck used various types of transitions, such as dissolves, irises, stars and vertically slanting wipes, whereas Itami exclusively uses dissolves, apart from the final scene's fade-out/fade-in between the Japanese paddy field and the field in Manchuria (1996). The insert shots of Japanese scenery and traditional culture, which for Okumura obscure the relationship of cause and effect in Fanck's narrative (1987), but also clearly resemble and likely echo the Tourism Bureau's campaigns to introduce Japan as an attractive destination, are more numerous in *Samurai's Daughter*. Yet, Itami was 'forced' to cut several hundred feet, as he states, and he inserted the final shots of the soldier in Manchukuo only unwillingly (Itami 1961 [1937]: 246; Kishi and Nogami 2012: 33). These examples demonstrate Itami's lack of complete control on the editing process, but also that the NHK's assessment of Itami's 'lifeless' version as 'merely correcting' some geographical inconsistencies misses the point (1986: 127).

The generally accepted story, based on Richard Angst's statement, is that every scene was shot twice, with the same actors and at the same locations; the staff worked with Fanck in the morning and Itami in the evening (Hansen 2001: 190; High 2003: 161; NHK 1986: 130). Itami, too, declared that 'every shot of the "Japanese version" (international version) was made separately', first because of the different languages used, second because the Japanese financiers wished to keep a print in Japan and third because 'Fanck's way of directing was unsatisfactory to the Japanese' (1961 [1937]: 245). These statements seem to suggest two discrete films, one directed by Itami and the other by Fanck, each based on one script written mainly by Fanck. Consequently, the editing process is underexplored and the existence of 'alien' shots of Manchukuo and shots that look extremely alike is ignored.

Yomota points out the difference in the way that Mitsuko is presented in the two films:

> Hara's first scene [in FV] shows her walking sedately through a Japanese garden, the camera following her and showcasing pagodas and the *torii* in the water. In Itami's version, on the other hand, when Mitsuko hears about Teruo coming back she animatedly throws some fish food ... into

the air. A humorous musical score accompanies a sequence of shots of koi carps and deer. What characterizes Itami's version is . . . the complete indifference to the rhetoric of Nazi-German imagery. (2000: 41–2)

In 1973, however, Fanck remembered that Itami was unhappy about 'a Japanese girl' twirling: 'Itami argued that Hara should not express her joy to such an extent and redid the scene by having her walk more sedately' (342). The eventual selection of shots in the editing processes, of course, was a different matter, and significantly, the two scenes are found in both versions, and thus query the preceding ideological deductions. Mitsuko runs and twirls in both versions (Figure 6.1), which first contradicts Fanck's claim that he used only his own shots, 'apart from when I had made a mistake concerning Japanese customs' (342), and second questions the extent of Itami's control over the directing of actors with regard to Fanck's style being somehow 'unsatisfactory' (1961 [1937]: 245). At least, Itami does not show Mitsuko stumbling into a small bush – likely an outtake that Fanck decided to include in his final edit – and her voice in *New Earth* is slightly calmer and lower in pitch.

Generally, a very close viewing of the films confirms that the vast majority of scenes, and particularly those with actors, use discrete footage.

FIGURE 6.1 *Mitsuko running through the garden.*

FIGURE 6.2 *The globe scene.*

Yet, in many instances the visuals are so similar that only a frame-by-frame comparison reveals slight differences in the position of the head, the eyes or a limb, the movement of costume or the camera angle.[4] At times, scenes shot for one version seem also to have been used in the other version, for instance, in Itami's 'globe scene', where Teruo explains the need to 'cultivate' Manchukuo and uses English-language dubbing for parts of Teruo's lines, breaking with Itami's principle of acoustic authenticity and suggesting that he himself had not shot this scene for inclusion in his version (Figure 6.2.)

Many of the insert shots of landscapes or animals, however, seem to stem from a common stock of footage, from which sometimes different shots were selected. If these minute differences are also due to a controversy about distribution rights, as Itami claims (1961 [1937]: 245), the project at this point certainly does not signify the successful cooperation between newly forged allies, given that the Japanese partners shouldered the lion's share of the exploding costs.

---

[4]Contrary to Angst's account, however, most of the location shooting with Itami must have taken place during the day and not in the evening, given the natural daylight in these scenes and the early sunset in Japan.

The films display a large number of differences, varying in level of degree: Itami realized Fanck's script, as he was supposed to, and of course used English instead of German for the non-Japanese dialogue. But he also twisted some of the material either during shooting or editing – it is impossible to determine, for instance, whether a scene was cut in the editing room or already on set. Furthermore, the way he edited his selection of landscape shots and material from the Mantetsu documentaries into his film results in a very different atmosphere and image of Japan. Three interrelated aspects, namely the relative importance of human characters and the landscape as a character itself; the treatment of militarism and associated ideologies; and what Hayashi termed 'the real' versus 'the symbolic' (1936), are particularly important because of their impact on the two directors' personas, on general categorizations of the project itself and on interpretations of the contested timeframe from which it emerged.

Symbolism versus the real

Itami's more pragmatic approach can be observed in various places throughout the film. Some seemingly simple examples include the characters in his version speaking more Japanese, in particular in the Buddhist priest's speech to Teruo and Father Kanda's talk about Japan's overpopulation, for which Fanck used German voice-over narration, and also Mitsuko's English teacher (played by resident Swiss architect Max Hinder).[5] Gerda, as in Fanck's version, enters Iwao and Mitsuko's hotel room to enquire about Mitsuko's emotional state after Teruo had stated his resistance against their marriage. She explains the reason of her visit in Japanese, but different to her faultless delivery of the sentence in *Samurai's Daughter*, she stumbles over the last part of the sentence and Iwao[6] tells her in English 'That's alright: She [*nodding towards Mitsuko*] also knows some English.' Actress Ruth Eweler genuinely looks nervous before her Japanese dialogue, and it appears that Itami decided to use this blooper. Not only does it make the situation appear more natural regarding the characters' language proficiencies and the respective courtesies towards one's host country and a guest, it also avoids Fanck's symbolic depiction of 'ideal types' and showing them as

---

[5]Hinder sympathized with the National–Socialist regime; he organized a travelling exhibition with the telling title 'Großdeutschland' (Greater Germany) in 1938 (Hack 1996: 93), and propagated 'Japan' as an ally after his move to Germany in 1940 (Bieber 2014: 991–4).
[6]On an amusing side note that demonstrates the perils of a polyglot co-production: Eweler in this scene appears to be very confused about the languages: as she opens the door in the English–Japanese version, she begins speaking in German ('*Oh pardon. Verzeihen Sie.*'), after which Hayakawa replies to her in English. In Fanck's version, she speaks the same German lines, but then squeezes in an 'Excuse me', before beginning her lines in Japanese.

representatives of their countries in the best light. A final example of such seemingly small but impactful changes relates to Fanck's baseless claim that he acquiesced in Itami's mise-en-scène to avoid mistakes in the representation of Japanese customs: Gerda is at the Yamato house, on Iwao's invitation. In Fanck's version, Mitsuko serves them their meal (Figure 6.3), but Itami has the maid serve all three of them, which weakens Fanck's image of Mitsuko as a 'typical, subservient' Japanese girl, and is also a much more realistic depiction of an upper-class household.

The dramatic, twenty-minute-long climax of Teruo rescuing Mitsuko from the volcano was for Fanck and his team an opportunity to play out their strengths and expertise in mountain-film-making, for which they had been invited. Itami, however, again reacted against Fanck's setting up of symbolic traits by adding more authentic but also dramatic nuances. Hansen reiterates conventional readings of Fanck when interpreting the scene's dominant use of extreme long shots of the two protagonists as signifying 'the relationship between people and nature [. . .] in which human will becomes meaningless in the face of the overpowering greatness of the surrounding nature' (1997a: 41). The same convention is still used, often in action movies, to emphasize the obstacles the protagonists are facing, but without diminishing the impression of willpower. The framing here clearly

FIGURE 6.3 *Mitsuko serving dinner.*

shows Fanck's predominant interest in the landscape, but it also stresses the protagonists' mental strength, which drives them up the volcano and back down again. Because the road up the mountain is blocked, Teruo takes a shortcut by swimming through a hot, volcanic lake. He takes off his shoes and subsequently scrambles up the active volcano in his (asbestos) socks. The burns and injuries to his feet are 'symbolic' in that they denote his 'physical proficiency' and 'powerful masculinity' – these were duly noted in Germany (*Steglitzer Anzeiger* 7.4.1937; *Die Wehrmacht* 9.4.1937; cited in Fanck 1938: 73) – and are emphasized voyeuristically by close-ups on his feet and images of smoke and bubbling lava emerging from the rocks (Figure 6.4).

In *New Earth*, Teruo merely wades through a river in his sturdy boots, and it is Mitsuko who throws away her sandals when she finds them cumbersome in the mountainous terrain; they later serve as a useful marker for Teruo to find her. Their strenuous ascent up the mountain, in most parts and unfortunately for both cast and crew, must have been indeed shot twice, showing Itami's opposition to Fanck's symbolic choice of costume. Contrary to expectations, however, Itami's film presents us with the more dramatic climax. Fanck's collection of 'hellish' images of bubbling lava, smoke, vertiginous precipices and upward-tilting camera angles is somewhat at

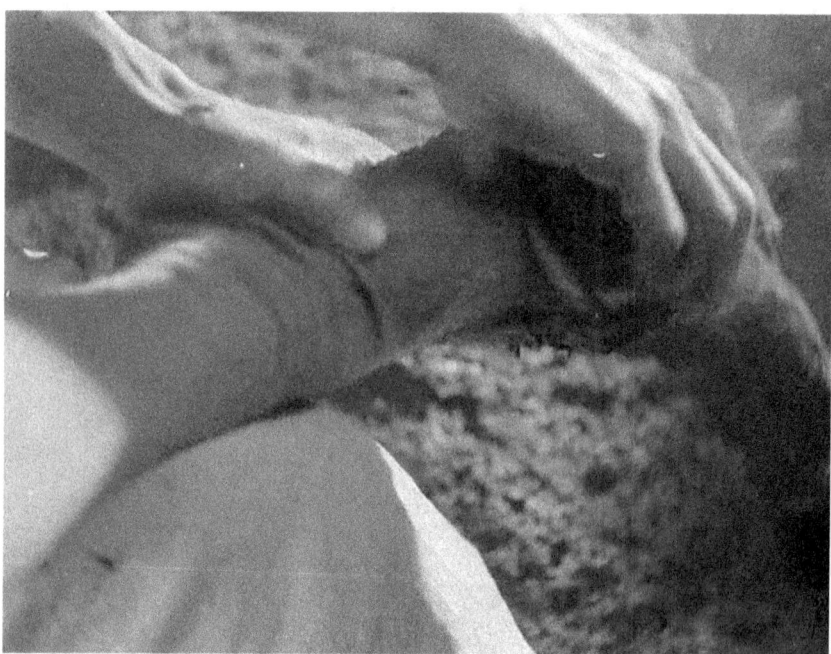

FIGURE 6.4 *Teruo's injured feet.*

odds with the relatively unexciting – even anticlimactic – resolution of Teruo's rescue mission: he approaches Mitsuko and gently puts his hand on her shoulders to turn her around from the crater to face him. Itami, however, more closely follows a conventional narrative, including thrill and suspense. Mitsuko, wearing her wedding kimono, stands at the abyss. She staggers a little, and overlapping images of clouds, smoke, rocks and her face, together with a pivoting camera, evoke a feeling of vertigo. A similar sequence appears earlier in Fanck's version, but by being embedded into Mitsuko's journey up the mountain, rather than the climax at the abyss, it is less dramatic in impact. Itami intensifies the cuts between her face and downward landscape shots (the camera tilting down a crater, a rapid mountain creek and falling cherry petals) by threatening music. A shot of a Buddha (also found in Fanck's version) quickly dissolves into a whirring paper windmill, which is then kaleidoscopically multiplied. The editing here results in a strong feeling of disorientation, reattributed to Mitsuko by a cut to her face. She shuts her eyes, staggers and dramatic music sets in. In the left corner of the frame a figure wearing a kimono briefly flashes up just to fall down the steep mountain face. The camera follows the rapid downward movement, flying down the mountain, amid falling rocks and a small avalanche. This quick dramatic sequence is resolved by a beautiful, serene shot of the empty kimono fluttering through mid-air. A tilt up to the summit where Mitsuko had stood shows only a white towel lying on the rock, which is then later found by Teruo. The following shot reveals Mitsuko lying on a ledge, where Teruo picks her up (Figure 6.5). While her flawless appearance motivated an American reviewer's criticism as unrealistic – 'Volcano ledges in this country are well-padded to insure nice, easy landing. Maybe' (Will 1937) – it nevertheless fits better with the next scene in terms of continuity.

Teruo carries his fiancée down the mountain – a rather mundane but nevertheless arduous feat – and into a mountain hut. When she comes to, the camera pans with her gaze and reveals the dark wedding kimono hanging from a peg on the wall. The next cut shows her looking underneath her blanket, discovering that she wears her under-kimono and, embarrassed, she pulls the blanket up to her face. Teruo, who had been tending to her and stroking her hair while she was unconscious, quickly reassures her that she need not worry about 'that'. This charming scene leads to their emotional reconciliation: Mitsuko tells him about her feelings for him and Teruo breaks down, calling himself an 'idiot'. The scene ends with a close-up of their faces in profile, their noses almost touching. The tenderness in this scene makes the couple appear very human and real. A fade-in presents the conclusion to this subplot: wedding presents are arranged on small trays, accompanied by triumphant music.

For his rescue scene, Fanck combined shots of the couple and the material shot early on of Mount Asama's eruption, to add his signature dramatic mountain rescue amid brutal natural forces. After Mitsuko discovers the

FIGURE 6.5 *Teruo picks up Mitsuko – Itami uses the same shot, minus the superimposition.*

injuries on Teruo's feet, the volcano erupts and causes destruction. Mitsuko appears to have fainted, and Teruo carries her down the mountain while the volcano spews lava and stone, destroying one of Tsuburaya or Asano's miniature farmhouses. Shots of the couple are interrupted by shots of natural disaster, and they barely make it into the hut. Exceptionally, Fanck used Itami's footage of the actors, as indicated by Teruo wearing his boots, but crucially these are in Teruo's dream, as signified by the use of superimpositions and rhythmic editing, reminding one greatly of the protagonist's dream in *Kagami*. These editing decisions result in the action becoming less immediate or 'real'. Moreover, the prominence of nature shots leaves little room for emotions: Fanck ends the scene in the hut earlier than Itami, and consequently the couple does not come as close to one another (Figure 6.6).

The wedding is completely missing from Fanck's edition, which in the light of entire narrative so far being built upon the question whether they would or would not be married disappoints expectations. Rather, he resolves the narrative with Teruo's waking up in a garden and seeing Mitsuko, as a vision of Japaneseness, wearing a kimono and playing the *koto* (Figure 6.7). Itami omits this image of Japanese femininity, seemingly taken straight from a *Yokohama shashin*. Instead, he depicts the newly-weds walking down a country road together.

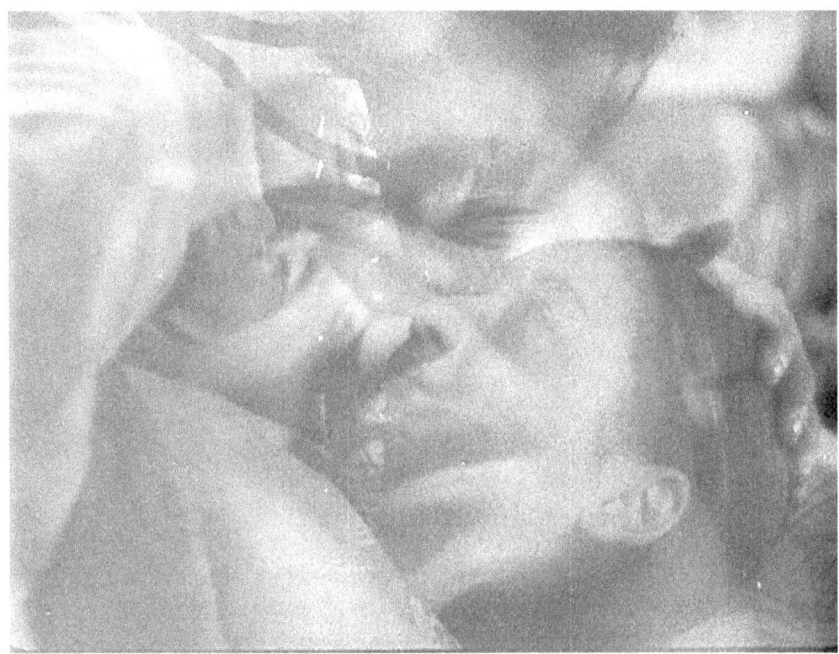

FIGURE 6.6 *Superimpositions signifying Teruo's dream.*

FIGURE 6.7 *Mitsuko playing the* koto.

In summary, Hansen's assertion that Itami's scenes on the volcano are less dramatic does not ring true (1997a: 54). We are dealing with two different kinds of drama. While largely prescribed by Fanck's script, the drama in Itami's edition is based on and revolves around the people; in Fanck's film human emotions take a back seat to nature and symbolism.

Human nature: People and landscapes

In his rather uncharacteristic venting about *New Earth* in December 1936, Itami commented on one main point of difference – and dispute – between himself and Fanck:

> 'The Japanese don't understand mountains.' 'The Japanese can't film the beauty of mountains.' [...] This sort of comment put me off a little. Fanck said: 'To present the mountain's expression in this moment is difficult' whereas I'd have liked to say: 'It is much more difficult to capture a person's expression at a given moment'. I like mountains. People, however, are much more interesting in terms of emotions. (Sawamura 1936: 10)[7]

Disparate emphases on the people actually living within the landscape comprise the main difference between *New Earth* and *Samurai's Daughter*, with the former focusing more on people's lives – despite the titles suggesting otherwise. Therefore, somewhat surprisingly, landscape scenes in Itami's version sometimes are longer and at least as dramatic as in Fanck's, regardless of political or ideological agendas or implications. For Fanck, nature was one of the protagonists, while in Itami's films the action takes place within the landscape naturally. In Itami's *Peerless Patriot*, the defeated Ise no Kami retreats into a mountain forest to hone his skills with a mountain ascetic hermit. By carrying culturally specific connotations of the mountain asceticism (*shugendō*) practised by the *yamabushi* (mountain monks), the landscape here is not entirely neutral, but the mountains are a place, not a character.[8] And this fundamental stylistic difference between the directors – that could have worked either to make a well-rounded film or to doom the project – is visible from the very beginning. Itami's 'bundling together' of the 'picture-postcard shots' that Fanck dispersed throughout his version has been interpreted as a sign of his unhappiness with Fanck's visual emphasis (Yamamoto 2004: 78), and at first glance, it might appear as a stop-gap

---

[7] This statement was also included in a collection of details and rumours, published post-release and critical of the films' quality and the project's political background (Nishimura 1937).
[8] Fanck's visual connotation of 'mountains' and 'the sacred' is not unrelated to the Japanese context. On sacred mountains in Shinto, see for example Earhart (1968; Suzuki 2007).

measure to get them out of the way of his narrative. However, his sequence in the beginning is even longer than Fanck's collage of shots of Mount Fuji, volcanoes and the sea, and it works very well to set the mood for his film.

The opening scene of sunrise over the Inland Sea, accompanied by calm music, is followed by a fisherman bringing his boat ashore. A shot of Mount Fuji glimpsed behind the nets hung up to dry eventually tracks back to reveal men and women sitting around a fire at the beach, underneath the iconic volcano. Itami's cutting between scenes of the 'symbol of Japan' and the lives of the people in its vicinity makes use of the mountain-as-symbol with the potential for different interpretations in different contexts (Bernstein 2008: 59–63). The sequence continues with various images of the national symbol but always brought into context with what actually makes the nation: people living and working in villages at the foot of the mountain. Therefore, Hansen's reading of Fanck's use of the volcano as stereotypical imagery and her observation that Itami used fewer landscape shots in general, and of Mount Fuji in particular, miss this nuance (1997a: 54). In both versions, Mount Fuji appears again in the scene in which Teruo returns home to his birth family. Fanck inserted a shot of pilgrims into the sequence that shows Teruo walking down a country road and looking at the mountain. He is wearing national costume, a kimono for the first time in the film, and the cutting on action between him walking towards the national symbol and the pilgrims also walking away from the camera and towards the mountain, again, is symbolic and makes an ideological statement about the spiritual relationship of 'the Japanese man' to his nation, as signified by the volcano. In his parents' house, Teruo wakes up a changed man 'beneath' Mount Fuji, the dissolve (or 'tear jerker') transition slowing down time to evoke a deep impact on the audience (Figure 6.8).

In *New Earth*, Teruo wears the Western-style clothes appropriate for a modern, educated man, as he walks down the road. A POV shot reveals Mount Fuji, a cut back to Teruo's face shows him affected emotionally, followed by a pan back to the mountain and Teruo walking into the frame, which momentarily combines both man and the symbol of Japan. The pilgrims, however, are omitted and thus Fanck's spiritual component is rejected in favour of human emotion. In both films, Teruo's return to the farm follows and is motivated by his visit to his old Buddhist teacher to consult him about his crisis regarding individual freedom. As the priest Ikkan Oshō lays out the need to relinquish individual desires for the national good, Fanck uses shots of the temple interior and religious symbols, accompanied by a suggestive 'spiritual', percussion-heavy soundtrack. Itami, however, cuts between shots of the two men walking and of Mount Fuji as the symbol for Japan to which Teruo is about to return. Lying down to sleep in his parents' house, he remembers his first view of the mountain, followed by more shots of the volcano. However, and crucially, the overwhelming majority of these show Mount Fuji in the background of people performing farming and manual

FIGURE 6.8 *Teruo waking up beneath Mount Fuji.*

labour. Not only does this echo Itami's exposition scene with its emphasis on people, it also manifests his somewhat obscure interpretation of Fanck's 'people without space motif' as 'the idea of returning to the soil and honest, rural labour' (Itami 1936). For Teruo, this homecoming here is less spiritual than emotional, and it takes place in Japan.

The connection between the landscape and the people within it plays a crucial role in both films, and this motif is firmly initiated in the narrative by the scene of the earthquake at the Kandas' house, after the opening sequence and before we meet Teruo and Gerda on the ship. Again, both versions are very similar in terms of footage. But their impact differs as a result of editing and slightly but significantly altered dialogue. In *New Earth*, the same shot of the sea breaking on rocks that Fanck had used earlier in his exposition is accompanied by the powerful sound of waves. The sound continues after a cut to the interior of the house with Teruo's little sister Emiko sitting in front of a tiered platform (*hina dan*), which houses the dolls for the dolls' festival. In Itami's version, with its witty use of sound, she is holding a little paper boat and moves it back and forth, the sound of waves continuing and matching the toy's motion.[9] Yet, the

---

[9] The boat also appears in Fanck's film, when Emiko asks her mother if 'big brother went away on such a ship?'

sound continues and only through association seems to change with the visuals as the camera pans right, to her father sorting rice, then further to her mother grinding the rice in a mortar. In both films, it is Emiko who makes us aware of the impending danger. In *Samurai's Daughter*, she is kneeling on the floor and turns to see the dolls beginning to shake on their pedestal. Itami, with his focus on human interaction, chose to have her stand in the doorframe, listening to her parents' conversation about Teruo's coming home. A rumbling, clicking sound starts and a cut to the rice-mortar, from which a similar sound had emerged before, shows the rice grains moving slightly. Hansen cites this scene as an example of Itami's rejection of Fanck's stereotypes by depicting the family as frightened during the earthquake, in contrast with the 'Asian stoicism' they display in *Samurai's Daughter*, projecting an image of Japanese bravery in the face of adverse natural forces (1997a: 54–5). Yet, the little girl is just as frightened in both versions and runs into her mother's arms, and her parents' disquieted looks are similar; on the visual level there is no more 'Asian stoicism' in Fanck's than in Itami's version (Figure 6.9). The editing, however, and changes in the dialogue alter the respective meaning made by the two versions concerning the notions of 'samurai bravery' and national character:

FIGURE 6.9 *Little Emiko being scared.*

Cuts between the startled faces, Mrs Kanda exclaiming 'an earthquake' and Mr Kanda repeating the words serve to confirm the danger in both versions, but Fanck breaks the interpersonal connection by insert shots of a picture dangling on the wall and a rack with two swords shaking slightly. Both films then share a take of Emiko standing in the doorframe before running past her father and into her mother's arms, who embraces her tightly. The earthquake sequence in Itami's version is twenty seconds longer and is characterized by rhythmic cutting between shaking and falling objects and the family's frightened faces. It also depicts more damage and eventually, even the wall starts to crack, before – as in Fanck's edition – the dolls tumble. Fanck signifies the end of the earthquake by Mr Kanda's hand steadying the swaying teakettle. He then turns towards his daughter:

> **Kanda Kōsaku (FV):** Emiko, you are great. It was such a strong earthquake, but *you weren't even a bit frightened.*

Itami uses a close-up of Emiko's face as she – still held by her mother – turns and looks at the room and sees the rice in the mortar calming down, as is the music. Her father addresses her:

> **Kanda Kōsaku (IV):** Emiko, you are great. It was such a strong earthquake, but *you didn't cry.*

He thus appreciates that she might have been frightened but did not express her fear through tears, and then distracts her and returns to everyday life by telling her to look after her dolls that have all fallen over. Hence, the family does not appear to be any more stoic in either version, but the emphasis on bravery is absent in Itami's version, which makes the scene seem more ordinary. The impression of 'authenticity' is achieved by focusing on family life and family relationships, rather than emphasizing bravery, more specifically 'samurai-lineage bravery', as indicated in *Samurai's Daughter* by a shot of swords shaking during the earthquake.

Geopolitics: Spatial logic and militaristic expansion

More important in terms of the message of bravery, however, is the transition from this scene to the next, where we meet Teruo and Gerda for the first time on board of the steamship to Japan. In *Samurai's Daughter*, Kanda's message about bravery is underlined, corroborated and generalized by a vertical wipe to Teruo, leaning against the railing and facing the camera. He takes up Kanda's words:

Teruo (FV): To be brave. The Japanese people have been trained to be brave by this country's natural forces. By the many earthquakes, volcanoes, typhoons. A tough environment and little land for so many people.

Gerda stands next to him, listening intently. When Teruo turns to her, he again faces the audience in a close-up, followed by a cut to Gerda's understanding expression. In this scene, Gerda represents the target audience, whom Teruo directly addresses. Itami interrupts the repeated message about Japanese bravery, first by the playful insertion of a close-up of Emiko's paper boat and then by a dissolve from the toy, with its tiny Hinomaru flag stuck on top, to the steamship moving into the frame from the right. Only then do we see Teruo explaining the environmental impact on the national character to Gerda:

Teruo (IV): Yes, volcanoes, earthquakes and [*turning around to look out at the coast*] typhoons have made the Japanese people brave and calm.

Serenity supplements and tempers bravery, and the scarcity of land, which initiates the plot line of 'people without space' is left unmentioned and thus does not set up the plot.

Fanck divided his film into two main acts – followed by a short third act titled 'Manchuria' – through the image of the opposing forces of 'West Wind' and 'East Wind'. These signify the advance of 'tempting' but eventually unsuitable and even destructive influences from the West (Gerda, Western individualism, Western technology and, allusively, the storm of 'Communism') and the advent of restorative, indigenous Eastern currents. The image of east wind and west wind as opposing, ideological forces had been evoked previously in Pearl S. Buck's novel *East Wind: West Wind* (1930), which was published in Germany in 1934. According to Kawakita, the novel inspired Fanck's script with is subjects of an arranged marriage, native traditions and Western influences in China (1966). In Fanck's vision, the left and right side of the frame become geographical markers of 'West' and 'East', as if looking at a map. Hence, the ship from Germany enters the frame from the left, and the smoke from the funnel blows off towards the right when Teruo, in his infatuation with Gerda and 'the West', remarks that the wind just happens to blow from the West. After he told Gerda about his betrothal to Mitsuko and realized his difficult situation, he notices that 'the wind is now coming from the East once again'; the observation being confirmed by a cut to smoke moving right to left (Figure 6.10).

The wind motif, implicitly, is about cultural differences and the impossibility of a relationship between Gerda and Teruo despite their mutual attraction. The metaphorical use of 'east wind' and 'west wind' evokes one of the most

FIGURE 6.10 *Spatial logic.*

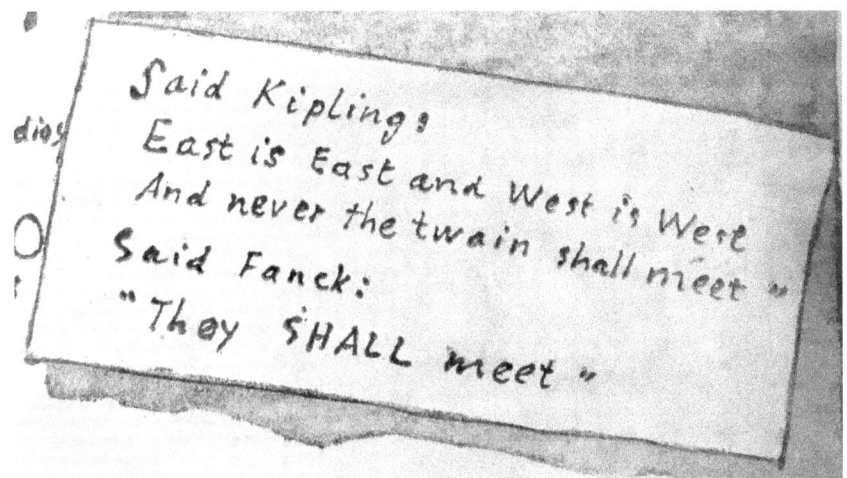

FIGURE 6.11 *A detail from a Tōwa advertisement for 'Japan's premiere* [sic] *export film'.*

memorable, but also 'most misquoted and misunderstood' (Buda 2006: n.p.) line of Kipling's 'Ballade of East and West' (1889): 'Oh, East is East and West is West and never the twain shall meet'. The Japanese producers, interested in a profitable meeting, utilized the maxim – in Kipling's sense and in the spirit of the Anti-Comintern Pact – for their advertising campaign (Figure 6.11), but in the film, the gap appeared insurmountable.

> **Gerda** (IV and FV): East wind and west wind . . . will always blow from different directions.

Itami dismisses the 'hard structuring' through the intertitles, but he kept parts of Fanck's spatial logic, tailored to the American market. Gerda is 'American' and the ship from America enters the frame from the right ('East'), but, strikingly, in the conversation the chimney smoke constantly moves in the 'opposite direction'. The shots are edited in 'the wrong way around', despite the lines referring to 'West' and then 'East' as in Fanck's edition. Either Itami was indifferent, or he introduced this irritation deliberately, possibly to undermine the visual enforcement of spoken messages by demonstrating the arbitrariness of the editing process. Fanck kept his structuring convention of East and West throughout *Samurai's Daughter*; even the national flags that decorate the ship and the protagonists standing beneath them are arranged accordingly (Figure 6.12), Itami adopted the convention, but, contrary to the direction the boat came from, he staged 'America', signified by the Stars and Stripes, on the left and the Japanese flag on the right side of the frame. The War Flag of the Imperial Japanese Army in Fanck's version, perhaps

FIGURE 6.12 *Itami uses the same setting, with the Hakenkreuz and Imperial Army flags replaced by the Stars and Stripes and Hinomaru respectively.*

significantly, is replaced by the national flag, Hinomaru. But in the next shot, Itami uses the same set design as Fanck had, but a long shot as opposed to Fanck's medium shot: Teruo and Gerda suddenly stand beneath the Japanese and the German flag respectively; and hence the flags carry no meaning as towards the protagonists' nationalities. In the second instance prominently displaying the flags, Fanck also uses the Hinomaru, but he also breaks the 180-degree rule in order to maintain his spatial logic, and therefore filmmaking standards in favour of his symbolism: while in the first shot, Teruo had lent against the railing with his back, Gerda and he now face the very same railing, but the 'left' still signals West/Germany (Hakenkreuz) and 'right' equals East/Japan (Hinomaru) (Figure 6.13).

Itami's replacement in the previous scene of the military flag by the national one could have been a mere continuity mistake, as the flags seem to be playing musical chairs in both versions, but an interpretation that links this choice to his critical posture towards the negative qualities associated with militarism is supported by various other changes he made with regard to aggressive expansionism and its ideological foundations. It is unlikely that Fanck was completely conversant with these nuances, but Itami's insider position enabled him to twist the mise-en-scène to have a

FIGURE 6.13 *Fanck violating the 180-degree rule (Itami here uses the Stars and Strips and the Hinomaru, and in a sense keeps the spatial logic).*

subtle effect on possible meanings read from the audiovisual signals. For instance, as *naginata* and *kyūdō* were part of girls' education at the time, together with swimming or gymnastics, Mitsuko's comprehensive education as depicted in Fanck's version seems authentic (Figure 6.14). Itami, however, omitted the *naginata* training from Mitsuko's education towards wifehood (Yamamoto 2004: 78–9). With naginata training becoming compulsory in girls' schools in 1936 in context with 'wartime militarist education' (Bennett 2010: 160), Itami excluded the most ideologically charged aspect from this montage scene.

Neither did he include the most obvious reference to the Anti-Comintern Pact: in Fanck's version, before Gerda leaves Japan, she and Iwao stand on the cliffs, overlooking the stormy sea and the rocky coast, the strong wind providing the background sound (Figure 6.15). Iwao (whose name translates as 'rock') tells Gerda about the 'dangerous storm blow[ing] across the world'. This storm threatens Germany from the East and Japan from the West, and therefore it is clear that it must originate in the Soviet Union as the centrally located eye of the communist hurricane. In the spirit of the newly minted agreement, Iwao tells Gerda to 'convey to your country that here, in the Far East, a nation on its rocky island is keeping watch. This storm will break on its walls'.

FIGURE 6.14 *Shooting the naginata scene.*

FIGURE 6.15 *'A dangerous storm is blowing across the world'.*

The dialogue is visually reinforced by cuts between close-ups on Iwao's solemn expression, Gerda listening intently, and shots of bamboo bending in the wind and of stormy waves breaking on rocks. Fanck had initiated this motif in the first act on the ship, when Teruo tells Gerda about dangerous storms from central Asia having broken on Japanese rocks in the two thousand years of Japanese history. Iwao's later repetition corroborates the message. In Itami's version, Teruo also had alluded to dangerous storms from the continent, but then referred to the Mongolian invasion 'under Genghis Khan' having crashed against the Japanese cliffs. This line has two implications: first, it contains a factual mistake – the invasions took place under Kublai Khan – which, intentionally or not, might have irritated the knowledgeable audience. Assuming Genghis Khan, the 'scourge of Europe' sprung from German imagination, Itami chose not to correct this blunder. Second, the contemporary meaning of these storms is made less allusive and therefore 'subliminal' through a reference to an actual historical event, well-known by the domestic audience. The 'rock scene' is entirely missing from *New Earth* and it appears to have been 'squeezed' into Fanck's film, indicating Fanck's subsequent tailoring of his film towards topical developments and German audiences.

The division into a German–Japanese and an English–Japanese version allowed Fanck to include strong references to Germany in his version, such as Gerda's nationality, the hakenkreuz flag, Mitsuko's German lessons and the use of German music (the hiking song *Der frohe Wandersmann*, 1822, von Eichendorff). Likewise, Itami added a few reference points for a specifically American audience. Some are merely 'translations', such as the use of the Stars and Stripes and Mitsuko's English lessons. There is, however, a more significant digression from Fanck's film and a nod towards America regarding *people without space*, the 'most interesting' of Fanck's ideas (Itami 1961 [1937]). In *Samurai's Daughter*, the theme is centred on Teruo's desire to go to Manchukuo. Looking at a globe with Gerda, he tells her:

> **Teruo** (FV): I'm Japanese, and I want to live for Japan. But look here, this country, Manchukuo [*map of Manchukuo*], is twice as big as your Germany or my Japan [*Manchurian landscape*]. There still is new earth in abundance [*large stubble fields*], which could feed many more people, if it was cultivated properly [*horses pulling a threshing sledge*]. But first, peace and order must be created [*Asia express, plane, boy scouts, soldiers*]. And that is the mission of the Japanese people. We have to perform enormous development work there [*donkey-powered grain mill, construction work, new houses, cars*]. And we will perform it.

Needless to say, this has been discussed as one of the most openly propagandistic elements in the film and understood as backing up the National Socialist 'drive to the East' through inwardly directed Orientalism. The same motif in Itami's version remains unexamined although it makes an even clearer statement to his (American) target audience, as well as coeval Japanese discourse. As in Fanck's version, Teruo explains to Gerda, that Manchukuo is 'twice as big' as Japan; but the rest of his lines are strikingly different.

> **Teruo** (IV): [With] less than half the number of people [*shots of a train and large plains*]. There's work to be done [*plains, train*]. For me, my son and their sons [*Great Wall, villages, people working in fields, shepherds*] . . . but the climate is bad. Cold in winter and hot in summer. We'll pioneer in Manchukuo as the Americans pioneered in California [*farmers working, cultural treasures, temples, monuments*].

This line supports the topical Japanese discourse on expansion by referring to American westward expansion as a model. As Tamanoi points out, Robert Seeley's 1883 book *The Expansion of England*, which theorized various parts of the globe as 'quite empty' and therefore ideal for English colonialization, had become an important text in the Japanese discourse on colonialism after the Russo-Japanese War (2008: 16). At a conference of the Japanese Institute of Oriental Studies in 1935, participants referred to Seeley with regard to the imperial project in Manchukuo, but also to North America as a model empty space for settlement (2008: 17), evoking the Californian myth. Had the film been screened in the United States, it could, at the most, have been imagined to evoke an understanding of Japanese actions through this comparison. The American *Variety*'s reviewer picked up on this negatively, however, criticizing *New Earth* as 'propaganda for both home and domestic consumption. Several spots in the story dwell upon the fact that Japan is very much overpopulated and develops [sic] the idea that Manchuokuo [sic] is a good place to go in for large-scale farming along Western lines' (Will 1937). The Americans had completed their 'expansion', but the Germans were just about to begin. Yet, the idea of a 'manifest destiny' to cultivate the wilderness and the significance of 'California' as a mythical landscape of abundance to be achieved through hard work by the 'right people' are common to all three national contexts. Of course, both German and Japanese nationals had participated in America's endeavour, a history still part of the cultural repository, as seen for instance in Trenker's film *The Emperor of California* (Der Kaiser von Kalifornien, 1935), which ascribes the successful expansion to German abilities. Similarly, as Wald shows, the 'pioneer narrative' narrated the hard work by Japanese immigrant as central to American successful westward expansion (2016: 80–1). For the Japanese, however, 'California' also denoted national humiliation, as the 'paradise' became unobtainable with the California Alien Land Law of 1920, directed against further Japanese immigration. At the same time, it stood for a second chance for national prestige in a second California, as the Law provided reason for many first-generation settlers to leave California and go to Northern China, soon to become Manchukuo, and put their first-hand knowledge to work there (Azuma 2005: 80–2). In the German context, the most blatant example of the monster born out of the union of the manifest destiny discourse, racism and the California myth is found in 1942, in Himmler's 1942 inhuman polemic *Der Untermensch* that legitimates the 'drive to the East': 'Badly used fertile soil that could be a paradise, Europe's California, but in reality, is neglected and desolate' (1942: 2). Yet, the German reviews of *Samurai's Daughter* mention 'living space' directly only about three times in over fifty pages of Fanck's selection of articles, the issue of the individual versus the group taking precedence (Fanck 1938). Following the release of the two *New Earth* in Japan, however, the phrase 'new land' – the connection to the film indicated by parentheses – was used in reports on Japanese 'soldiers of the hoe' leaving for Manchukuo or Brazil (*Asahi Shinbun* 20.06.1937; *Asahi Shinbun* 14.04.1939), which demonstrates the films' participation in ongoing discourses on the empire's expansion.

Itami still slightly changes the implications, as the dialogue alters Teruo's determination to go to Manchukuo towards the more personal motif of creating a new livelihood for his family, which reminds one of Fanck's 1935 idea. What is more striking, however, again is the editing of the Manchukuo scene: many of the shots with actors are more or less identical in both versions, especially in the beginning, when Teruo is driving the tractor and Mitsuko is standing in the field with their baby boy. The musical score by Yamada and with lyrics by Kitahara Hakushū (*Aoi sora mirya*), performed mainly by a male soloist in *Samurai's Daughter* and by a men's choir in *New Earth*, promises a new soil to be discovered by the east wind, somewhere beyond the clouds. In Fanck's version, Teruo and Mitsuko look around and see large, fertile fields and two other Japanese farmers cultivating it with tractors; there is also a shot of the soldier standing on a pile of straw. There is no indication of any 'traditional' manual labour being performed, and hence, the sequence of several tractors ploughing the large, flat, fields with the wide horizon in the background stands in stark contrast with the previous scene of small, terraced paddy fields filled with toiling farmers. It also fits with the discourse on 'construction' and 'cultivation' in a backward region that was initiated in the globe scene. In Itami's edition, however, Teruo's POV shots reveal a very different vista, also reminding us of Itami's version of the globe scene: he turns to the left and sees farmers manually bundling straw. Then he turns to the right, and a sequence of shots shows herds of cattle in broad pastures, flocks of sheep in the mountains, led by a shepherd, Manchurians on horseback and a donkey. The visual impression is vibrant and lively due to the montage of shots with alternating horizontal lines of action. The following sequence shows people winnowing grain and a small, pigtailed child with

FIGURE 6.16 *The 'donkey-mill' in Fanck's version, with the small boy out of frame.*

a bare behind supervising a donkey-operated mill that Fanck had used in his 'globe-scene' to signify the region's backwardness (Figure 6.16). Itami's depiction of Manchukuo reflects a life of everyday farm work rather than the promotional images of the technologically advanced state of affairs in 'utopia'. *New Earth*'s images show what people are actually doing in Teruo's destination; they are less 'symbolic' than Fanck's legitimization of the 'drive to the West' through a juxtaposition of what has to be changed and what has already been achieved. Apart from the burden of a manifest destiny to tame the wilderness, Fanck's version indicates no hardship related to this endeavour. Itami, however, brings up the very real, everyday problem of the extreme climate in Teruo's monologue in the globe scene and also shows hard, manual labour. Because this scene was shot 'according to Itami's script' (Itami 1961 [1937]: 244), and he therefore exerted greater influence than in any other part of the film, it carries specific significance in terms of representational power struggles, and clearly demonstrates his concern with authenticity.

A second, pragmatic problem concerning emigration to Manchukuo was that the land actually belonged to someone else, despite being imagined as 'empty space', ready to be discovered, possessed and cultivated, as expressed in the final scene's musical score. Directly addressing the issue of militarist expansionism, it is unsurprising that most accounts focus on the propaganda inherent in this scene, as personified by the soldier character, to point out the director's ideological differences (e.g. Hansen 1997a: 55). The soldier appears twice in the final scene of *Samurai's Daughter*, once in the montage of vistas of Manchukuo discussed earlier, and then at the very end. In *New Earth*, he merely appears at the end, as a small silhouette, slowly turning his back to the camera and walking away before the screen fades to black. But there is more to this scene than merely the ending: as with the startlingly militaristic final act in *Nippon* (Chapter 1), the 'soldier' appears to be a late, contextually founded addition to the story. In various announcements of the plot, the film ends with Mitsuko laying the baby on the 'soft soil. A ray of brilliant sunshine. The end' (e.g. in *Ōsaka Mainichi Shinbun* 03.08.1936). Since the iconic soldier is a clear reference to military expansion, or a military pact, this supports the idea that Fanck altered the film in response to political developments, and Itami did not, or perhaps differently. It also explains Nogami's statement that Itami inserted the soldier against his will (2012: 33), as he likely planned to end the film according to the script.

Fanck's mise-en-scène follows his logic of the 'left' and 'right' side of the frame as geographical signifiers of 'West' and 'East'. Consequently, the soldier in both his appearances in the scene faces the left, and hence the direction where two 'threats' reside: China and communism (Figure 6.17).

FIGURE 6.17 *The soldier guarding the settlers.*

At the end of the scene – and the film – he turns towards the camera and smiles as he observes the young settler family. The fact that the new soil had to be acquired by force remains unspoken, the soldier protects and guards; he does not conquer. A close-up on his smiling face then shows his expression turning serious; his gaze breaks the fourth wall. This technique addresses the audience, whom he reassures of his steadfastness and determination (to protect the world from communism), the bayonet gleaming in the foreground, as the screen fades to black.

Itami only shows the soldier at the very end. The narrative and spatial relation between him and the protagonists – established through eye-line match cutting in Fanck's film – remains totally ambiguous. A long shot shows Mitsuko and Teruo sitting down and engaging with their child, then a quick dissolve shows a soldier standing on a grassy hill in a distance. The low (or bad) contrast makes his facial expression in this long shot impossible to decipher. And, more importantly, he is situated in the left half of the frame, facing the right. According to the script's logic, this would mean 'East', and therefore 'Japan'. As discussed before, Itami sometimes used this logic in his version, altered to match the different nationalities. For this final scene he either decided to ignore the convention, broke it deliberately or he has the soldier facing 'Japan'. Without further extramedial resources, an interpretation – beyond the soldier's lacking integration into the narrative – would be unsound. A possible direction of such an interpretation, however, is indicated by an earlier scene: at the beginning of both versions, preceding the earthquake, the Kandas receive a telegram with news of Teruo's return to Japan. Mrs Kanda looks at the postman with a concerned expression (Figure 6.18).

> Mrs. Kanda: Oh my, I don't really like telegrams . . .
> Postman (FV): There are good telegrams, too!

We learn that this is, indeed, a 'good telegram', as it brings news of their son's return, but Mrs Kanda's initial reaction remains unclear in Fanck's edition. Itami, however, readdresses the topic in the 'globe scene', following the equation of expansionism to California and to Manchukuo:

> Teruo (IV): Thousands of our People died whilst [. . .]. My own brother died [. . .].
> Gerda (IV): Oh, you had a brother?
> Teruo (IV): Yes, an elder brother. That's why I could be adopted . . .

This alteration of the dialogue is important for two reasons. First, Itami contextualizes Teruo's adoption within his family situation. The later scene of Hideko and her father leaving the hotel after their (undisclosed) disappointing talk with Teruo is the same in both versions: Hideko and her father walk out of the revolving doors, looking dejected (Figure 6.19).

FIGURE 6.18 *Mrs Kanda receives the telegram.*

FIGURE 6.19 *His birth family is disappointed by Teruo's attitude.*

But Itami's version had already shown them at the harbour, intending to greet Teruo. Hideko comes down the boarding ramp of the NYK liner to inform her father that they came in vain, as the ship had arrived early. In her Western-style dress, she then leads her father through modern Tokyo. Teruo's subsequent rejection thus has an even stronger impact. We also understand Hideko's literal 'guiding role' to her father. After the death of the eldest son and Teruo's adoption, she now carries the oldest child's responsibilities to care for her parents, even if this involves the ill-reputed job of a factory girl that Itami had criticized in Fanck's script. Second, Itami adds the most remarkable nuance in terms of 'authenticity' to his version: from Teruo's mentioning of his older brother, we suddenly realize that the Kandas must have received a 'bad' telegram before, possibly about a son *not* coming back to them. It is unclear whether this brother was a soldier at arms, or a 'soldier of the hoe', but this nuance makes one ponder whether the soldier in Itami's final scene is not gazing back towards Japan after all. Itami reminds us that people were actually dying for the conquest; I did not see this nuance being picked up in any of the numerous reviews.

Finally, Itami also rejected the intertitle 'Manchukuo'. He cuts directly from a long shot of farmers working in paddy fields to a grassy plot that is being broken by the Komatsu tractor. Although, in the previous scene, Teruo's birth father had told the newly-weds that 'there is no land for so many people. You two must think about this, too. There are too many people in Japan. There are too many people', the next act could actually take place anywhere: in Hokkaido for instance, or at the agricultural institute where it had been shot. It is only about two minutes into the scene that we get a chance to look around with Teruo and see, among other scenes of agricultural labour, a Manchurian-looking man on horseback and the little bare-bottomed, pigtailed (and therefore 'Chinese-looking') boy, providing geographical markers. Directly after seeing the boy, Teruo decides to place his son into the furrow. His line of dialogue 'You, *too*, shall become a child of this soil' ('*Bōzu omae* mo *tsuchi no ko ni naru yo*') thus makes more sense than in Fanck's version, as – in interplay with the visuals – it connects the baby with the people already living on the land, rather than making him the first generation of manifest destiny. It is perhaps for this very reason that the soldier appears vague and without a specific mission in Itami's final scene.

This idea is supported by Itami's use for the Manchukuo scene of the first and third stanza of the common score, *Aoi sora mirya*, in contrast to the first and second used in Fanck's film. The first stanza is about 'our land' beyond the clouds, which the east wind shall discover. The second one specifically mentions the need to cross the ocean and cover a great distance to find land in abundance, and hence is a clear reference to Manchukuo. In the third stanza, the tractor is rumbling and the east wind shall gaze at our soil: 'You and I are young Japan, and wherever one lives the sun shines high.' While the third stanza used by Itami is by no means 'harmless' in the context of military expansion and agro-colonialism, I find it still significant that Itami skipped the second stanza, whose final lines 'I can already see the wide fields' in Fanck's version provide the acoustic background for a pan from a close-up on Mitsuko to an eye-level match long shot of the soldier. Itami ends the song (after the second stanza) before the visual markers of Manchukuo, thus avoiding the double enforcement of the message by audiovisual signals. The remainder of his final scene is accompanied by instrumental music, which is slowly replaced by the sound of a tractor passing by the young family. The film could, narratively, visually and acoustically have ended here. The following two shots of the soldier have an entirely different, instrumental soundtrack. Not only is the disaccord signified by the sound, but the optical quality is also remarkably incongruous with the otherwise characteristically excellent cinematography by Angst, Riml, Ueda and Staudinger (Figures 6.20 and 6.21). Itami's reported unwillingness to 'add' the soldier manifests in the material: the actor being partially off-frame together with the low-contrast and grainy image suggests perhaps a test roll that was certainly not intended for inclusion in the end product, and not by Itami. Like the soldier facing 'East' instead of 'West', Itami had wanted to give the film a different direction.

FIGURES 6.20 *The first impression of the soldier in Itami's New Earth (Courtesy of the National Film Archive of Japan).*

FIGURE 6.21 *Itami's soldier as a small silhouette in the background (Courtesy of the National Film Archive of Japan).*

Itami's changes are indicative of the various transcultural strands of representational and political ideologies that he reacted against in Fanck's script, albeit within contractual restrictions. He directed and edited his version with a more authentic (to him) and less suggestive symbolic descriptions of contemporary currents in mind, but it is also clear that *New Earth* was not a film he would have author-directed on his own. However, regarding the image of Japan Itami's version projected for international consumption, his twisting of the militaristic aspects discussed earlier was too subtle: *New Earth*'s most important anticipated target market was the United States, and *Variety*'s foreign correspondent remarked on the Manchurian topic and concluded that the Japanese government was involved, 'with the idea of slipping over a hunk of propaganda for both home and foreign consumption' ('Will' 1937). Ultimately, because of the many changes of topics and people involved the films went through, it is difficult to say where Itami actively intervened, and which divergences are due to external influences. A case in point is a scene on the ship to Japan, where Teruo and Gerda admire the impressive technology in the engine room:

> **Gerda** (FV): Wonderful, such a machine! [*louder, over the machinery noise*] Won-der-ful, such a ma-chine!
> **Teruo** (FV): We built it! And woe to our old Nippon, if we had not learned this from you at the very last moment.

In Itami's version, we hear Gerda say: '... these machines ... don't you think so' but the rest of the dialogue is unintelligible; the machinery more or less drones out their voices for about ten seconds. Consequently, the attribution of Japan's modern achievements to Western knowledge is absent here. Yet, it remains unclear whether this was a conscious move on Itami's part. If Yamada Kōsaku had complained that his composition for the climax in Fanck's version had been rendered inaudible by the volcano's rumbling due to the poor sound editing (Daibō 2010: 21–3), the technological problems regarding sound were generally more pronounced in Itami's film. *New Earth* demonstrates that films have multiple authors, and that technology always plays a part as well. And as with the 'confusion' of Genghis Khan and Kublai Khan with regard to the 'divine winds' that saved Japan from Western invasions, it is possible that at some point towards the very end of an overlong, exhausting and frustrating project, some of those involved stopped even caring.

The matter at hand was that different, often competing, versions of reality exist at any given time, and that neither of the two directors was 'free', in the sense of being autonomous. The multiple expectations and agendas piled onto the project were certainly more restrictive and influential than the usual studio- or mountain environments. While the very possibility of capturing an ultimate version of the multi-nuanced and, after all, subjective 'authentic' experience is highly questionable, it is nevertheless fair to say that some approaches are more based in representational traditions than others and can (but not necessarily must) be distorted by Orientalist patterns. It was this distortion and the associated agendas that Itami reacted against when directing and editing a Japanese film for outward projection, according to the original plan, but keeping his domestic audience in mind. The fact that the entire undertaking ended, once more, in disappointment for everyone concerned, however, is not surprising – at least in hindsight. The project's very environment – political, cultural, hierarchical and transnational – and too many expectations and aspirations as towards its effect on the individuals involved, determined its inability to live up to its grandiose proclamations, despite the directors' offering of two visions of Japan's reality in their respective takes on the script. And while various 'images of Japan' are available, as Itami acknowledged in his preface to *New Earth*, not all may be equally valid in a given context. It is this very context that determines which viewpoints are speakable, representable and being received.

7

Repercussions

Coming to terms with *New Earth*

Itami

Japan no longer has peasants. Nor has it poor people. There are only soldiers and the rich, who live in magnificent Western buildings, sit on chairs wearing Western clothes and move only in order to perform some grandiose mission; that is the kind of export films these people talk about. Whoever is able to make such a film might make it. It is impossible for me.

(ITAMI 1961 [1944]): 176)

I get a headache every time I hear the name of that monstrosity.

(ITAMI ABOUT *NEW EARTH* IN HIGH 2003: 162)

Itami's stance regarding the authenticity of the Japan represented on screen was obviously one of the main factors for the project *New Earth* resulting in two distinct films. The preceding quotation stems from an essay on 'Film and national characteristics' (*Eiga to minzokusei*), published in the film journal *Eiga Hyōron* in 1944. Here, Itami reacts to the government's continuing desire for export films to increase Japan's international status, but is strongly opposed to the distortion of lived reality these kinds of films project. *New Earth* played a pivotal role for his evaluation of projects originating in the same 'dream of export', but with an increasing nationalist and militarist twist in the context of the Second World War at its height. Following his experiences with the German–Japanese co-production, Itami was weary towards this use of film for purposes other than intrinsically cinematic.

This already becomes clear in January 1937, in or just after *New Earth*'s final post-production stages. Itami here appears to have recollected himself following his rare outburst in the *Kinema Nyūsu* interview a few weeks prior (Chapter 2). In a newspaper article about *New Earth,* he stresses Fanck's 'strong nerves' that saw the production to an end, a veiled reference to the problems on set. Stating that the film 'certainly is beautiful', even 'too beautiful', and that not much psychological depth was required from Hara in her role as Mitsuko, he also makes clear that this was not a film he would have made himself, but he never attacks Fanck personally (*Ōsaka Mainichi Shinbun* 07.01.1937). In fact, he repeats that despite all problems, the German director always remained friendly and collected, and even in the previous more 'shocking' piece, he makes clear that Fanck 'unlike other foreigners' did not act condescendingly towards his Japanese cast and crew (*Ōsaka Mainichi Shinbun* 07.01.1937; Sawamura 1936). But still, professionally, the project was a disaster. Itami agreed to co-direct for the sake of film export, but was very sceptical following his experience. The best way forward was to concentrate on improving the quality of Japanese films and to just wait for foreign distributors to come forward by themselves: '[With *New Earth*] I have come to be painfully aware of the fact that, if we – just thinking about foreign markets – irrationally produce films directed at foreigners, it will result in the same mess as with the Yokohama shops for foreigners' (*Ōsaka Mainichi Shinbun* 07.01.1937; Sawamura 1936).[1]

But how did *New Earth* impact on Itami's work and his persona? Both directors were, inevitably, strongly involved in this peculiar film and its story. Consequently, the project, its various contexts and political developments interacted not only in the constructions of their personas but also, in certain aspects and on a micro-level, on the popular understanding of this particular slice of history, as becomes clear through a more detailed examination of the film's place in Itami and Fanck's careers.

Itami never directed a film that he had not scripted himself, with this notable exception. And most of his scripts were based on original works by others; out of thirty-four scripts, sixteen were his original work, and out of his signature films, only *Chuji Makes a Name for Himself*. Itami's forte was turning visions into screenplays. That he was a better writer than a director is already apparent in Inagaki's assessment of his first work, *Vicissitudes of Revenge* (Adauchi ruten, 1928), and later in a review of *Frivolous Servant* in 1935 (*Asahi Shinbun* 01.06.1935; Saeki 1987: 166–7). *New Earth* was the only film in his career in which he had almost no control over the material.

---

[1] Itami later once again likened *New Earth* to a 'product from Yokohama', cheaply produced, 'exotic' objects specifically made for export, which were out of line with Japanese aesthetic sensibilities and domestically derided for their low quality, but sold profitably abroad (1961 [1944]).

It is not surprising that he attempted to capitalize on his strengths by writing the alternative, eventually rejected, script. For the Japanese critics, Itami could not compensate for this lack of control with only his directing abilities, and his film never stood on its own. With Fanck's version replacing his, and the overwhelmingly negative reviews, *New Earth* represented a downturn in Itami's career. For instance, Kumagai refused Ufa's offer to co-direct a film in Germany 'because of Itami's example' (Hara 1937d). To dismiss *New Earth* as 'not really his film', therefore, does not do the situation justice. When the introspective Itami states that he 'learned just a little about my own foolishness and that is all there is to it' we ought to take this statement seriously (1961 [1937]: 244). He did not linger on the project, but it became a part of his life and his public persona.

Critical discourse then and now divides Itami's career into pre- and post– *New Earth*, the film a watershed between success and failure.[2] *New Earth* had tapped into contemporary discursive currents and, intentionally or not, an underlying continuity developed in terms of discourse and motifs. In his subsequent works, Itami commented on these motifs by giving them his personal spin. The most obvious change is that *jidaigeki* specialist Itami directed a *gendaigeki* directly after *New Earth*. *Hometown* (Furusato, 1937) was made in a gruelling work schedule under Tōhō's central producer system (Itami 1961 [1937]: 246). Based on the eponymous *shin kabuki* play (1936) by socialist writer Kaneko Yōbun (1893–1985), the film 'depicts the heroine's isolation by her family as she is unable to adapt to the life in her old hometown when returning after her graduation from Women's University in Tokyo' (Kokuritsu Gekijō 1995: 97; *Yomiuri Shinbun* 28.04.1937). This 'social tragedy of an intellectual woman' (*Yomiuri Shinbun* 30.04.1937) takes up the topics of class struggle, gender struggle and of choices made in the light of changing social structures. However, far from merely victimizing Kitako (Natsukawa Shizue) and blaming her 'old-fashioned' family and village, the story is more complex. She goes back to the city and suffers a year of hardships before returning home, but in doing so she has to compromise her worldview (Tsumura 1937). Unlike Teruo's homecoming in *New Earth*, there is no satisfying happy ending. Assuming a link to *New Earth* here is not far-fetched, since *Hometown* was announced as an opportunity for Itami to regain his good name after the debacle (Tsumura 1937; *Asahi Shinbun* 28.03.1937a). Reviewers also referred to the co-production when giving Itami full responsibility for this subsequent failure (Tsumura 1937; *Asahi Shinbun* 28.03.1937a). Seen as lacking in 'poetic sentiment', *Hometown* failed to fulfil expectations. The rural hometown (*furusato*) is a well-used topos of Japanese cultural representation, evoking emotions of belongingness and nostalgia; pre-war examples include Mizoguchi's *A*

---

[2]E.g. Kitagawa (1961: 452; Sharp 2011: 51–3).

Song of Hometown (Furusato no uta, 1925) or *Izu Dancer* (Izu no odoriko, 1933, Gosho) (Wada-Marciano 2008: 24–32). The countryside had also figured as a solution in *New Earth*, when Teruo returns to his birth family's village and back to being 'fully Japanese'. Yet, in *Hometown*, the nostalgia is questionable. Her hometown cannot remedy the problems Kitako encountered in the city. Both topoi are ambivalent, void of a stable, morally superior standpoint. An idealized return to traditions is not easily feasible for the individual. 'Selfish and vain' Kitako (Tsumura 1937) also contrasts starkly to *New Earth*'s Mitsuko, the ideal of Japanese womanhood.

Itami's last film as a director, *The Giant* (Kyojin den, 1938), was one in a row of many adaptations of Victor Hugo' *Les Misérables* (1862), known in Japan as *Ah, No Mercy* (Ā mujō). Hara's star persona as an 'international actress' connects *New Earth* with *The Giant*, as she plays the Cosette character, Chiyo, alongside *jidaigeki* superstar Ōkōchi Denjirō. But 'internationality' became a matter of critical contempt directed at Itami. One critic specifically took umbrage with the 'obnoxiously Western' (*bata kusai*) depiction of the Japanese characters (Tsumura 1938). He charged Itami with disappointing chronotopic expectations: 'after having gone through the trouble of transposing the original work into Japan in terms of place and into the Meiji Period in terms of time, he presents a picture that seems as if the study of crucial things like "Meiji Period" or "the Japanese" has been disregarded in the process of adaptation' (Tsumura 1938). The discussion turned towards the question of authenticity, as it had with Itami's '*gendaigeki* wearing a topknot'. The use of superimposed Japanese subtitles in scenes where Chiyo and her lover, English tutor Seike Ryōma ('Marius', played by Sayama Ryō), converse in English was criticized as affected on Itami's part (Tsumura 1938; 'K' 1938). Hara had already been seen taking English lessons in *New Earth,* and it does not seem unlikely that two lovers would use a foreign language to converse in private, but in 1938, the highly sensitized discourse linked the notion of a foreign language to questions of nationhood. 'Japaneseness' and the characteristics conceived to be exclusive and endemic to it – the 'national character' (*minzokusei*) – loomed large. Itami takes up precisely that issue in his essay 'Film and National Characteristics', linked to the notion of representing this supposed 'national character' to the outside world in political contexts (1961 [1944]). This is also one of his few later, direct references to *New Earth*. His labelling it a 'pitiful example of a mongrel with an indistinct nationality' follows from his understanding of the relation between film and its cultural environment (1961 [1944]: 178). For Itami, 'films that do not reflect the daily life of the nation are not films. Art is a flower growing out of the people's lives.' Art, in this sense, is *descriptive* of its cultural environment. Students of English were part of the Meiji Period, and he depicted two of them. The deliberate tailoring of films towards foreign audiences – as with the 'mongrel' *New Earth* – distorts the reflected image of a national environment, because export films have to scale the 'national fence' (*minzoku no kaki*), a nation's 'distinctive manners, customs and language', the height of which determines the ease of border-crossing. Films 'specifically directed at foreign audiences', in their search for internationality, lose or distort their authenticity (1961 [1944]: 174).

Unsurprisingly, with his understanding of what Japan 'looked like', Itami diverged from the official standpoint as formulated by the Cabinet Information Bureau (*Naikaku jōhō kyoku*), which was concerned with film policies beginning in December 1940. Their 'establishment of national film' (*kokumin eiga no juritsu*) was closely connected to requirements of war and aimed at producing 'national films' to foster a 'strong national spirit' through the depiction of 'central national norms and values' (Salomon 2008: 67–9). As art and film thus came to be considered as *prescriptive*, defining a true state of being Japanese, according to official ideology, the negative evaluation of Itami's work changed in focus. *New Earth* almost acting as a fulcrum, the critical focus shifted from 'historical authenticity' to 'national authenticity', which was discursively reasserted by a recourse to tradition. An interesting instance of this rhetoric in transnational action is found in Tsumura's article in the English-language magazine *The XXth Century*, which was published in Shanghai from 1941 to 1945, financed by the German Foreign Office. Writing about 'sword-fighting plays' starring Ōkōchi, Hasegawa, Kataoka and others, he consequently also addresses Itami's films:

> In spite of the underlying heroism, however, the authorities prohibited the production of such films when they ran too contrary to historical facts. As a result of this, inferior 'sword-fighting films' have disappeared almost entirely, while films dealing with typical events in the history of 'Nippon Bushido', with minute description of customs and manners, are being encouraged. (1942: 437)

At a time in which discourse sought affirmation, raising questions about the prescribed status quo was certainly difficult. When, in 1931, Itami had asked for future films to insist on 'the right things', his vision was far removed from a discourse that sought to mobilize the general public (1961 [1931]: 16).

His forced withdrawal from active directing occurred in 1938, after the release of *The Giant* and a relapse of his tuberculosis during its production (Ōta 1996: 2). Following very negative reviews, Itami 'without a word in protest or in his own defence ... silently retired from the scene' and officially left Tōhō in late 1940 (Nogami 2006: 38). Despite his declining health, he wrote scripts, essays and articles out of a combination of financial need and a desire for writing that can be deduced from the sheer volume of his work. He also commented on the work of young scriptwriters. Hashimoto Shinobu sent him *Rashomon* for his opinion (Yoshimoto 2000: 183), and after Itami's death in 1946, the script went to Kurosawa through Saeki. Although *New Earth* failed to secure international appreciation for Japanese film, Itami was, after all, peripherally involved in a film that succeeded in this goal.

One of his last scripts is *The Life of Muho Matsu* (Muhō Matsu no isshō, 1942), 'one of the finest and most moving films produced during the war years' (Jacoby 2008: 69). Itami had joined Nikkatsu in February 1941, when his condition had slightly improved, and he intended to direct this film himself, as a comeback. When this proved impossible, Inagaki took over and decided to censor the script 'voluntarily', so that it would be released (Ōta 1996: 3–5). Still, a mutual attraction between the uncultivated rickshaw puller Matsugurō and the widow of an officer of the imperial army had to remain unthinkable, and those scenes, among others, were deleted during post-production censorship. Itami's premonition that this 'was not the best material for the *zeitgeist*' proved true (1961 [1941]a: 249). Films had been officially declared as *dangan* (bullets) in the service of the war effort in 1941 (Ōta1995: 6), and these 'bullets' were not to be used to question ideals. In 1943, when *Muho Matsu* was first released, Itami wrote a forceful piece condemning the wartime government as incompetent and the war itself as foolish (1961 [1943]: 182). In the light of the lives already lost, he urged politicians to use diplomatic measures to end the war. Itami's script for *Dare Your Life* (Fushaku shinmyō) was another daring, non-conformist choice of material, based on the eponymous novel (1939) by Yamamoto Yūzō (Itami 1961 [1941]b). Itami made it into a *jidaigeki* on the Shimabara Rebellion (1637–38), a mostly peasant uprising against abusive superiors (Harrington 2013). According to Hirano, the portrayal of the horrors of war, of an ideology that drives people to their death and of the average person's unwillingness to fight the hopeless war of their superiors led to its banning (2001: 225). Considering the commotion around *Muho Matsu*, the banning of *Dare Your Life*, of *Cotton Version of the Record of Great Peace* (Momen taiheiki) and of the essay discussed earlier, all within two years, Itami's description of his work as 'not the best material for the *zeitgeist*' was a conscious decision with regard to his artistic integrity.

Reconsidering the assessment of *New Earth* as the immediate cause of the 'pathetic' end of Itami's career (High 2003: 158), it now appears as an accelerator rather than a generator. The interplay of various factors was responsible for the downturn. First, Itami's tuberculosis often impeded is work. Already in 1929 Inagaki took over the second part of *Hell of Ten Thousand Flowers 2* (Zoku manka jigoku, 1929) and *A Samurai's Career* (Ehon musha shugyō, 1929) due to 'serious health issues' (Kishi 1953: 199; Tomita 1997: 69). Hence, Itami's relinquishing his work on set of *New Earth* to his assistant director Saeki – often interpreted as his psychological withdrawal from the project is neither unprecedented nor surprising considering the physical strains of climbing steep mountains

FIGURE 7.1 *Angst, Itami and Staudinger shooting on location.*

and shooting in extreme heat (Figure 7.1). Second, *New Earth* had severely restricted Itami as an 'author-director', foreshadowing subsequent developments. Itami registered his disapproval of the shift towards a producer system that curbed the directors' powers, relegating them from 'supervisors' (*kantoku*) to *metteurs en scène* (*enshutsu*) as in his work on *Hometown* (Satō 2001: 105–6; Itami 1961 [1937]). Third, his take on things clashed with the *zeitgeist*. The discourse Itami excelled in, the witty questioning and deconstruction of tropes of cultural representation, had broken down in favour of more assertive images.

Itami's critical stance towards the wartime regime, best represented in his 1946 essay on wartime responsibility, is prominent in assessing his reputation – also with regard to *New Earth*. In contrast to other directors, his health prevented him from being drafted into the army or more actively into mass mobilization measures, and his early death in 1946, at a critical juncture between two ideological systems, facilitates the shaping of his persona and it being editing out of the wartime narrative. In his obituary in the *Yomiuri Shinbun*, the by now problematic *New Earth* was still listed among his 'representative works' (25.09.1946). Yet, within a few weeks, the editorial intervention into his persona began: the Occupation censors deleted from a *tanka* (Japanese verse form in five lines and thirty-one syllables) from an essay on Itami, dating from 1942. Itami here expressed a surprisingly pro-war attitude (Hirano 2001: 230–1). The poem could have been seen as detrimental to the Occupation authorities' re-education efforts and to Itami's persona as a positive, reinforcing example of a moralist, following his essay on wartime responsibility. And neither the *tanka* nor a postcard text with a similar thrust published in *Eiga Hyōron* in January 1942 (Salomon 2011: 170) is included in the collection of his works (Itami 1961, 1971).

New Earth plays a pivotal role in the construction and assessment of Itami's persona, either as a memory to be repressed or as an instance of victimization, which culminates in scholarly discourse that considers the ordeal of his cooperation with Fanck responsible for his final collapse in 1938 and, by implication, his death in 1946 (e.g. High 2003: 163). Conversely, Saeki attributes the ensuing bout of tuberculosis to the skiing trip they took after having finished editing *New Earth* (Saeki 1987: 163), possibly another reason for Itami's absence from the premiere. Still, the a posteriori linking of the end of his career and his death to this unpopular part of Itami's oeuvre seems to cement the dichotomy of victim and perpetrator, and runs counter to Itami's own emphasis on the importance of taking responsibility for one's actions. Seen within Itami's oeuvre as a director, screenwriter, critic and essayist, it emerges as a positive instance rather than a problematic moment. It would have been easy to join the bandwagon of 'national policy films', especially after *New Earth* had been contextualized with the Anti-Comintern Pact. Also, his later, puzzling statements are coherent: once a war has broken out, even a pacifist at heart may wish for his country to win for various reasons, fear of the devastating consequences of a loss being one of them (Saeki 1987: 208). Itami's position may not necessarily have been anti-war, but, as expressed in his 'nonsense films', he took a continuous stance against authority for authority's sake.

New Earth originally represented an interlude in Itami's overall oeuvre, outwardly in terms of genre and of shared directorial authority, but more significantly, in dealing with a definite, assertive description of a homogenized national entity. Eventually it turned into a rupture. Like his three final films, *New Earth* had been criticized as lifeless, a judgement that continued well into the post-war period (e.g. Kishi 1974: 38). This assessment implies Itami's emotional detachment from the project and its product, but perhaps misses the point. As his mid-production diary entry shows, Itami was disillusioned, indeed:

> On your way to work in the morning, when you come to a place where the entire studio can be seen at a glance, stop for a moment and think about this: Within that small arena, a whole lot of people are running around making a big fuss. How silly! When you understand the silliness of it all, your spirit can stand still while only your body goes on into the studio. (Itami's journal entry of 11.09.1936; cited in Nogami 2006: 44)

Yet, he nevertheless applied himself to depicting in his version something closer to how he understood the reality of 'Japan' in 1936 that this film, after all, was supposed to reflect and project.

Fanck

The film's premiere in Berlin ... conveyed strong impressions, because it illustrates vividly this great East Asian nation's healthy attitude towards the concepts of blood, soil, nation, family.

(*BERLINER MORGENPOST*, 25.3.37; CITED IN FANCK 1938: 28)

What is this 'Blood and Soil' actually supposed to mean? I never got it. . . . In short: The Japanese weren't National Socialists of course. . . . Every farmer in the world is attached to his earth, to his soil. What's that got to do with National Socialism? This is just plain stupid! It is a farmer's connection to the ground. . . . Well, of course I've heard the expression 'Blood and Soil' but I never understood the meaning.

(FANCK; CITED IN WEIGEL 1976: 28)

In Fanck's case, the attempt for a more nuanced approach is more complicated, not least because he put himself openly and consciously at the forefront of the film project and within a decidedly political context. When he arrived in Japan, he stressed, 'I want to film the spirit of mountain-secluded Japan, and introduce the real Japan throughout the West. The German Nazi spirit (*nachi seishin*) is an ideal formed out of synthesis with Fichtean philosophy,[3] and it seems to me that this matches ideally with the Japanese spirit' (*Ōsaka Nichinichi Shinbun* 09.02.1936). This statement invites various interpretations, but it appears to me that Fanck here – on his first official day in Japan – presents himself as a man with an important mission and as a representative of his country. The fostering of goodwill for his film-making mission through the evocation of a kindred mentality does not seem out of the ordinary, bearing in mind that 'Nazi' was the regular term used for 'National Socialist' or even 'Germany' by the Japanese

---

[3] Johann Gottlieb Fichte (1762–1814) was one of the founders of German idealism and greatly influenced by Kant. His *Addresses to the German Nation* (Rede an die deutsche Nation, 1806) aimed at defining the very German nation and was crucial in the uprising against Napoleon, but also inspired German nationalism and ideas of ethnic superiority for decades to come (see McGuire 1976). In 1933, Leni Riefenstahl, on Fanck's suggestion, presented Hitler with the first edition of Fichte's collected works (Ryback 2008: 100–4). Despite not being the most influential on Hitler's ideology, Fichte played a prominent part, as the volumes' well-read state suggests (Ryback 2008: 100–4).

media, rather than by Fanck. He had been invited to understand, culturally translate and represent the Japanese spirit, and his speech is geared towards this aspect. On the other hand, a close observation of his statements made in very different circumstances, for instance in 1935, before the production began, in 1937 and 1938 following *New Earth*'s release and the conclusion of the Anti-Comintern Pact, and in the 1960s, when he narrated his own life in his autobiography, shows poignant fluctuations and contradictions. When Fanck worked on the film and took up topics of popular and national interest, he increased his power position in the discourse that circulated and was enforced by these topics. In the particular frameworks of Japan and Germany in the mid-1930s, to keep a foothold in an increasingly state-controlled industry meant to be involved in ideologically informed power structures. After 1945, despite several personal and structural continuities, a changed discursive environment demanded different manoeuvrings. By observing the flows of arguments, claims, contradictions and positions taken in his utterances, we are able to discern, rather than his 'true' intentions, the very volatility of these positions. Before this more unstable background, what questions was *New Earth* (or *Samurai's Daughter* in the German context) supposed to answer for Fanck and how did it impact on his career and persona?

The plain reason given by his widow for his taking on the project are financial difficulties (Hansen 1997a: 47). Fanck was unable to keep to a budget, constantly acquiring and selling artwork and valuable books, depending on the fluctuations of his assets (Horak 1997b: 7). It is no coincidence that he cites 'artistic freedom' from financial concerns as the 'most pressing problems of German film' in 1933 (Fanck 1997 [1933]). Fanck strove towards – and regarded himself as – his ideal of the author-director who 'not merely stages another's ideas and thoughts' (Fanck 1997 [1933]). This (head-)strong vision was also the reason for his clash with Itami over the represented image of Japan. Hayashi retrospectively described Fanck as 'headstrong and wilful' and mentioned a nickname Fanck was given – presumably behind his back – by his Japanese crew: *Panku* (flat tyre), likely referring to the problem of getting things 'rolling' due to Fanck's stubbornness (Hayashi 1978: 50). His strong authorial vision and personal style made his films clearly distinguishable, but at the same time impeded his work

Fanck had always been working on the 'periphery of the mainstream film industry' (Bock and Bergfelder 2006: 116), partly due to his independent character, but also because he was known to wait for hours or days for particular cloud formations, lighting or snowfall, and few producers were willing to spend vast amounts of time and money for films with little plot and without proper scripts. For Steiner Daviau, Fanck's later 'freezing out' as a director was not primarily politically motivated, but due to the high cost of his productions and the fact that 'months of shooting in the mountains, far away from any control was intolerable for Goebbels'

(2002: 128). In his 1973 account, Fanck makes the political context responsible for the collapse of his career and argues that he was sidelined because he initially rejected party membership (1973: 317). He also cites *The Eternal Dream* (Der ewige Traum, 1934) as the first instance of direct, ideologically founded hostility. According to Fanck, Goebbels disliked the idea of a heroic, French and therefore 'non-German', protagonist ascending a French mountain (1973: 321–2). Moreover, the production company Cine-Allianz was jointly owned by two Jewish business partners, one of them, Gregor Rabinowitsch, apparently a pet-enemy of Goebbels (Prawer 2005: 98). Fanck insinuates that consequently the film had almost no advertising and ran only in some theatres: 'My most beautiful and accomplished film thus remained almost unknown' (1973: 317– 18). Goebbels, however, remarks on 21 October 1934: '*Eternal Dream*. A magnificent mountain film by Fanck' (2006b: 123). This assessment does not sound very hostile, but to try and discern objective truths and falsehoods in these various statements is futile. It is more productive to notice the author taking both an external and an internalized point of view: Fanck points the camera at himself.

Fanck argues that he was financially distraught after Goebbels blocked *The Sinking of the Sisto* because of its 'pacifist message' of five nationalities working together to rescue the crew; and this was just when Kawakita approached him (Fanck 1973: 328–9). And in Japan, he remembers, it was 'quite dangerous' for him to meet Jewish director Joseph von Sternberg as he visited the resort town Karuizawa (Figure 7.2). Ambassador Dirksen,[4] 'a very fine man and anti-Nazi', told him to keep the meeting secret, but after predictable press attention, Fanck was ordered to the NSDAP's Japan branch; he claims he did not go (Fanck 1976: 10).

In the light of a letter to his mother in which Fanck praises Hitler for fulfilling Fichte's nationalist philosophical ideals, his decision to remain 'unorganized', at least initially, was not primarily out of ideological opposition (Horak 1997a: 34). Asked in 1973 why he did not leave the country after 1933, like many of his colleagues, Fanck's answer reveals a long period of working through memory to arrive at a tolerable version of the past:

---

[4]Incidentally, Japan's 'first foreign co-production of the postwar period' (Sharp 2017), partly originated in this visit. Sternberg saw Fanck's total control over the project, something he aspired to for his own work (Mizuno 2009: 13). In 1953, with Kawakita and Ōsawa reinstated, the two producers Sternberg and Tsuburaya Eiji came together once more and repeated history: *The Saga of Anatahan* (Anatahan, 1953, Sternberg) was planned both as a revival of Sternberg's troubled career and to disseminate an 'accurate image' of Japan. Ultimately, according to Mizuno's account of the production, they could not agree on this authentic image (Mizuno 2009: 19). Supposed to be released in various countries, *Anatahan* was re-edited two times for different target audiences (Mizuno 2009: 19).

I think in democratic terms. The National Socialists were voted for by the outright majority, ninety per cent even, a fact that is not considered anymore today. What else was I supposed to do? No. Had the communists won, I had thought the same way: I have to abide; they hold the majority. I am no revolutionary who stands on barricades and does pointless things. (Fanck 1976: 23–4)

Regardless of his own political or ideological convictions, like everybody else in the new regime, Fanck had to appeal to the powers that be in order to have a chance of reviving his career. *Bergfilm*, as he understood it, and himself as its originator, was at its end. By 1935 he had not 'author-directed' a film since *The Eternal Dream* (1934). Two subsequent ideas remained unmade: *Avalanche* (Die Lawine) and *The Sinking of the Sisto*, the latter not even a mountain film. Trenker and Riefenstahl developed the style into new directions, and in 1935 Fanck declared his 'alpine film oeuvre' to be over (Fanck 1997 [1935]). Still, given the emigration of talent at the time, it is surprising that 'one of the commercially most successful directors of the Weimar Period' (Horak 1997b: 7) had to go to Japan to make his next film, vying for funding, as seen in his earliest article concerning the project (Fanck 1935). In this article, Fanck compares his new project to *Condottieri* (1937),

FIGURE 7.2 *The meeting in Karuizawa. Left to right: Max Hinder (?), Fanck, Itami, Sternberg, Hara.*

a planned German–Italian co-production about the Italian national hero Giovanni de Medici (1498–1526), initiated by the Italian government and to be co-directed by and starring his former pupil, Luis Trenker (Bock and Bergfelder 2006: 480–1). Trenker's success in obtaining state support for a German–Italian co-production provided a reason for Fanck to expect help for his own endeavour. When it premiered in Stuttgart on 24 March 1937, the day after *Samurai's Daughter*'s gala premiere, *Condottieri* received more attention in the press (*Film-Kurier* 1937d). It was also given the same rating as *Samurai's Daughter* and was voted 'Best Film Representing Natural Beauty and Artistic Treasures' in the Biennale of 1937. Most reviewers, however, 'found *Condottieri* strong on visuals but weak on plot', and it was banned in 1945 (Baskins 2011: 182). Trenker's earlier plagiarizing of one of Fanck's scripts for his own *Mountains in Flames* (Berge in Flammen, 1931) had caused a latent rivalry between them, probably also due to Fanck's falling fortunes, whereas Trenker seemed to be on the rise. After the war, Trenker managed to return to and attract public interest as an expert on things alpine, something his former mentor had aspired to but failed to achieve, a comparison that might help to explain Fanck's acrimonious and vehement 'corrections' of his public image in 1973.

The career of Fanck's other 'disciple', Leni Riefenstahl, is as legendary as it is contentious. When Fanck wrote his first announcement of his new project in Japan, the state-commissioned *Triumph of the Will* had already been released and highly awarded. While Fanck was in Japan, Riefenstahl made her monumental series about the Olympic Games of 1936, which won the highest national and several international awards. Having himself directed a film on the Winter Olympics in 1928 (*The White Stadium*), Fanck was surpassed by Riefenstahl and by Trenker. He was also bypassed by new developments and trends:

> In an attempt to control the articulation of fictional worlds, only a small proportion of films were shot outdoors or on location. Directors functioned above all as facilitators, not as distinctive auteurs. Film was to be artful and accessible, not intellectual or esoteric. Features of the Third Reich favoured carefully crafted artificial realms and showed a predilection for studio spaces, costume design and script logic. (Rentschler 2002: 141–2)

Time was over for the pioneer of mountain films. Ultimately, his work and persona no longer resonated with the current atmosphere.

In this light, it is interesting to note that his opportunistic tendencies strengthened during and after the making of *New Earth*, which supports the theory of opportunism rather than targeted intentions from the onset: in a press conference before the Berlin premiere, Fanck claimed that he went to Japan to obtain beneficial input for Germany with regard to 'ideals', such as the leader principle (1937c). And indeed, apart from motifs in the film that can be partly explained through the processes of resemblance and recognition in cultural translations (see Chapter 4), there are two blatant instances in his version's dialogue and mise-en-scène. Teruo explains his adoption to Gerda, the journalist and stand-in for the German audience, as follows: 'So that the ancestral line may not break. The blood must be maintained'. And Gerda, taking notes, remarks, 'A nice custom! This will be particularly interesting for us'. Teruo's explanation does not make much sense regarding his adaptation and betrothal to Mitsuko, but fits neatly into the German exclusionist discourse on ancestry based on blood and race (see also Chapter 4). Gerda's subliminally muttered side-remark regarding the usefulness of this 'Japanese ideal' for Germany supports the ideology in the film's target environment, and equally was supposed to improve Fanck's position. Without the need to address the German discourse, Itami's dialogue is strikingly different and an appropriate or authentic representation of this particular costume of adopting 'son-in-laws': 'So that the family name may not stop'. Gerda merely says, 'Fine custom, very interesting'. Visually, Fanck's aim to fit himself and the film into the ideological currents is best seen in the scene of Teruo's visit to the Buddhist temple: as Teruo and the priest Ikkan Oshō walk to the temple, a long shot shows the building surrounded by a fence constructed of *manji* (swastika) symbols, alternately left- and right facing (*omote manji*, representing 'infinite mercy' and *ura manji*, representing 'intellect and strength') (Figure 7.3). It almost goes without saying that the

FIGURE 7.3 *The* manji *fence.*

FIGURE 7.4 *A close-up shot of Teruo.*

following close-up on the priest as he begins his speech about the national community taking precedence over the individual, and on Teruo listening thoughtfully, are taken before the background of the National Socialist–appropriated right-facing swastika, or hooked cross (*hakenkreuz*) to firmly link the message to the German context (Figure 7.4).[5] It is at this point, I argue, that Fanck lacked professional respect for the Japanese objectives in the endeavour, and had the German target discourse take over. At the press conference, Fanck made the connection of his film and the current ideology unambiguous, as he explained 'harakiri' as the highest manifestation of heroism: the process consisting of 'slitting one's entire belly and intestines (by the way, in the shape of a *hakenkreuz*)' (1937c: 13). This and other topics are not found in the film because he 'only understood [their relevance] during his work in Japan' (1937c: 14). The opportunism discerned in his persona as constructed by his vita and writings is problematic, and it appears to be founded in a desire to be recognized for what he saw himself to be, but within adverse circumstances.

---

[5]Ironically, Fanck links the priest's message to 'Shinto', despite the scene taking place in a Buddhist temple. This is another instance of insufficient awareness regarding the 'original' as well as the objective taking precedence over the source context.

None of Fanck's films before *New Earth* contain openly political allusions, despite his personal convictions that may have included aspects of national (not necessarily nationalist) and *völkisch* thoughts. Regarding the film's original title, *People Without Space*, it stands to reason that this choice of topic stemming from Fanck's ideas for the script before his arrival in Japan was related to Hack's position as co-president of the German–Japanese Society and his lobbying for sympathy for Japanese actions in Manchuria after 1931 (see Chapter 1). Furthermore, one of the paramount goals for Kawakita and his partners was not to repeat a clichéd 'Madame Butterfly story'. In this sense, to pick up a very contemporary topic that at the same time resonated with the global discourse, specifically of course in the two contracting countries, Japan and Germany, seemed to be the way forward, and the eventual product addresses this very issue. Therefore, for Fanck, this film and his subsequent comments also became a decisive step taken on his career path in National Socialist Germany. On the other hand, to relegate part of his auteurial power to the 'politically dictated subject matter' he points out in the film in 1938 went against his principles, and as seen from the abundant landscape shots, the master of mountain film eventually got the better of him, which might also explain his overt placing of *Samurai's Daughter* into the hegemonic ideology after his return. A reviewer for *Der Deutsche Film* duly identified the 'overlong' second part of Teruo rescuing Mitsuko from the volcano as Fanck's tour de force, displaying his 'bravura' even when detrimental to the film (*Der Deutsche Film* 1937); contradicting comments in Japan implying that these shots disguise the ideological content (Hansen 1997a: 67). Goebbels criticized these scenes and did not award the film the highest rating of 'politically and artistically especially valuable'.

In the following, Fanck made several short films from the footage collected in Japan, but, for a prolific film director with an impressive career in terms of critical acclaim and output, his career faltered remarkably. His star kept descending despite the 'propaganda piece' *Samurai's Daughter* and the evaluation of his camera style as 'markedly German' in a meeting of the Reich Film Chamber in 1937 (Horak 1997a: 59). From 1938 to 1939, he directed Bavaria Studio's *A German Robinson* (1940) in South America, but claims to have been assigned his unit production manager 'for political surveillance' and complains about rigorous cuttings, which indicates that he had lost control over his work (Fanck 1973: 147). The film was banned after the war, yet Brandlmeier argues that it was 'one of those propaganda films that constantly undermined themselves ... much to Goebbels's displeasure' (2008: 223), a response that not only explains the post-production changes but also Fanck's falling into oblivion as a feature film director. Eventually, he made two culture films for Riefenstahl-Film GmbH, *Josef Thorak* (1943) and *Arnold Breker* (1944), edited from material initially produced on commission by Albert Speer's agency 'Generalbauinspektor Berlin' for

The Führer Constructs His Capital (*Der Führer baut seine Hauptstadt*), (Kropp 2009: 109). Riefenstahl's company was not under the Propaganda Ministry's command but associated with *Braunes Haus* (Brown House), the NSDAP's national headquarters. Hence, neither Fanck nor Riefenstahl directly worked under Goebbels, both citing personal conflicts as the reason (Horak 1997a: 38; Riefenstahl 1994 [1987]: 280). Fanck earned well during this employment: 4,000 Reichsmark per month was almost twice the average wage of a worker in 1940 (Horak 1997a: 48; Bundesministerium der Justiz 2011). On April Fool's day 1940, he finally joined the NSDAP – for the Riefenstahl-Film assignments according to Zimmermann (2005: 515), or 'out of opportunism', as Steiner Daviau claims (2002: 128). These two reasons do not contradict one another, but despite these steps, Fanck never made another film.

After the war, several of his films were banned under category C of the 'Principles for Inter-Allied Censorship of German Film' by the Allied Information Committee (Short 1996: xi): *A German Robinson* was described as 'National Socialist Propaganda', the précis repeating the usual split of form and content: 'Excellent shots of Chile, Patagonia and Tierra del Fuego made by the 1939 Fanck Film Expedition, story "hammy" and full of propaganda' (Kelson 1996: 17). *Arno Breker* and *Joseph Thorak* fell under 'Nazi Art Propaganda' (Kelson 1996: 142–3). The short *Winter Journey Through Southern Manchuria* (Winterreise durch Südmandschurien, 1938) is categorized as a 'Japanese film': 'Average production and photography, propaganda' (Kelson 1996: 147–8). *Samurai's Daughter* is also listed as a Japanese film, with 'strong nationalist Japanese propaganda' (Kelson 1996: 69). Its current association with German propaganda was not self-evident in 1945. Horak argues that Fanck's post-war failure to revive his career was due to a large part to the 'post-war German film industry [consisting] almost entirely of the same group of people as during the war'; they had excluded Fanck from their group already in 1933, because they considered him to be 'on the scrap heap' (1997a: 65–6).

His work came once more to public attention in 1957 through mountain film festivals. He also managed to sell a few scripts, but his career as a director was over. Later, a benefactor bought the copyrights for his films and paid him a monthly pension, improving his financial situation, at least. He died in Freiburg in 1974, his reputation still unclear and subject to dispute. For instance, Yomota's conclusion that the defeat of the Axis destroyed Fanck's career and he 'left Germany for Chile, never again made a film, and died a broken man in 1974' (Yomota 2000: 79) calls to mind, but also confuses Fanck with the several high-ranking party members who fled to South America to avoid persecution after the fall of the regime under which they had thriven. Fanck's career ended before 1945, and this was not connected to the fall of the political system. He also married his third wife, almost fifty years his junior, in 1972, so the notion of 'broken' perhaps applies more to his problematic reputation and difficult post-war career than his personal life.

The very temporal focus on the Third Reich elucidates the rhetorical acts in Fanck's autobiography and also in his other writings about himself as a director and about his position within the film industry. For his acts of writing, Fanck drew on abundant material. Not only did he keep a profuse amount of letters, drafts of articles and scripts, but the specific historical times on which Fanck focuses in his 1973 autobiography – the *Weimar Republic and the Third Reich* – are also powerful resources. Remembering is always interpretive and specific to the occasion and time of writing. And these contexts are 'charged politically' because who is authorized to remember and forget is contested and changes over time (Smith and Watson 2001: 24). If history is perhaps not always 'written by the victors', it is at least hard to write history – as autobiographers do – against the hegemonic point of view and remain credible.

Fanck struggled to revive his career and reputation: on the occasion of the release of *Samurai's Daughter*'s re-edited version, not very imaginatively titled *Cherry Blossoms, Geisha and Volcanoes* (Kirschblüten, Geishas und Vulkane) by Globus Film in 1958, he wrote a piece on the film and attached three pages of review snippets to signify its earlier success, omitting the many ideology-related excerpts that took up so much space in his 1938 publication (ca.1960). Attempting also to achieve television screenings, he advertised the spectacular volcano scenes and represents the film as a historical document (Fanck ca.1970). He also claims that the film had been inconvenient to the wartime regime anyway and had disappeared from Third Reich screens when Molotov came to Berlin for negotiations with Hitler (likely in 1940), because 'two scenes with anti-communist tendencies' and the final scene in Manchuria would have antagonized the Russians (Fanck ca.1970). However, according to Fanck's interpretation in 1973, German television rejected *Samurai's Daughter* because of ideological concerns regarding the notion of blood and soil, which he strongly refutes. He also argues that he had 'completely depoliticized' the film by cutting relevant scenes (1973: 361–3).

The rejection of his 'most beautiful film' (1973: 361–3) and the impossibility of re-establishing his career was an emotional blow for someone defining himself so much through his work. Fanck was also aware that his persona was connected to the notion of National–Socialist propaganda, specifically with regard to Kracauer's work (Rentschler 1990: 144). His autobiography is therefore defensive in tone when it comes to the time between 1933 and 1945. *New Earth/Samurai's Daughter* takes a prominent place in his narration of the past precisely because, in popular discourse, it is regarded as the beginning of his collaboration with the regime. This film, in his memory, was the one on which his professional and personal post-war life hinged. A very poignant indicator for Fanck having felt under pressure to 'rectify' the account is the strange story he tells in his autobiography about the ship's late departure from Marseille to Japan and Goebbels's off-handed reaction to Fanck's request for money to cover the four additional days on land (see Chapter 2). Given the amount of press attention and advertising in Japan that covered every minute detail about the project, the absence of a report on the ship being late and the meticulously planned schedule being in jeopardy is more than surprising. In fact, the *Suwa Maru* did increase speed on its way from London due to a technical problem and in order to arrive in Marseille one day early for repair works. But she stayed in port for only two days, thus leaving Marseille one, not four days later, keeping the scheduled fortnightly service for each port and arrived in Kobe as scheduled on 8 February 1936.[6] Even if the passengers had to stay off-board for this additional day, it is highly unlikely that Fanck had to cable either Goebbels or Kawakita out of acute financial distress. In retrospect, Fanck inflated a real event in order to contrast Japanese and German support of his project, which would then prove his distance from the German regime.

And while returning from Japan in February 1937, he claims, the news of the German army marching into Prague filled him with consternation: 'We Germans could not afford such a breach of promise' (Fanck 1973: 360). Given the context of the German invasion of Czechoslovakia, the 'promise' most likely refers to the Munich Pact, signed on 29 September 1938.[7] German troops entered Prague on 15 March 1939. Fanck seems to confound his journey in 1937 with his return from South America after shooting *A German Robinson* in spring 1939. In his attempts of coming to terms with the past, Fanck puts his most contested film, *Samurai's Daughter*, and his alleged increasing wariness towards German politics in the same timeframe; this story thus becomes yet another 'character witness'.

Fanck's writing displays an autobiographer's concern to explain how he has arrived at where he was in 1972/1973, but he also attempts to fix the past from the present. His image was created, not least by himself but also by various persons and in diverse contexts. The publisher's cutting of almost 50 per cent out of Fanck's autobiography represents yet another gap: between Fanck's persona as originally constructed by himself and the persona presented by the publisher. The missing final paragraph – which he explicitly asked the publisher to attach – expressed his gratitude for the many 'splendid reviews' and 'enthusiastic fan letters' he received throughout his career: 'I have given enjoyable and uplifting hours to countless Millions

---

[6] I am grateful to Horie Makoto of the NYK Maritime Museum Yokohama for providing me with the information for this section.
[7] This agreement between Italy, France, Britain and Germany ceded the 'Sudeten German territory' in Czechoslovakia to Germany. Widely regarded as a step to prevent Hitler's threatened military eastward expansion, it could neither prevent the fall of Czechoslovakia in March 1939 nor Hitler's subsequent 'drive to the East'.

[of people]; thus my life has had a reason after all' (Fanck ca.1969). In his autobiography Fanck narrates himself as a victim rather than a collaborator, but the subject position he took in writing his past lacks critical distance. Back in the 1930s and beyond, it is the evident opportunism behind Fanck's willingness to cooperate with the regime – as apparent in his writings more than in his films – that leaves a bitter aftertaste. Examining Fanck's position as a director of a specific genre in dramatically changing contexts, however, showed he was not the Third Reich's 'appointed director' as which he often appears with regard to *New Earth*. Still, he was also not opposed to using his surroundings to keep or improve his own standing within the increasingly complex power nexus of Germany in the 1930s. And *Samurai's Daughter/ New Earth* played a pivotal role in this regard. Especially when it comes to people remembering the Third Reich, the notion of 'telling the truth' or 'deceiving' is at the forefront of many analytical approaches. Fanck's public persona encourages analyses along this line. At the same time, however, there are no easily definable demarcation lines between collaboration and non-collaboration, and these were also not the only options available, as Itami pointed out in his essay on individual responsibility:

> Of course, theoretically, an intellectual problem should be treated as an intellectual problem throughout; there should be no scope for an intersection with concepts of right or wrong. But it is impossible to analyze the behaviour of human beings as living, organic entities in a purely logical manner. In other words, once an intellectual problem becomes connected to human behaviour, it changes into an intricate complex of intentions and emotions. That is why the judgement of right and wrong can intervene with the intellectual phenomenon of ignorance. (1961 [1946]: 209)

Contemporary commentary on *New Earth* confirms Itami's position as the moral winner and Fanck's post-war reputation as a collaborator. Is it then the case that 'Fanck won out' (High 2003: 150)? Momentarily remaining within the schema of victim or perpetrator, or of winner or loser in history, we can certainly conclude that the project did not hurt Itami's reputation as much as it did Fanck's. Considering that both directors intensely disliked the experience of their joint film-making and that this project took on a life of its own that went beyond their controls and impacted on their personas and the stories told about Japanese and German wartime relations, 'winners and losers' of history become very unstable as an always-already context-dependent category.

Conclusion

Dear Mr Itami, I am probably the only one to understand the hopeless nature of the task you were facing when you decided not only to assist me in directing, but also to make your own version of a topic that you had not devised and that therefore could not but remain foreign to you in its essential elements. And, most of all, that forced an artistic style on you that was not your own.... When you now read from the German reviews to which joyful degree I have succeeded in benefiting your fatherland, you will perhaps understand today what I could never really convey to you then because of the language gap: 'I must observe your Japan from a simplifying perspective, from a thousand kilometres up high.... I must not lose myself in the details of differentiating the Japanese soul, which I had indeed observed through my artistic empathy, but which I could not have presented to European audiences who were supposed to get a notion of the Japanese people for the very first time'.

(FANCK 1938: 8–9)

Fanck had proclaimed it his goal to satisfy both Western and Japanese audiences (Aoyama 1936: 91), but the project succeeded in neither, despite its undeniable success at the box offices. In Japan its depiction of the country engendered heated discussions, and Goebbels, one of the most influential members of the German audience, was less than impressed. General 'Western audiences', apart from the markets served by Fanck's version, never saw the film. But still, the German–Japanese joint film production *New Earth/ Samurai's Daughter* has attracted attention for the past eighty years. The primary impetus for reopening the discussion arose from the realization of the very amount of energy – in terms of money, but also individual effort and aspiration – invested in the project, which became obvious when going through the scrapbooks, photo albums, collections of documents and footage that the participants and the films produced. This, often very personal, dynamism, together with apparent historical and temporal inconsistencies, made the attribution to exclusively political objectives highly unlikely, and the very existence of two competing films challenges the use of this 'first German-Japanese co-production' to represent a harmonious relationship of kindred spirits. Finally, I was interested in learning more about the Japanese side's investments in the project that had been left behind German concerns. The desire for clearly drawn lines is understandable but problematic when approaching *New Earth* and its temporal and spatial contexts, as these desires, rather than stories told by the project itself, can shape our approach to the text, as Gerow points out (2008). My own desire was to understand the complexity and personal motives behind the façade, even on the danger of getting entangled in the webs of histories. In order to gain an improved understanding of this film – and, in extension, of historical cultural texts in general – a comprehensive and open approach that pays attention to 'inconsistencies in the style, conflicts over its interpretation, and the multifaceted history of [the] text' is indispensable (Gerow 2008: 4). I have attempted to approach and understand *New Earth*'s 'multifaceted history' in a way as simple as possible – but not simpler.

Agger's argument that '[g]enre, cultural traditions and national and international relations constitute a broader notion of intertextuality which is practically indispensable in the interpretation of works' significant relational features and the traditions to which they belong' (1999: n.p.) applies all the more to *New Earth*. National/cultural borders are more fluid, 'auteurial intentions' are more complex, as is their interplay with the industry and politics, and the processes of input and change in transnational encounters are more intricate.

In many instances, criticisms of Fanck's image of Japan and purported resistance to Japanese input for their distorting Orientalist lens and attitude are justified, for example, regarding his emphasis and representation of 'samurai bravery' that Itami had criticized early on. Fanck went on to tailor his version of Japan specifically to the needs of his – by then – German audience, and indeed, the image of Japan as a nation of samurai that it corroborated rather than questioned could usefully be put into the service of the National–Socialist regime. When it comes to Fanck's situatedness within the project, apart from the undoubtedly attractive adventure and flattering prestige he received, the main impetus seems to have been financial and career-related concerns. Careful examination, however, shows its irregularity, in that both the production and the film were set in a place completely foreign to the European Alps, Fanck's natural habitat. He worked with an unfamiliar cast and crew as opposed to his Freiburg School. A novelty for him, the film had to be fully scripted as stipulated by the contract. He – and others – knew that he was not gifted as a scriptwriter and many of his actors were not actors in the usual sense, but enthusiastic sports people. In summary, despite the many indulgences undoubtedly granted to the foreign guest, he worked in an unfree environment, probably similar to new restrictions in the German film world that had already caused him discomfort. But he, Angst and his film team produced some striking imagery indeed. It is also apparent that he did attempt to showcase contemporary Japan, which is quite pronounced in the first part of the film, but that his own dream of Japan, the political context and his passion for the depiction of mountains – or volcanoes – took over.

However, focusing entirely on the Western gaze comes dangerously close to ending the discussion by assuming that everything originates in and is ultimately directed at the Western representer (Said 2003: 3). The resulting denial of the Other's materiality and too easy attribution to the Western eye (or German lens) misses crucial parts of the story. Arguably, Fanck later used the same framework by declaring himself as charged with the role of the Western representer and the sole author, but it became obvious that the nationalized dichotomy was difficult to uphold. Mutual interaction occurred, and despite the supposed lack of 'German propaganda' in Itami's version (Yomota 2000: 41–2), the existence of 'Japanese propaganda' in Itami's *New Earth* as well as in Fanck's *Samurai's Daughter* for German-speaking countries makes the idea of a German National Socialist (fascist)/Japanese (therefore-non-fascist dichotomy) lose its significance. Each side clearly influenced the other, and it was only at the point of intersection of their multifarious objectives that this project could happen. Neither participant was forced into it, neither enjoyed the process or reaped substantial benefits from it; the perpetrator–victim dichotomy collapses as well. Already in 1937, Itami's epigraph to his version questioned the very representation of the project as collaboration, as did Fanck's – far less-cited – statement about his dislike of the project in a letter from Japan to Paul Kohner, head of Universal's European division and associate producer of his *SOS Iceberg*: 'I'd rather scale calving icebergs in Greenland or float around on ice-floes than shoot a film here in Japan' (02.09.1936, *Fanck Documents*), which does not fit that well into the usual accounts. The rupture grew out of a confrontation of two different views of Japan and hence two different objectives in representing its image, the discourse about which, as time went by, moved from the cinematic–cultural to the ideological–political.

Various political, personal, industrial and cultural interests converged into what was to become *New Earth*, some of them similar, or connected, to those resulting in the most obvious political context, the conclusion of the Anti-Comintern Pact in November 1936. At a specific temporal juncture, both events became related. Seemingly obvious political agendas behind the production were confusing, at times chaotic and always contested from within by power struggles about authority and authenticity. Fanck put this connection into service in the course of the production and exhibition, but negated it post-1945. The same applies to Kawakita, whose later statements very much resemble Fanck's: 'My only regret about this project was that some overseas people thought the picture was farfetched [*sic*] justification for Japan's takeover of Manchuria because (1) the young couple at the end decides to make their life together in Manchuria and (2) the Japanese title was *New Land* (Atarashiki Tsuchi)' (Kawakita N. 1988: 21). To deny power and agency to the Japanese partners would be myopic. They were idealistic to a certain degree, but not naïve; and as business people they shouldered a significant portion of costs, risked their reputation and utilized the film and its discursive environments for their own purposes. But still, even with Kawakita's subsequent distribution contracts, the outcome was not what they had wished for, not in terms of the film itself, its international success, nor its anticipated trigger effect on further, substantial co-productions and exports. And while post-war readings of this almost-pre-war film turn coeval comments around to blame Fanck for the failure and take responsibility away from Itami, the Japanese director emerges from this story far removed from a passive victim. He refuted rumours that he took 'silent revenge' by sabotaging the film, declared the project as 'pointless' and as a year-long waste of his efforts (Itami 1961 [1937]: 246), but he also shaped it subtly. The understanding of *New Earth* as a negative turning point in his career is corroborated by coeval reviews of his later films, but not by the contemporary reception of his following written works, be it the script for *The Life of Muho Matsu* (1942) or his numerous topical essays. These pieces were as critical of ideological and political currents as his trademark 'iconoclastic' period films. His *New Earth* certainly was not iconoclastic, due to its restrictive framework, but it was still problematic, in terms of the topic prescribed by a foreigner and its emphasis on human relations rather than national characteristics selected expressly for outward projection. What all participants had in common, however, was the wish to see the project through (for various reasons), which then led to the split into two versions.

In his epigraph to *New Earth* Itami politely calls it 'one subjective version of reality'. In their work, Fanck and Itami both are concerned with 'authenticity', but a close look reveals that these are indeed different versions or 'types' of authenticity. Fanck stressed the 'authenticity' of the scenes shown on screen in terms of their not being 'tricks'. In *New Earth*, he was charged with the uncharacteristic task of representing an authentic and foreign national essence. In contrast to Fanck's authenticity in terms of 'form', Itami was concerned with the authenticity of the version of lived experience as he understood it, a trait that became problematic in a prescriptive rather than descriptive discursive environment. Authenticity played a prominent role in the discourses on *New Earth*, but, as the differences between the versions and the reception of the films demonstrate, the notion became even more complicated on the level of the often-hierarchical structures of transnational encounters that underlie the co-production, even more so in the highly politicized environment before the outbreak of the Second World War.

The reception in Germany was unspectacular, but in Japan – understandably given the grandiose announcements and great expectations – the (mis-)representation of 'us' was a major point of comment and contempt. On the other hand, Japanese commentators had suggested topics that were authentically Japanese to them and that they had wished to see included in the film. Some of them, such as the impact of the natural environment on the national character, were included but with a German twist, and it also remains open to question, what kind of film could have satisfied the majority of Japanese with an adequate representation – directed to the outside – of how they perceived their realities. Authenticity is not the self-evident notion it represents itself to be, and its very emptiness as a signifier sets up endeavours based on the notion as failures from the very beginning, as seen with the history of export films, 'national disgrace films' and the star-crossed co-production discussed in this book. Yet, film was still considered, theorized and proclaimed as a medium with a high potential to capture and disseminate lived reality.

Authenticity as a means to an end

Dibbler disagreed. 'Apart from anything else', he declared, 'it wouldn't look right.' But it's the real Ankh-Morpork, Uncle', said Soll. 'It's got to look *exactly* right. How can it not look right?' 'Ankh-Morpork doesn't look all that genuine, you know', said Dibbler thoughtfully. 'Of course it's bloody genuine!' snapped Soll, the bonds of kinship stretching to snapping point. 'It's really there! It's really itself! You can't make it any more genuine. It's as genuine as it can get!'. Dibbler took his cigar out of his mouth. 'No, it isn't', he said. 'You'll see.' . . . Dibbler had been right. The new city was the old city distilled. Narrow alleys were narrower, tall buildings taller. Gargoyles were more fearsome, roofs more pointed. . . . It looked far more like Ankh-Morpork than Ankh-Morpork ever had.

(PRATCHETT 1991: 201, 208)

Irie's observation that '*New Earth* brought several new types of vision to Japanese film' (1996: 13) can be extended beyond the technical aspects it addressed, such as the famed zoom lens, screen processing and exotic types of dissolves. The extraordinary project, which drew from various contexts and pretexts, brought 'Japan' itself into deep focus. The film was supposed to make Japan visible on-screen. But even if Fanck, as stated in his address to Itami in 1938, had been able to 'distil' an essence out of the multiplicity of everyday life through his telephoto lenses and romanticist aesthetics, his representation would still not have been innocent and objective, but purpose-driven and subjective. The same applies to Itami's film, which he tweaked in reaction to Fanck's version of reality. The romantic idea of an ephemeral essence is necessarily void, but seems to keep its attractiveness through changing circumstances. There are situations where a quality formerly perceived as authentic is pushed from its pedestal, to be replaced by another. A temporally close example is the National Socialists' banning of modern artistic expressions, understood as authentic to the artist's experiences of modern Germany, but then suddenly un-German and hence inauthentic. The idea that there was an authentic Japan to represent and that this would be easily identified and somehow translated while still keeping its authentic quality underscores the entire project, in its German and Japanese contexts, and in both nationalist discourses the currency of this thought was high:

> For the political unity of the nation consists in a continual displacement of its irredeemably plural modern space, bounded by difference, even hostile nations, unto a signifying space that is archaic and mythical, paradoxically representing the nation's modern territoriality, in the patriotic, atavistic temporality of Traditionalism. (Bhabha 1990: 300)

Many versions of reality are real because they are grounded in an individual's or a group's lived experiences. But which of these can become dominant, or even 'heard', depends on individual positioning, as apparent from the sharp domestic criticism of Itami's version, which, seen from today, is as good a film as the restrictive framework allowed for. With regard to competing versions of past events, Morris-Suzuki argues that the 'nation's ownership of a particular past' is challenged by outside points of view (1997: 5), an argument that turns a spotlight on the relationship of citizens and official versions of national histories. Similarly, *New Earth* was part of a discourse on the ownership of a particular image of Japan at a time when the hegemonic image was changing, and the power to represent such an image was connected to hierarchies. In the international film project, the questions of how to portray the correct image and who would succeed in doing so were related to issues of power. The fact that the ownership of this highly publicized picture eventually was seen to go to the foreign director and was determined by his gaze was of consequence in this discourse.

The importance assigned in the project to authenticity, and the authority to determine its absence or presence, raises crucial questions about the economy of truth in such international encounters. Explicitly intending to move beyond stereotypes, the Japanese aimed at representing an alternative version of themselves by first inviting Fanck and eventually resorted to Itami intervening. *New Earth* therefore also brings into perspective the ready subscription to the idea of representational authority and authenticity based on the 'insider' position; as Faris puts it, the assumption that giving a camera to a member of the society to be represented 'somehow solves the problem of power and conceptual imposition' (1992: 171). A case in point is the convincing logic of Itami's frequently mentioned omission (or bundling at the beginning) of the picture postcard scenery generally ascribed to Fanck's orientalizing eye (e.g. Yamamoto 2004: 78). Yet, the automatic attribution of Itami's strategy to his position as a cultural insider who would resist and therefore avoid inauthentic tourism campaign-like shots is not conclusive, because exactly this quality was pointed out by an American reviewer of his version: 'First reel is devoted largely to shots which cover every inch of Japan, which could be of possible interest to the tourist' (Will 1937), and in fact, they are not much different from the Tourism Bureaus advertising brochures that also relied on received, beautiful sights, seemingly untouched by modern developments.

The return to an 'authentic', meaning 'traditional', Japaneseness drove *New Earth*'s narrative as well as relevant discourses in Japan, for example with regard to the return of the doctrine of the 'good wife and wise mother' as embodied by Mitsuko. Fanck's image of Japan – not so much due to his film's visuals that included modern aspects, too, but due to the plotline of a return to being authentically Japanese driving and concluding the narrative, within a discursive environment that equalled 'authentic' with 'traditional' and therefore with pre- or at best early modern – could only result in a received, anachronistic understanding of what Japan is. Such topics, of course, resonated with similar discourses in Germany, which explains their easy entry into the plot. Yet, pointing out Orientalizing images in a cultural artefact can be an important analytical step, but focusing entirely on the Western gaze comes dangerously close to ending the discussion by assuming that everything originates in and is ultimately directed at the Western representer (Said 2003: 3). This kind of 'Meta-Orientalism' that denies the Other's materiality too easily attributes everything to the Western eye (or German lens) and consequently misses crucial parts of the story. Arguably, Fanck later used the same framework by declaring himself as charged with the role of the Western representer and the sole author. However, mutual interactions took place between Fanck and his Japanese environment, between Itami and Fanck and, of course, between Hollywood-loving Itami and film as a transnational medium. Regardless of the dominant intention behind the production, the problem of how to translate Japanese culture for foreign audiences was at the centre of what Fanck called his mission – a skopos-driven, audiovisual cultural translation. The general questions remain whether translators should actually aim at staying as close to the original as possible (Nornes 1999) and whether Fanck would have been able to do so, and if such a translation would have reached the anticipated audience. Processes of cultural translations depend on knowledge of both contents but often occur based on moments of recognizing similar patterns. For instance, Fanck had predicted a charming effect of Hara's grammatically slightly incorrect German and her accent on the German audience, and Kawakita

Kashiko, reporting from the German premiere, labelled Hara's German as 'cute' and predicted international stardom based on the enthusiastic audience responses to her appearances on the stage (Kawakita 1937). For Fanck and the German audience Hara's German evoked sympathy, and arguably fascination with someone other, because it appeared authentic, both on-screen and on-stage. When something is already known, it appears to be all the more authentic, in the foreign as well as in the local context. And therefore, neither Hara nor the film itself broke stereotypes.

Continuities

New Earth was yet another, even more highly publicized, attempt to open Western markets for Japanese films as well as to redress (mainly Western) misrepresentations of Japan. Its forerunners left their marks, both in terms of visual style and motif and regarding the almost breathless Japanese media coverage of this much-anticipated, final international breakthrough for Japanese film. Consequently, *New Earth* harks back to earlier discourses and images, be it *Yokohama shashin*, the Tourism Bureau's campaigns, *Nippon* and *Kagami*, Fanck's aesthetics between the two aesthetics of the Weimar Republic and the Third Reich or personal continuities. And, strikingly with regard to the Anti-Soviet implications of at least half of the outcome, composer Yamada Kōsaku's previous experience with a Soviet–Japanese film demonstrates the difficulties brought about by a politicized environment and transnational representational traditions, regardless of personal efforts.

Big Tokyo (Daitōkyō, 1933), a collaboration between Soviet film-maker Vladimir Shneiderov and the Tokyo Asahi newspaper, emerged out of very similar concerns: the authentic representation of the contemporary Japanese experience within the politically charged context after Japan's move to power in the region with the annexation of Manchukuo (Fedorova 2014). *Big Tokyo* was also reported on extensively in Japan, only to be followed by disappointment after its release. Like *New Earth*, *Big Tokyo* resulted in two versions, one for Soviet and another for Japanese audiences. And it also brought forth criticisms regarding its misrepresentation of Japan's reality, as for instance with regard to Shneiderov's emphasis on gender equality, as signified by the many working women in the film. While *New Earth*'s depiction of Mitsuko conformed to images of Japanese femininity as promulgated in the West as well as by Japanese publications, the sturdy women of *Big Tokyo* provoked 'discontent among Japanese viewers, and one reviewer even called the characters at a construction site "women who look like men"' (Fedorova 2014: 111). In terms of style more a documentary than a drama film, *Big Tokyo* arguably gives a more realistic impression of 1930s everyday Japan than *New Earth*, with its romantic stressing of the 'Japanese spirit', but it is equally biased in terms of the ideological agendas at its heart that focus on Soviet discursive needs. While Yamada with his compositions had 'wished to create an image of a powerful, modernized country that still cherished culture' the political environment resulted in a very different image (Fedorova 2014: 121). As with *New Earth*, Yamada was sorely disappointed by the deletion of his pieces in favour of music perceived by the Soviet side as more fitting for their own domestic audiences. In the light of the increasing Japanese presence on the continent, 'Soviet audiences had to be provided with an exotic image of an underdeveloped country that tried to copy everything from the West' (Fedorova 2014), which led to the use of popular jazz songs, instead of Yamada's syncretic compositions, and a stressing in the narrative and voice-over narration of Japan's underlying ancientness under a modern veneer (Fedorova 2014: 114). The political and industrial contexts add to the fact that 'the translator's interpretation remains partial, both incomplete in omitting irrecoverable aspects of the foreign text and slanted towards what is intelligible and interesting in the receiving culture. It also reflects the cultural and financial interests of publishers, the gatekeepers who decisively exercise the power to admit or exclude foreign works' (Venuti 2013: 112–13). And of course, these characteristics also reflect the personal or professional interests of the translators or representers. *Big Tokyo* displays yet another similarity with *New Earth* that simultaneously points to stylistic and thematic continuities and the context-dependency of interpretation: Fedorova describes the voice-over commentary for a rural scenery in *Big Tokyo* as follows: '"The countryside has electricity, but the land owned by peasants is very small. People have to work with their hands, Fields are narrow, like small kale yards. A tractor won't be able to turn here." This comment suggests the extent to which Japanese peasants stood to benefit from Soviet-style collectivization that would give them broad lands easily cultivable by machines' (2014: 114). At the same time, the aural and visual signals would have corroborated the 'people without space' discourse that bolstered the production's political context, and they also foreshadow much of *New Earth*'s Manchurian subplot.

Taking the idea of continuity further, with Yamada having composed the puppet first state's national anthem and the song about the blue skies and wide fields of Manchukuo that Teruo sings while driving his tractor, a booklet Yamada edited in 1940 for the Manchukuo Immigration Association (*Manshū Ijū Kyōkai*) is of interest. An extensive collection of 'Songs on the cultivation of Manchuria' (*Manshū kaitaku kakyokushū*), it also contains Teruo's song, *Aoi sora mirya*. But more strikingly, the young woman on the cover, wearing farmer's garb and smiling brightly into the sun while working the large field, looks very much like Mitsuko. An aesthetic continuity – of which this image is one example – developed regarding the depiction of pioneer life in Manchukuo. While *New Earth* drew from pre-existing stylistic conventions of Manchuria (and Japan), it went on to feed into and influence subsequent discourse and representation. Apart from the political context, this was certainly also due to Fanck and Angst's strong visuals, and the extensive advertising campaigns that dispersed these images widely and deeply. And to take this idea even further, as with the casting of Isamu Kosugi as the desperate farmer in Uchida's *Earth* (Chapter 5), I cannot help but think of the famous still of Hara Setsuko's character Yukie in Kurosawa's first post-war film *No Regrets for Our Youth* (Waga seishun ni kuinashi, 1946). The last part of this critical commentary of the wartime regime's impacts on individual lives shows Yukie working hard in her in-laws' fields, looking exhausted, dishevelled and sweaty, in what appears to me a (perhaps unconscious) negative homage to the picture-book-like image of Mitsuko in 'Farmers Paradise' Manchukuo.

These flows demonstrate the persistence – and therefore power – of images. And the continuities go even further, as in its Japanese context the international project *New Earth* foreshadows the persistent discourse about what is seen as being 'authentic' and who is considered to be a spokesperson with the right to represent it on national and international screens? The domestic criticism, specifically of Itami's version, and also of the project in general, points to an 'aesthetic nationalism'. As Beard points out with regard to recent Canadian cinema, 'Canadian movies must not simply be Canadian, but Canadian in a particular way' (2013: n.p.), a statement hinting at the complex relations between the intentions of agents involved and the industrial and political contexts. In 1938, Fanck explained that the Japanese producers invited a German director to make this film because, 'except for us Germans, probably no other *Kultur-Volk* is as unpopular internationally as the Japanese' – hence, the need for 'positive propaganda' (1938: 109). Despite the previous, failed attempts, film was still considered to be an appropriate means to influence the international perception of a group of people, at a time of growing nationalism. This tension between the national and the international with regard to Japan as it was represented on-screen was picked up by Kurosawa in the context of *Rashomon* winning the Venice International Film Festival's Grand Prix and the American Academy's Award for Best Foreign Film in 1951 and 1953 respectively:

> Japanese critics insisted that these two prizes were simply reflections of Westerner's curiosity and taste for Oriental exoticism, which struck me then, and now, as terrible. Why is it that Japanese people have no confidence in the worth of Japan? Why do they elevate everything foreign and denigrate everything Japanese? (1999: 90–1)

In 1937, despite criticism, Japanese audiences and critics still widely preferred Fanck's version of *New Earth* and, by extension, of Japan. Later scholarly discussions attributed the film's critical success in Germany to the Propaganda Ministry's orders and, in Japan, to the audience's curiosity, rather than to some sort of value, artistic, industrial, personal or otherwise. This doubly self-conscious gaze continues to complicate international cultural relations as well as Japan's self-definition vis-à-vis 'the West'.

> While Japanese films have benefited from the strong appeal of exoticism among many Western viewers until now, the latest outcome may suggest that the cultural difference can sometimes blind the viewer's ability to understand and empathise. (Ishitobi 2011)

Ishitobi's report on Miike Takashi and Kawase Naomi's *not* winning an award at Cannes in 2011 reminds one of Kurosawa's grievance as well as of Japanese reactions to 'national disgrace films' in the 1920s and 1930s, and therefore Kawakita's motive for embarking on *New Earth*. Within this rhetoric, Japanese films either succeed because of Western desire for mere exoticism (not good, thought-provoking or entertaining films) or fail due to Western ignorance (about Japan, not about its cinematic output).

Fanck's version is still being discussed and reshown in Japan, and slowly Itami's version seems to find its way out of the archival vaults. This endurance is also an indication of the continuous struggle to define what Japan is, in this case played out on the silver- or laptop screen. A recent documentary-style short film by Australian film-maker David Anthony Parkinson, *Love Japan* (Nihon ga daisuki desu, 2014), showcased Japan's diverse cities in a slow-motion travelogue. It was praised for expressing the director's 'love and respect' for Japan, as well as revealing its beauty in a way that even 'the Japanese had been unaware of' (*The Huffington Post Japan* 2014), almost paraphrasing of the rhetoric surrounding Fanck and *New Earth*. Mobilizing the outsider's gaze, behind and before the camera, in order to discover new facets of something familiar is not necessarily problematic. An outsider position allows for an alternative approach, informed by a different background and understanding, and therefore can constructively supplement inside points of view. But it is within the long history of representational struggles in the international arena that such assessments suggest a deeper-seated issue: too strong a desire for the representation and recognition by others suggests a certain degree of insecurity. But arguably, as explored here, Japan's image has been used and distorted according to others' agendas, and despite various attempts at self-representation the cultural flows were unequal, characterized and determined by nationalized hierarchies.

Even disregarding an explicit ideological agenda, the complex problem of cultural bias pervades – and misleadingly facilitates – projects that deal with representing 'others' to 'us'. The 'translator must somehow control the unavoidable release of meanings that work only in the translating language. Apart from threatening to derail the project of imitation, these meanings always risk transforming what is foreign into something too familiar or simply irrelevant' (Venuti 2013: 109). It is because of the aforementioned power of the image that – especially in politically charged contexts – representers, and maybe even more so foreign representers, bear a special responsibility for the way their images can be interpreted and for how they interact with the wishes and ambitions of those they are representing.

Interpretation, of course, is also what happens while writing a history out of past events. The end product of the processing of aspects of the past is nothing else but representation, and therefore it is equally purpose-driven. Telling the past as it really was is as impossible as filming the really real; today's representations of the past – as Itami said with regard to *jidaigeki* – the present or the future will always be in the light of and in response to the concerns of today (1961 [1933]: 25–6). *New Earth*, as an historical event and an historical artefact, demonstrates how the perspective on such events by critical research competes with familiar, 'catchy' narratives. The propensity of such narratives to keep reproducing themselves is related to the specific (historical) territory they occupy, even more so if this territory is transnational, which brings with it multiple and often contradicting interpretations and versions of events – or films. The practices of memory and the politics of history here detach themselves from wider discourses about a critical coming to terms with the past, a tendency that results in the aforementioned self-reproduction of familiar and hence satisfying narratives. This not only concerns approaches to film history but also interpretations of transnational encounters. The individual agencies, structural constraints and inconsistencies that *New Earth* allows us to observe bring the past to life as a network of agendas, forces, breaks and continuities. A critical memory and history culture as well as an understanding of processes of cultural translation and interpretation require fundamental research: a detailed investigation of relevant artefacts and the people involved in their production, political events, personal movements and industrial contexts leads to a different perspective on such events and a more critical (film) historical thinking.

In this respect – as imagined by Kawakita Kashiko in October 1936 when she recalled the film team returning from Mount Yakedake (1936b) – *New Earth* became a 'great film'. It did not open up the international market to Japanese film, but its very existence and the plurality of texts it engendered opened up a window to a small but densely populated slice of the contested epistemological territory of the world at the brink of war.

APPENDIX 1

Plot summary and credits

Plot summary

Yamato Teruo returns to Japan after eight years of studying natural sciences in Germany.[1] He comes back to Japan to place his newly acquired knowledge into the service of his country. However, during his stay in Europe he learned Western ideas of individualism and free choice: Teruo faces a dilemma. He, as a farmer's son, had been adopted by the rich Yamato family and is engaged to their daughter Mitsuko who waits for his return. Due to his 'infiltration' with Western values and his attraction to the German journalist Gerda Storm who accompanies him on the ship, he feels that he cannot marry Mitsuko. We see Japan through the journalist's eyes, who remarks on the modernity of Japanese industry, and we also learn about the 'dangerous winds' coming from the middle of Asia that threaten Japan from the West and Germany from the East. *Ostwind* (east wind): the rest of the film is a story along the lines of the 'return of the lost son'. Teruo's old childhood teacher, the Buddhist priest Ikkan Osshō, Gerda and Teruo's sister Hideko, a 'modern' factory girl working in a silk mill, help him return to his roots, where the foremost importance is the group, not the individual. Moreover, we learn about the scarcity of space and fertile soil in Japan and the necessity to go to Manchuria in order to pacify and cultivate the country. Gerda is commissioned by Yamato Iwao, Teruo's adoptive father, to convey to Germany that the 'dangerous storms' will break on Japanese rocks. In the meantime, Mitsuko, who is convinced that Teruo does not want to marry her, decides to commit suicide by throwing herself into a volcano. Teruo convinces his family's elders about his changed attitude and learns about Mitsuko being missing. He chases after her and manages to find and rescue her. His birth father, the farmer Kanda Kōsaku, again impresses on them the hardships of cultivating the small fields of Japan and feeding the too large population. The end of the film sees the young couple married, and with a baby boy, in the large, fertile fields of Manchukuo. A soldier, looking out to the West, watches over them and their fellow settlers.

---

[1] This plot summary is based on Fanck's version.

Credits

	Samurai's Daughter	*New Earth*
Production	J.O. Studio and Tōwa Shōji Dr. Arnold Fanck-Film	J.O. Studio and Tōwa Shōji
Producers	Kawakita Nagamasa Ōsawa Yoshio Arnold Fanck	Kawakita Nagamasa Ōsawa Yoshio
Distribution	Terra AG	Tōwa Shōji
Director	Arnold Fanck Itami Mansaku	Arnold Fanck Itami Mansaku
Assistant director	Walter Tjaden	
Script	Arnold Fanck	Arnold Fanck
Camera	Richard Angst	Richard Angst
Camera assistants	Walter Riml Ueda Isamu Hans Staudinger	Walter Riml Ueda Isamu Hans Staudinger
Stage design	Yoshida Kenkichi	Yoshida Kenkichi
Costumes	Matsuzakaya Department Store	Matsuzakaya Department Store
Miniatures	Asano Mōfu	Asano Mōfu
Editing	Arnold Fanck Alice Ludwig Kishi Fumiko	Itami Mansaku Saeki Kiyoshi Alice Ludwig Nogami Teruyo Kishi Fumiko
Special effects	Tsuburaya Eiji	Tsuburaya Eiji
Music	Yamada Kōsaku (new pieces, apart from three older ones)	A selection of Yamada Kōsaku's (as Kôsçak Yamada) older works, adapted by (his pupils) Aoki So and Ito Noboru
Lyrics	Kitahara Hakushū Saijō Yaso	Kitahara Hakushū Saijō Yaso
Orchestra	New Symphonic Orchestra (Shin kōkyōgakudan)	Chuo Symphonic Orchestra, (Chūō kōkyōgakudan)

APPENDIX 1

Conducted by	Yamada Kōsaku	Ito Noboro (as Novol Itoh)
Sound	Nakaōji, Teiji	Nakaōji, Teiji
Recorded on	RCA High Fidelity	RCA High Fidelity
Premiere in Japan	Teikoku Gekijō, Taishōkan, Musashinokan Theatres, 11 February 1937	Teikoku Gekijō Theatre, 3 February 1937
Premiere in Germany	Capitol am Zoo, Berlin, 23 March 1937	n/a
Length of original version	126 min.	114 min.
Length of version available on DVD	106 min.	n/a
Black/white	Languages: Japanese and German	Languages: Japanese and English
Cast		
Yamato Mitsuko	Hara Setsuko	Hara Setsuko
Yamato Teruo (né Kanda)	Kosugi Isamu	Kosugi Isamu
Gerda Storm	Ruth Eweler	Ruth Eweler
Yamato Iwao	Sessue Hayakawa	Sessue Hayakawa
Buddhist priest Ikkan Oshō	Nakamura Kichiji	Nakamura Kichiji
Kanda Hideko	Ichikawa Haruyo	Ichikawa Haruyo
Kanda Kōsaku	Takagi Eiji	Takagi Eiji
Teruo's mother	Tokiwa Misako	Tokiwa Misako
Kanda Emiko	Murata Kanae	Murata Kanae
Oiku, Mitsuko's nurse	Hanabusa Yuriko	Hanabusa Yuriko
German/English teacher	Max Hinder	Max Hinder

APPENDIX 2

Feature films shown to Fanck in Japan (February–March 1937)[1]

Backstreet Symphony (Uramachi no kōkyōgaku) (1935), Dir. Watanabe Kunio, Japan: Nikkatsu.[2]
Bride Contest (Hanayome kurabe) (1935), Dir. Shimizu Yasujirō, Japan: Shōchiku.
Chorus of One Million (Hyakumannin no gasshō) (1935), Dir. Tomioka Atsuo, Japan: J.O. Studios.[3]
Chuji Makes a Name for Himself (Chūji uridasu) (1935), Dir. Itami Mansaku, Japan: Shinkō.[4]
The Frivolous Servant (Kimagure kaja aka Sengoku kitan: Kimagure kaja) (1935), Dir. Itami Mansaku, Japan: Chiezō Productions.
The Girl in the Rumour (Uwasa no musume) (1935), Dir. Naruse Mikio, Japan: P.C.L.
Green Horizon (Midori no chiheisen) [two parts] (1935), Dir. Abe Yutaka, Japan: Nikkatsu.
Kouta Tsubute: Bird-Chasing Oichi (Kouta tsubute: Torioi Oichi) (1936), Dir. Tsuburaya Eiji, Japan: J.O. Studios[5]

---

[1]Kawakita often uses short titles for popular films (Kawakita 1936a). Where possible, I have completed them and added information on the year of release, the director and the producing studio, for an impression of the types of films and the range of studios. I mostly draw on Galbraith's list of Tōhō productions, also for the English titles (Galbraith 2008), and the *Complete List of Japanese Movies*, 1899–1945, compiled by Shutsū and Nagata. The officially participating J.O. and P.C.L. Studios represent a relatively large share of the films in comparison with the two major studios Nikkatsu and Shōchiku: (Shōchiku: 5; Nikkatsu: 4; P.C.L.: 3; J.O.: 3; Chiba: 1; Shinko: 1; Onga Geijutsu Kenkyūjo: 1). The overwhelming majority of the films are *gendaigeki*, all but one *jidaigeki* are Itami's iconoclastic films.
[2]Starring Kosugi Isamu, this hugely popular film won first place in the first ever Tokyo Nichinichi Shinbunsha All Japan Film Contest (Shutsū and Nagata 2008: 146).
[3]J.O.'s first feature film (Galbraith 2008: x).
[4]Itami Mansaku's first talkie.
[5]Tsuburaya Eiji's first directorial work was released on 19 March 1936 (Shutsū and Nagata 2008: 463).

The Life of a Woman in the Meiji Era (Meiji ichidai onna) (1935), Dir. Tasaka Tomotaka, Japan: Nikkatsu/Irie Productions.
The Man, the Woman and the Boys (Kare to kanojo to shōnentachi) (1935), Dir. Shimizu Hiroshi, Japan: Shōchiku.
Only this One Night (Semete koyoi o) (1935), Dir. Shimizu Yasujirō, Japan: Shōchiku.
A Portrait of Shunkin (Shunkinshō: Okoto to Sasuke), (1935), Dir. Shimazu Yasujirō, Japan: Shōchiku.
Princess Kaguya (Kaguya hime) (1935), Dirs. Aoyagi Nobuo and Tanaka Yoshitsugu, Japan: J.O. Studios.[6]
Theatre of Life (Jinsei gekijō) (1936), Dir. Uchida Tomu, Japan: Nikkatsu.
Three Sisters with Maiden Hearts (Otome gokoro sannin kyōdai) (1935), Dir. Naruse Mikio, Japan: P.C.L.
Wife, be like a Rose! (Futari zuma: Tsuma yo bara no yō ni) (1935), Dir. Naruse Mikio, Japan: P.C.L.[7]
The Young Gentleman at University: Sunny Days (Daigaku no wakadanna: Nippon hare) (1934), Dir. Shimizu Hiroshi, Japan: Shōchiku.[8]
Youth Across the River (Kawa mukō no seishun), (1933), Dir. Kimura Sotoji, Japan: Onga Geijutsu Kenkyūjo.[9]

---

[6]Tsuburaya Eiji's self-developed methods and shooting techniques for achieving stunning photographic effects were first put into action in *Princess Kaguya*, including superimpositions and a miniature model of Kyoto. It is possible that Tsuburaya's appointment to *New Earth* where he introduced a new rear-projection system and likely also worked with the miniature models is connected to Fanck's viewing of *Princess Kaguya*.
[7]Based on Nakano Minoru's *shinpa* play *Futari Zuma* (Shutsū and Nagata 2008: 801), it is most likely the first Tōhō film (when the company was not yet consolidated under that name) that made its way to U.S. screens (Galbraith 2008: 7). Thus, it provided a point of reference for the project *New Earth* as an export film.
[8]Part four and the first sound film of the *Wakadanna* series (Shutsū and Nagata 2008: 715).
[9]Shutsū and Nagata describe this film as a 'tendency film' (*keikō eiga*), depicting the hardships of life in a rural village and that of factory workers in the city (Shutsū and Nagata 2008: 316).

APPENDIX 3

Filmography Arnold Fanck

1913 *4628 Meters Upwards on Skies: The Ascent of Monte Rosa* (4628 Meter hoch auf Skiern. Besteigung des Monte Rosa), (13 September): participation.[1]

1920 *The Wonders of Skiing, Part 1* (Das Wunder des Schneeschuhs, Teil 1), Germany: Berg- und Sportfilm (BSF), (October): director, producer, actor, script, camera, editor.

1920 *Masters of Water* (Die Meister des Wassers), Germany: BSF: producer.

1921 *Taking the Jungfrau Train into the Perpetual Ice* (Mit der Jungfraubahn in die Regionen des Ewigen Eises), Germany: BSF: producer.

1921 *Jiu-Jitsu: The Invisible Weapon* (Jiu-Jitsu. Die unsichtbare Waffe, 1921), Germany: BSF: producer.

1921 *The Great Boxing Match Dempsey-Carpentier* (Der große Boxkampf Dempsey-Carpentier), Germany: BSF: producer.

1921 **Battling the Mountain* (Im Kampf mit dem Berge), Germany: BSF (22 September): director, producer, script, camera, editor.[2]

1921 *Moritz the Dreamer* (Moritz der Träumer. Wie sich Moritz die Erschaffung der Welt vorstellt), Germany: BSF: producer.

1922 *The Dying Town* (Die sterbende Stadt), Germany: BSF (11 August): producer.

1922 **The Wonders of Skiing Part 2* (Das Wunder des Schneeschuhs. 2. Teil), Germany: BSF (20 October): director, producer, actor, script, camera, editor.

1922 *Pomperly's Battle with his Ski* (Pömperly's Kampf mit dem Schneeschuh), Germany: BSF: director (with Holger Madsen), script (with Holger Madsen), producer.

1922 *The German Tournament 1922* (Die deutschen Kampfspiele 1922), Germany: BSF: producer.

1922 *Football Match Earth – Mars* (Fußballwettspiel Erde – Mars), Germany: BSF: producer.

---

[1]In order to indicate the volume of Fanck's film-related activity, I have listed all films in which he was involved and his respective function(s). The credits and dates are mainly from the German Film Institute's *Filmportal* [Online]. Fanck's major feature films are marked with an asterisk. Re-editions and re-release dates are given in square brackets. Where a release date was available, this is indicated; censorship dates are available from www.filmportal.de.

[2]Music composed by Paul Hindemith.

1922 *A Great Trip: A Sailing Film and What Cameraman Huckebein Experienced While Shooting* (Auf rauschender Fahrt. Ein Segelsportfilm und was Operateur Huckebein bei seiner Aufnahme erlebte), Germany: BSF: producer.
1922 *Ali Baba and the Forty Thieves* (Ali-Baba und die 40 Räuber), Germany: BSF (12 February): producer.
1922 *Chufu* (Chufu), Germany: BSF: producer.
1923 *1000 Dollars Reward* (1000 Dollar Belohnung), Germany: BSF: producer.
1923 *Saving Franz* (Franzens Lebensrettung. Ein Erlebnis unter den Wilden), Germany: BSF: producer.
1923 *The Human Heart* (Das Herz des Menschen), Germany: BSF: producer.
1924 **Mountain of Destiny* (Der Berg des Schicksals), Germany: BSF (10 May): director, producer, script, editor, camera.
1924 *The Cloud Phenomenon of Majola* (Das Wolkenphänomen von Maloja), Germany: BSF: director, camera, editor.
1924 *Lotte in High Demand* (Die begehrte Lotte oder Welch entzückende Füßchen), Germany: BSF: producer.
1924 *The Wolf of the Dead* (Der Toten-Wolf), Germany: BSF: producer.
1925 *The White Art* (Die weiße Kunst), Germany: BSF (12 February): producer, editor.[3]
1925 *Rowing* (Das Rudern), Germany: BSF: producer.
1926 *South Tyrol* (Südtirol. Ein Vorposten deutscher Kultur), Germany: BSF (7 March): camera, producer.
1926 **The Holy Mountain* (Der heilige Berg), Germany: BSF/Universum-Film AG (Ufa) (17 December): director, script, editor.
1927 *Winter Sports in the Black Forest* (Wintersport im Schwarzwald), Germany: BSF: producer.
1927 *The Big Leap (Der große Sprung), Germany: Ufa (20 December): director, script, editor.
1928 **The White Stadium* (Das weiße Stadion), Switzerland: Olympia Film AG (Zurich), (20 March): director, editor.
1928 *Fight for the Matterhorn* (Der Kampf ums Matterhorn), Germany: Hom-Film GmbH (27 November (1934 sound version)): script.
1928 *Om mani padme hum* (Om mani padme hum), Germany: Dr. Wilhelm Filchner (10 January): editor.
1929 **The White Hell of Pitz Palu* (Die weiße Hölle vom Piz Palü), Germany: H. R. Sokal-Film GmbH (11 October) (1930: English language sound version; 1935: German language sound version): director (with G. W. Pabst), story, script, editing.
1930 *Avalanche aka *Storm over Mont Blanc* (Stürme über dem Montblanc), Germany: Althoff-Amboss-Film AG (Aafa), (25 December): director, script, editor.[4]
1931 *White Frenzy (Der weiße Rausch, Neue Wunder des Schneeschuhs), Germany: H. R. Sokal-Film GmbH, commissioned by Aafa, (10 December): director, script, editor.

---

[3]Short documentary; edited from *The Wonders of Skiing*.
[4]Fanck's first, post-synced sound film.

1932 *Fleeting Shadows* (Fliehende Schatten), Germany: Flugfilm Syndikat (12 April): editor.
1933 *SOS Iceberg (SOS Eisberg), Germany/United States: Ufa/Universal Pictures Corporation Co. Inc./: director (with Tay Garnett), (22 September): script, editor.[5]
1934 *Eternal Dream (Der ewige Traum), Germany/France: Cine-Allianz (31 March): director (with Henri chomet, script, editor.[6]
1934 *North Pole: Ahoy!* (Nordpol: Ahoi!), Germany/United States: Ufa/Universal Pictures Corporation Co. Inc. (18 April): idea.
1934 *The Whale* (Der Walfisch II –Verarbeitung), Germany: Ufa: director.
1934 *Seals* (Die Seehunde),[7] Germany: Ufa (14 September): director.
1934 *Badinga, King of Gorillas* (Badinga, der König der Gorillas), Germany: Terra-Filmkunst Gmbh (Terra): script.
1935 *How to Film Skiing* (Training zum Skifilmen), Germany: Terra: director.
1935 *Ski Records* (Höchstleistungen im Skilauf), Germany: Terra (23 May): director, script.
1936 *The Wilderness Is Dying!* (Die Wildnis stirbt!), Germany: Arbeitsgemeinschaft für Film- und Forschungs-Expeditionen (13 November): director (following Hans Schomburgk's edit), sound-editor.
1937 **The Samurai's Daughter* (Die Tochter des Samurai; Atarashiki tsuchi (1943 as *Die Liebe der Mitsu*; 1958 as *Kirschblüten, Geishas und Vulkane*)), Germany/Japan: Dr. Arnold Fanck-Film (Berlin); J.O. Studios; Tōwa Shōji (Tokyo: 11 February; Berlin: 23 March): director, producer, script, editor.
1938 *Little Hans* (Hänschen klein), Germany: GbR Dr. A Fanck/Dr. F. W. Hack Berlin (10 June): director, producer, camera,
1938 *Imperial Buildings in the Far East* (Kaiserbauten in Fernost), Germany: Dr. Arnold Fanck Tokyo (28 July): director, producer.
1938 *Winter Journey Through Southern Manchuria* (Winterreise durch Südmandschurien: Aufnahmen der japanischen Fanck-Expedition), Germany: Dr. Arnold Fanck (Tokyo), (10 November): director, producer.
1939 *On New Paths* (Auf neuen Wegen), Germany: Ufa: director.
1940 *Rice and Wood in the Mikado's Realm* (Reis und Holz im Lande des Mikado), Germany: Ufa: director.
1940 **A German Robinson* (Ein Robinson. Das Tagebuch eines Matrosen), Germany: Bavaria-Filmkunst GmbH (25 April): director, script, editor.
1940 *From Patagonia to Tierra del Fuego* (Von Patagonien nach Feuerland), Germany: Bavaria: director.
1941 *Spring in Japan* (Frühling in Japan), Germany: Ufa: director.
1941 *Japan's Holy Volcano* (Japans heiliger Vulkan), Germany: Ufa: director.
1941 *Battle for the Mountain* (Kampf um den Berg. Eine Hochtour vor 20 Jahren), Germany: Ufa: director.

---

[5] The American edition was co-directed by Tay Garnett.
[6] The French version, *Eternal Dream* (Rêve éternel), was co-directed by Henri Chomette and premiered in Paris in April 1934.
[7] *North Pole: Ahoy! The Whale* and *Seals* appear to be short documentaries made from footage collected during shooting *SOS Iceberg* in Greenland.

1943 *Joseph Thorak* (Joseph Thorak - Werkstatt und Werk), Germany: Kulturfilm-Institut GmbH; Riefenstahl-Film GmbH (November): director (with Hans Cürlis).

1944 *Impressions from Japan's Coastlines* (Bilder von Japans Küsten), Germany: Dr. Arnold Fanck-Film (Berlin); J.O. Studios; Tōwa Shōji: director.

1944 *The Atlantic Wall* (Atlantik-Wall), Germany Ufa-Sonderproduktion GmbH: director.

1944 *Arno Breker* (Arno Breker - Harte Zeit, starke Kunst), Germany: Kulturfilm-Institut GmbH; Riefenstahl-Film GmbH: director (with Hans Cürlis).

1950 *Foehn* (Föhn), Germany: H.R. Sokal-Produktion; Rolf Hansen-Film GmbH (10 October): script.[8]

1956 *Tetje and Fiedje 1* (Tetje und Fiedje: Wie sie einst zu einem Paar Skier kamen), Germany: H.R. Sokal-Film GmbH; Dr. Arnold Fanck: director.[9]

1956 *Tetje and Fiedje 2* (Tetje und Fiedje: Wie sie einst eine Füchsin fangen wollten), Germany: H.R. Sokal-Film GmbH; Dr. Arnold Fanck: director.

1956 *Tetje and Fiedje 3* (Tetje und Fiedje: Wie sie einst beinahe ihre smucke Deern erwischt hätten), Germany: H.R. Sokal-Film GmbH; Dr. Arnold Fanck: director.

1956 *Tetje and Fiedje 4* (Tetje und Fiedje: Wie sie einst Skifahren lernten), Germany: H.R. Sokal-Film GmbH; Dr. Arnold Fanck: director.

1956 *Small Tent - Great Love* (Kleines Zelt und große Liebe), Germany: Bavaria (05 October): idea.

1965 *White Frenzy: Then and Now* (Der weiße Rausch - einst und jetzt: Die Geschichte des Skilaufs von Anfang an), Germany: Insel-Film GmbH & Co. (09 December): consulting director.[10]

---

[8] Remake of *Piz Palu* (1929).
[9] The *Tetje and Fiedje* short film series uses material from the pre-war films featuring Guzzi Lantschner and Walter Riml as the eponymous comedian duo (likely *White Frenzy*, *The Great Leap*, and *North Pole, Ahoy!*).
[10] The film is compiled from various works, including Fanck's *White Frenzy* (1931) and *The Wonders of Skiing* (1920 and 1922).

APPENDIX 4

Filmography Itami Mansaku[1]

1928[2] *Peace on Earth* (aka All's Right with the World; Tenka taiheiki; 天下太平記), Dir. Inagaki Hiroshi, Japan: Chiezō Productions (Kataoka Chiezō Purodakushon) (Chie Puro) (15 June), Itami: script.
1928 *The Wandering Gambler* (aka Vagabond Gambler; Hōrō zanmai; 放浪三昧), Dir. Inagaki Hiroshi, Japan: Chie Puro (28 July), Itami: actor, script.[3]
1928 *Young Genji* (aka Genji Boy; Genji kozō; 源氏小僧), Dir. Inagaki Hiroshi, Japan: Chie Puro (3 October), Itami: script.
1928 *Vicissitudes of Revenge* (Adauchi ruten; 仇討流転), Dir. (also script) Itami Mansaku, Japan: Chie Puro (25 November).[4]
1928 *Hell of Ten Thousand Flowers 2, Part 1* (Zoku manka jigoku: dai ippen; 続万花地獄　第一篇), Dir. Itami Mansaku (also actor and script), Japan: Chie Puro (31 December).[5]
1929 *Hell of Ten Thousand Flowers 2, Part 2* (Zoku manka jigoku: dai nihen; 続万花地獄　第二篇), Dirs. Inagaki Hiroshi and Itami Mansaku (also actor and script), Japan: Chie Puro (15 February).[6]
1929 *A Samurai's Career* (aka Picture Book on Knight Errantry; Ehon musha shugyō 絵本武者修業), Dir. Inagaki Hiroshi, Japan: Chie Puro (7 June), Itami: script.
1930 *Beyond the Spring Breeze* (Harukaze no kanata e; 春風の彼方へ), Dir. Itami Mansaku (also script), Japan: Chie Puro (14 March).

---

[1]This filmography is based mainly on: Hirano (2001; Galbraith 2008; Jacoby 2008: 88–90; Shutsū and Nagata 2008; Yamane 1997). I have adopted English translations when available; otherwise the translations are my own. Extant films are marked with an asterisk.
[2]If in doubt, I have adopted the release dates in Shutsū and Nagata's catalogue of Japanese feature films from 1899 to 1945 (Shutsū and Nagata 2008).
[3]Based on Itami's original script *Date Mondo* (伊達主水, 1927).
[4]Based on the *rakugo* piece-cum-*kabuki* play *Kaidan Botan Dōrō* by Sanyūtei Enchō (see Leiter and Yamamoto 1997: 257–8). It has been adapted for the screen several times, the first version likely being a *kabuki* performance in 1910.
[5]Based on Yoshikawa Eiji's novel *Manka jigoku* (1929).
[6]Itami collapsed during the production and Inagaki finished it alone. Itami consequently was not involved in the final part of the trilogy, released 15 February 1929.

1930 *Here Comes Young Genji* (Genji kozō shutsugen; 源氏小僧出現), Dir. Itami Mansaku (also script), Japan: Chie Puro (1 August).

1930 *Kodenji's Escape* (Nigeyuku Kodenji; 逃げ行く小伝次), Dir. Itami Mansaku (also script), Japan: Chie Puro (10 August).[7]

1931 *Famous Young Genji* (Gozonji Genji kozō; 御存知源氏小僧), Dir. Itami Mansaku (also script), Japan: Chie Puro (15 January).

1931 *The Thirteenth Year of the Genroku Era* (Genroku jūsan nen; 元禄十三年), Dir. Inagaki Hiroshi, Japan: Chie Puro (1 May), Itami: script.[8]

1931 *Cheerful Kon Chusuke Part 1* (Kaikyō Kon Chūsuke zenpen; 快侠金忠輔前篇), Dir. Soga Masashi (as Furitsu Rankyō), Japan: Chie Puro (29 May), Itami: script.[9]

1931 *Cheerful Kon Chusuke Parts 2 & 3* (Kaikyō Kon Chūsuke chūhen kohen; 快侠金忠輔 中篇・後篇), Dir. Soga Masashi, Japan: Chie Puro (5 June), Itami: script.

1931 *Golden Boy Rikitaro* (aka Rikitaro Kinteki; Kinteki Rikitarō; 金的力太郎), Dir. Itami Mansaku (also script), Japan: Chie Puro (1 July).[10]

1931 *Fireworks* (Hanabi; 花火), Dir. Itami Mansaku (also script), Japan: Chie Puro (26 August).

1932 *Peerless Patriot* (aka Unrivaled Hero; Kokushi Musō; 国士無双), Dir. Itami Mansaku, Japan: Chie Puro (14 January) [*Kinema Junpō* Place 6].[11]

1932 *The Life of a Foul Murderer* (aka Professional Killer; Yamiuchi tosei; 闇討渡世), Dir. Itami Mansaku (also script), Japan: Chie Puro (3 June).[12]

1932 *Togitatsu's Revenge* (Togitatsu no utare; 研辰の討たれ), Dir. Itami Mansaku (also script), Japan: Chie Puro (17 November).[13]

1933 *The Dice Tattoo* (aka The Tatooed Gambler; Irezumi chōhan;[14] 刺青奇偶), Dir. Itami Mansaku (also script), Japan: Chie Puro (14 January).

1933 *A True Tokyoite's Kagura* (Edokko kagura; 江戸っ子神楽), Dir. Itami Mansaku (also script), Japan: Chie Puro [unfinished].[15]

---

[7]Based on John Galsworthy's play *Escape* (1921) (Shutsū and Nagata 2008: 897). Its cinematic adaptation, *Escape*, by British director and producer Basil Dean was released in the United States in September 1930, a mere month before Itami's film reached the Japanese cinemas.
[8]Based on Hayashi Fubō's (Hasegawa Kaitarō) original work (*Ninjō misui*, 刃傷未遂).
[9]Based on Yoshikawa Eiji's serial *Kon Chūsuke* (1930).
[10]Inspired by Ferenc Molnár's play *Liliom* (1919), which had already been turned into a film by Frank Borzage in 1930, and later by Fritz Lang in 1934 (Yamane 1997: 78).
[11]*Peerless Patriot* is based on Iseno Shigetaka's (1903-1982) original idea. The origin of 'one of the best *jidaigeki* films of the silent era' (Iwasaki 1961: 150) is contested. The reason being the contemporaneous penchant for made-up authors (like James Maki) and the alternative reading of the name Iseno Shigetaka as *Ise no jūseki* ('heavily responsible for Ise'). However, most sources agree that the original is, indeed, by Iseno and the script by Itami (Itami and Shiga 1961: 77; Iwasaki 1961: 150; Yamane 1997: 90; Shutsū and Nagata 2008: 475). 21 minutes extant; Held by National Film Archive Japan.
[12]Based on Muramatsu Shōfū's (Muramatsu Giichi) novel *Ningen kikin* (1931).
[13]Based on Kimura Kinka's kabuki play *Togitatsu no utare* (1925).
[14]Based on Hasegawa Shin's eponymous novel (1932).
[15]Based on a novel by Hasegawa Shin.

1934 *A Migrating Bird's Souvenirs of the Kiso Valley* (Wataridori Kiso miyage; 渡鳥木曾土産), Dir. Itami Mansaku (also script); Japan: Chie Puro (14 January).[16]

1934 Feb. 8: *Encyclopaedia of Budo* (aka Bushido Handbook; Budō taikan; 武道大鑑), Dir. Itami Mansaku (also script), Japan: Chie Puro (8 February) [*Kinema Junpō* Place 4.][17]

1934 *The Story of the Forty-Seven Loyal Retainers: Scroll of Bloodshed, Scroll of Revenge* (Chūshingura ninjōhen fukushuhen; 忠臣蔵刃傷篇復讐篇), Dir. Itō Daisuke, Japan: Nikkatsu (17 May), Itami: script and assistant director.

1935 *Chuji Makes a Name for Himself* (aka *Chuji in His Heyday*; Chūji uridasu; 忠次売出す), Dir. Itami Mansaku (also script), Japan: Shinkō Kinema (28 February) [Itami's first talkie; *Kinema Junpō* Place 4].

1935 **Frivolous Servant* (aka *Capricious Young Man*; lit. *Rare Story of the Era of Warring States: The Whimsical Youth*; Sengoku kitan: Kimagure kaja; 戦国気譚: 気まぐれ冠者), Dir. Itami Mansaku (also script), Japan: Chie Puro (30 May).[18]

1936 *Akanishi Kakita (aka The Letter; Akanishi Kakita; 赤西蠣太), Dir. Itami Mansaku (also script), Japan: Chie Puro (18 June) [*Kinema Junpō* Place 5].[19]

1936 *The Peony Lantern* (Botan dōrō, 牡丹燈籠), Dir. Nobuchi Akira, Japan: Rengō Eiga Sha (R.E.S), Itami: script [unfinished].[20]

1937 *New Earth (Atarashiki Tsuchi; 新しき土), Dir. Itami Mansaku,[21] Japan/Germany: J.O. Studios, Tōwa Shōji (3 February).

1937 *Hometown (Furusato; 故郷), Dir. Itami Mansaku (also script), Japan: J.O. Studios (1 May).[22]

1937 *Gonza and Sukeju (Gonza to Sukejū; 権三と助十), Dir. Itami Mansaku (also script), Japan: J.O. Studios (8 October).[23]

1938 *The Giant (aka Tale of a Giant; Kyojin den; 巨人伝), Dir. Itami Mansaku (also script), Japan: J.O. Studios (Tōhō Eiga (Tokyo) Co. Ltd.) (11 April).[24]

1942 *Dare Your Life* (Fushaku shinmyō; 不惜身命), Itami (script) [unrealized].[25]

1943 *Cotton Version of the Record of Great Peace* (Momen taiheiki; 木綿太平記), Itami (script) [unrealized].

1943 **The Life of Muho Matsu* (aka The Life of Matsu the Untamed; Muhō Matsu no isshō; 無法松の一生), Dir. Inagaki Hiroshi, Japan: Daiei (28 October), Itami: script.[26]

---

[16] Based on Saeki Kiyoshi's original idea.
[17] Based on Yamate Saichirō's (Iguchi Chōji) novel *Ichinen yojitsu* (1933).
[18] According to Thornton, the film is a homage to Douglas Fairbanks in *The Three Musketeers* (1921, Fred Niblo (Thornton 2008: 45). Held by National Film Archive Japan.
[19] Based on Shiga Naoya's novel (1918). The first work after the revival of cooperation between Chiezō Productions and Nikkatsu. Available on DVD.
[20] Based on Sanyūtei Enchō's *rakugo* piece-cum-*kabuki* play *Kaidan Botan Dōrō* (1884).
[21] I concur with the conventional interpretation and attribute the script solely to Fanck (Itami 1961: 244; Shutsū and Nagata 2008: 56). Held by National Film Archive Japan.
[22] Based on Kaneko Yōbun's play (1936). Held by National Film Archive Japan.
[23] Based on Okamoto Kidō's shin kabuki play (1926). Held by National Film Archive Japan.
[24] Based on Victor Hugo's *Les Misérables* (1862). Held by National Film Archive Japan.
[25] Based on Yamamoto Yūzō's novel (1939).
[26] Based on Iwashita Shunsaku's novel *Tomishima Matsugurō den* (1941). Available on DVD.

1948 *Children Hand in Hand* (Te o tsunagu kora; 手をつなぐ子等), Dir. Inagaki Hiroshi, Japan: Daiei (30 March), Itami: script.[27]

1950 *I'm A Bodyguard* (Ore wa yōjinbō; 俺は用心棒), Dir. Inagaki Hiroshi, Japan: Tōyoko Eiga (19 February), Itami: script [working title: *Mukashi o ima ni*].[28]

1952 *53 Stations of the Wind of Love* (Koikaze gojūsan tsugi; 恋風五十三次), Dir. Nakagawa Nobuo, Japan: Tōei Kyoto (8 May), Itami: script [working title: *Tōkaidō hizakurige*]. [29]

1955 *Bad Boy Makes a Name for Himself* (Akutarō uridasu; 悪太郎売出す) Dir. Arai Ryōhei, Japan: Daiei (19 October) [script by Fuji Yahirō, based on Itami's *Chuji Makes a Name for Himself*].

1958 *The Life of Muho Matsu* (aka The Life of Matsu the Untamed aka The Rickshaw Man; Muhō Matsu no isshō; 無法松の一生), Dir. Inagaki Hiroshi, Japan: Tōhō (22 April), Itami: script [Golden Lion, 1958 Venice Film Festival].[30]

1964 *Children Hand in Hand* (Te o tsunagu kora; 手をつなぐ子等), Dir. Hani Susumu, Japan: Shōwa Eiga (28 March), Itami: script.

1965 *The Life of Muho Matsu* (aka The Life of Matsu the Untamed aka The Rickshaw Man; Muhō Matsu no isshō; 無法松の一生), Dir. Misumi Kenji, Japan: Daiei (28 April), Itami: script.[31]

1986 *Peerless Patriot* (aka The Unrivaled Hero; Kokushi musō; 国士無双), Dir. Hosaka Nobuhiko, Japan: Sanreniti (25 October) [script by Kikushima Ryūzō, based on original idea by Iseno Shigetaka and Itami Mansaku].

---

[27] Available on DVD.
[28] Based on Tamura Ichiji's children's book (1944).
[29] Based on Yoda Yoshikata's original work. An Edo Period 'Road Movie' (Tōei 1992: 11).
[30] Available on DVD.
[31] A 1963 version directed by Murayama Shinji uses a screenplay by Itō Daisuke (Hirano 2001: 232). Available on DVD.

REFERENCES

Abegg, Lilly (1937), 'Die neue Erde; Ein deutsch-japanischer Film', *Frankfurter Zeitung* - Reichsausgabe, 03 March: 111–3.
Abel, Jonathan E. (2012), *Redacted: The Archives of Censorship in Transwar Japan*, Berkeley: University of California Press.
Adachi-Rabe, Kayo (2002), 'Unsichtbarer Tod: Mori Ogais "Geschlecht der Abe" in der Verfilmung von Kumagai Hisatora, Versuch einer Neubewertung', *Japonica Humboldtiana*, (6): 167–82.
Agger, Gunhild (1999); 'Intertextuality revisited: Dialogue and negotiations in Media Studies', *Canadian Aesthetics Journal*, 4. Available Online: http://www.uqtr.uquebec.ca/AE/vol_4/gunhild.htm (accessed 09 September 2012).
Aldinger, Karin (2005), *Propaganda Audiovisuell - Nationalsozialistische Propaganda in Film- und Wochenschau*, München: GRIN-Verlag.
Anderson, Benedict (1993), *Imagined Communities: Reflections on the Origin and Spread of Nationalism*, London: Verso.
Anderson, Joseph L. and Donald Richie (1982 [1959]), *The Japanese Film: Art and Industry*, Princeton: Princeton University Press.
Aoyama, Toshimi (1936), 'Atarashiki tsuchi tokushū: Atarashiki tsuchi o okuru Anorudo Fanku', *Eiga no Tomo*, (70): 90–1.
Asad, Talal (2010 [1986]), 'The concept of cultural translation', in Mona Baker (ed.), *Critical Readings in Translation Studies*, 7–27, New York: Routledge.
Asahi Shinbun (24.05.1926), 'Dairokkan': 6.
Asahi Shinbun (05.06.1926), '*Bushidō* o goran': 2.
Asahi Shinbun (01.06.1935), '*Kimagure kaja*: Chiezō no nansensu mono': 7.
Asahi Shinbun (13.11.1935), 'Raishun nihon o otozureru: Yamaeigaō Doitsu no Fanku hakase': 11.
Asahi Shinbun (29.02.1936), '*ZaoZaō no juhyō* satsuei no kushin': 7.
Asahi Shinbun (15.03.1936), 'Fankuhan *Zaō Seifuku*': 9.
Asahi Shinbun (18.04.1936), 'Fanku hakase no omegane ni futari': 2.
Asahi Shinbun (13.05.1936), 'Fanku eiga haiyujin kimaru: Shuen wa Hara Setsuko': 2.
Asahi Shinbun (10.06.1936), 'Shineiga hyō: *Akanishi Kakita*: 6.
Asahi Shinbun (30.06.1936), 'Teikoku gekijō de *Hikyō Nekka* (Mantetsu)': 7.
Asahi Shinbun (27.08.1936a), 'Fanku shi kako seifuku': 11.
Asahi Shinbun (27.08.1936b), 'Gaimusho ga "kantoku": Kokusai eiga kyōkai no jinyō o kyōka, zokuzoku kokusakumono o fugiri': 11.
Asahi Shinbun (18.12.1936), 'Nichidoku ginmaku kyōtei: *Atarashiki tsuchi* fugiri – raiharu ryōkoku ga dōji ni': 2.
Asahi Shinbun (12.02.1937), 'Akatsuki nō hosō: Fanku hakase to Hara Setsuko san': 2.

Asahi Shinbun (13.02.1937), 'Rishū no ame yo kokotutekina nippon': 2.
Asahi Shinbun (11.03.1937), 'Toki, kyōkan, himei ... miokuri kyōsō Hara chan no shuppatsu': 11.
Asahi Shinbun (13.03.1937), 'Setsuko san bokoku o hanaru': 11.
Asahi Shinbun (28.03.1937a), 'Hōgakai no sekigahara: Burokkusen no naka ni maku o kiru sakuhinsen': 5.
Asahi Shinbun (28.03.1937b), 'Wadai tobidasu ginmaku: Hara jō Berurin de shuen gaikokan no musume ni funshite': 13.
Asahi Shinbun (11.04.1937), 'Hara Setsuko no eiga ni Yamada Kōsaku shi Doitsu e: Fu hakase no *Gaikōkan no Musume*': 13.
Asahi Shinbun (27.04.1937), 'Setsuko wa hogaraka Berurin kara sunappu godai': 5.
Asahi Shinbun (04.05.1937), '*Atarashiki tsuchi* Pari e': 13.
Asahi Shinbun (20.05.1937), '*Atarashiki tsuchi*': 5.
Asahi Shinbun (20.06.1937), '*Atarashiki tsuchi* e no shute': 10.
Asahi Shinbun (02.07.1937), 'Manshū no "*Atarashiki tsuchi*" ni': 3.
Asahi Shinbun (01.08.1937), 'Kaikoku nihon o shudai *Atarashiki tsuchi* no mukau o haru yushutsu eiga *Taifun* no shindatsu': 4.
Asahi Shinbun (14.04.1939), '*Atarashiki tsuchi* Manshūkuo e': 1.
'*Atarashiki tsuchi* Manshūkuo de mo daijū' (24.02.1937), *Newspaper, Title Illegible*: n.p.
Atkins, E. Taylor (2001), *Blue Nippon: Authenticating Jazz in Japan*, Durham: Duke University Press.
Atlantic Wall (Atlantik-Wall) (1944), Dir. Arnold Fanck, Germany: Ufa Sonderproduktion GmbH (Berlin).
Auslin, Michael R. (2011), *Pacific Cosmopolitans: A Cultural History of U.S.-Japan Relations*, Cambridge, MA: Harvard University Press.
Azuma, Eiichiro (2005), *Between Two Empires: Race, History, and Transnationalism in Japanese America*, New York: Oxford University Press.
B, F. v. (1919), 'Harakiri', *Lichtbild-Bühne*, 12 (52): 19.
Balázs, Béla (1984 [1931]), 'Der Fall Dr. Fanck', in Helmut H. Diederichs and Wolfgang Gersch (eds), *Der Geist des Films: Artikel und Aufsätze 1926-1931*, (2), 287–91, München: Carl Hanser.
Banks, Marcus (1992), 'Which films are the ethnographic films?', in Peter Ian Crawford and David Turton (eds), *Film as Ethnography*, 116–29, Manchester: Manchester University Press.
Barrett, Gregory (1992), 'Comic targets and comic styles: An introduction to Japanese film comedy', in Arthur Nolletti and David Desser (eds), *Reframing Japanese Cinema: Authorship, Genre, History*, 210–26, Bloomington: Indiana University Press.
Barshay, Andrew E. (1988), *State and Intellectual in Imperial Japan: The Public Man in Crisis*, Berkeley: University of California Press.
Baskett, Michael (2008), *The Attractive Empire: Transnational Film Culture in Imperial Japan*, Honolulu: University of Hawai'i Press.
Baskins, Cristelle (2011), 'A storm of images: Italian Renaissance art in Luis Trenker's *Condottieri* (1937)', *The Italianist*, 31: 181–204.
Bäumler, Ernst (1988), *Die Rotfabriker: Familiengeschichte eines Weltunternehmens*, München: Piper 1988.

Baxandall, Michael (1985), *Patterns of Intention: On the Historical Explanation of Pictures*, New Haven: Yale University Press.
Beard, William (2013), 'Aesthetic nationalism in English-Canadian cinema', *Senses of Cinema*, 69: n.p. Available Online: http://sensesofcinema.com/2013/feature-articles/aesthetic-nationalism-in-english-canadian-cinema/ (accessed 25 June 2014).
Beba-Woche (1926), 'Japan-ein neues Filmland', (4): cover page.
Benesch, Oleg (2014), *Inventing the Way of the Warrior: Nationalism, Internationalism, and Bushido in Modern Japan*, Oxford: Oxford University Press.
Bennett, Alexander (2010), 'Japan: Naginata', in Thomas A. Green and Joseph R. Svinth (eds), *Martial Arts of the World: An Encyclopedia of History and Innovation*, Vol. 2, 158–62, Santa Barbara: ABC-CLIO.
Berliner Lokalanzeiger (27.03.1937), 'Setsuko Hara in Berlin', 74 (55): n.p.
Bernardi, Joanne (2001), *Writing in Light: The Silent Scenario and the Japanese Pure Film Movement*, Detroit: Wayne State University Press.
Bernstein, Andrew (2008), 'Whose Fuji?: Religion, region, and state in the fight for a national symbol', *Monumenta Nipponica*, 63 (1): 51–99.
Berque, Augustin (1992), 'Identification of the self in relation to the environment', in Nancy R. Rosenberger (ed.), *Japanese Sense of Self*, 93–101, Cambridge: Cambridge University Press.
Bhabha, Homi K. (1990), 'Dissemination: Time, narrative, and the margins of the modern nation', in Homi Bhabha (ed.), *Nation and Narration*, 291–322, London: Routledge.
Bieber, Hans-Joachim (2009), '*Die Tochter des Samurai*. Deutsch-japanische Filmproduktionen in der NS-Zeit', in Dagmar Bussiek and Simona Göbel (eds), *Kultur, Politik und Öffentlichkeit: Festschrift für Jens Flemming*, 355–77, Kassel: Kassel University Press.
Bieber, Hans-Joachim (2014), *SS und Samurai. Deutsch-japanische Kulturbeziehungen 1933-1945*, München: Iudicium.
Blinn, Miika (2008), 'The dubbing standard: Its history and efficiency. Implications for film distributors in the German film market', *DIME Working Papers on Intellectual Property Rights*, 57. Available online: www.dime-eu.org/files/active/0/WP57-IPR.pdf (accessed 12 June 2016).
Bock, Hans-Michael and Tim Bergfelder (2006), *The Concise Cinegraph: Encyclopaedia of German Cinema*, New York: Berghahn Books.
Bogner, Thomas (1999), 'Zur Rekonstruktion filmischer Naturdarstellung am Beispiel einer Fallstudie. Natur im Film *Der heilige Berg* von Dr. Arnold Fanck', PhD Thesis, Universität Hamburg.
Bordwell, David (2007), 'Another Bologna briefing', 6 July. Available online: www.davidbordwell.net (accessed 30 July 2013).
Borkin, Joseph (1978), *The Crime and Punishment of IG Farben*, New York: The Free Press.
Botschaft von Japan (2009), 'Koichi Kishi – ein japanischer Musiker', *Neues aus Japan*, 52. Available online: www.de.emb-japan.go.jp (accessed 30 July 2011).
Boyd, Carl (1981), 'The Berlin-Tokyo axis and Japanese military initiative', *Modern Asian Studies*, 15 (2): 311–38.
Brandlmeier, Thomas (2008), *Kameraautoren: Technik und Ästhetik*, Marburg: Schüren Verlag.

Brecht, Bertolt (1964 [1936]), 'Alienation effects in Chinese acting', in John Willett (ed.), *Brecht on Theatre: The Development of an Aesthetic*, 91–9. London: Methuen.
Bremer Zeitung (28.02.1937), 'Die Tochter des Samurai': n.p.
Buda, Janusz (2006), 'Rudyard Kipling's The Ballad of East and West', *Waseda University Faculty of Commerce*. Available online: www.f.waseda.jp/buda/texts/ballad.html (accessed 17 March 2012).
Bundesarchiv Berlin (13.06.2012), 'Friedrich Wilhelm Hack', [Email] Message to author.
Bundesministerium der Justiz (2011), 'Sozialgesetzbuch (SGB) Sechstes Buch (VI): Anlage 1 Durchschnittsentgelt in Euro/DM/RM'. Available online: http://www.bundesrecht.juris.de (accessed 02 March 2012).
Chiba, Nobuo (1987), *Eiga joyū no Shōwa*, Tokyo: Daiwa Shobō.
Chiba, Nobuo (1995), *Hara Setsuko Denki*, Tokyo: Shoeisha.
Corazza, Heinz (1937), *Die Samurai. Ritter des Reiches in Ehre und Treue*, München: Zentralverlag der NSDAP, Franz Eher Nachf.
Culver, Annika A. (2013), *Glorify the Empire: Japanese Avant-Garde Propaganda in Manchukuo*, Vancouver: UBC Press.
Daibō, Masaki (2010), 'Todokanai merodi: Nichidoku gassaku eiga *Atarashiki tsuchi* no eiga ongaku ni miru Yamada Kōsaku no risō to genjitsu', in Sugino Kentarō (ed.), *Eiga to neishon*, 1–34, Kyoto: Mineruba Shobō.
Dalby, Liza (2001), *Kimono: Fashioning Culture*, London: Vintage.
Davis, Darrell William (1996), *Picturing Japaneseness: Monumental Style, National Identity, Japanese Film*, New York: Columbia University Press.
Der Deutsche Film (1937), 'Filme des Monats: Die Tochter des Samurai', 1 (11): 333–4.
Der Film (1919), 'Das Museum Umlauff als Filmfundus', 4 (19): 29.
Der Film (1937a), 'Cocco-Tobis-Nippon', 10 April, (15): n.p.
Der Film (1937b), 'Richard Angst fährt wieder nach Japan', 12 July, (24): n.p.
Deutsche Filmexport GmbH, Berlin (1936–1938), 'Exportlizenzen', *Fanck Documents*, Filmmuseum München.
Drew, William M. (2003 [1996]), 'Kiyohiko Ushihara's *Shingun* (Marching On): "Banzai" for a high-flying silent classic'. Available online: www.gildasattic.com/shingun.html (accessed 20 June 2012).
Duara, Prasenjit (2003), *Sovereignty and Authenticity: Manchukuo and the East Asian Modern*, Lanham: Rowman & Littlefield Publishers.
Dyer, Richard (2007), *Stars*, London: British Film Institute.
Earhart, H. Byron (1968), 'The celebration of Haru-Yama (Spring-Mountain): An example of folk religious practives in contemporary Japan', *Asian Folklore Studies*, 27 (1): 1–24.
Ebisaka, Takashi (2004), 'Nichidoku gassaku eiga *Atarashiki tsuchi* o megutte: sono 2', *Teikyō Kokusai Bungaku*, 17: 37–84.
Eiga Engeki Naihō (25.02.1937), '*Atarashiki tsuchi* no nishū sō agedaka': 1.
Eiga Mainichi (07.07.1936), 'Fanku eiga hajimete geki no kuranku, Itami kantoku no shidō ni': n.p.
Eisner, Lotte (1973), *The Haunted Screen: Expressionism in the German Cinema and the Influence of Max Reinhardt*, London: Secker and Warburg.

Elsaesser, Thomas (1994), 'Moderne und Modernisierung: Der deutsche Film der dreißiger Jahre', *montage-av*, 3 (2): 23–40.
Elsaesser, Thomas (2000), *Weimar Cinema and After: Germany's Historical Imaginary*, London: Routledge.
Enami, Nobukuni (ca 1905), 'Iris Garden in Horikiri Tokyo'. Available online: www.t-enami.org (accessed 28 October 2013).
Enrich, Enric (2005), 'Legal aspects of international film co-production'. Available online: www.obs.coe.int/online_publication/expert/coproduccion_aspectos-juridicos.pdf.en (accessed 29 September 2011).
Erste Internationale Filmzeitung (17.08.1918), 'Harakiri', 12 (33): 24.
Fanck, Arnold (1935), 'Shinto: Dr. Arnold Fanck über das Projekt eines japanischen Filmes', *Film-Kurier*, 17 (170): 4.
Fanck, Arnold (02.09.1936), 'Letter to Paul Kohner', *Fanck Documents*, Filmmuseum München.
Fanck, Arnold (1937a), '*Atarashiki tsuchi* nihon fukiri ni saishite', *Yomiuri Shinbun*, 03 February: 6.
Fanck, Arnold (1937b), 'Nihon no sōgōteki inshō (1)', *Asahi Shinbun*, 25 January: 9.
Fanck, Arnold (1937c), 'Pressekonferenz', *Fanck Documents*, Filmmuseum München.
Fanck, Arnold (1938), *Die Tochter des Samurai: Ein Film im Echo der Deutschen Presse*, Berlin: Ernst Steiniger.
Fanck, Arnold (ca 1969), 'Manuskript für *Er führte Regie mit Gletschern, Stürmen und Lawinen*'. Available online: www.antiquariat.de (accessed 02 July 2010).
Fanck, Arnold (ca. 1970), 'Die Tochter des Samurai', *Fanck Documents*, Filmmuseum München.
Fanck, Arnold (1973), *Er führte Regie mit Gletschern, Stürmen und Lawinen. Ein Filmpionier erinnert sich*, München: Nymphenburger.
Fanck, Arnold (1976), 'Interview mit Arnold Fanck by Herman Weigel', *Filmhefte*, 5 (2): 3–29.
Fanck, Arnold (1997 [1933]), 'Das Problem der künstlerischen Freiheit des Autors und Regisseurs im Film. (1933)', in Jan-Christopher Horak and Gisela Pichler (eds), *Berge, Licht und Traum. Dr. Arnold Fanck und der deutsche Bergfilm*, 171–3, München: Bruckmann.
Fanck, Arnold (1997 [1935]), 'Anfang und Ende meines alpinen Filmschaffens (1935)', in Jan-Christopher Horak and Gisela Pichler (eds), *Berge, Licht und Traum. Dr. Arnold Fanck und der deutsche Bergfilm*, 173, München: Bruckmann.
Fanck, Arnold (1997 [1937], 'Rundfunkvortrag in München (1937)', In Jan-Christopher Horak and Gisela Pichler (eds), *Berge, Licht und Traum. Dr. Arnold Fanck und der deutsche Bergfilm*, 180–2, München: Bruckmann.
Fanck, Matthias (2009), *Weisse Hölle – Weisser Rausch: Arnold Fanck, Bergfilme und Bergbilder 1909-1939*, Zürich: AS Verlag.
Fanck Documents (1936) 'Zadankai', [translated into German], 09.02.1936, Filmmuseum München.
'Fanku hakase ikkō' (1937), Kawakita Memorial Film Institute.
Fedorova, Anastasia (2014), '*Big Tokyo* (1933) and the ideology of sound', *Japanese Slavic and East European Studies*, 35: 103–27.

Ferguson, Jane M. (2018), 'Flight school for the spirit of Myanmar: Aerial nationalism and Burmese-Japanese cinematic collaboration in the 1930s', *South East Asia Research*, 26 (3): 268–82.
Film-Kurier (1935a), 'Hinter den Film-Kulissen Japans: Der Trust herrscht', 09 July, 17 (157): 1–2.
Film-Kurier (1935b), 'Mäzene in Japan: Kulturfilm-Produktion ohne geschäftliche Rücksichten', 20 August, 17 (193): 1.
Film-Kurier (1936), 'Herbst in Japan', 21 January, 18 (17): 2.
Film-Kurier (1937a), 'Empfang der Stadt Leipzig für Setsuko Hara', 16 March, 19 (88): 3.
Film-Kurier (1937b), 'Erweiterung der deutsch-japanischen Filmbeziehungen: Rahmenabkommen der Tobis mit Japan', 10 April, 19 (82): n.p.
Film-Kurier (1937c), 'Chinesischer Besuch in der Tobis', 23 March, 19 (69): 2.
Film-Kurier (1937d), 'Condottieri', 25.03.1937, 19 (71): n.
Film-Prüfstelle Berlin (1933), 'Zulassungskarte für Bildstreifen: *Kagami*', 22. September, Frankfurt am Main: Deutsches Filminstitut.
Filmwoche (20.03.1935), 'In die weite Welt', 13 (12): 2.
Flüggen, Christian (1920), 'Harakiri', *Deutsche Lichtspiel-Zeitung*, 8 (7): 2.
Foreign Affairs Association of Japan (1926), *The Japan Yearbook 1926*, Tokyo: Foreign Affairs Association of Japan.
Foreign Affairs Association of Japan (1933), *The Japan Yearbook 1933*, Tokyo: Foreign Affairs Association of Japan.
Foreign Affairs Association of Japan (1934), *The Japan Yearbook 1934*, Tokyo: Foreign Affairs Association of Japan.
Foreign Affairs Association of Japan (1939), *The Japan Yearbook 1938-1939*, Tokyo: Foreign Affairs Association of Japan.
Foucault, Michel (1980), 'Truth and power', in Colin Gordon (ed.), *Power/Knowledge: Selected Interviews and Other Writings 1972-1977 by Michel Foucault*, 109–33, Harlow: Harvester Press.
Foujita, Tsuguharu (as Tsuguji) (1937), 'A biased view of the Japanese cinema', in Tadashi Iijima, Akira Iwasaki and Kisao Uchida (eds), *Cinema Yearbook of Japan 1936-1937*, 32–4, Tokyo: Sanseido.
Fox, John P (1982), *Germany and the Far Eastern Crisis 1931-1938: A Study in Diplomacy and Ideology*, Oxford: Clarendon.
Freiberg, Freda (2000), 'Comprehensive connections: The film industry, the theatre and the state in the early Japanese cinema', *Screening the Past: An Online Journal of Media and History*, (11). Available online: www.latrobe.edu.au/screeningthepast (accessed 24 November 2012).
Fu, Poshek (2003), *Between Shanghai and Hong Kong: The Politics of Chinese Cinemas*, Stanford: Stanford University Press.
Furukawa, Takahisa (2003), *Senjika no nihon eiga*, Tokyo: Yoshikawa Kobunkan.
Galbraith, Stuart (2008), *The Tōhō Studios Story: A History and Complete Filmography*, Lanham: Scarecrow Press.
Galliano, Luciana (2002), *Yōgaku: Japanese Music in the Twentieth Century*, Lanham: Scarecrow Press.
Gartenlaube (1933), 'Roberts Nurblond', (19): n.p.

Geertz, Clifford (1988), 'Being there: Anthropology and the scene of writing', in *Works and Lives: The Anthropologist as Author*, 1–24, Stanford: Stanford University Press.
Gerow, Aaron (2001), 'The word before the image', in Dennis C. Washburn and Carole Cavanaugh (eds), *Word and Image in Japanese Cinema*, 3–35, Cambridge: Cambridge University Press.
Gerow, Aaron (2008), *A Page of Madness: Cinema and Modernity in 1920s Japan*, Ann Arbor: The University of Michigan.
Gerow, Aaron (2010), *Visions of Japanese Modernity: Articulations of Cinema, Nation, and Spectatorship, 1895-1925*, Berkeley: University of California Press.
Goebbels, Joseph (1987), *Die Tagebücher von Joseph Goebbels: Sämtliche Fragmente; Teil 1, Aufzeichnungen 1924-1941*, Vol. 3, ed. Elke Fröhlich, München: K.G. Saur.
Goebbels, Joseph (2006a), *Die Tagebücher von Joseph Goebbels. Teil 1, Aufzeichnungen 1923-1941*, Vol. 2 (3), ed. Elke Fröhlich, München: K. G. Saur.
Goebbels, Joseph (2006b), *Die Tagebücher von Joseph Goebbels. Teil 1, Aufzeichnungen 1923-1941*, Vol. 3 (1), ed. Elke Fröhlich, München: K. G. Saur.
Goebbels, Joseph (2006c), *Die Tagebücher von Joseph Goebbels. Teil 2, Diktate 1941-1945*, Vol 4, ed. Elke Fröhlich, München: K. G. Saur.
Gōto, Nobuko (2014), *Yamada Kōsaku: tsukuru no de wa naku umu*, Tokyo: Mineruba Shobō.
Graichen, Gisela and Horst Gründer (2005), *Deutsche Kolonien. Traum und Trauma*, Berlin: Ullstein.
Hack, Annette (1996), 'Die Deutsch-Japanischen Gesellschaften: 1888-1945', in Günter Haasch (ed.), *Die Deutsch-Japanischen Gesellschaften von 1888 bis 1996*, 1–441, Berlin: Edition Colloquium.
Hack Documents ('Hack-Papiere'), held by Prof. Bernd Martin, Historisches Seminar, Universität Freiburg.
Hake, Sabine (2002), *German National Cinema*, London, New York: Routledge.
Hall, Robert K., ed. (1949), *Kokutai no Hongi: Cardinal Principles of the National Entity of Japan*, Cambridge, MA: Harvard University Press.
Hansen, Janine (1997a), *Arnold Fancks Die Tochter des Samurai: Nationalsozialistische Propaganda und Japanische Filmpolitik*, Wiesbaden: Harrassowitz.
Hansen, Janine (1997b), 'Auf den Wunsch meines Führers', in Jan-Christopher Horak and Gisela Pichler (eds), *Berge, Licht und Traum. Dr. Arnold Fanck und der deutsche Bergfilm*, 125–41, München: Bruckmann.
Hansen, Janine (2001), '*The New Earth*: A German-Japanese misalliance in film', in Aaron Gerow and Abe Mark Nornes (eds), *In Praise of Film Studies: Essays in Honor of Makino Mamoru*, 184–98. Victoria: Kinema Club; Traffort Publishing.
Hansen, Janine (2007), 'Celluloid competition: German-Japanese film relations, 1929-45', in Roel Vande Winkel and David Welch (eds), *Cinema and the Swastika: The International Expansion of Third Reich Cinema*, 187-98, New York: Palgrave Macmillan.
Hara, Setsuko (1937a), 'Hara Setsuko berurin tayori (chū)'. *Tōkyō Nichinichi Shinbun*, 17 April: n.p.

Hara, Setsuko (1937b), 'Hara Setsuko berurin tayori (jo)', *Tōkyō Nichinichi Shinbun*, 16 April, n.p.
Hara, Setsuko (1937c), 'Hara Setsuko berurin tayori (ka)', *Tōkyō Nichinichi Shinbun*, 07 May: n.p.
Hara, Setsuko (1937d), 'Watakushi no jikai sakuhin', *Ōsaka Mainichi Shinbun*, 02 April: n.p.
Harrington, Ann M. (2013), 'Shimabara Rebellion (1637–1638)', in Louis G. Perez (ed.), *Japan at War: An Encyclopedia*, 381-2, Santa Barbara: ABC-CLIO.
Hartmann, Rudolf (2003), 'Japanische Studenten an der Berliner Universität: 1920-1945', *Kleine Reihe*, (22): 201.
Hasegawa, Nyozekan (1932), *Nihon fashizumu hihan*, Tokyo: Ōhata Shoten.
Haukamp, Iris (2014), 'Fräulein Setsuko Hara: Constructing an international film star in nationalist contexts', *Journal of Japanese and Korean Cinema*, 6 (1): 4–22.
Hayakawa, Sesshū (1936), 'Sesshū: Sekai ginmaku ni kaerisaku – *Atarashiki tsuchi* no kien', *Asahi Shinbun*, 24 December: 2.
Hayashi, Bunzaburō (1936), '*Atarashiki tsuchi* to Fanku', *Kinema Junpō*, 01 Spetember, (586): 2.
Hayashi, Bunzaburō (1978), 'Anorudo Fanku no koto', in Tōwa Kabushiki Kaisha (eds), *Tōwa no hanseki*, 50, Tokyo: Tōhō Tōwa Kabushiki Kaisha.
Hazumi, Tsuneo (1936a), 'Fanku hakase ni tazuneku (1): Nihon no yama o toshite', *Yomiuri Shinbun*, 12 November: 5.
Hazumi, Tsuneo (1936b), 'Fanku hakase ni tazuneku (2): Nihon no yama no miryoku', *Yomiuri Shinbun*, 13 November: 5.
Heidegger, Martin (1927), *Sein und Zeit*, Tübingen: Max Niemeyer.
Hempenstall, Peter and Paula Mochida (2005), *The Lost Man: Wilhelm Solf in German History*, Wiesbaden: Otto Harrassowitz Verlag.
Herzberg, Georg (1937), 'Die Tochter des Samurai/Capitol', *Film-Kurier*, 24 March, 19 (70): 2.
High, Peter B. (2003), *The Imperial Screen: Japanese Film Culture in the Fifteen Years' War, 1931-1945*, Madison: University of Wisconsin Press.
Himmler, Heinrich and SS-Hauptamt, eds (1942), *Der Untermensch*, Berlin: Nordland.
Hirano, Kyoko (1992), *Mr. Smith Goes to Tokyo: Japanese Cinema Under the American Occupation, 1945-1952*, Washington, DC: Smithsonian Institute.
Hirano, Kyoko (2001), 'Japanese filmmakers and the responsibility for war: The case of Itami Mansaku', in Marlene J. Mayo and J. Thomas Rimer (eds), *War, Occupation and Creativity: Japan and East Asia, 1920-1960*, 212-32, Honolulu: University of Hawai'i Press.
'Hisokani fukumen no tateyakusha' (27.11.1936), *Newspaper, Title Illegible*: n.p.
Hobsbawm, Eric and Terence Ranger (1993), *The Invention of Tradition*, Cambridge: Cambridge University Press.
Hōchi Shinbun (15.02.1936), 'F. hakase raichō o ki ni kokusai eiga no hayari': n.p.
Hoffmann, Hilmar (1996), *The Triumph of Propaganda: Film and National Socialism, 1933-1945*, Oxford: Berghahn Books.
Honma, Fujio (1933), 'Eiga *Nippon*: Kokujokuteki eiga o miru', *Asahi Shinbun*, 8th March: 9.
Horak, Jan-Christopher (1997a), 'Dr. Arnold Fanck: Träume vom Wolkenmeer und einer guten Stube', in Jan-Christopher Horak and Gisela Pichler (eds),

Berge, Licht und Traum. Dr. Arnold Fanck und der deutsche Bergfilm, 15–67, München: Bruckmann.
Horak, Jan-Christopher (1997b), 'Vorwort', in Jan-Christopher Horak and Gisela Pichler (eds), *Berge, Licht und Traum. Dr. Arnold Fanck und der deutsche Bergfilm*, 7–11, München: Bruckmann.
Hori, Hikari (2017), *Promiscuous Media: Film and Visual Culture in Imperial Japan, 1926–1945*, London: Cornell University Press.
Horne, Charles F. and Walter F. Austin (1998), *Source Records of World War I*, Lewiston: E. Mellen Press.
Hospers, John (1976 [1946]), *Meaning and Truth in the Arts*, Chapel Hill: University of North Carolina Press.
Howard, Christopher (2010), 'From the Reverse-Course Policy to High-Growth: Japanese International Film Trade in the Context of the Cold War', PhD Thesis, University of London, School of Oriental and African Studies, London.
Hu, Tse-Yue G. (2010), *Frames of Anime: Culture and Image Building*, Hong Kong: Hong Kong University Press.
The Huffington Post (2014), 'Nihon ga daisuki desu. Ōsutoraria no eizō sakka ga totta Nihon ga utsukushī', 28 July. Available from: www.huffingtonpost.jp (accessed 13 June 2016).
Hughes, David W. (2007), 'Folk music: From local to national to global', in Alison Tokita and David W. Hughes (eds), *The Ashgate Research Companion to Japanese Music*, 281–302. Aldershot: Ashgate.
Hughes, David W. (2008), *Traditional Folk Song in Modern Japan: Sources, Sentiment and Society*, Folkestone: Global Oriental.
Hugo, Victor (1862), *Les Misérables*, Paris: A. Lacroix, Verboeckhoven & Cie.
Ichikawa, Haruko (1937), 'Kazan o idaku josei', *Asahi Shinbun*, 11 February: 4.
Iida, Shinbi (1976), 'Kumagai Hisatora', in Kinema Junpōsha (ed.), *Kinema Junpō: Nihon eiga kantoku zenshū*, 151, Tokyo: Kinema Junpōsha.
Illustrierter Film-Kurier (1930), 'Yakichi der Holzfäller', (1633): 9.
Illustrierter Film-Kurier (1937), 'Ein Dr. Arnold Fanck Film: *Die Tochter des Samurai*', special edition (8).
Inaga, Shigemi (2007), 'Modern Japanese arts and crafts around Kyoto: From Asai Chu to Yagi Kazuo with special reference to their contact with the West (1900–1954)', in *Traditional Japanese Arts and Crafts in the 21st Century: Reconsidering the Future from an International Perspective*, 47–74, Kyoto: International Research Center for Japanese Studies.
Inaga, Shigemi (2010), 'Crossing axes: Occidentalism and orientalism in modern visual representations of Manchukuo (1931–1945)', in *Orientalism/Occidentalism: Languages of Cultures vs. Languages of Description*, 93–113, Moscow: Russian Institute for Cultural Research.
Inui, Tsuneyoshi (1937a), 'Nihontekina mono (1): Futatsu no *Atarashiki tsuchi* ni kanshite', *Kōchi Shinbun*, 30 April: n.p.
Inui, Tsuneyoshi (1937b), 'Nihontekina mono (2): Futatsu no *Atarashiki tsuchi* ni kanshite', *Kōchi Shinbun*, 1 May: n.p.
Inui, Tsuneyoshi (1937c), 'Nihontekina mono (3): Futatsu no *Atarashiki tsuchi* ni kanshite', *Kōchi Shinbun*, 2 May: n.p.
Inui, Tsuneyoshi (1937d), 'Nihontekina mono (1): Futatsu no *Atarashiki tsuchi* ni kanshite', *Kōchi Shinbun*, 3 May: n.p.

Irie, Yoshiro (1996), 'Curator's choice/ Jōeisakuhin kaisetsu', *NFC Newsletter*, 8: 12–3.
Isaac, Benjamin (2006), 'Proto-racism in Graeco-Roman antiquity', *World Archaeology*, 38 (1): 32–47.
Ishitobi, Noriki (2011), 'Cannes hopefuls return empty-handed, but not disheartened', *Asahi News*, 05 June: n.p. Available online: www.asahi.com/e nglish/TKY201106040178.html (accessed 13 October 2011).
Ishiwari, Osamu, Toshiro Maruo and Hoji Tani (2005), *Hajime ni kigeki ariki: Shimizu Hiroshi, Ozu Yasujirō, Naruse Mikio, Yamanaka Sadao, Itami Mansaku soshite Saitō Torajirō*, Tokyo: Waizu Shuppan.
Itami, Mansaku (1936), 'Interview Itami', *Fanck Documents*, Filmmuseum München.
Itami, Mansaku (1961), *Itami Mansaku Zenshū*, ed. Naoya Shiga, Tokyo: Chikuma Shobō.
Itami, Mansaku (1961 [1931]), 'Shinjidaieiga ni kansuru kōsatsu', in Naoya Shiga (ed.), *Itami Mansaku Zenshū*, Vol. 1, 5–16, Tokyo: Chikuma Shobō. [Original publication: *Eiga kagaku kenkyū*, April].
Itami, Mansaku (1961 [1933]), 'Shinjidaieiga no sonzairiyū no tsuite', in Naoya Shiga (ed.), *Itami Mansaku Zenshū*, Vo. 1, 25–31, Tokyo: Chikuma Shobō. [Original publication: *Asahi Shinbun*, serialized April 20–2, 25–6].
Itami, Mansaku (1961 [1937]), 'Itami Mansaku hōdan o yomu', in Naoya Shiga (ed.), *Itami Mansaku Zenshū*, Vol. 2, 244–7, Tokyo: Chikuma Shobō. [original publication: *Eiga Fan*, July].
Itami, Mansaku (1961 [1938]), 'Jidaieiga no engi ni tsuite', in Naoya Shiga (ed.), *Itami Mansaku Zenshū*, Vol. 1, 97–103, Tokyo: Chikuma Shobō. [Original publication: *Nihon Eiga*, July].
Itami, Mansaku (1961 [1941]a), '*Muhō Matsu no isshō* ni tsuite', in Naoya Shiga (ed.), *Itami Mansaku Zenshū*, Vol. 2, 248–52, Tokyo: Chikuma Shobō. [Original publication: *Eiga Junpō*, 21 December].
Itami, Mansaku (1961 [1941]b), 'Fushaku shinmyō', in Naoya Shiga (ed.), *Itami Mansaku Zenshū*, Vol. 3, 327–88, Tokyo: Chikuma Shobō.
Itami, Mansaku (1961 [1943]), 'Sensō chūshi o nozomu', in Naoya Shiga (ed.), *Itami Mansaku Zenshū*. Vol. 1, 181–3, Tokyo: Chikuma Shobō.
Itami, Mansaku (1961 [1944]), 'Eiga to minzokusei', in Naoya Shiga (ed.), *Itami Mansaku zenshū*, Vol. 1, 173–80, Tokyo: Chikuma Shobō. [original publication: *Eiga Hyōron*, March]
Itami, Mansaku (1961 [1946]), 'Sensō sekininsha no mondai', in Naoya Shiga (ed.), *Itami Mansaku zenshū*, Vol. 1, 205–14, Tokyo: Chikuma Shobō [original publication: *Eiga Shunjū*, August].
Itami, Mansaku (1964 [1940]), 'Engi shidōron sōan', in Sannosuke Matsumoto (ed.), *Gendai Nihon shisō taikei, Vol 14: Geijutsu no shisō*, Tokyo: Chikuma Shobō. [Original publication: *Eiga enshutsugaku dokuhon*, December].
Itami, Mansaku (1971), *Itami Mansaku essei shū*, ed. Kenzaburō Ōe, Tokyo: Chikuma Shobō.
Itami, Mansaku (1997 [1933]), 'Kare to katsudō', in Mika Tomita (ed.), *Chie puro jidai: Kataoka Chiezō, Inagaki Hiroshi, Itami Mansaku- shadatsu ni, entāteinmento*, 33–4, Tokyo: Firumu Ātosha.
Iwamoto, Kenji (2004), 'Nashonarizumo to kokusaku eiga', in Kenji Iwamoto (ed.), *Nihon eiga to nashonarizumo 1931-1945*, 7–27. Tokyo: Shinwasha.

Iwasaki, Akira (1937), 'Die neue Erde', *Der Film*, (10): n.p.
Iwasaki, Akira (1961), *Eigashi*, Tokyo: Tōkyō Keizai Shinpōsha.
Jacoby, Alexander (2008), *A Critical Handbook of Japanese Film Directors: From the Silent Era to the Present Day*, Berkeley: Stone Bridge Press.
Japan Times (04.02.1937), 'World premiere of New Earth at Imperial Theatre': n.p.
Japan Weekly Chronicle (1936), 'Emigration to Manchukuo', 1800: 27.
Jung, Uli (2013), 'Fanck, Arnold', in Ian Aitken (ed.), *The Concise Routledge Encyclopedia of the Documentary Film*, 244–5, New York: Routledge.
'K' (1938), 'Shineiga hyō: Kyojinden Tōhō Tōkyō sakuhin', *Yomiuri Shibun*, 16 April: 3.
Kabayama, Aisuke (1937), 'Confidential letter to Fanck', 10 February, *Fanck Documents*, Filmmuseum München.
Kajino, Ena, Seiji Chōki and Hermann Gottschewski (2011), *Kishi Kōichi to ongaku no kindai: Berurin firu o shiki shita nihonjin*, Tokyo: Seikyusha.
Kanzog, Klaus (1994), *'Staatspolitisch besonders wertvoll': Ein Handbuch zu 30 deutschen Spielfilmen der Jahre 1934 bis 1945*, München: Schaudig & Ledig.
Katō, Tetsurō (2005), 'Personal contacts in German-Japanese cultural relations during the 1920s and early 1930s', in Christian W. Spang and Rolf-Harald Wippich (eds), *Japanese-German Relations, 1895-1945: War, Diplomacy and Public Opinion*, 119–38, London: Routledge.
Kattelle, Alan D. (2003), 'The amateur cinema league and its films', *Film History*, 15 (2): 238–51.
Kawakita, Kashiko (1936a), 'Fanku eiga-shohei yori kansei made', *Eiga no Tomo*, (70): 94–5.
Kawakita, Kashiko (1936b), 'Yutakana dojō e no suteishi', *Eiga no tomo*, December issue: 66–7.
Kawakita, Kashiko (1937), 'Wasurekataki no wa Hara Setsuko no kao', *Hōchi Shinbun*, 20 April: n.p.
Kawakita, Kashiko (1966), '*Atarashiki tsuchi* no seisaku-1936', *Tōwa shinekurabu*, 8: 1.
Kawakita, Kashiko (1968), 'Tōwa Shōji Goshigaisha monogatari', in Tōwa Kabushiki Kaisha (eds), *Tōwa no 40 nen: 1928-1968*, Tokyo: Tōwa Kabushiki Kaisha.
Kawakita, Kashiko (1973a), '*Atarashiki tsuchi* no seisaku-1936', in Kawakita Kashiko, *Eiga hitosuji ni*, 46–52, Tokyo: Nihon Tosho Centre.
Kawakita, Kashiko (1973b), *Eiga hitosuji ni*, Tokyo: Nihon Tosho Senta.
Kawakita, Kashiko and Tadao Satō (1991), *Eiga ga sekai o musubu*, Tokyo: Sojusha.
Kawakita, Nagamasa (1937a), 'Deutscher Film und Japan', Film-*Kurier*, 08 April, 19 (81): 3.
Kawakita, Nagamasa (1937b), 'Ōbei eigakai angyō', *Nippon Kinema Nichinichi Shinbun*: n.p.
Kawakita Nagamasa (1955), 'Aisaku eiga jidai: Sekai joyū no tanjō', *Yomiuri Shinbun*, 27 June: 2.
Kawakita, Nagamasa (1988), *My Recollections*, Tokyo: Tōhō-Tōwa Co. Ltd.
Kelson, John F. (1996 [1951]), in Kenneth R. M. Short (ed.), *Catalogue of Forbidden German Feature and Short Film Productions Held in Zonal Film*

Archives of Film Section, Information Services Division, Control Commission for Germany, (BE), Trowbridge: Flick Books.
Kettler, Constanze (2011), *Die Instrumentalisierung Preußens im nationalsozialistischen Propaganda-Spielfilm*, München: Grin Verlag.
Kida, Sho (2010), *Hara Setsuko: aruga mama ni ikite*, Tokyo: Asahi Shinbun Shuppan.
Kiernan, Ben (2007), *Blood and Soil: A World History of Genocide and Extermination from Sparta to Darfur*, New Haven: Yale University Press.
Kinematograph (1927a), 'Bushido', 08 May, 21 (1055): 2.
Kinematograph (1927b), 'Filmkritische Rundschau: *Bushido*', 15 May, 21 (1056): 19.
Kinematograph (1933), 'Die neue Kontingentverordnung', 01 July, 27 (125): 1.
Kirchmann, Kay (2005), 'Szenen eines Kampfes. Die Wolkenbilder des Dr. Fanck', in Lorenz Engell, Bernhard Siegert and Joseph Vogl (eds), *Wolken: Archiv für Mediengeschichte*, Vol. 5, 117–29, Weimar: Verlag der Bauhaus-Universität Weimar.
Kirihara, Donald (1992), *Patterns of Time: Mizoguchi and the 1930s*, Madison: University of Wisconsin Press.
Kishi, Matsuo (1953), 'Itami Mansaku', in *Nihon eigajin den*, 191–206, Tokyo: Hayaka Shobō.
Kishi, Matsuo (1974), 'Itami Mansaku', in *Kinema Junpō: Nihon eiga kantoku zenshū*, 36–8, Tokyo: Kinema Junpōsha
Kishi, Fumiko and Teruyo Nogami (2012), 'Henshūsha no omoide', in Toshio Takasaki and Shinya Aoki (eds), *Atarashiki tsuchi*, 30–3, Tokyo: Kinema Junpōsha.
Kitagawa, Fuyuhiko (1937), 'Futatsu no *Atarashiki tsuchi* ni tsuite: Itami Mansaku no tachiba', *Eiga Shudan*, April issue: 24–5.
Kitagawa, Fuyuhiko (1961), 'Eiga no hito Itami Mansaku', in Naoya Shiga (ed.), *Itami Mansaku Zenshū*, Vol. 3, 447–58, Tokyo: Chikuma Shobō.
Klee, Ernst (2009), *Das Kulturlexikon zum Dritten Reich: Wer war was vor und nach 1945*, 2nd edn, Frankfurt am Main: S. Fischer.
Knopp, Guido (2003), *Hitler's Women*, New York: Routledge.
Köck, Johannes (n.d.), 'Vom Zufall zur Steuerung des Filmlandes Tirol'. Available online: www.cinetirol.com/de (accessed 15 March 2012).
Kokumin Shinbun (17.05.1936), 'Atarashiki tsuchi: seisaku iyoiyo kaishi.': n.p.
Kokumin Shinbun (11.03.1937), 'Ashita made yōi': n.p.
Kokumin Shinbun (02.04.1937), 'Hara jō berurin monogatari': n.p.
Kokuritsu Gekijō Kindai Kabuki Nenpyō Hensanshitsu (1995), *Kindai kabuki nenpyō: Kyōto hen*, Tokyo: Yagi Shoten.
Koni Bideo (2005), 'Hikyō Nekka', *Mantetsu Kiroku Eigashū*, 9.
Körber-Abe, Sven (2010), 'Japans Filmanfänge – Teil 2: Industrie und staatlicher Einfluß', *OAG Notizen*, (6): 394.
Kracauer, Siegfried (1984), *Von Caligari zu Hitler: Eine psychologische Geschichte des deutschen Films*, Frankfurt am Main: Suhrkamp.
Kracauer, Siegfried (2004 [1947]), *From Caligari to Hitler: A Psychological History of the German Film*, Princeton: Princeton University Press.
Kramer, Sven (2009), 'Versuch über den Propagandafilm. Zu Leni Riefenstahls Dokumentarfilmen aus den dreißiger Jahren', in Jörn Glasenapp (ed.), *Riefenstahl Revisited*, 71–99, München: Fink.

Krebs, Gerhard (1994), 'Von Hitlers Machtübernahme zum Pazifischen Krieg (1933-1941)', in Gerhard Krebs and Bernd Martin (eds), *Formierung und Fall der Achse Berlin-Tokyo*, 11-26, München: Iudicium.
Krebs, Gerhard (2009), *Das moderne Japan, 1868-1952*, München: Oldenbourg.
Kreimeier, Klaus (1999), *The Ufa Story: A History of Germany's Greatest Film Company, 1918-1945*, Berkeley: University of California Press.
Kreimeier, Klaus (2002), *Die Ufa-Story: Geschichte eines Filmkonzerns*, Frankfurt: Fischer.
Kreiner, Josef, ed. (1984), *Deutschland - Japan: Historische Kontakte*, Bonn: Bouvier.
Kropp, Alexander (2009), '"Vom Generalbauinspektor genehmigt."- Albert Speers Medienpolitik als "Generalbauinspektor für die Reichshauptstadt" (GBI) zwischen 1937 und 1944', in Udo Margedant, Heinrich Quaden and Michael Klein (eds), *Verantwortungsvolle Wissenschaft. Festschrift zum Akademischen Forum zur 122. Cartellversammlung des Cartellverbandes Katholischer deutscher Studentenverbindungen, Samstag, 3. Mai 2008, Universität Bonn*, 101-9, Stuttgart: Klein.
Krug, Hans-Joachim (2001), *Reluctant Allies: German-Japanese Naval Relations in World War II*, Annapolis: Naval Institute Press.
Kunisaki, Aya (2006), '1920 nendai (1920-1926) Berurin ni okeru Hata Toyokichi (1892-1956)', *The Institute for Theatre Research, Departmental Bulletin*, (6): 141-56.
Kurosawa, Akira (1999). 'From *Something like an Autobiography*', in Gilbert Adair (ed.), *Movies*, 83-91, London: Penguin Books.
Kyōto Nisshutsu Shinbun (08.03.1937), 'Hara Setsuko berurin e': n.p.
L. B. (1919), 'Harakiri, Die Geschichte einer jungen Japanerin', *Kinematograph*, 31 December: n.p.
La Cinématographie Francaise (1937), 'Nagamasa Kawakita prépare un film franco-nippon', (967): 9.
Lancashire, Terence (2011), *An Introduction to Japanese Folk Performing Arts*, Farnham, Surrey: Ashgate.
Leims, Thomas (1990), 'Das Deutsche Japanbild in der NS-Zeit', in Josef Kreiner and Regine Mathias (eds), *Deutschland-Japan in der Zwischenkriegszeit*, 441-62, Bonn: Bouvier.
Leiter, Samuel and Jirō Yamamoto (1997), *New Kabuki Encyclopedia: A Revised Adaptation of Kabuki Jiten*, Westport: Greenwood Press.
Lichtbild-Bühne (1931), 'Japan', 24 (169): 15-6.
Lichtbild-Bühne (1933), '*Kagami*: Ufa-Kulturfilm - Ufa Palast am Zoo', 26 (239): n.p.
Lichtbild-Bühne (1935a), 'Japan zeigt europäische Filme', 28 (244): n.p.
Lichtbild-Bühne (1935b), 'Japanische Produktionskosten', 28 (234): 57-8.
Lidchi, Henrietta (1997), 'The poetics and the politics of exhibiting other cultures', in Stuart Hall (ed.), *Representation: Cultural Representations and Signifying Practices*, 151-208, London: Sage.
Lindholm, Charles (2008), *Culture and Authenticity*, Oxford: Blackwell Publishing.
Loewy, Hanno (1999), 'Das Menschenbild des fanatischen Fatalisten. Oder: Leni Riefenstahl, Bela Balasz und Das Blaue Licht', *KOB*, 1-35. Available online: http://kops.ub.uni-konstanz.de/volltexte/2000/569/ (accessed 05 October 2010).

Loiperdinger, Martin (2004), 'Filmzensur und Selbstkontrolle', in Wolfgang Jacobsen, Anton Kaes and Hans Helmut Prinzler (eds), *Geschichte des deutschen Films*, 534–7, Stuttgart: Metzler.
Mainichi Shinbun (25.03.1936), 'Akanishi Kakita no go mensō ni F hakase no kyōtan': n.p.
Mainichi Shinbun (02.04.1936), 'F hakase no kyōdō kantoku: Itami Mansaku seishiki judaku': n.p.
Makino, Mamoru (2001), 'Rethinking the emergence of the Proletarian Film League of Japan (Prokino)', in Aaron Gerow and Abe Mark Nornes (eds), *In Praise of Film Studies: Essays in Honor of Makino Mamoru*, 14–44, Victoria: Kinema Club; Traffort Publishing.
Maltarich, Bill (2005), *Samurai and Supermen: National Socialist Views of Japan*, Oxford: Peter Lang.
Manvell, Roger (1974), *Films and the Second World War*, London: Dent & Sons.
Martin, Bernd (1995), 'Japan and Germany on the path towards war: Mutual influences and dependencies', in Bernd Martin (ed.), *Japan and Germany in the Modern World*, 207–38, Oxford: Berghahn.
Martin, Bernd, ed. (1995), *Japan and Germany in the Modern World*, Oxford: Berghahn Books.
Martin, Bernd and Susanne Kuß, eds (2003), *Deutsch-chinesische Beziehungen, 1928–1937: 'Gleiche' Partner unter 'ungleichen' Bedingungen. Eine Quellensammlung*, Berlin: Oldenbourg Akademieverlag.
McClain, James L. (2002), *Japan: A Modern History*, New York: W.W. Norton.
McDonald, Keiko (2000), *From Book to Screen: Modern Japanese Literature in Films*, Armonk: M.E. Sharpe.
McGilligan, Patrick (2013 [1997]), *Fritz Lang: The Nature of the Beast*, Minneapolis: University of Minnesota Press.
McGuire, Michael D. (1976), 'Rhetoric, philosophy and the volk: Johann Gottlieb Fichte's addresses to the German nation', *Quarterly Journal of Speech*, 62 (2): 135–44.
Mehl, Margaret (2014), 'Going native, going global: The violin in modern Japan', *The Asia Pacific Journal: Japan Focus*, 12 (48): 1–13.
Meskill, Johanna and Margarete Menzel (1966), *Hitler & Japan: The Hollow Alliance*, New York: Atherton Press.
Miller, John Scott (2009), *The A to Z of Modern Japanese Literature and Theatre*, Plymouth: Scarecrow Press.
Mishima, Kaoru (2005), 'Berurin no chōshū ni todokerareta "nihon no seiyō ongaku": Kishi Kōichi no kangaeru "nihon ongaku", azumidashita "seiyō ongaku"', *Bulletin of Institute for Interdisciplinary Studies of Culture, Doshisha Women's College of Liberal Arts*, (22): 145–64.
Mitsui, Toru (1997), 'Interactions of imported and indigenous musics in Japan: A historical overview of the music industry', in Alison J. Ewbank and Fouli T. Papageorgiou (eds), *Whose Master's Voice? The Development of Popular Music in Thirteen Cultures*, 152–74, Westport: Greenwood Press.
Miyao, Daisuke (2007), *Sessue Hayakawa: Silent Cinema and Transnational Stardom*, London: Duke University Press.
Miyao, Daisuke (2013), *The Aesthetics of Shadow: Lighting and Japanese Cinema*, London: Duke University Press.

Mizumachi, Seiji (1937), 'Bonsaku Atarashiki tsuchi no shokon', Kinema Junpō, 11 March, (604): 1.
Mizuno, Sachiko (2009), 'The Saga of Anatahan and Japan', *Spectator*, 29 (2): 9-24.
Modan Nippon (1935), 'Cover page', 11 (10).
Moeller, Felix (2000), *The Film Minister: Goebbels and the Cinema in the Third Reich*, Stuttgart: Edition Axel Menges.
Moore, Allan (2002), 'Authenticity as authentication', *Popular Music*, 21 (2): 209-23.
Moreck, Kurt (1929), 'Die Kulturelle Mission des Kinos', in Edmund Bucher and Albrecht Kindt (eds), *Film Photos wie noch nie*, 39-41, Frankfurt am Main: Kindt & Bucher Verlag.
Mōri, Masato (2006), *Kishi Kōichi eien no seinen ongakuka*, Tokyo: Kokusho Kankokai.
Morris-Suzuki, Tessa (1997), 'Global memories, national accounts: Nationalism and the rethinking of history'. Available online: www.nuim.ie/staff/dpringle/igu_wpm/morris.pdf (accessed 05 June 2005).
Morris-Suzuki, Tessa (2015 [1998]), *Re-Inventing Japan: Time, Space, Nation*, New York: Routledge.
Mrugalla, Andreas (2002), 'Die Einsamkeit des heimkehrenden Kulturwanderers: Ein Grundmotiv in der historischen Erzählprosa Inoue Yasushis', PhD Thesis, Westfälische Wilhelms-Universität, Münster.
Mund, Gerald (2006), *Ostasien im Spiegel der deutschen Diplomatie: die privatdienstliche Korrespondenz des Diplomaten Herbert v. Dirksen von 1933 bis 1938*, Stuttgart: Franz Steiner.
Nakai, Masakazu (1951), 'Shikisai eiga no omoide', *Eiga no Tomo*, September: n.p.
Nakanishi, Susumu (1985), 'The spatial structure of Japanese myth: The contact point between life and death', in Earl Roy Miner (ed.), *Principles of Classical Japanese Literature*, 106-29, Ann Arbor: U.M.I. Books on Demand.
National Film Center Tokyo (2005), *Hakkutsu sareta eiga tachi 2005*. Available online: www.momat.go.jp/FC/NFC_Calendar/2005-07-08/kaisetsu.html (accessed 11 April 2010).
NHK [Nippon Hōsō Kyōkai] Dokyumento Shōwa Shuzaihan, eds (1986), *Tōkī wa sekai o mezasu: kokusaku to shite no eiga*, Tokyo: Kadokawa Shoten.
NHK [Nippon Hōsō Kyōkai] Dokyumento Shōwa Shuzai han, eds (1987), *Hitorā no shigunaru: Doitsu e keisha shita hi*, Tokyo: Kadokawa Shoten.
Nippon Hyōron (18.02.1937), 'Jūnin no ichiryū kantoku': n.p.
Nippon Kinema Nichinichi Shinbun (January 1936), 'Sanjūman en motte norikomu Fanku hakase': n.p.
Nippon Kinema Nichinichi Shinbun (26.03.1936), 'Kyakuhon dakkō no F hakase: Itami Mansaku to Tanaka Kinuyo ni sesshō kaishi': n.p.
Nippon Kinema Nichinichi Shinbun (10.07.1936), '*Atarashiki tsuchi* satsuei kyōkō': n.p.
Nippon Kinema Nichinichi Shinbun (22.07.1936), '*Atarashiki tsuchi* doitsu eigohan, nihonhan to tomo ni seisaku': n.p.
Nishimura, Masami (1937), '*Atarashiki tsuchi* ruporutāju', *Kinema Junpō*, 21 March, (606): 13.
Nitobe, Inazō (1899), *Bushido: The Soul of Japan*, Philadelphia: Leeds & Biddle.

Nitobe, Inazō (1901), *Bushido: Die Seele Japans, eine Darstellung des japanischen Geistes*, trans. Ella Kaufmann, Tokyo: Shokwabo.
Nogami, Teruyo (2006), *Waiting on the Weather: Making Movies with Akira Kurosawa*, trans. Julie Winters Carpenter, Berkeley: Stone Bridge Press.
Nornes, Abé Markus (2003), *Japanese Documentary Film: The Meiji Era Through Hiroshima*, Minneapolis: University of Minnesota Press.
Nygren, Scott (2007), *Time Frames: Japanese Cinema and the Unfolding of History*, London: University of Minnesota Press.
Oberhauser, Robert (1937), 'Deutscher Film am Hofe des Mikado', *Rheinische Landeszeitung*, 19 March: n.p.
Ogawa, Naoko (2005), 'Eiga kenkyū no saikentō: Saihakken sareta *Bushidō* no ichizuke o rei ni shite', *Bulletin of International Research Center for Japanese Studies* 31 (October): 235–55.
Ohata, Tokushiro (1976), 'The Anti-Comintern Pact, 1935–1939', in James William Morley (ed.), *Deterrent Diplomacy: Japan, Germany, and the USSR 1935–1940*, New York: Columbia University Press.
Okumura, Masaru (1987), 'Futatsu no *Atarashiki tsuchi*', notes for talk given at *Japan Society of Image Arts and Sciences Meeting*, Tokyo: Nihon University.
Orbach, Danny (2008), 'Japan through SS eyes: Cultural dialogue and instrumentalization of a wartime ally', *European Studies*, (7): 115–32.
O'Reagan, Tom (2002), 'Australian cinema as national cinema', in Allan Williams (ed.), *The Concept of National Cinema*, 89–136, London: Rutgers.
Ōsaka Jiji Shinpō (03.02.1933), 'Kenran! Eiga no haru o koka ni yobu': 5.
Ōsaka Mainichi Shinbun (09.02.1936), 'Ame ni kagureta yama ni urami': n.p.
Ōsaka Mainichi Shinbun (03.08.1936), 'Eiga monogatari: Fanku eiga', n.p.
Ōsaka Mainichi Shinbun (07.01.1937), '*Atarashiki tsuchi* wa tashikani kirei': 13.
Ōsaka Nichinichi Shinbun (09.02.1936), 'Akogare no nihon e: sangakueiga ō Fanku hakase': n.p.
Ōsaka Nichinichi Shinbun (24.03.1936), 'Fanku eiga kyakuhon shinchoku shite': n.p.
Ōta, Yoneo (1995), 'Eiga *Muhō Matsu* no isshō saisei (II): "Eiga hō" to eiga tōsei no jidai', *Ōsaka Geijutsu Daigaku Kiyō* (18): n. p.
Ōta, Yoneo (1996), 'Eiga *Muhō Matsu* no isshō saisei (III): Senjika no eigajintachi', *Ōsaka Geijutsu Daigaku Kiyō* (19): n. p.
Oyabe, Zenichirō (1924), *Jingisu Kan wa Minamoto Yoshitsune nari*, Tokyo: Fuzanbō.
P (1919), '*Harakiri*: Pressevorstellung im Marmorhaus', *Der Film*, 4 (51): 39–40.
Pamphlet: Japanischer Abend (29.02.1934), 'Koichi Kishi – Ein japanischer Komponist und Filmdirektor', Deutsches Filminstitut, Frankfurt am Main.
Pander, Hans (H.P.) (1927), 'Filmschau: *Bushido*', *Der Bildwart: Blätter für Volksbildung*, 5 (7): 478–9.
Pfeiffer, Lorenz and Henry Wahlig (2012), *Juden im Sport während des Nationalsozialismus: Ein historisches Handbuch für Niedersachsen und Bremen*, Göttingen: Wallstein.
Pollock, Sheldon (1993), 'Deep orientalism? Notes on sanskrit and power beyond the Raj', in Carol A. Breckenridge and Peter van der Veer (eds), *Orientalism and the Postcolonial Predicament: Perspectives on South Asia*, 76–133, Philadelphia: University of Pennsylvania Press.

Powers, Nina (2007), 'Mountain and fog', *Cabinet* (27): n.p. Available online: www.cabinetmagazine.org (accessed 02 March 2013).
Prange, Gordon W., Donald M. Goldstein and Katherine V. Dillon (1985), *Target Tokyo: The Story of the Sorge Spy Ring*, New York: McGraw-Hill.
Pratchett, Terr (1991), *Moving Pictures: A Discworld Novel*, London: Corgi Books.
Prawer, Siegbert Salomon (2005), *Between Two Worlds: The Jewish Presence in German and Austrian Film, 1910–1933*, New York: Berghahn Books.
'Premiere of the New Earth' (03.02.1937), Tokyo: Tōwa Shōji.
Princeton Alumni Weekly (1927), 'Japanese association formed', 28 (3): 74.
Pruys, Guido Marc (2009), *Die Rhetorik der Filmsynchronisation: Wie ausländische Spielfilme in Deutschland zensiert, verändert und gesehen werden*, La Vergne: Lulu Press.
Reichsführer SS (1942), *Der Weg zum Reich*, Berlin: Deutscher Schulverlag.
Reischauer, Haru Matsukata (1986), *Samurai and Silk: A Japanese and American Heritage*, 269–71, Cambridge, MA: Belknap Press of Harvard University Press.
Rentschler, Eric (1990), 'Mountains and modernity: Relocating the Bergfilm', *New German Critique*, (51): 137–62.
Rentschler, Eric (2002), 'The testament of Dr. Goebbels', in Alan Larson Williams (ed.), *Film and Nationalism*, 137–51, London: Rutgers University Press.
Rhodes, Anthony (1976), *Propaganda the Art of Persuasion: World War II*, New York: Chelsea House.
Richie, Donald (1974), *Ozu: His Life and Films*, Berkeley: University of California Press.
Richie, Donald (2001), *A Hundred Years of Japanese Film*, Tokyo: Kodansha International.
Riefenstahl, Leni (1994 [1987]), *Memoiren: 1902–1945*, Frankfurt am Main: Ullstein.
Roach, Joseph R. (2007), *It*, Ann Arbor: University of Michigan Press.
'Ruth Eweler: Ein Filmstar aus dem Sauerland' (1999), *Jahrhundert-Geschichten*, [TV programme], WDR Siegen, 26 July.
Ryback, Timothy W. (2008), *Hitler's Private Library: The Books That Shaped His Life*, New York: Alfred A. Knopf.
S-k. (1937), 'Japan erstrebt Weltmarktformat: Günstige Abschlüsse mit der Tobis-Cinema', *Film-Kurier*, 14 March (86): n.p.
Saeki, Kiyoshi (1987), 'Itami san no enshutsu', in Shohei Imamura et al. (eds), *Tōki no jidai*, Vol. 3, 156–67, Tokyo: Iwanami Shoten.
Said, Edward W. (1993), *Culture and Imperialism*, New York: Knopf.
Said, Edward W. (2003 [1978]), *Orientalism*, London: Penguin Books.
Saito, Kenta (2007), 'The Man Who Shot Zao: Tsukamoto Koji', Yamagata International Documentary Film Festival. Available Online: www.yidff.jp/2007/cat075/07c077-e.html (accessed 25 September 2011).
Sakai, Naoki (1991), 'Return to the West/return to the East: Watsuji Tetsuro's anthropology and discussions of authenticity', *boundary 2*, 18 (3): 157–80.
Sakisaka, Itsurō (1937), 'Nihon o miru gan', *Asahi Shinbun*, 21 February: 9.
Sallitt, Dan (2010), 'Escaped from the archives: Tomu Uchida's "Earth" (1939)', *Mubi*. Available online: http://mubi.com/notebook/posts/escaped-from-the-archives-tomu-uchidas-earth-1939 (accessed 12 April 2013).

Salomon, Harald (2008), 'Das Herr (Rikugun): Ein japanischer Propagandafilm aus dem Jahr 1944', *Japonica Humboldtiana*, (12): 59-149.
Salomon, Harald (2011), *Views of the Dark Valley: Japanese Cinema and the Culture of Nationalism, 1937-1945*, Wiesbaden: Harrassowitz.
Salzburger Festspielhaus (1930), *Madame Butterfly. (Die kleine Frau Schmetterling). Tragödie einer Japanerin*, Salzburg: Kiesel.
Sander-Nagashima, Berthold J. (2006), 'Naval relations between Japan and Germany', in Christian W. Spang and Rolf-Harad Wippich (eds), *Japanese-German Relations, 1895-1945: War, Diplomacy and Public Opinion*, 40-56, New York: Routledge.
Sanyō Shinbun (06.03.1937), '*Atarashiki tsuchi*: Teikokukan no "nihonhan" o miru': n.p.
Sasō, Tsutomu (2005), *Mizoguchi Kenji zensakuhin kaisetsu*, Tokyo: Kindai Bungeisha.
Satō, Tadao (1982), *Currents in Japanese Cinema*, trans. Gregory Barrett, Tokyo: Kodansha International.
Satō, Tadao (1991), 'Kaidai, kaisetsu', in Kawakita Kashiko and Tadao Satō (eds), *Eiga ga sekai o musubu*, 220-320, Tokyo: Sojusha.
Satō, Tadao (1995), 'Hara Setsuko', in Kinema Junpōsha (ed.), *Nihon eiga jinmen jiten: Joyū hen*, 393-401, Tokyo: Kinema Junpōsha.
Satō, Tadao (1997), *Nihon eigashi*, Tokyo: Iwanami Shoten.
Satō, Tadao (2001), *Eiga to shinjitsu*, Tokyo: Chūō Kōron Shinsha.
Satō, Tadao (2008), *Kenji Mizoguchi and the Art of Japanese Cinema*, ed. Aruna Vasudev and Padgaonkar Latika, trans. Brij Tankha, New York: Berg.
Satow, Morihiro (2006), 'Representing "Old Japan": *Yokohama Shashin* and the visual culture of the late 19th century', *Iconics*, (8): 37-54.
Sawamura, Tsutomu (1936), 'Eiga kaiwai: tanpen Nihon no sangaku', *Kinema Nyūsu*, (December): 10-11.
Schalek, Alice (1925), *Japan: Das Land des Nebeneinander*, Breslau: Ferdinand Hirt.
Schiweck, Ingo (2001), '*… weil wir lieber im Kino sitzen als in Sack und Asche' Der deutsche Spielfilm in den besetzten Niederlanden 1940-1945*, Münster: Waxmann.
Schmidlechner, Florian (2011), '"Der Jude mit der roten Badehose": Jüdische Helden, Stereotypen und Antisemitismus im Trickfilm bis 1945', in Barbara Eder, Elisabeth Klar and Ramón Reichert (eds), *Theorien des Comics: Ein Reader*, 303-20, Bielefeld: Transcript Verlag.
Schu. (1937), 'Skikata kanei: Richard Angst und Walter Tjaden erzählen', *Film-Kurier*, 19 (11): n.p.
Schuster, Ingrid (1988), *Vorbilder und Zerrbilder: China und Japan im Spiegel der deutschen Literatur 1773-1890*, Bern: Peter Lang.
Segawa, Yūji (2017), *Atarashiki Tsuchi no shinjitsu*, Tokyo: Heibonsha.
Seidensticker, Edward (1990), *Tokyo Rising: The City Since the Great Earthquake*, New York: Knopf.
Seigle, Cecilia Segawa (1993), *Yoshiwara: The Glittering World of the Japanese Courtesan*, Honolulu: University of Hawaii Press.
Shanhai Nippō (04.06.1937a), 'Hoshōkin jumanen "OK": *Atarashiki tsuchi* fukiri made no ikisatsu': n.p. [Originally published in the *Hōchi Shinbun* 03 December 1936].

Shanhai Nippō (04.06.1937b), 'Chūgoku minshū dantai ga yokoyari': n.p.
Sharp, Jasper (2011), *Historical Dictionary of Japanese Cinema*, Lanham: Scarecrow Press.
Sharp, Jasper (2017), 'The saga of Anatahan', *All the Anime*. Available online: http://blog.alltheanime.com/the-saga-of-anatahan/ (accessed 15 August 2017).
Shibasaki, Atsushi (2011), 'Activities and discourses on international cultural relations in modern Japan: The making of KBS (Kokusai Bunka Shinko Kai), 1934–53', *Journal of Global Media Studies*, 8 (March): 25–41.
Shōchiku (10.02.1937), 'Fanku kantoku ga Doitsu ni motte kaeru doitsu han'.
Shōchiku, eds (1996), *Shōchiku hyakunenshi*, Tokyo: Shōchiku Kabushiki Kaisha.
Short, Kenneth R. M (1996), 'Introduction', in Kenneth R. M. Short (ed.), *Catalogue of Forbidden German Feature and Short Film Productions held in Zonal Film Archives of Film Section, Information Services Division, Control Commission for Germany, (BE)*, i–xvii, Trowbridge: Flick Books.
Shutsū, Akio and Tetsurō Nagata (2008), *Nihon gekieiga sōmokuroku: Meiji 32-nen kara Shōwa 20-nen made*, Tokyo: Nichigai Asoshietsu, Hatsubaimoto Kinokuniya Shoten.
Sierek, Karl (2018), *Der lange Arm der Ufa Filmische Bilderwanderung zwischen Deutschland, Japan und China 1923–1949*, Wiesbaden: Springer.
Silverberg, Miriam (1991), 'The modern girl as militant', in Gail Bernstein (ed.), *Recreating Japanese Women*, 239–66, Berkeley: University of California Press.
Silverberg, Miriam (2007), *Erotic Grotesque Nonsense: The Mass Culture of Japanese Modern Times*, Berkeley: University of California Press.
Smith, Sidonie and Julia Watson (2001), *Reading Autobiography*, Minneapolis: University of Minnesota Press.
Soda, Kazuhiro (2007), 'Yamagata eigasai', *Kansatsu eiga no shūhen*. Available online: http://documentary-campaign.blogspot.com/2007_10_01_archive.html (accessed 13 August 2011).
Sommer, Theo (1962), *Deutschland und Japan zwischen den Mächten 1935-1940*, Tübingen: Mohr.
Sontag, Susan (1987 [1975]), 'Fascinating fascism', in *A Susan Sontag Reader*, 305–25, Harmondsworth: Penguin.
Soyama, Naomori (1937), 'Warera no tachiba to Angusuto: Awasete Shimazaki Kiyohiko shi ni kotau', *Kinema Junpō*, 606: 113–14.
Spalding, Lisa (1992), 'Period films in the prewar era', in Arthur Nolletti and David Desser (eds), *Reframing Japanese Cinema: Authorship, Genre, History*, 131–44, Bloomington: Indiana University Press.
Spang, Christian W. (2003), 'Wer waren Hitler's Ostasienexperten? (2)', *OAG Notizen*, (5): 10–25.
Spranger, Eduard (1937), 'Eduard Spranger an Käthe Hadlich, 22. Februar 1937 (Tokyo-Omori/Omori-Hotel)', *Scripta Paedagocica Online*. Available online: http://opac.bbf.dipf.de/editionen/spranger-hadlich (accessed 25 March 2012).
Standish, Isolde (2000), *Myth and Masculinity in the Japanese Cinema: Towards a Political Reading of the 'Tragic Hero'*, Richmond: Curzon.
Standish, Isolde (2005), *A New History of Japanese Cinema: A Century of Narrative Film*, London: Continuum.
Stehr, Nico and Hans von Storch (2010), *Klima, Wetter, Mensch*, Opladen: Barbara Budrich.

Steiner Daviau, Gertraud (2002), 'Arnold Fanck und Luis Trenker: "Regisseure für Hollywood"', in Friedbert Aspetsberger (ed.), *Der Bergfilm: 1920-1940*, 125-42, Innsbruck: Studienverlag

Steinweis, Alan E. (1991), 'Weimar culture and the rise of National Socialism: The Kampfbund für deutsche Kultur', *Central European History*, 24 (4): 402-23.

Sugimoto, Etsu Inagaki (1925), *A Daughter of the Samurai*, Garden City: Doubleday.

Sugimoto, Etsu Inagaki (1935), *Eine Tochter der Samurai*, Hamburg: Krüger.

Sugimoto, Shunichi (2005 [1934]), 'Itami Mansaku: Sono hito to geijutsu', in Osamu Ishiwari, Toshiro Maruo and Hojji Tani (eds), *Hajime ni kigeki ariki: Shimizu Hiroshi, Ozu Yasujirō, Naruse Mikio, Yamanaka Sadao, Itami Mansaku soshite SaitoTorajiro*, 110-15, Tokyo: Waizu Shuppan. [Original publication: *Eiga Geijutsu Kenkyū*, July 1934].

Sutā (1937), '*Atarashiki tsuchi* o okuru: Anorudo Fanku', 05 January, (88): 2.

Suzuki, Masataka (2007), 'Mountain religion and gender', in *Sangaku shugen (Japanese Mountain Religion): Mountain Religion and Shugendo in Japan*, 57-83, Tokyo: Nihon Sangaku Shugen Gakkai.

Tajima, Nobuo (2009), 'Fighting behind the scenes: Developments in German Far East policy, 1935-1936', in Akira Kudo, Nobuo Tajima and Erich Pauer (eds), *Japan and Germany: Two Latecomers to the World Stage, 1890-1945*, 199-237, Folkestone: Global Oriental.

Takada, Jirō (1937), 'Kokujoku eiga: *Atarashiki tsuchi* o mite', *Hokkoku Shinbun*, 09 April: n.p.

Takahashi, Toshio (2012), 'Modaniti to nihon kaiki: *Atarashiki tsuchi* no Hara Setsuko no miryoku', in Masaaki Harada and Shinya Aoki (eds), *Hara Setsuko: 13 nin no miwaku no hiroin shashin de furikaeru 28 nen no joyū jinsei*, 164-7, Tokyo: Kinema Junpōsha.

Tamanoi, Mariko (2008), *Manshū: kōsaku suru rekishi*, Tokyo: Fujiwara Shoten.

'Tanaka Kinuyo o zessan, Itami kantoku ni mo kōshō' (26.03.1936), *Newspaper, Title Illegible*: n.p.

Tansman, Alan, ed. (2009a), *The Aesthetics of Japanese Fascism*, London: University of California Press.

Tansman, Alan, ed. (2009b), *The Culture of Japanese Fascism*, London: Duke University Press.

Taylor, James and Warren Shaw (1997), *Dictionary of the Third Reich*, London: Penguin.

Teito Nichinichi Shinbun (09.02.1936), 'Taisaku ni sakidatte shōhin o seisaku': n.p.

Terada, Yoshitaka (2007), 'Introduction', in Yoshitaka Terada (ed.), *Authenticity and Cultural Identity: Performing Arts in Southeast Asia*, 1-8, Osaka: National Museum of Ethnology.

Thode-Arora, Hilke (1992), 'Die Familie Umlauff und ihre Firmen - Ethnographica-Händler in Hamburg', *Mitteilungen aus dem Museum für Völkerkunde Hamburg*, 22: 143-58.

Thompson, Kristin and David Bordwell (2003), *Film History: An Introduction*, London: McGraw-Hill.

Thornton, Sybil Anne (2008), *The Japanese Period Film: A Critical Analysis*, Jefferson: McFarland.

Toepser-Ziegert, Gabriele and Hans Bohrmann (1984), *NS-Presseanweisungen der Vorkriegszeit: Edition und Dokumentation*, München: K. G. Saur.
Tōei (1992), *Chronicle Toei – Kuronikuru Tōei: 1947-1991*, Tokyo: Tōei Kabushiki Gaisha.
Tōhō Tōwa, eds (1978), *Tōwa no hanseiki: 50 Years of Tōwa: 1928-1978*, Tokyo: Tōhō Tōwa Kabushiki Kaisha.
Tōkyō Jiji Shinpō (13.02.1936), 'Fanku hakase gaimushō hōmon': n.p.
Tokyo-tō Shinbun (28.03.1936), 'Itami Mansaku kantoku o shōdaku ka': n.p.
Tomita, Mika, ed. (1997). *Chie Puro Jidai: Kataoka Chiezō, Inagaki Hiroshi, Itami Mansaku: Shadatsu ni, entāteinmento*, Tōkyō: Firumu Ātosha.
Tomita, Mika (2005), 'Taishō jidai no nichidoku aisaku eiga *Bushidō* ni miru nihon hyōshō', *Katsudō hōkoku* (12): 69-73.
Trinh, T. Minh-ha (1994 [1989]), 'Outside in inside out', in Jim Pines and Paul Willemen (eds), *Questions of Third Cinema*, 133-49, London: British Film Institute.
Tsuji, Hisakazu and Akira Shimizu (1987), *Chūka denei shiwa: ichi heisotsu no nitchū eiga kaisōki 1939-1945*, Tokyo: Gaifusha.
Tsumura, Hideo ('Q') (1937), 'Shineiga hyō: shijō ni koboshi Minosuke to Natsukawa no *Furusato* (J.O. sakuhin)', *Asahi Shinbun*, 28 April: 5.
Tsumura, Hideo ('Q') (1938), 'Shineiga hyō: Kyojinden (Tōhō Eiga)', *Asahi Shinbun*, 16 April: 4.
Tsumura, Hideo (1942), 'Stars of Japan', *The XXth Century*, June issue: 431-40.
Turquan, Jean (1937), 'Nagamasa Kawakita réalisera un Film Franco-Japonais', *La Cinématographie Francaise*, (966): 24.
Uchida, Kimio (1936), '*Atarashiki tsuchi* nichieihan', *Kinema Junpō*, (601): 1.
Uchida, Kimio (1937), 'Futatsu no *Atarashiki tsuchi*', *Kinema Junpō*, 21 February: n.p.
Ushihara, Kiyohiko (1933a), 'Eiga "Nippon" no mondai: guken issoku (jo)', *Asahi Shinbun*, 9 March: 9.
Ushihara, Kiyohiko (1933b), 'Eiga "Nippon" no mondai: guken issoku (ge)', *Asahi Shinbun*, 10 March: 9.
Variety (1937a), 'Kawakita, Japanese prod.-distrib, denies any Nippon-Nazi pix deals', (126): 23.
Variety (1937b), 'Modern's "New Earth"', (127): 27.
Venuti, Lawrence (1995), *The Translator's Invisibility: A History of Translation*, London: Routledge.
Venuti, Lawrence (2010 [1993]), 'Translation as cultural politics', in Mona Baker (ed.), *Critical Readings in Translation Studies*, 65-79, New York: Routledge.
Venuti, Lawrence (2013), 'How to read a translation', in Lawrence Venuti (ed.), *Translation Changes Everything: Theory and Practice*, 109-15, New York: Routledge.
Vlossak, Elizabeth (2010), *Marianne or Germania? Nationalizing Women in Alsace, 1870-1946*, Oxford: Oxford Universtiy Pres.
von Vietsch, Eberhard (1961), *Wilhelm Solf: Botschafter zwischen den Zeiten*, Tübingen: Wunderlich.
Wada-Marciano, Mitsuyo (2008), *Nippon Modern: Japanese Cinema of the 1920s and 1930s*, Honolulu: University of Hawai'i Press.
Wahl, Christ (2008), 'Inside the robot's castle: UFA's English-language versions in the early 1930s', in Tim Bergfelder and Christian Cargnelli (eds), *Destination*

London: German-Speaking Emigrés and British Cinema, 1925–1950, 47–61, New York: Berghahn Books.
Wald, Sarah D. (2016), *The Nature of California: Race, Citizenship, and Farming Since the Dust Bowl*, Seattle: University of Washington Press.
Washburn, Dennis C. (2001), 'The arrest of time: The mythic transgressions of *Vengeance Is Mine*', in Dennis C. Washburn and Carole Cavanaugh (eds), *Word and Image in Japanese Cinema*, 318–41, Cambridge: Cambridge University Press.
Watsuji, Tetsurō (1935), *Fūdo ningengakuteki kōsatsu*, Tokyo: Iwanami Shoten.
Watts, Craig (2001), 'Blood Spear, Mt. Fuji: Uchida Tomu's conflicted comeback from Manchuria', *Bright Lights Film Journal*, 33: n.p. Available online: http://brightlightsfilm.com/33/tomu1.php (accessed 13 February 2012).
Weigel, Herman (1976), 'Von Fanck und seinem Handwerk', *Filmhefte*, 5 (2): 31–4.
Weinstein, Valerie (2014), 'Reflecting chiral modernities: The function of genre in Arnold Fanck's transnational Bergfilm *New Earth* (1936–37)', *Alterity and Affinity: Encounters between German-Speaking Countries and East Asia*, 34–51, New York: Berghahn Books.
Weisse Wand (n.d.), 'Kleine Geschichte der Synchronisation'. Available online: www.weisse-wand.info/pdfs%20synchro/kleine%20gesch.pdf (accessed 11 August 2012).
Welch, David (1999 [1994]), *Modern European History 1871–2000: A Documentary Reader*, New York: Routledge.
Welch, David (2001 [1983]), *Propaganda and the German Cinema*, London: Oxford University Press.
Wells, Henry W. (2002), 'Michiyuki', in John Gassner and Edward Quinn (eds), *The Reader's Encyclopedia of World Drama*, 564, New York: Courier Dover.
Wendt, Bernd Jürgen (2000), *Das nationalsozialistische Deutschland*, Opladen: Leske Budrich.
White, Hayden (1987), *The Content of the Form: Narrative Discourse and Historical Representation*, Baltimore: Johns Hopkins University Press.
'Will' (1937), 'The New Earth (Japanese made)', *Variety*, 125 (3 March): 13.
Williams, Alan (2002), 'Introduction', in A. Williams (ed.), *Film and Nationalism*, 1–22, London: Rutgers.
Witte, Karsten (1993), 'Film im Nationalsozialismus', in Wolfgang Jacobsen, Anton Kaes and Hans Helmut Prinzler (eds), *Geschichte des deutschen Films*, 119, Stuttgart: JB Metzler.
Wollen, Peter (1972), *Signs and Meaning in the Cinema*, Bloomington: Indiana University Press.
Yamada, Kōsaku, ed. (1940), *Manshū kaitaku kakyokushū*, Vol. 1, Manshū Ijū Kyōkai, Tokyo: Hakubi Shuppansha.
Yamaguchi, Seison (2002 [1937]), 'Berlin im Frühling 1937: Tagebuch, 1. April-9. Juni', trans. Tanja Schwanhäuser, *Kleine Reihe*, 21, Berlin: Mori-Ōgai-Gedenkstätte der Humboldt-Universität zu Berlin.
Yamamoto, Naoki (2004), 'Fukei no (sai)hakken – Itami Mansaku to *Atarashiki tsuchi*', in Kenji Iwamoto (ed.), *Nihon eiga to nashonarizumo: 1931–1945*, 63–102. Tokyo: Shinwasha.
Yamamoto, Yūzō (1979 [1923]), *Dōshi no hitobito: Gikyokushū*, Tokyo: Nihon Kindai Bungakukan.

Yamane, Sadao (1997), 'Itami Mansaku', in Kinema Junpōsha (ed.), *Nihon Eiga Jinmei Jiten: Kantoku hen*, 77–9 Tokyo: Kinema Junpōsha.
Yamato Nippō (21.02.1937), 'Fanku to Itami no sōi: *Atarashiki tsuchi* doitsuhan o mite': n.p.
Yanagizawa, Fumitaka (2014), 'Ānorudo Fanku kantoku no *Zaō: Shirogane no rappu* wa nakatta', *Yamagata Daigaku Kankyō Hozen Sentā*, 17: 57–76.
Yokohama Bōeki Shinbun (28.06.1935), 'Hamakko sutā': n.p.
Yomiuri Shinbun (24.05.1926), 'Tōa no *Bushidō*': 9.
Yomiuri Shinbun (15.07.1926), 'Mata mo ōshū no gakudan ni nihon no meika': 3.
Yomiuri Shinbun (29.06.1929), 'Shōchiku haikyūsha berurin ni iyoiyo hōga no ōbei shinshutsu': 10.
Yomiuri Shinbun (28.08.1929), 'Beikoku e arawareru: 10 su bon no Shōchiku eiga': 10.
Yomiuri Shinbun (03.09.1929), 'Nichidoku eigahaikyū no shinjigēto setsuritsu: Shōchiku, Nikkatsu o chūshin to shite': 10.
Yomiuri Shinbun (11.03.1935), 'Itami kantoku jihyō o dasu: Rokuon setsubi fuman de': 10.
Yomiuri Shinbun (24.07.1935), 'Kokujoku eiga no yushutsu fusegu: Aratani torishimari rei': 7.
Yomiuri Shinbun (28.12.1935), 'Kamera no shi ni utau: Setsugaku nihon no seibi': 4.
Yomiuri Shinbun (21.01.1936), 'Sangaku eiga seisaku ni shin puro tanjō Fanku hakase raigetsu yōka raichō': 7.
Yomiuri Shinbun (25.01.1936), 'Fanku hakase no *Tochi naki hitobito* ni kankeisha keikai': 15.
Yomiuri Shinbun (09.02.1936), 'Yama nomi de naku yamato damashī mo': 3.
Yomiuri Shinbun (10.02.1936), 'Sanka gokuhan de tsukuru: *Tsuchi naki hitobito*': 10.
Yomiuri Shinbun (07.06.1936), 'Sensen mata ijō: Shihon hyakumanen no shineiga kaisha-Takarazuka no Kobayashi-shi ga shinshutsu': 7.
Yomiuri Shinbun (06.08.1936), 'Wafuku de tozan': 3.
Yomiuri Shinbun (25.08.1936), 'Tsū ni natta Kosugi Isamu': 3.
Yomiuri Shinbun (03.11.1936), 'Fanku hakase mo kikoku': 7.
Yomiuri Shinbun (27.11.1936), 'Fanku hakase no miyage "nekka"': 5.
Yomiuri Shinbun (08.04.1937), 'Kokujoku eiga to wa kore da': 5.
Yomiuri Shinbun (20.04.1937a), 'Dokusai nachi no dan: *Atarashiki tsuchi* no Eberajo ginmaku kara taikyo meirei': 5.
Yomiuri Shinbun (20.04.1937b), 'Wazukaishita kanojo no kingan: Itami Mansakushi dan; Fankushi ni mo sekinin, Kosugi Isamukun dan': 5.
Yomiuri Shinbun (27.04.1937), 'Honnendo ginmaku besuto 3 ni Kosugi, Yamada, Kawamura no 3 yū': 5.
Yomiuri Shinbun (28.04.1937), 'Shineiga hyō: "Sekinin wa moto ni" Minosuke no shojōsaku': 5.
Yomiuri Shinbun (30.04.1937), 'Kōkoku: Eiga *Furusato* hoka / Nihon Gekijō hoka': 6.
Yomiuri Shinbun (06.06.1937), '*Atarashiki tsuchi* ni fundai: shina de konichi kai': 4.
Yomiuri Shinbun (29.07.1937), 'Beisuijōgun ya Hara Setsuko jō': 3.
Yomiuri Shinbun (24.11.1937), 'Samurai no musume': 3.
Yomiuri Shinbun (25.09.1946), 'Itami Mansaku (eiga kantoku) shikyo': 2.

Yomiuri Shinbun (08.01.1954), 'Fanku ni midasareta: *Atarashiki tsuchi* de sutā no isu e': 4.
Yomiuri Shinbun (03.10.1990), 'Manshū kokusaku eiga no roke': 12.
Yomota, Inuhiko (2000), *Nihon no joyū*, Tokyo: Iwanami Shoten.
Yoshida, Junji (2006), 'Origins of Japanese film comedy and questions of colonial modernity', PhD Thesis, University of Oregon.
Yoshimoto, Mitsuhiro (2000), *Kurosawa: Film Studies and Japanese Cinema*, Durham: Duke University Press.
Young, Louise (1998), *Japan's Total Empire: Manchuria and the Culture of Wartime Imperialism*, Berkeley: University of California Press.
Zhang, Yingjin (2004), *Chinese National Cinema*, New York: Routledge.
Zimmermann, Peter (2005), 'Propagandafilme der NSDAP', in Peter Zimmermann and Kay Hoffmann (eds), *Geschichte des dokumentarischen Films in Deutschland*, Vol. 3: *Drittes Reich*, 505-29, Stuttgart: Reclam.

FILMOGRAPHY

The Abe Clan (Abe ichizoku) (1938), Dir. Kumagai Hisatora, Japan: Tōhō.
Advancing Italy (Yakushin Itari), no further information.
Akanishi Kakita (Akanishi Kakita) (1936), Dir. Itami Mansaku, Japan: Chiezō Productions.
Album of Snowy Mountains (Yukiyama no arubamu; Album der Schneeberge) (1939), Dir. unclear, Japan.
Anti-Communist Crusaders (Bōkyō jūjigun) year unclear, Dir. unclear, Japan: Ōsaka Mainichi Shinbunsha.
Arnold Breker (Arno Breker – Harte Zeit, starke Kunst) (1944), Dir. Arnold Fanck, Germany: Ufa (Riefenstahl-Produktion; Kulturfilm-Institut GmbH).
Ascent of the Mont Blanc: 15,781 Feet High (1902), Dir. Frank Ormiston-Smith, United Kingdom: Warwick Trading Company.
La Bataille (The Danger Line) (1923), Dirs Sessue Hayakawa and Édouard Émile Violet, France: Le Film d'Art.
Big City: A Chapter on Labour (Daitokai rōdō-hen) (1929), Dir. Ushihara Kiyohiko, Japan: Shōchiku.
Big Tokyo (Daitōkyō) (1933), Dir. Vladimir Shneiderov, Japan/USSR: Tokyo Asahi/Mezhrabpomfilm.
Bonfire (Kagaribi) (1928), Dir. Hoshi Tetsuroku, Japan: Shōchiku.
Burning Sky (Moyuru ōzora) (1940), Dir. Abe Yutaka, Japan: Tōhō. [German version: *Nippon's Wild Eagles* (Nippons wilde Adler), (1942).]
Bushido: The Iron Law (Bushido: Das eiserne Gesetz) (1926), Dirs Carl Heiland and Kako Zanmu, Germany/Japan: Deutsch-Nordische Film-Union GmbH (Berlin)/Tōa Tojin.
The Cheat (1915), Dir. Cecil B. De Mille, USA: Jesse L. Lasky Feature Play Company.
Chuji Makes a Name for Himself (Chūji uridasu) (1935), Dir. Itami Mansaku, Japan: Shinkō.
Chūshingura [two parts] (1934), Dir. Itō Daisuke, Japan: Nikkatsu.
The Comrade's Song (Senyū no uta; Das Lied des Kameraden) (1939), Dir. Richard Angst, Japan: Tōhō.
Condottieri (1937), Dir. Luis Trenker and Werner Klingler, Italy/Germany: Consorzio per il film Condottieri.
The Conquest of Mount Zaō (Zaō seifuku) (1936), Dir. Arnold Fanck, Japan: Arnold Fanck Productions-Japan Tourism Bureau (?).
Contemporary Japan (Gendai Nippon) (1937), Dirs Fujita Tsuguharu and Suzuki Shigeyoshi, Japan: Tōa Hassei Nyūsu Eiga Seisakujo.

Crossroads (Jūjiro; Im Schatten des Yoshiwara]) (1928), Dir. Kinugasa Teinosuke, Japan: Shōchiku.
The Dawn of Manchuria and Mongolia (Manmō kenkoku no reimei) (1932), Dir. Mizoguchi Kenji, Japan: Irie Productions (Shinkō).
Diary of Chuji's Travels (Chūji Tabi Nikki) (1927), Dir. Itō Daisuke, Japan: Nikkatsu.
Die Nibelungen (Die Nibelungen: Siegfrieds Tod) (1924), Dir. Fritz Lang, Germany: Decla-Bioscop AG.
Do Not Hesitate, Young Folks (Tamerau nakare wakōdo yo) (1935), Dir. Taguchi Tetsu, Japan: Nikkatsu.
Earth (Tsuchi) (1939), Dir. Uchida Tomu, Japan: Nikkatsu.
Emergency Era Japan aka *Japan in Time of Crisis* (Hijōji Nippon) (1933), Dir. Kondō Iyokichi, Japan: Ōsaka Mainichi Shinbunsha.
The Emperor of California (Der Kaiser von Kalifornien) (1935), Dir. Luis Trenker, Germany: Luis-Trenker-Film.
The Eternal Dream (Der ewige Traum; Rêve éternel) (1934), Dirs Arnold Fanck and Henri Chomette, Germany/France: Cine-Allianz.
Eternal Heart (Eien no kokoro; Yakichi der Holzfäller) (1928), Dir. Sasaki Keisuke, Japan: Shōchiku.
Fire Festival (Himatsuri) (1985), Dir. Yanagimachi Mitsuo, Japan: Seibu Sezon Group.
Five Scouts (Gonin no sekkōhei) (1938), Dir. Tasaka Tomotaka, Japan: Nikkatsu.
Fourth Opus (Daiyon sakuhin) (1932), Dir. Kishi Kōichi, Japan: Kishi Productions.
Frivolous Servant (Kimagure kaja) (1935), Dir. Itami Mansaku, Japan: Chiezō Productions.
A German Robinson (Ein Robinson) (1940), Dir. Arnold Fanck, Germany: Bavaria-Filmkunst.
The Giant (Kyojin den) (1938), Dir. Itami Mansaku, Japan: Tōhō.
Girls in Uniform (Mädchen in Uniform, Seifuku no shojo) (1939), Dirs Leontine Sagan and Carl Froelich, Germany: Deutsche Film-Gemeinschaft.
Godzilla (Gojira) (1954), Dir. Honda Ishirō, Japan: Tōhō.
The Great Love (Die große Liebe) (1942), Dir. Rolf Hansen, Germany: Ufa.
Ground for Divorce (Der Scheidungsgrund) (1937), Dir. Carl Lamac, Deutschland: Moldavia Film.
Harakiri (1913), Dir. Harry Piel, Germany: Eiko-Film GmbH (Berlin).
Harakiri (1919), Dir. Fritz Lang, Germany: Decla-Film-Gesellschaft Holz & Co.
Haru: Spring (Haru, Im Frühling: Ein Film von japanischen Frühlingsfesten) (1934), Dirs Kishi Kōichi and Nicholas Kauffmann, Japan/Germany: Kishi Productions/Ufa.
Head Hunters of Borneo (Die Kopfjäger von Borneo) (1936), Dir. Viktor von Plessen, Germany/Netherlands: N.V. Handels-Maatchappij Tampico.
Hell of Ten Thousand Flowers 2, Part 1 (Zoku manka jigoku: dai ippen) (1928), Dir. Itami Mansaku, Japan: Chiezō Productions.
Hell of Ten Thousand Flowers 2, Part 2 (Zoku manka jigoku: dai nihen) (1929), Dirs Inagaki Hiroshi and Itami Mansaku, Japan: Chiezō Productions.
The History of Skiing in Japan (Nihon sukī hattatsu shi) (1936), Dir. Arnold Fanck, Japan–Germany: Arnold Fanck Productions-Japan Tourism Bureau (?).

The Holy Mountain (Der heilige Berg) (1926), Dir. Arnold Fanck, Germany: Berg- und Sportfilm GmbH/Ufa.
Hometown (Fujiwara Yoshie no furusato) (1930), Dir. Mizoguchi Kenji, Japan: Nikkatsu.
Hometown (Furusato) (1937), Dir. Itami Mansaku, Japan: J.O. Studios.
I was Jack Mortimer (Ich war Jack Mortimer; Namae no nai eiga) (1935), Dir. Karl Froelich, Germany: Froelich-Film GmbH.
Imperial Buildings in the Far East (Kaiserbauten in Fernost. Aufnahmen der japanischen Fanck-Expedition) (1938), Dir. Arnold Fanck, Germany: Dr. Arnold Fanck (Tokyo) on commission by Terra-Filmkunst GmbH (Berlin).
Izu Dancer (Koi no hana saku: Izu no odoriko) (1933), Dir. Gosho Heinosuke, Japan: Shōchiku.
The Japanese Girl (Nihon musume, Japan yin thwe) (1935), Dir. Nyi Pu, Burma/Japan: A1 Film/P.C.L.
Joseph Thorak (Joseph Thorak, Werkstatt und Werk) (1943), Dirs Hans Cürlis and Arnold Fanck, Germany: Ufa (Riefenstahl-Produktion; Kulturfilm-Institut GmbH).
A Journey Through Manchuria (Manshū no tabi) (1937), Dir. unclear, Japan [Manchukuo]: Mantetsu Eiga Seisakujo.
Kagami (Kagami: Traditionen im Hause des Japaners aka Spiegel) (1933), Dirs Kishi Kōichi and Wilhelm Prager, Japan/Germany: Kishi Productions/Ufa.
Know Your Enemy: Japan (1945), Dir. Frank Capra, USA: US War Department.
The Land of Cherry Blossoms (Das Land der Kirschblüte) (1930s), Dir. unclear, Germany: Degeto.
The Life of Muho Matsu (Muhō Matsu no isshō) (1943), Dir. Inagaki Hiroshi, Japan: Daiei.
The Lion Dance (Kagami jishi) (1935), Dir. Ozu Yasujirō, Japan: Shōchiku.
Little Hans (Hänschen Klein) (1938), Dir. Arnold Fanck, Germany: Dr. Arnold Fanck-Film.
A Living Doll (Ikeru ningyō) (1929), Dir. Uchida Tomu, Japan: Nikkatsu.
A Love in Heaven (Tengoku ni musubu koi) (1932), Dir. Gosho Heinosuke, Japan: Shōchiku.
Love Japan (Nihon ga daisuki desu) (2014), Dir. David Parkinson, Australia: Moonship Picture.
The Love-Mad Music Teacher (Kyōren no onna shishō) (1926), Dir. Mizoguchi Kenji, Japan: Nikkatsu.
The March of the *Japanese Second Army to the Battle of Liaoyang* (Das 2. Kaiserlich-Japanische Regiment auf dem Weg nach Liaoyang) (1904), Dir. Jules Greenbaum, Germany: Deutsche Bioscope.
Marching On aka *The Army Advances* (Shingun) (1930), Dir. Ushihara Kiyohiko, Japan: Shōchiku.
Metropolis (1926), Dir. Fritz Lang, Germany: Ufa.
Mister Japan (Misutā Nippon) (1931), Dir. Murata Minoru, Japan: Nikkatsu.
Mount Zaō (Zaō san) (1935), Dir. Tsukamoto Kōji, Japan: amateur film.
Mountain of Destiny (Berg des Schicksals) (1924), Dir. Arnold Fanck, Germany: Berg- und Sportfilm GmbH.
Mountains in Flames (Berge in Flammen; Les Monts en flammes) (1931), Dirs Luis Trenker and Karl Hartl/Luis Trenker and Joe Hamman, Germany/France: Les Films Marcel Vandal & Charles Delac.

Mud and Soldiers (Tsuchi to heitai) (1939), Dir. Tasaka Tomotaka, Japan: Nikkatsu.
Musume (Karakuri musume) (1927), Dir. Gosho Heinosuke, Japan: Shōchiku.
My Japan (1945), Dir. unclear, USA: US Treasury Department, War Finance Division.
New Earth (Atarashiki tsuchi [IV]) (1937), Itami Mansaku, Japan/Germany: Tōwa Shōji/Arnold Fanck Productions.
Nippon: Love and Passion in Japan (Nippon: Liebe und Leidenschaft in Japan) (1932), Dir. Carl Koch, Germany/Japan: Ufa/Tōwa Shōji.
No Regrets for Our Youth (Waga seishun ni kuinashi) (1946), Dir. Kurosawa Akira, Japan: Tōhō.
Olympia (Olympia) [two parts] (1938), Dir. Leni Riefenstahl, Germany: Olympia Film GmbH.
A Page of Madness (Kurutta ichipeiji) (1926), Dir. Kinugasa Teinosuke, Japan: Kinugasa Productions.
Peace on Earth (Tenka taiheki), 1928, Dir. Inagaki Hiroshi, Japan: Chiezō Productions.
A Pebble by the Wayside (Robō no ishi) (1938), Dir. Tasaka Tomotaka, Japan: Nikkatsu.
Peerless Patriot (Kokushi musō) (1932), Dir. Itami Mansaku, Japan: Chiezō Productions.
The People's Oath (Kokumin no chikai; Das Heilige Ziel) (1938), Dir. Nomura Hiromasa, Japan: C.T.N.
Poem of the Sea (Umi no uta) (1932), Dir. Kishi Kōichi, Japan: Kishi Productions.
Priest of Darkness (Kōchiyama Sōshun) (1936), Dir. Yamanaka Sadao, Japan: Nikkatsu.
Prince Achmed's Adventures (Die Abenteuer des Prinzen Achmed) (1926), Dirs Lotte Reiniger and Carl Koch, Germany: Comenius-Film GmbH.
Rashomon (Rashōmon) (1950), Dir. Akira Kurosawa, Japan: Daiei.
A Samurai's Career (Ehon musha shugyō) (1929), Dir. Inagaki Hiroshi, Japan: Chiezō Productions.
The Samurai's Daughter (Die Tochter des Samurai; Atarashiki tsuchi [FV]) (1937), Dir. Arnold Fanck, Japan/Germany: Tōwa Shōji/Arnold Fanck Productions.
Secluded Jehol (Hikyō Nekka) (1936), Dir. Akutagawa Kōzō, Japan [Manchukuo]: Mantetsu Eiga Seisakujo.
A Song of Hometown (Furusato no uta) (1925), Dir. Mizoguchi Kenji, Japan: Nikkatsu.
SOS Iceberg (SOS Eisberg) (1933), Dirs Arnold Fanck and Tay Garnett, Germany/United States: Deutsche Universal-Film AG (Ufa)/Universal Pictures Corporation Co. Inc.
Storms over Mont Blanc aka *Avalanche* (Stürme über dem Montblanc) (1930), Dir. Arnold Fanck, Germany: Althoff-Ambos-Film AG (AAFA Film).
Street Juggler (Machi no tejinashi) (1925), Dir. Murata Minoru, Japan: Nikkatsu.
The Summer Battle of Osaka (Ōsaka natsu no jin) (1937), Dir. Kinguasa Teinosuke, Japan: Shōchiku.
Ten Minutes Mediation (Jippunkan no shisaku) (1932), Dir. Kichi Kōichi, Japan: Kishi Productions.
Theatre of Life (Jinsei gekijō) (1936), Dir. Uchida Tomu, Japan: Nikkatsu.

Third Opus (Daisan Sakuhin) (1932), Dir. Kishi Kōichi, Japan: Kishi Productions.
This Was Japan (1945), Dir. Basil Wright, UK: Crown Film Unit.
The Time of Tempei: Mysterious Thief Samimaro (Tempei jidai: Kaitō Samimaro) (1928), Dir. Koishi Eiichi, Japan: Shōchiku.
Tragedy of a Marriage (Kekkon higeki) (1929), Dir. Higashibōjō Yasunaga, Japan: Nikkatsu.
Triumph of the Will (Triumph des Willens) (1935), Dir. Leni Riefenstahl, Germany: Reichsparteitagfilm der L. R. Studio-Film (Berlin).
Verdun (Verdun, souvenirs d'histoire) (1931), Dir. Léon Poirier, France: Compagnie Universelle Cinématographique.
Vicissitudes of Revenge (Adauchi ruten) (1928), Dir. Itami Mansaku, Japan: Chiezō Productions.
Wandering Gambler (Hōrō zanmai) (1928), Dir. Inagaki Hiroshi, Japan: Chiezō Productions.
White Frenzy (*Der weiße Rausch, Neue Wunder des Schneeschuhs*) (1931), Dir. Arnold Fanck, Germany: H. R. Sokal-Film GmbH.
The White Stadium (Das weiße Stadion) (1928), Dirs Arnold Fanck and Othmar Gurtner, Switzerland: Olympia-Film AG.
Wife! Be Like a Rose (Tsuma yo bara no yō ni) (1935), Dir. Naruse Mikio, Japan: P.C.L.
Winter Journey Through Southern Manchuria (Winterreise durch Südmandschurien) (1938), Dir. Arnold Fanck, Germany: Ufa.
Writings on Love and Marriage (Renai to kekkon no sho) (1936), Dir. Abe Yutaka, Japan: Nikkatsu.
Yoshiwara (1937), Dir. Max Ophüls, France: Milo Film.
Yoshiwara: Japanese City of Lust (Yoshiwara, die Liebesstadt der Japaner) (1920), Dir. Arthur Bergen, Germany: Zelnik-Mara-Film GmbH.
Youth Across the River (Kawamukō no seishun) (1933), Dir. Kimura Sotoji, Japan: Onga Keijutsu Kenkyūjo.
Zao: Silver Frenzy (Zaō: Shirogane no rappu) (1936), Dir. Arnold Fanck, Japan: Arnold Fanck Productions-Japan Tourism Bureau (?).

INDEX

Abe Clan, The (1938)   108
Abegg, Lily   77
Abe ichizoku. See Abe Clan, The (1938)
Abe Yutaka   94
Adauchi ruten. See Vicissitudes of Revenge (1928)
Advancing Italy   104
adventure films   14, 55
Afifa studios   30
Agfa   56, 56 n.1
Aida Masae. *See* Hara Setsuko
Akanishi Kakita (1936)   62, 88, 115
Akashi Ushio   29
Akutagawa Kōzō   151
Album of Snowy Mountains (1939)   82
Allgeier, Sepp   54
Allied Information Committee   209
Amakasu Masahiko   150
American-Chinese co-production (*The Good Earth*, 1937)   92
anachronism   134, 160
Anatahan. See Saga of Anatahan, The (1953)
Anderson, Joseph L.   8
Angst, Richard   54, 58, 63, 65, 81, 82, 93, 152, 161, 189, 215, 222
Anti-Comintern Pact (1936)   5, 8, 13, 21, 48, 52, 80, 83, 85, 90, 93–5, 97, 99, 101, 103, 104, 177, 179, 200, 202, 215
Anti-Communist Crusaders   104
anti-Japanese propaganda films   13
archetypes   109, 128, 130, 132, 134
Arita, Hachirō   98
Arlberg skiing technique   94
Army Department   64

Arnold Breker (1944)   208, 209
'Aryan Paragraph' (*Arierparagraph*)   112
Asahi Shinbun   5, 60, 66, 110, 138, 220
Asano Mōfu   36
Ascent of the Mont Blanc: 15,781 Feet High (1902)   54
Asia Express   9, 151
Association of Independent Filmmakers (*Jiyū Eigajin Renmei*)   89
Association of National-Socialist Stage and Film Artists. *See* Fellowship of German Artists club (*Kameradschaft der deutschen Künstler*)
Association of Revolutionary Asians (*Die Vereinigung der revolutionären Asiaten/Kakumeiteki Asiajin Kyōkai*)   35
Autumn in Japan (1935)   145
Avalanche (Die Lawine)   204
avant-garde   31, 48
Axis powers   5, 13, 89, 209

Bälz, Erwin Toku   94
Bando Tsumasaburō   30
Bantsuma Tachibana Universal   30
Bavaria Studio   208
Being and Time (*Sein und Zeit*, Heidegger)   110, 112
Berg des Schicksals. See Mountain of Destiny (1924)
Berge in Flammen. See Mountains in Flames (1931)
Bergfilm. See mountain film
Berg- und Sportfilm GmbH Freiburg (BSF)   54

Berlin   5, 21, 31, 37, 43
Berliner Tageblatt   39
Betz, Hans-Walter   58
Big City: A Chapter on Labour (1929)   32, 37, 38, 41–2
Big Tokyo (1933)   66, 67, 220–1
binational co-production   11, 21, 49, 90, 105
binational relations   57, 74, 83, 95
binational trade agreements   149
Bōkyō jūjigun. See Anti-Communist Crusaders
Bolshevism   103
Bonfire (1928)   32, 36, 38–9, 41
bon odori   142
Brown House (*Braunes Haus*)   209
Buchholz, Karl   58, 60
Buck, Pearl S.   92, 175
Bullerian, Hans   35
Burmese-Japanese co-production   67
Burning Sky (1940)   94
Bushido: Das eiserne Gesetz. See *Bushido: The Iron Law* (1926)
Bushido: Die Seele Japans (*Bushido: The Soul of Japan*, Nitobe Inazō)   29
Bushido: The Iron Law (1926)   29–31, 51
bushidō (*self-sacrifice*)   29

Cabinet Information Bureau (*Naikaku jōhō kyoku*)   197
California   182, 183, 186
California Alien Land Law (1920)   182, 183
camera technology   118–19
Canaris, Wilhelm Franz   90, 103
Capitol am Zoo theatre   74
censorship   58, 61, 63, 75, 127
Cheat, The (1915)   27, 127
Cherry Blossoms, Geisha and Volcanoes (1958)   210
Chiba Bank   71
Chiezō Production (Chie Puro)   30, 61, 62, 87
China
   Kawakita's relations to   32, 57
   political relations with Germany   26, 28, 91
   political relations with Japan   26, 28, 49, 51, 147, 155, 185
Chomette, Henri   67
Chuji Makes a Name for Himself (1935)   61, 62, 194
Chūji uridasu. See *Chuji Makes a Name for Himself* (1935)
Cine-Allianz   203
Climate: An Anthropological Consideration (*Fūdo: ningen gakuteki kōsatsu*, Watsuji Tetsurō)   110, 138
Cocco-Tobis-Nippon (C.T.N)   81, 83, 91
collaboration   7–9, 13, 26, 30, 42, 52, 62, 74, 87, 90, 101
colonialism   182
colonization   147, 182
commodification   14
communism   91, 175, 185
Communist International (Comintern)   90
Comrade's Song, The (1939)   82
Condottieri (1937)   204–5
Contemporary Japan (1937)   65, 99, 101
Cotton Version of the Record of Great Peace (1943)   198
Critique of Japanese Fascism (*Nihon fashizumu hihan*, Hasegawa Nyozekan)   123
Crossroads (1928)   31
Cultural Affairs Division (*Gaimushō bunkabu*)   57, 98–9
culture
   cross-fertilization   25
   differences   175
   exchange   26, 31, 56, 57
   films (*bunka eiga*)   81, 151
   history   7, 224
   identity   121, 123
   impact of   45
   isolationism   42
   and political relations   4
   relations   223
   representation   199

traits   17
translation   18–19, 22, 42, 43, 66, 73, 105, 108, 110, 111, 113, 117, 118, 128, 139, 146, 158, 206, 219, 224
Western   25

Dagover, Lil   28
Daiichi Eiga   63
Daisan sakuhin. See Third Opus (1932)
Daitokai rōdō-hen. See Big City: A Chapter on Labour
Daitōkyō. See Big Tokyo (1933)
Danger Line, The (1923)   27, 128
Dare Your Life (Fushaku shinmyō)   198
Das 2. Kaiserlich-Japanische Regiment auf dem Weg nach Liaoyang. See March of the Japanese Second Army to the Battle of Liaoyang, The (1904)
Das Land der Kirschblüte. See Land of Cherry Blossoms, The (1930s)
Das weiße Stadion. See White Stadium, The (1928)
Daughter of the Samurai, A (Etsu Inagaki Sugimoto)   74
Dawn of Manchuria and Mongolia, The (Manmo kenkoku no reimei)   149
de Medici, Giovanni   205
Der Deutsche Film   208
Der ewige Traum/Rêve éternel. See Eternal Dream, The (1934)
Der Film   77, 81
Der Führer baut seine Hauptstadt. See Führer Constructs His Capital, The
Der heilige Berg. See Holy Mountain, The (1926)
Der Kaiser von Kalifornien. See Emperor of California, The (1935)
Der Scheidungsgrund. See Ground for Divorce (1937)
Der Untermensch (Himmler)   183

Der Weg zum Reich. See Road to the Reich, The
Deutsch-Nordische Universal Film (DNFU)   30, 51
Diary of Chuji's Travels (Chūji tabi nikki, 1927)   61
Die große Liebe. See Great Love, The (1942)
Die Kopfjäger von Borneo. See Head Hunters of Borneo (1936)
Die Nibelungen (1924)   31
Die Tochter des Diplomaten/Gaikōkan no musume. See Diplomat's Daughter, The
Die Tochter des Samurai (Samurai's Daughter). *See New Earth (Atarashiki tsuchi)*
Die weiße Hölle vom Piz Palü. See White Hell of Piz Palu (1929)
Diplomat's Daughter, The   80
Directors' Guild of Japan (Nihon eiga kantoku kyōkai)   126
discourse   9, 19–20, 23, 27, 73, 109, 110
   on authentic Japaneseness   146
   contemporary   50
   on cultural representation   26
   German   78, 101, 112, 118, 121, 148, 153, 206, 207, 219
   global   208
   ideological   11, 67, 87, 147
   intellectual   123
   Japanese   5, 22, 45, 101, 123, 136, 138, 148, 182, 219
   media   137
   militarist-expansionist   155, 160
   on modernity   145
   nationalist   8, 22, 136, 218
   National-Socialist   112
   Orientalist   41, 182
   political   14, 22, 83, 101, 102
documentary films   49, 59, 66, 80, 118, 120, 151
Do Not Hesitate, Young Folks (1935)   131
Dōshi no hitobito (Comrades)   63
Dr. Arnold Fanck-Film Berlin-Tokyo   58

dubbing 39–40

Earth (Tsuchi, Nagatsuka) 127
Eastern art, impact on European culture 43
East Wind: West Wind (Buck) 175
editing process 30, 37, 45, 47, 63, 151, 160–4, 168, 173, 177, 183, 191
Ehon musha shugyō. See Samurai's Career, A (1929)
Eien no kokoro. See Eternal Heart (1928)
Ein Robinson. See German Robinson, A (1940)
Eisner, Lotte 13
Elsaesser, Thomas 13
Emergency Era Japan (1933) 88
Emperor of California, The (1935) 182
entertainment tax and German film censorship 75
Ertl, Hans 54
Eternal Dream, The (1934) 67, 203, 204
Eternal Heart (1928) 32, 42
Ethics (Rinrigaku, Watsuji Tetsurō) 112
ethnographic film 118, 120, 151
Etsu Inagaki Sugimoto 74
European films 31, 51, 52
Eweler, Ruth 5, 58, 63, 68, 79, 129, 130, 164, 164 n.6
Exclusion Act against Japanese immigration to the US (1924) 26
exotic subjects in German film 28, 29
Expansion of England, The (Seeley) 182

'family state' (kazoku kokka) 6
Fanck, Arnold 1, 6–9, 7 n.2, 8 n.3, 11, 13–20, 22, 23, 26, 31, 32, 34, 42, 45, 48, 50, 52–54, 56–7, 59, 63, 68, 72, 74–5, 77–84, 89, 90, 93, 95, 96, 98, 99, 101–4, 107–11, 113–20, 122–6, 128, 130, 132, 134–7, 141, 144, 146, 148–50, 151, 152, 154–60, 162, 170, 173, 183–6, 188, 191, 194, 200–9, 213, 215, 217–20, 222, 223. See also individual works
autobiography 210–12
background 115–16, 120–1
banning of films 209
concerns on landscape shooting 137–9
discrepancies with Itami 64–6, 81
division of film 175
and earthquake sequence 174
end of career 209–10
geographical inconsistencies 143
and his ideological systems 87
image of Japan 214, 219
impression on Tokyo 139–40
and including references to Germany 181
initial discussions with Itami 62
and landscape scenes 60, 61, 73, 166, 170–2
loan from Terra 67, 69
persona 86, 116, 211
re-establishing his career 210
reputation 58, 86, 94, 149, 150, 201, 209, 210, 212
rescue scene 167–8
rivalry with Trenker 205
spatial logic 177, 178
symbolic depiction of 'ideal types' 164–5
visual style 55, 145, 162, 170
Fanck Film Studios (Fanku eiga satsueijo) 69
Faust (Goethe) 134
February 26 Incident (ni ni roku jiken) 59, 62
femininity 36, 130, 132, 168, 220
Fichtean philosophy 201, 203
Fighting League for German Culture (Kampfbund für deutsche Kultur, KfdK) 36
'Film and National Characteristics' (Eiga to minzokusei, Itami) 193, 196
film and politics 67, 89, 92
film drama (geki eiga) 62, 65

Film Law 127
Fire Festival (1985) 145
First World War 26, 28, 98
Five Scouts (1938) 127
Foreign Affairs Association of Japan (*Nihon Gaiji Kyōkai*) 85
foreign films
 in Japan 11, 26, 27, 81 n.7
 regulations of in Germany 44
Foreign Ministry 57, 97–9
Fourth Opus (Daiyon sakuhin) 43
Frankfurter Zeitung 77
'free cutting' technique 55
Freiburg School of filmmaking 54, 118, 214
French-Japanese co-production 82
Friedrich, Caspar David 55
Frivolous Servant (1935) 61, 64, 194
From Caligari to Hitler (Kracauer) 13
fūdo, concept of 110, 113, 122 n.4
Fūdo (Watsuji Tetsurō) 138
Führer Constructs His Capital, The 209
Fuji Shashin Film K. K. 56
Fujita Tsuguharu (Fujita Tsuguji/ Léonard Tsuguharu Foujita) 31–2, 69
Fujiwara Yoshie no furusato. *See Hometown* (1930)
Furitsu Rankyō. *See* Soga Masashi
Furtwängler, Wilhelm 43
Furusato no uta. *See Song of Hometown, A* (1925)
Fushimi Akira 30

Gallone, Carmine 80
Garnett, Tay 67
geisha-themed works 27
gendaigeki 32, 41, 59, 61, 64, 88, 114, 115, 125, 130, 195
Gendai Nippon. *See Contemporary Japan* (1937)
'Generalbauinspektor Berlin' 208
Genghis Khan 155, 181, 191
Genghis Khan is Minamoto Yoshitsune (*Jingisu Kan wa Minamoto Yoshitsune nari*, Oyabe Zenichirō) 155

genre 38, 54, 60, 62, 65, 86, 114, 118, 142
Germain, André 31
German-American co-production. *See also SOS Iceberg* (1932) 55
German audience 6, 42, 109–11, 213, 214, 219, 220
German Film Law (1934) 50
German films 13, 22, 26, 28, 39, 44, 77. *See also individual film titles*
 boycott of 83
 re-evaluation 86
German Foreign Office 94, 95, 97, 197
German-Italian co-production 205
German-Japanese co-production 9, 11, 21, 26, 29, 42, 44, 50–2, 58, 62, 67, 68, 80, 87, 94, 101, 104, 193, 213, 214, 216
German Japanese Society (DJG) 75
German Robinson, A (1940) 93, 120, 208, 209, 211
Germany 5, 12, 14, 34, 42, 48, 77, 79, 83–4, 91, 101, 111, 118, 119, 147, 179, 201, 202, 212
 discourse 78, 101, 121, 148, 153, 206, 207, 219
 exhibition of foreign films in 44
 expansionist discourse 7, 148
 interest in Japanese culture 30
 persecution of Jews 83
 politics 211
 propaganda 7, 13
 relations with China 91
 relations with Japan 4, 5, 7–9, 11, 21, 22, 28, 49, 79–80, 83, 91, 97, 101, 104
Giant, The (1938) 196, 197
Girls in Uniform (1931) 58
Glimpses of New Japan (Shigeyoshi Suzuki) 69
Globus Film 210
Gloria Palast theatre 2, 74
Godzilla (1954) 20
Goebbels, Joseph 5, 6, 44, 58, 74–6, 79, 86, 94–6, 103, 122, 159, 202, 203, 208, 209, 211, 213
Gojira. *See Godzilla* (1954)

Gonin no sekkōhei. See Five Scouts (1938)
Good Earth, The 92
Gosho Heinosuke 31, 145
Grand Prix, Venice International Film Festival 222
Greater Japan Film Association (*Dai Nippon Eiga Kyōkai*) 50, 57
Great Love, The (1942) 78
Ground for Divorce (1937) 130

Haas, Wilhelm 95
Hack, Friedrich Wilhelm 48, 58, 75, 83, 90, 94–7, 99, 101–3, 154–5, 208
Hanabusa Yuriko 63
Hänschen Klein. See Little Hans (1938)
Harakiri (1913) 28–9, 31, 51, 161
Hara Setsuko 5, 7 n.2, 21, 108, 116, , 136, 162, 194, 196, 219, 220, 222
   casting for *New Earth* 63
   symbolising Japan 122, 129–32, 134, 155
   world tour in 1937.. 74–7, 79–83, 148
Hasegawa Nyozekan 123, 197
Hashimoto Shinobu 197
Hata Toyokichi 52
Hayakawa Ichirō 150, 155
Hayashi Bunzaburō 34, 35, 40, 42, 58, 94, 95, 107, 113, 114, 117, 145, 160, 202
Hayashida Shigeo 150
Head Hunters of Borneo (1936) 58
hegemonic ideology 208, 210, 218
Heidegger, Martin 110, 112
Heiland, Karl 29–31, 51
Hell of Ten Thousand Flowers 2 (1929) 198
Hess, Rudolf 6
Hijōji Nippon. See Emergency Era Japan (1933)
Himatsuri. See Fire Festival (1985)
Himmler, Heinrich 5, 183
Hirota Kōki 90, 98, 147

Hitler, Adolf 6, 12, 42, 78, 79, 91, 95, 101, 103, 150, 203
Holl, Loo 29
Hollywood films 26
Holy Mountain, The (1926) 55, 116, 120
Home Ministry (*Naimushō*) 50, 69
Hometown (1930) 145, 195–6, 199
'hometown' (*furusato*) themed films 145, 146
Hōrō zanmai. See Wandering Gambler (1928)
Hoshi Tetsuroku 60
human emotions 24, 25, 34, 139, 164, 167, 168, 170–2, 200, 212

Ichikawa Haruko 134
Ichikawa Haruyo 63
Ich war Jack Mortimer/Namae no nai eiga. See I was Jack Mortimer (1935)
Ikeda Tadao 30
Ikeru ningyō. See Living Doll (1929)
Imperial Buildings in the Far East (1938) 150
Im Schatten des Yoshiwara. See Crossroads (1928)
Inagaki Hiroshi 61, 62, 87, 194, 198
industrialization 27
Inoue Yasushi 45
international co-production 51, 61, 66, 94
International Film Association of Japan (*Kokusai Eiga Kyōkai*) 50, 57, 99
International Film Inc. (*Kokusai Eiga Kabushikigaisha*) 49
international (*kokusai*) films 26, 27, 30, 57, 73, 101, 136
international recognition of Japan, issue of 26, 55, 66
International Tourism Bureau 57, 59, 60
Intra-Asian film trade relations 27 n.2
Irie Takako 131, 217
Isamu Kosugi 222

Itami Mansaku   7–9, 8 n.3, 11, 13–16, 20, 22–4, 61, 63, 68, 71–3, 77, 78, 81, 87, 89, 102, 103, 113–17, 120–4, 130, 132, 134, 137, 140, 143, 150, 156, 160, 162, 164, 166–7, 177, 178, 183, 185, 193–201, 214–19, 222–4. *See also individual works*
  absence from programme and advertisement material   72, 73, 78
  anti-militarist reputation   159
  death of   199–200
  depiction of Manchukuo   184
  discrepancies with Fanck   64–6, 81
  and earthquake sequence   174
  exposition scene   172
  focus on human interaction   173
  genres   87–8
  geographical corrections   157–8
  lack of control on *New Earth*   194–5
  and landscape scenes   170, 171
  meeting with Fanck   62
  persona   200
  projecting for international consumption   190
  reference points for American audience   181, 182
  rejection of intertitle 'Manchukuo'   188
  representation of Japanese customs   165
  reputation   212
  and scene of soldier   185, 186, 189
  scenes on volcano   168, 170
  sound editing   161, 191
  version of 'globe scene'   163, 183, 186
Itō Daisuke   61
Iwasaki Akira   27, 77
I was Jack Mortimer (1935)   104
Izu Dancer (1933)   145, 196

Japan   12, 13, 22, 23, 48, 58, 90–1, 125, 157, 202, 213
  authenticity, notion of   14–19, 26–8, 31, 40, 51, 56, 67, 73, 78, 85, 86, 101, 105, 108–11, 113, 114, 116, 119, 122–5, 128, 130, 136, 142, 147, 149, 150, 154–6, 160, 193, 196, 197, 206, 216–20
  bravery image of   110, 138, 173
  climate and landscape   110, 124, 144–6, 150
  culture   43, 44, 50, 51, 138, 219
  discourse in   5, 22, 45, 101, 123, 136, 138, 148, 182, 219
  emigration   182–3
  expansionist policies   91–2, 148, 178
  foreign politics   101, 104
  government   97, 190
  image in Western films   29
  importing European films to   31, 51, 52, 77, 81
  and militarism   87, 178
  modern   22, 34, 38, 66, 85, 146, 158–60, 215, 220
  Mongolian invasion of   155, 181, 191
  national characteristics   110, 111, 138
  propaganda   92, 153, 215
  relations with Germany   4, 5, 7–9, 11, 21, 22, 28, 49, 79–80, 83, 91, 97, 101, 104
  representation of   36, 37, 42, 43, 50, 51, 59, 64, 66, 68, 73, 77, 85, 95, 108, 109, 111, 121, 124, 146, 149, 150, 155, 156, 195, 223
  symbol of   171
  traditional lifestyle   132
  traditional music   16
  'victimization' of   89
  winter sports   60
  women   135, 136
Japanese-American co-productions   50
Japanese clothes (*wafuku*)   132, 134
Japanese Culture Ministry   93, 98
Japanese films   14, 19, 22, 37, 79, 136, 223. *See also individual film titles*

concept 59
export 11, 14, 21, 25–7, 29, 31, 32, 34, 42, 49, 50, 52, 53, 57, 59, 61, 68, 73, 94, 98, 99, 104, 105, 122, 145, 151, 158, 193, 197, 217
  with German participation 51
  internationalization of 2, 5, 9, 21, 26, 27, 49, 57, 85
  political use of 13 n.7
  problems faced by 30
  production 27, 31, 48, 51, 69
  quality 194
  reputation of 38, 50, 63
  technological developments in 43
  of wartime period 7
  on Western screens 27, 52, 220
Japanese Girl, The (1935) 57
Japanese Institute of Oriental Studies 182
'Japaneseness' 37, 43, 113, 122, 123, 126, 127, 130, 132, 145, 146, 158, 219
Jenkins-Ōsawa (J.O.) Studios 20, 56, 62, 63, 65, 67, 69, 71 n.5, 73, 114
jidaigeki 20, 29, 32, 38, 41, 61, 63, 88, 114, 115, 132, 158, 160, 195, 198, 224
Jinsei gekijō. See *Theatre of Life* (1936)
Jippunkan no shisaku. See *Ten-Minute Meditation*
Josef Thorak (1943) 208, 209
Journey Through Manchuria, A (1937) 151
Jūjiro. See *Crossroads* (1928)

Kabayama Aisuke 2, 56, 57, 71–3, 98
Kabayama Chūji 57
Kagami jishi. See *Lion Dance, The* (1935)
Kagami: Traditions in the Japanese House 42–52, 58, 59, 118, 134, 168, 220
Kagaribi. See *Bonfire* (1928)
Kaiserbauten in Fernost. See *Imperial Buildings in the Far East* (1938)
Kako Zanmu 29, 30

Kamata Studios 32
Kami Kyōsuke 150
Kaneko Yōbun 195
Karakuri musume. See *Musume* (1927)
Kataoka Chiezō 61, 62, 197
Kauffman, Nicholas 81
Kawakita Kashiko 1, 2, 7–9, 11, 20, 24, 26, 31, 32, 34–6, 42, 50–3, 55–9, 61, 63–5, 67, 69, 74, 77, 79–83, 92–8, 102, 104, 149, 154, 175, 203, 203 n.4, 208, 211, 215, 216, 219–20, 223, 224
Kawakita Memorial Film Institute 57
Kawakita Nagamasa 1, 7 n.2, 11, 20, 25, 26, 42, 53, 74, 77, 96, 97, 122 n.4
Kawamukō no seishun. See *Youth Across the River* (1933)
Kawamura Reikichi 126
Kawase Naomi 223
Kekkon higeki. See *Tragedy of a Marriage* (1929)
Kida Zenso 81
Kido Shirō 32–3, 57
Kikugoro VI 49
Kimagure kaja. See *Frivolous Servant* (1935)
kimono 132, 134, 168
Kimura Sotoji 64
Kinema Junpō 31, 78, 125, 151
Kinema Nyūsu, interview with Itami 194
Kinugasa Teinosuke 24, 31, 78, 121
Kirschblüten, Geishas und Vulkane. See *Cherry Blossoms, Geisha and Volcanoes* (1958)
Kishi Kōichi 42, 43, 45, 47–51
Kishi Puro (Kishi Film Productions) 44, 48, 51
Kishi Scientific Film Research Institute (*Kishi Gakujutsu Eiga Kenkyū Sho*) 43
Kitagawa Fuyuhiko 61, 65, 123, 157
Kitahara Hakushū 183
Kitamura Komatsu 30
Know Your Enemy: Japan (1945) 13
Kobayashi Ichizō 52, 71 n.5
Koch, Carl 34, 35, 38

Kōchiyama Sōshun. See Priest of Darkness, The (1936)
Kōda Nobu 66 n.4
Kodomo no maki. See On Children (1937)
Kohner, Paul 215
Koi no hana saku/Izu no odoriko. See Izu Dancer (1933)
Kokkō Film 81, 91
Kokumin no chikai/Das Heilige Ziel. See Oath of the People, The (1938)
Kokushi musō. See Peerless Patriot (1932)
Kōkyōkyoku 'Meiji shōka'. See Sinfonia 'Inno Meiji' (1921)
Konoe Fumimaro (Prince) 50
Kosugi Isamu 4, 63, 116, 125–7, 130
Kouta Katsutarō 142
Kracauer, Siegfried 13, 55, 86, 87
Kublai Khan 155, 181, 191
Kulturfilm 149
Kumagai Hisatora 74, 79–81, 108, 136, 195
Kume Masao 102
Kurosawa, Akira 25, 198, 222, 223
Kwangtung territory 147
Kwantung Army 154, 155
Kyojin den. See Giant, The (1938)
Kyōren no onna shishō. See Love-Mad Music Teacher, The (1926)

La Bataille. See Danger Line, The (1923)
La Fille du Samouraï. See New Earth (*Atarashiki tsuchi*)
Lamaists. See Tibetan Buddhists
Land of Cherry Blossoms, The (1930s) 49
Lang, Fritz 28, 30, 32
Lantschner, Guzzi 86
leader principle (*Führerprinzip*) 6, 6 n.1
League of Nations 26, 48
League of Nations Commission of Enquiry 147
Les Misérables (1862) 196
liberalism 87, 112, 113, 123

Life of Muho Matsu, The (1942) 198, 216
Lion Dance, The (1935) 49, 50
Little Hans (1938) 119
Living Doll (1929) 125
Love in Heaven, A (1932) 69, 108
Love Japan (2014) 223
Love-Mad Music Teacher, The (1926) 32, 34
Ludwig, Alice 58, 160
Lytton Commission 147

Machi no tejinashi. See Street Juggler (1925)
Madame Butterfly (Puccini) 25, 28
Mädchen in Uniform. See Girls in Uniform (1931)
Maki, James 30
Malten, Wilhelm 44, 47
Manchukuo Immigration Association (*Manshū Ijū Kyōkai*) 221
Manchukuo (Manchuria) 4, 5, 7, 11, 38, 48, 49, 51, 57, 67, 74, 91, 92, 102, 108, 109, 127, 145, 147–55, 161, 163, 181, 183, 184, 186, 190, 216, 220, 221
Manchurian Industrial Spearhead Immigration Group 149
Manchurian Motion Picture Company (*Man'ei*) 150
'manifest destiny' 182–4, 188
Manshū no tabi. See Journey Through Manchuria, A (1937)
Marching On (The Army Advances, 1930) 49
March of the Japanese Second Army to the Battle of Liaoyang, The (1904) 28
Marco-Polo Bridge Incident (Lugouqiao Incident, 1937) 83
Marunouchi ondo 142
Matsukata Otohiko 57, 71 n.5
Matsuoka Yōsuke 147
Meiji Restoration 29, 32, 61, 80, 114
Meta-Orientalism 219
Metropolis (1926) 28, 32
michiyuki 156
Miike Takashi 223

militarist-expansionism 155, 184
'Millions to Manchuria' plan 4
Ministry of Education, Science and Culture 50, 99
Mishima Issei 142
Mister Japan (1931) 125
Misutā Nippon. See Mister Japan (1931)
Mizoguchi Kenji 32, 149
Modan Nippon (magazine) 132
Modern Film Corporation 83
modernity 134, 142, 145, 225
modernization 27
Momen taiheiki. See Cotton Version of the Record of Great Peace (1943)
montage sequence 45, 140, 179, 183
Mori Iwao 29
Mori Ōgai 45
Motoori Norinaga 110
mountain film 20, 54–5, 60, 62, 86–7, 94, 115, 204–5
Mountain of Destiny (1924) 55
Mountains in Flames (1931) 205
Mount Asama 137, 167
Mount Fuji 15, 36, 37, 144, 171
Mount Zao (1935) 59, 60
Moyuru ōzora. See Burning Sky (1940)
Mud and Soldiers (1939) 127
Muhō Matsu no isshō. See Life of Muho Matsu, The (1942)
Mukden Incident (1931) 147
Munich Pact (1938) 211
Mushanokōji Kintomo 5, 79, 90
music fusion 15–16
music production 66–7
Musume (1927) 31
My Japan (1945) 13
'My wish for the end of war' (*Sensō chūshi o nozomu*, 1943) 88

naginata training 179
Nakamura Kichiji 63
Nakayama Shinpei 142
nansensu shin jidaieiga 87, 115, 117
narrative films 32, 49, 56, 61, 118, 119, 137, 158
Naruse Mikio 59

'national disgrace film' (*kokujoku eiga*) 27, 37, 42, 52, 65, 69, 127, 223
national equality 27
National Film Archive Japan 9
national films 197
national identity 121, 126, 127, 136, 156
nationalism 7 n.2, 79, 113, 130, 146, 222
nationalist ideology 23, 113
National Museum of Modern Art Tokyo 9
national policy (*kokusaku*) film 89, 99, 101
national prestige 18, 78, 104, 105
National Socialism 86, 111, 112, 201, 207, 208
NationalSocialist German Worker's Party (Nationalsozialistische Deutsche Arbeiterpartei) 6 n.1, 56 n.1, 203, 209
Natsukawa Shizue 195
Natsume Sōseki 45
Nazism 11, 12, 20, 80, 87, 201, 209
New Earth (*Atarashiki tsuchi*) 2, 4–14, 7 n.2, 8 n.3–4, 16–22, 24–6, 29, 32, 35–8, 42, 43, 45, 47–52, 85–7, 90, 91, 93, 94, 104, 105, 108–13, 122, 136, 193–200, 205–10, 212–16, 221–4. See also Fanck, Arnold; Itami Mansaku
 authenticity of landscapes 137–9
 cast and crew 56, 60, 63, 125–32, 134
 Chinese reaction and 91–2
 controversies and noncooperation 64–5, 163
 critics 73, 122, 123
 distribution rights 67, 69, 71, 163, 216
 ethnographic endeavours and encounters 117–23
 Fanck's shots 54–5, 118, 134–5
 Fanck's version *vs.* Itami's version 157–62
 governmental involvement in 97–8

Itami's cooperation in 89
Manchukuo in 147–56
musical score 66–7
people and landscapes 170–4
politics of editing 160–4
premieres, reception and
  release 71–5, 77–9, 82–4, 93,
  104, 123, 124, 139, 202, 217
pre-production phase 58
producing authentic image of
  Japan 116, 118, 120
production and costs 53, 56–7,
  59, 68–9, 83, 93, 155, 202
promotion 79, 82
rating and reviews 75–7
rejection by German
  television 210
rural locations 144–6
scenes of steelworks and silk
  factory 98
screening of uncut version 91–2
script 8, 9, 16, 23, 49, 56, 58, 62,
  63, 65, 68, 81, 87, 98, 101, 102,
  107, 108, 117, 119, 120, 155
selecting Itami as co-director 61
selling 82
shooting 56, 60, 62, 63, 65,
  68, 121
spatial logic and militaristic
  expansion 174–91
success 78
symbolism vs. real 164–70
'things typically Japanese'
  (*nihontekina mono*) 123–4
in United States 83, 182
urban location 139–43
'new' period films (*shin
  jidaieiga*) 87, 88
Nihon ga daisuki desu. See *Love Japan*
  (2014)
Nihon musume/Japan Yin Thwe. See
  Japanese Girl, The (1935)
nihon shōkai films 99
Nikkatsu Studios 32, 34, 57, 61–3, 71,
  71 n.5, 130, 198
*Nippon: Liebe und Leidenschaft in
  Japan*. See *Nippon: Love and
  Passion in Japan* (1932)

Nippon: Love and Passion in Japan
  (1932) 27, 31–44, 51, 68, 81,
  87, 94, 95, 158, 185, 220
Nippons wilde Adler. See *Nippon's
  Wild Eagles* (1942)
Nippon's Wild Eagles (1942) 94
Nitobe Inazō 29
No Regrets for Our Youth
  (1946) 222
NSDAP. See NationalSocialist German
  Worker's Party
Nuremberg Rally (1936) 13

Oath of the People, The (1938) 82
Ogasawara Takeo 81
Okada Kenichi 99
Okajima Tsuyako 29
Ōkōchi Denjirō 61, 196, 197
'Old Japan' 15, 47, 132, 140,
  144, 145
Olympia films 81
Olympic Games (1936) 205
Olympic Winter Games (1940) 82
On Children (1937) 69
'Operation Nekka' (*Nekka sakusen*,
  1933) 155
Oriental tradition, image of 36, 47,
  48, 146
Ormiston-Smith, Frank 54
Ōsaka natsu no jin. See *Summer Battle
  of Osaka, The* (1937)
Ōsawa Yoshio 56, 57, 63, 69, 93 n.7,
  203 n.4
Ōshima Hiroshi 90, 95–8, 103, 108
Ōtani Takejirō 32, 71, 78
Ott, Eugen 103
Oyabe Zenichirō 155
Ozu Yasujirō 5, 30, 49

Pabst, G. W. (Georg Wilhelm) 55
Page of Madness, A (1926) 24, 27
'Paradise Manchuria' (*rakudo
  manshū*) 148
Peace on Earth (1928) 61
Pebble by the Wayside, A (1938) 127
Peerless Patriot (1932) 88, 115, 170
People Without Space. See *New Earth
  (Atarashiki tsuchi)*

people without space (*Volk ohne Raum*) 5, 102, 109, 159, 172, 175, 181, 221
Photo Chemical Laboratory Film Studios (P.C.L.) 57, 63, 67, 71 n.5
Picturesque Japan 69, 99
Piel, Harry 28
Poem of the Sea (Umi no uta) 43
political cooperation 21, 74, 97, 104
political developments 8, 21, 63, 85, 86, 96, 97, 103, 104, 114, 194
political ideologies 190
political motivation 83
political reconciliation 28, 30
popular music 67
post-war narratives 8
power 17, 27, 87, 120, 122
Prager, Wilhelm 43
Priest of Darkness, The (1936) 63, 132
'Principles for Inter-Allied Censorship of German Film' 209
Proletarian Film Movement in Japan 77
propaganda 9, 23, 109, 184
  and aspirations 12–14
  elements 182
  films 38, 64, 93, 93 n.7, 149, 151
  German 7, 13, 209
  Japanese 92, 153, 209, 215
  National Socialist 8, 209, 210
  political 7, 8, 22, 107–8
Propaganda Ministry 43, 58, 91, 98, 103, 209, 222
proto-fascist sentiments 13, 86

'The question of those responsible for the war' ('*Sensō sekininsha no mondai*,' Itami) 88

Rabinowitsch, Gregor 203
racial equality 26
racialized thinking 111
Raindrop Prelude (Chopin) 115
Rashomon (1950) 25, 198, 222
'real', notion of 114–17
Rèhé annexation 155

Reich Film Chamber 208
Reich Music Chamber 36
Reichskulturkammergesetz (Reich Culture Chamber Law) 44
Reichskulturkammer (Reich Culture Chamber) 43
Reiniger, Lotte 35
Renai to kekkon no sho. See Writings on Love and Marriage (1936)
Ribbentrop, Joachim von 83, 90, 94, 95, 98, 103
Riefenstahl, Leni 81, 86, 87, 116, 130, 204, 205, 209
Riefenstahl-Film GmbH 208
Riml, Walter 54, 58, 60, 189
ritual suicide 28, 29, 69
Road to the Reich, The 112
Robō no ishi. See Pebble by the Wayside, A (1938)
Roosevelt, Theodore 57
Rudyard Kipling's *The Ballad of East and West* 177
Rueck, Minna 58
Russia. *See* Soviet Union
Russo-Japanese War (1904–5) 147, 182
ryōsai kenbo ('Good Wife and Wise Mother' doctrine) 131–2, 134

Sacred Rice (Seinaru kome) 62
Saeki Kiyoshi 198, 200
Saga of Anatahan, The (1953) 203 n.4
Said, Edward W. 48
Saijō Yaso 142
Sakai Naoe 95, 96
Sakisaka Itsurō 123–4, 128
Salzburger Festspielhaus 36
Samurai's Career, A (1929) 198
Sawamura Tsutomu 65
Sayama Ryō 196
Schacke, Otto 31
Schneeberger, Hans 54
Schneider, Johannes (Hannes) 94
Secluded Jehol (Hikyō Nekka) 151
Second Sino-Japanese War (1937) 13, 83
Second World War 8, 83, 193, 216

Seeley, Robert   182
*Senyū no uta/Das Lied des Kameraden.
    See Comrade's Song, The* (1939)
Serupan   102
Sessue Hayakawa   5, 20, 27, 28, 63,
    83, 127–8, 149
Shadows of the Yoshiwara (1929). *See
    Crossroads* (1928)
Shiga Naoya   88
Shigeyoshi Suzuki   69
shin kabuki   195
Shinkō Kinema   62, 115
Shirai, Matsujirō   71
Shneiderov, Vladimir   66, 220
Shōchiku European Distribution
    Company (*Shōchiku eiga ōshū
    haikyū kabushiki kaisha*)   33
Shōchiku Studios   29, 30, 32–4,
    49, 57, 62, 63, 69, 71, 73, 78,
    108, 143
short films   9, 43, 47, 49, 54, 59, 104,
    145, 149, 150, 152, 208, 223
silent cinema   30, 40, 67
Sinfonia 'Inno Meiji' (1921)   16
Sinking of the Sisto, The   203, 204
Social Darwinism   6 n.1
Society for International Cultural
    Relations (*Kokusai Bunka
    Shinkōkai*)   2, 50, 56, 57
Soga Masashi   30
Sokal, Henry   54
Solf, Lagi (So'oa'emalelagi)   34, 35,
    40, 43, 48
Solf, Wilhelm   35, 43, 56
Song of Hometown, A
    (1925)   145, 196
Sorge, Richard   103
SOS Eisberg. See SOS Iceberg (1933)
SOS Iceberg (1933)   55, 61, 67, 86,
    94, 215
sound film   39, 51
sound technology   39, 42, 57, 161
South Manchurian Railway Company
    (Mantetsu)   9, 48, 147, 151,
    152, 155
Soviet- Japanese film (*Big Tokyo*)   220
Soviet Union   5, 26, 67, 90, 91,
    147, 179
Soyama Naomori   73
Speer, Albert   208
Spranger, Eduard   122
SS (*Schutzstaffel*, Protection
    Squadron)   112
star persona   79, 124, 130, 132,
    136, 196
Staudinger, Hannes   58, 63, 189
stereotypes   109, 171, 173, 218, 220
Sternberg, Joseph von   203, 203 n.4
Stietencron, Georg Eduard Freiherr
    von   31, 32, 34, 61
Storms over Mont Blanc   87, 116
Street Juggler (1925)   31
Studio des Ursulines Paris   31
suicides   108. *See also* ritual suicide
Summer Battle of Osaka, The
    (1937)   78
Suzuki Denmei   41
Suzuki Shigeyoshi   64, 65, 69
sword-fighting films   197
swordplay   37, 38, 69

tachimawari   38
Taguchi Tetsu   131
Taishōgun Studios   61
Takagi Eiji   5, 63
Taki Rentarō   66 n.4
Tamagawa Studios   130
*Tamerau nakare wakōdo yo. See Do
    Not Hesitate, Young Folks*
    (1935)
Tanaka Kinuyo   32, 41, 63, 68, 131
Tasaka Tomotaka   127
*Tempei jidai: Kaitō Samimaro. See
    Time of Tempei: Mysterious
    Thief Samimaro, The* (1928)
'tendency' (*keikō*) films   61
*Tengoku ni musubu koi. See Love in
    Heaven, A* (1932)
Tenka taiheki. See Peace on Earth
    (1928)
Ten-Minute Meditation   43
Terra Film AG   67, 69, 79, 91,
    96, 150
Tetting, Carl   29
Theatre of Life (1936)   63, 125–7
Third Opus (1932)   43

Third Reich 78, 87, 205, 210, 212, 220
This Was Japan (1945) 13
Tibetan Buddhistm 151
Time of Tempei: Mysterious Thief Samimaro, The (1928) 32, 36, 38
Tjaden, Walter 58, 60, 108
Tōa Studios 29, 30, 51
Tōhō Tōwa 51–3, 56, 59, 82, 83, 93 n.7, 195, 197
Tokugawa Period (1603– 1868) 41, 62
Tokyo 2, 5, 12, 21, 58–9, 139–43
Tōkyō ondo 142
Tokyo Takarazuka Theatre Company 51
Tourism Bureau 102, 145, 161, 219, 220
Tōwa Shōji Ltd 1, 11, 31, 32–4, 51, 53, 64, 69, 81, 94, 95, 97, 150, 151
Traditionen im Hause des Japaners. See *Kagami: Traditions in the Japanese House*
Tragedy of a Marriage (1929) 34
Trans-Manchurian leg 148
Trans-Siberian Railway 74, 132, 148
Trenker, Luis 86, 87, 182, 204, 205
Triple Intervention (1895) 26
Triumph des Willens. See *Triumph of the Will* (1935)
Triumph of the Will (1935) 87, 205
Tsuburaya Eiji 20, 36, 60, 203 n.4
Tsuchihashi sound system 62
Tsuchi to heitai. See *Mud and Soldiers* (1939)
Tsukamoto Kōji 59
Tsuma yo bara no yō ni. See *Wife! Be Like a Rose* (1935)
Tsumura, Hideo 197
Tsuru Aoki 27
XXth Century, The 197
Typhoon (Taifun) 81, 82
Tyrolean Tourism Bureau 54

Uchida Tomu 125, 127, 222
Ueda Isamu 60, 110, 189
Ueki Masayoshi. See Kataoka Chiezō
Uemura Yasuji 57
ultra-militarism 58
Umlauff, Heinrich 28
United States 21, 26, 83, 92, 182, 190
Universal Picture 30, 94, 215
Universal Studios 55, 61
Universum Film AG (Ufa) 20, 31, 32, 34, 42–4, 49, 51, 54, 55, 81, 95, 150, 195
Ushihara Kiyohiko 32, 37, 40, 42, 49
utopia 151, 153, 184

Variety 182, 190
Venice International Film Festival 25, 222
Verdun (Verdun, 1931) 52
Versailles Treaty 96
Vicissitudes of Revenge (1928) 194
Violet, Édouard Émile 27
Visit Japan: Tourism Promotion in the 1920s and 1930s (2016) 9, 11
visual art 20, 67
voice-over narration 44, 47, 68, 119, 164, 221
von Dirksen, Herbert 71, 97, 103, 203

Waga seishun ni kuinashi. See *No Regrets for Our Youth* (1946)
Wakamatsu Tadaichi 96
Wandering Gambler (1928) 62
war criminals 89, 93, 93 n.7
Warring States period 34, 41
wartime films 93, 127
wartime mobilization 13
wartime responsibility 199, 200
Watsuji Tetsurō 110, 112, 138
Wedding March (Mendelssohn) 115
Weimar Republic 44, 112, 116, 220
Weimar Republic and the Third Reich (Fanck) 210
Western art 43
Western clothes (*yōfuku*) 132, 134, 156, 171
Western film-making techniques 93
Western life 25

Western markets   27, 220
Western music   16
White Hell of Piz Palu (1929)   55
White Stadium, The (1928)   55, 205
Wife! Be Like a Rose (1935)   59
Winter Journey Through Southern Manchuria, A (1938)   150, 209
Winterreise durch Südmandschurien. See *Winter Journey Through Southern Manchuria, A* (1938)
Writings on Love and Marriage (1936)   126

Yakichi the Woodcutter (Yakichi der Holzfäller). See *Eternal Heart* (Eien no kokoro, 1928)
Yamada Isuzu   126
Yamada Kōsaku   16, 20, 66, 66 n.4, 67, 69, 81, 82, 142, 149, 183, 191, 220–1
Yamamoto Yūzō   8, 23, 63, 89, 198
Yamanaka Sadao   61, 63, 87

Yokohama photography   144
Yokohama shashin   134, 168, 220
Yakushin Itari. See *Advancing Italy*
Yōkoso Nihon e: 1920–30 nendai no tsūrizumu to dezain. See *Visit Japan: Tourism Promotion in the 1920s and 1930s* (2016)
Yosano Akiko   35
Yosano Tekkan   35
Yosano Yuzuru   34, 35, 40
Yoshiwara (1937)   128
Youth Across the River (1933)   64
Yuasa Hatsue   36–7, 40, 43–5, 134
Yukiyama no arubamu/Album der Schneeberge. See *Album of Snowy Mountains* (1939)

Zaō san. See *Mount Zao* (1935)
zeitgeist   49, 77, 198, 199
Zoku manka jigoku. See *Hell of Ten Thousand Flowers 2* (1929)

www.ingramcontent.com/pod-product-compliance
Lightning Source LLC
Chambersburg PA
CBHW052112010526
44111CB00036B/1785